9.95

THE
DARIEN
DISASTER

THE DARIEN DISASTER

"Door of the seas . . . key of the Universe"

JOHN PREBBLE

MAINSTREAM PUBLISHING
EDINBURGH

Distributed in Canada by
DOUGLAS & McINTYRE, VANCOUVER

This edition published in Great Britain in 1978
by MAINSTREAM PUBLISHING COMPANY (EDINBURGH)
LTD, 5 Glen Street, Edinburgh.

Copyright © by John Prebble 1968

ISBN 0 906391 02 4

First published in England 1968 by
Martin Secker & Warburg Limited.

Printed in Great Britain by
Billing & Sons Limited.

Contents

Maps

FOR
IAIN CAMERON TAYLOR

The Noble Undertaking

"Then England for its treachery should mourn"
Edinburgh, April 1705

THE SAVAGE VOICE OF THE PEOPLE could be heard on the walls of
the Castle. The sentinels in the Half Moon Battery, the escort
company of the Town Guard drawn up in Palace Yard, had been
listening to it since dawn. From the embrasures of the battery,
down through blue peat-smoke and thin sunlight, over tall
chimneys and craw-step gables, they could see a violent torrent
from the Landmarket to Abbey Close: men, women and children,
horses, coaches, and overturned stalls, a foam of white faces at
windows and forestairs. The incessant cry of "No Reprieve!", on
a carrier wave of screams and obscenities, was losing its meaning
by repetition, but its throbbing menace still remained. In the
vaulted prison below the Great Hall of the Castle there may have
been nothing to hear but a man's heart-beat or the restless foot-
fall of a gaoler, nothing to disturb Thomas Green's confidence.
He smiled at the Keeper and said that he and his companions
would not die that day. Her Majesty's express would arrive from
London to save them, even at the foot of the gallows. Since
sentence had been passed, by the Judge and Assessors of the
High Court of Admiralty, since his *Dying Speech* had passed
through improving hands to the printer, the young man had
allowed no one to speak of his hanging as inevitable.

But hanging was that morning synonymous with justice, and
was plainly demanded by a mob which filled the main artery of
the city, fed by sixty capillary courts and wynds. All roads that
led to the six gates of Edinburgh were also crowded, by some
who had come on foot for fifty miles, armed with clubs and

swords to enforce payment for the wounded pride and spilt blood of the nation. Those who were not fighting to get into the city, were struggling to get out of it, by the College Kirk in the north and the Water Gate in the east. Here two roads embraced Caltoun Craigs and led to Leith, and each was choked with commons and gentility. Along the eastern road, past mud-walled parks and fields pricked by the green of young oats, the crowd was thicker, ineffectively controlled by scattered foot-soldiers and dragoons. By this way condemned pirates were customarily taken to the links at Leith, and on the grassy dunes, pointing north above the flood-mark, the gallows had been waiting two weeks for Captain Thomas Green, his mate John Madder, and his gunner James Simpson, of the English merchantman *Worcester*. Their last sight before they were hanged, if they were to be hanged, would be the white houses of Burntisland five miles across the Forth where their ship lay aground, its hold and cabins gutted, its masts stripped of canvas and yards.

In the palace of Holyroodhouse, behind the closed and guarded gates of Abbey Close, some of Her Majesty's Privy Councillors had gathered soon after dawn. They had come by coach from their town-houses in Cowgate and Canongate, or from their estates in the country, and they were shortly to travel up the Royal Mile to their Council Chamber in the Laigh Parliament House, there to decide whether the three seamen should be reprieved as the Queen advised, or should hang for piracy as the people demanded. None of them was anxious to make the journey, their arrival at Holyrood had been terrifying enough. The broad way of the Canongate, between splendid grey houses of square-hewn stone, had been full of angry men and women, surrounding the coaches, catching at bridles, hammering on varnished panels, thrusting inflamed faces through windows and leather curtains and spattering the Councillors with spittle as they shouted "No Reprieve!". There was now the unendurable thought of that odorous stretch of the High Street between the Netherbow Port and Parliament House, the heaps of timber, peat and dung that were the mob's traditional weapons of persuasion. It was not an atmosphere in which the Queen's principal servants could make a dispassionate decision.

Of the thirty members of the Council, nineteen had chosen to absent themselves and make no decision at all, as they had been absent from most of the Council's meetings since the trial a month before. The Marquis of Tweeddale, hot-tempered where his honour was concerned and proud of his general popularity, said that private affairs kept him on his estates but he was sure the Council would find a quorum without him. Lord Belhaven, a roaring patriot who liked to sing descant to the music of the mob, had previously pleaded prior duties to a house full of guests, and now, perhaps not inconsequentially, said that a course of diet kept him to his bed. The Earl of Crawford, also ailing, had "a violent cold and hoarseness" that prevented him from speaking. The Earl of Roxburgh, one of Her Majesty's Secretaries of State for Scotland, had written to say that had he been able to walk downstairs he would have been in town, but "I have got such a sprain that I don't know when I shall be able to travel". The Lord Justice Clerk, Cockburn of Ormiston, showed less imagination than might have been expected in an advocate. His son had recently gone to the west country, he said, and had taken all the horses. By such lies did great men protect public office and private reputation, and neglect their duty.

From hindsight that duty, in both law and common humanity, is now clear. The root of the evidence against Green and his crew was a drunken boast over a bowl of punch, the prosecution's case was enmeshed in medieval Latin and legal Doric, irrelevant and unintelligible to the accused and jury. The seven eminent advocates who acted for the defence appear to have presented no evidence, they did not submit their speeches for customary publication after the trial, and they left Edinburgh immediately in apparent fear for their safety. There is no record that the Judge either summed up, or gave direction in law to the jury beyond brief answers to some of their doubts as to the meaning of the prosecution's wordy quotations from the Law and the classics. None of the jurymen, five sea-captains and ten merchants, could be regarded as wholly impartial and disinterested, indeed it would have been difficult to find such a man in Scotland at that moment. Even so, a minority of them, closing their ears to the mob outside the court, could not agree with a verdict of guilty. All this the Privy Councillors had known for a month. Moreover, they now had before them affidavits sworn in London by sailors of the Scots ship *Speedy Return* which Green was accused of looting and burning. They clearly exonerated the crew of the *Worcester*, but the Councillors had set them aside on the specious excuse that they were "only attested copies". At the express wish of the Queen, but under emotional protest, the Councillors had already postponed the execution until to-day, April 11. Although they had entreated Anne that "no further reprieve might be granted", they had themselves voted for one yesterday, but, to their relief perhaps, had failed to secure the proper majority. Unlike their nineteen absent colleagues, these eleven men at least believed themselves obliged to make a decision, but they were held between conscience and expediency, between the knowledge that an express from London might arrive this morning with a full reprieve, and the realisation that the mob outside would be satisfied with nothing less than a hanging.

The mob had no doubts, no obligation to rationalise its passion in terms of duty and law and conscience. Its temper, always quick to ignite, had been further inflamed by a ballad written, or inspired, by Roderick Mackenzie, the embittered Secretary of the Company of Scotland, owners of the *Speedy Return*. In ugly verse, irresponsibly imaginative, it described how the brothers Robert and Thomas Drummond, captain and supercargo of that ship, had been bound and beheaded before they were thrown into the Indian Ocean. That innocent Scots should be so foully murdered by Englishmen was bad enough, worse that the victims should be two men who were heroes of Darien, survivors of Scotland's noble colony on the Isthmus of Panama. And that too, the mob was reminded, had been destroyed by the English.

Copies of the ballad fluttered among the raised fists and clubs when the gates of Holyrood were opened shortly before nine o'clock. Out came the Lord Chancellor's mace-bearer, bravely pacing the way as if he were to be welcomed by the respectful huzzas that normally greeted such a procession. Forty musketeers of Captain Robinson's Town Guard marched with bayonets fixed on either side of the nervous horses and gilded coaches. In the first rode the Chancellor, James Ogilvy, Earl of Findlater, Earl of Seafield, an unostentatious, beautiful man with a serene face and a gentle smile. He used both as curtain and outworks to the fortress of a dissembling mind, the greatest strength of which, it was said, was the faculty of knowing, without any exercise of reason, what should be done to please his sovereign. Yesterday this had naturally guided him to place a casting vote in favour of reprieve, but on the other hand he was aware that by respecting the Queen's present wishes he might be risking her future favour. "We are all sensible that it would do a vast deal of prejudice to Her Majesty's affairs in Parliament," he had written after an earlier meeting of the Council, "for all I speak with say that since God in his providence had discovered this barbarous murther, it will be hard if they be not allowed to put so just a sentence in execution against those who have taken the innocent blood of their fellow subjects."

With the Almighty thus involved as a witness for the prosecution, or at least an *ad hoc* member of the Privy Council, Seafield knew how this morning's business must go. That is, if the mob allowed him to reach the Laigh Parliament House. His courage, if cynical, was none the less resolute. Sitting back against the brocade and leather of his coach, his face pale and calm, he knew that there was not a man between Abbey Close and St. Giles who did not believe that he had conspired with the English, eight years before, to destroy the Company of Scotland and its colony, and in that sense was a greater villain than Green or Madder or Simpson.

The appearance of his livery, the Ogilvy lion on his arms, enraged the people outside the gates. All the way up Canongate they surged against the musketeers, clinging to Seafield's coach and yelling "No Reprieve!" In this wild, undignified manner, with the clang of hooves on the paving, Her Majesty's principal servants passed through the Netherbow Port and into a larger, more violent mob. Here men climbed over the dunghills and the kailwives' stalls to reach the coaches, to pelt them with stones, vegetables and dung, while women screamed abuse and encouragement from the windows and forestairs. The mace-bearer was brutally clubbed to his knees, and would have been killed had he not staggered into Milne Square and the offices of the Company of Scotland. The mob held the horses of Seafield's coach, struck at its emblazoned panels with sticks, fists and swords, thrust savage faces against its windows and yelled "No Reprieve!" to the calm face inside, until the swinging muskets of

Robinson's men beat them away. Slowly the coaches were able to move on, past the Tolbooth and Market Cross to Parliament Close. Here the buildings were the tallest in Europe, some of them newly-raised since the Great Fire, fourteen reaching storeys and each of them housing twenty families or more. At every window, on every stair, there were men, women and children crying "No Reprieve!"

When the doors of Parliament House closed on the Councillors, the mob entertained itself with songs and brawling, by hammering on the doors and shouting exhortations to the Council. Those who could not get into the close went up to the Castle ditch and shouted across the drawbridge. Within the Castle the Governor, Lord Leven (whose private opinion was that the accused should have been hanged without further debate) decided to damp down the anger of the mob by ordering away a battalion of Foot and a squadron of Horse to Leith sands. They came out of the Portcullis Gate by beat of drum, shining bayonets and ringing harness, down the Royal Mile to the Water Gate and the Leith Road. Some of the mob followed, singing and capering, but the greater part, distrusting great men behind locked doors, stayed where it was.

In their chamber below the great hall of the Estates, surrounded by the thumb-screws, the knives and pincers by which their predecessors had determined guilt or innocence, the Councillors debated for two hours. The noise of the mob, above their heads and beyond the doors, was a gentle, rushing murmur. There was nothing to say that had not been said, the delay came not from fresh discussion but from the need to stifle old doubts. The decision, when it was taken, was inevitable, and was made less by noble men in scarlet and ermine than by the foul mouths and hot temper of the people. "We came to be convinced," wrote Seafield, "that there was no possibility of preserving the public peace without allowing some that were thought most guilty to be execute." Green, Madder and Simpson were to hang that day as soon as they could be carried to the links at Leith, the rest of the *Worcester's* crew were reprieved for another week.

When a messenger had been sent to the Castle, the Councillors went in a body to tell the people, and Seafield spoke for them, standing at the open doors of Parliament House. What he said was called back through the mob, out of Parliament Close and down the Royal Mile. There were shouts of joy and cheers, and in this sudden, sunlit mood the Councillors hurried discreetly away. Seafield's coach had scarcely left the close when there was a shout that he had lied, that it was all a trick, that the murderers had been reprieved again. He bent forward behind the window, shaking his head, calling soundlessly to the mob, telling it to be patient for it would have satisfaction. Stones broke the glass and scattered him with splinters, hands clawed the coach to a halt, and angry voices yelled through the broken window. They would have Thomas Green and his bloody crew brought to execution or they would storm the Castle and burn the pirates alive. Seafield turned the handle of the door, pushed it open and stepped down into the street. Astonished by this arrogant act of courage, the mob parted to let him through. He walked calmly and slowly to the house of a friend.

And from Castle Hill, the beating of a drum. The Town Guard, led by Captain Robinson, was bringing the seamen down. As they came into the Landmarket there was a baying roar and then silence. Joseph Taylor, an English tourist, said that the appearance of the condemned men, their courage and their composure, moved many men to tears, and this may well have been so, for the enjoyment of all emotions was part of the public spectacle, and men who behaved well in face of death deserved and received some sentimental acknowledgement of a good performance.

Thomas Green's composure, as he walked between the bayonets, came less from courage, however, than from a continuing belief that he would yet be reprieved. He was innocent, he said, and why should this not be the truth when no man could hope to see God in mercy if he persisted in a lie? He was a strange young man, reserved, uncommunicative, and dedicated to duty. His *Dying Speech*, written some days before, sold by the same hands that circulated Mackenzie's ballad, declared that he had injured no man. "What the custom of pirates is, I thank God I know not, but I understand my accusers and persecutors will have you believe I think it is unnecessary to confess before men. Take what I have said as good Christians ought to do. If you have no charity you wrong yourselves and cannot hurt me." He was twenty-five. He had been given command of the *Worcester* when he was twenty-one. And his sad weakness was an addiction to strong liquors.

John Madder was no older than his captain, and was perhaps the more tragic figure, for he was a Scot, and might have escaped arrest had he not loyally surrendered himself. He knew that he was to die, and had no patience with Green's pathetic hope of a reprieve. His *Dying Speech*, like that of the silent gunner Simpson, had been written for him, and what either man thought, or truly said, cannot now be known.

Captain Robinson was counting heads as he marched with sword and sash. He said afterwards that there were eighty thousand armed men gathered outside the city, and so close together that one could have walked on their heads from Edinburgh to Leith sands. There were no tears now for the condemned, there was no compassion. That scene had been played in sequence, where best for dramatic effect, and the last act was evil confounded and virtue triumphant. The author of *A Letter from Scotland*, published three weeks later in London, said that the seamen were

> ... huzza'd, in triumph as it were, and insulted with the sharpest and most bitter invectives. Being come to the place of execution, good God what a moving sight was it to see those men stand upon the very varge of life, just launching into eternity, and at the same time see the whole multitude transported with joy. Some with pleasure asking: 'Why their countrymen did not come and save them?' Others, loading them with Scotch prayers, told 'em their old master would have 'em immediately. All of which they bore with invincible patience, like innocent men, English men and Christians, and made no other returns than by forgiving them, and desiring their charity.

Green's hope for a reprieve lasted almost until the end. Twice when the hangman tried to place the hood over his head he pushed it aside, looking anxiously along the road to Edinburgh. And then he understood. He stumbled on the ladder and would have collapsed but for Madder, who frowned at him, and by his own stoic resignation gave Green the courage to accept death.

"The tragedy was completed," said the *Letter*, "and from many points of hilly Edinburgh the bodies of the victims might be seen swinging on the sands of Leith. The national vengeance was more than satiated, and many of those who had been foremost in the strife were afraid to think of what they had done." Many, but not most. When the dead men were cut down, Robinson took Green's body to Mrs. Bartley's lodging-house, where the seaman had stayed before his arrest. He helped her to strip it, wash it, and coffin it, and later did the same for Madder and Simpson. But as he escorted the coffins for burial a flame of riot burst out again, and he fought the mob with a drawn sword at the door of the church.

Although the Council pardoned the rest of the *Worcester's* crew, without protest, there was little forgiveness or shame in Scotland. Too much was bitterly remembered. Ten years before, the nation had created a noble mercantile company, and three years later a colony on Darien that could have been the trading hub of the world. Nine fine ships, built or bought for this enterprise, had been sunk, burnt, or abandoned. Nearly half a million pounds sterling had been freely offered from Scotland's meagre purse, and that which had been taken was now without hope of return. Over two thousand men, women and children had left the Forth and Clyde for Darien, and never returned. They were buried on Panama, drowned in the Caribbean, rotting in Spanish prisons, or lost for ever as indentured servants in English colonies. There was scarcely a family in Scotland below the Highland Line that had not lost a son, or a father, a cousin, nephew or friend in this disaster. This was why Scotland hanged Thomas Green, Madder and Simpson, and this was why there could be no forgiveness.

Some weeks later, from the printing-house of James Watson in Craig's Close, there came another ballad, rejoicing in the confusion of England and the punishment of her pirates. It was called *A Pill for the Pork Eaters, or a Scots lancet for an English Swelling*.

> Then England for its treachery should mourn,
> Be forced to fawn, and truckle in its turn:
> Scots Pedlars you no longer durst upbraid
> And DARIEN should with interest be repaid.

"Trade will increase trade, and money will beget money"
London, May 1695

He was the original Scots Pedlar, the taunt first made in a sheet
of English doggerel, adopted as a sneer against all his countrymen, and later accepted by them in defensive pride. His only
known portrait is an illustration to one of his many pamphlets,
and it is grotesque enough to be taken for a caricature. Since it
was published while William Paterson was still alive it may well
have been an honest attempt at a likeness, and even in its crudity
there is something of the character more fully drawn by his
words and actions: a beaked, determined nose, mouth open to
release the passionate conviction of his thoughts, eyes melancholy
with disappointment. Like many men who respond to the instinctive spirit of their age he appeared to be in conflict with his, a
conscientious abstainer among great drunkards, tolerant in a
stifling atmosphere of bigotry, an advocate of national wealth
rather than private fortunes, an upstart deferred to by birth and
privilege, albeit never for long. What may be regarded as his
enduring monuments are also bizarre in comparison, the Bank of
England and a weed-choked ditch on Darien.

Idealistic, tactless, impatient with the turbid reasoning of his
contemporaries, it was not unnatural that the man should withdraw from the Bank at a moment when it was plainly certain to
succeed, but stubbornly serve the Darien undertaking in the face
of bitter and inevitable failure.

Much of his life is a mystery, unrecorded, unmentioned in the
thousands of words he wrote, and we have only the ribald scandal
of his enemies. Tradition places his birth at Skipmyre, in Dumfries, the son of a wealthy farmer, or a poor earth-breaker. He
grew up in the killing time, when Episcopacy rode a dragoon's
saddle at night against the conventicles, when families were dis-
persed, when good men of the western shires were transported or
went into exile for the glory of God and the preservation of their
skins. The same tradition says that his father gave him a good
schooling to prepare him for the Kirk, that at seventeen he was
carrying food and news to outlawed ministers in the hills above
the parish of Tinwald. He is also said to have been at Bothwell

Brig on the Clyde, when Monmouth's bright cuirass and the Graham's red plume came down on the Covenant, and that during the bloody persecution which followed he fled to England.

"He came from Scotland in his younger years," said his contemptuous enemy Walter Herries, "with a pack on his back, whereof the print may be seen." To Herries, Paterson was always the Scots Pedlar, once a real huckster and thereafter a trickster hawking the bright ribbons of his dreams to his countrymen. Whatever Paterson's youth was, it made him no ordinary man in vision or education. He wrote a good hand and reasoned clearly in it. He was an historian who had read widely, a theologian who understood that a faith without compassion was no religion at all. He had a practical knowledge of engineering, mathematics, finance and business, and was a diligent student all his life. Herries said that he abandoned his pedlar's tray after some years in England, and "seated himself under the wing of a warm widow near Oxford, where, finding that preaching was an easier trade than his own, he soon found himself gifted with an Anadab's spirit. Prophets being generally despised at home, he went on the *Propaganda fide* account to the West Indies, and was one of those who settled on the island of Providence a second time." Less colourfully, tradition says that he lodged with a relation in Bristol until he was 19, and when she died in 1674 she left him some small property which he used to buy himself a passage to the Caribbean. If this were so, it makes nonsense of the brave story that would have him standing in the ranks of the Lord at Bothwell Brig, five years later.

What he did during those seven or eight years in the West Indies is obscure, and he never wrote of them, except to give the authority of experience to his proposals for a colony. It is true that he built a reputation there for honesty and integrity, and it is possible that he traded as a merchant. Not unnaturally, it was said that he had spent some time as a buccaneer, an associate of Morgan, Avery and Sharpe, Dampier and Wafer, and those other forgotten men who beached their long-boats on crescent sands, smoked bull-hides beneath the palms, sacked Portobello and crossed the Isthmus like ancient heroes. When he returned to Europe, Herries said, his head was "full of projects, having all the achievements of Sir Henry Morgan, Batt. Sharp and the buccaneers in his budget." That he knew such men was more than likely, it was easy enough to meet them, or those who sailed with them, at Blewfields or in Port Royal. Robert Alliston, a veteran of Sharpe's raid on Portobello in 1679, was certainly his friend. And it was from Alliston perhaps, or Wafer, that Paterson first heard of Darien, the green and beautiful country on the northern coast of Panama, where the earth yielded fruit without cultivation, where noble, naked Indians knew the secrets of un-mined gold, and where lush mountain valleys led to the Pacific sea. There is no record that Paterson ever set foot upon Darien, or upon any part of the Central American mainland, and it might have been better for his countrymen if he had.

From the stories told by buccaneers he created his vision of a mercantile colony astride the Isthmus, a free-trading *entrepôt* of factories and forts where goods from the West could be ex-changed for goods from the East, a trading road between the Atlantic and Pacific, anticipating the Panama Canal by two hundred years and making the long voyage about Africa un-necessary. In one splendid paragraph he was to explain this later to his countrymen:

> The time and expense of navigation to China, Japan and the Spice Islands, and the far greatest part of the East Indies will be lessened by more than half, and the consumption of European commodities and manufactories will soon be more than doubled. Trade will increase trade, and money will beget money, and the trading world shall need no more to want work for their hands, but will rather want hands for their work. Thus this door of the seas, and the key of the universe, with anything of a sort of reasonable management, will of course enable its proprietors to give laws to both oceans, without being liable to the fatigues, expenses and dangers, or contracting the guilt and blood of Alexander and Caesar.

It is a character sketch of the man, imaginative, energetic, compassionate and naïve.

By the middle of the 1680s he was in Europe, hawking this dream. Robert Douglas, a Scots merchant who conducted his business in London, and who thought that Paterson was a garrulous bore who might become dangerous if taken seriously, later remembered that he was a familiar figure in Amsterdam coffee-houses, always talking about Darien. "He endeavoured to make a market of his wares in Holland and Hamburg," said Herries also, "but without any success. He went afterwards to Berlin, opened his pack there, and almost caught the Elector of Brandenburg in his noose, but that miscarried too."

From somewhere, the West Indies, Holland or Hamburg, Paterson acquired a small fortune, or at least the foundation upon which to build a small fortune, and when he set himself up in 1687 as a merchant in London, he was soon both successful and influential, the associate of other Scots merchants and of rich Jews like Joseph Cohen D'Azevedo. In London he also met Andrew Fletcher of Saltoun, the noble-minded Scots patriot who saw the inspired idea behind Paterson's lamentable habit of talking his audience into bored indifference. According to Dalrymple's *Memoirs*, Saltoun told Paterson to abandon his hope of European interest and to "trust the fate of his project to his own country-men, and to let them have the sole benefit, glory and danger of it." But Paterson had been too long away from Scotland. He rightly remembered it as poor in capital and resources, and, moreover, he was an internationalist, believing that no one nation could finance the scheme, or should enjoy its benefits.

He prospered in London. His industrious and enterprising mind, as well as his political principles which the Revolution had now made popular, brought him in contact with great men and new ideas. He helped to found a company, which lasted two hundred years, for supplying north London with piped water from the Hampstead hills, and later a similar company in Southwark of which he became treasurer. He is said to have been associated with Sir Theodore Janssen in the property development of the west, a scheme for noble squares and streets marching away from Lincoln's Inn Fields toward the village of Kensington. He wrote an intelligent proposal, which was ignored, for restoring a deplorably clipped coinage to its proper value. In 1693 he appeared before a Committee of the House of Commons on behalf of a mercantile group, explaining, with considerable skill, its scheme for credit upon Parliamentary security. When the Bank of England was formed next year upon this basis, he was one of its first directors, but he quarrelled with the others and resigned in 1695. Although men respected his intellect and his genius, few can have liked him. He was humourless, tiresome, and depressingly serious about all things. "When he appeared in public," said Herries, "he appeared with a head so full of business and care, as if he had Atlas's burden on his back. If a man had a fancy to be reputed wise, the first step he took to make way was to mimic Paterson's phiz. Nay, some persons had such a conceit of the miracles he could perform that they began to talk of an engine, to give the island half a turn round, and send the Orkneys where the Isles of Scilly stand."

Only a man like Saltoun could have admired Paterson's rigid honesty, his contempt for the corruption upon which politics, religion and trade flourished. He hated "bribery, cheating, designed cheating, wilful bankruptcy, and fraud and likewise theft, and so far from being a lesser or inferior degree thereof, they are the worst and most heinous of all. It seems strange that those who invented the hanging of thieves did not begin with this sort first."

He lived in Denmark Street, a pleasant terraced house in the parish of St. Giles and on the edge of Soho fields. The name of his wife, her character, descent and appearance are lost in the darkness that fills so much of Paterson's life. Herries said that she was "a red-faced coffee-woman, a widow in Birchin Lane".* Whether she was or not, she was loyal to her husband, took his pedlar's pack as a burden for her own shoulders, and what remains of her lies some yards inshore from Caledonia Bay on Darien.

The Spring of 1695 began as it had begun in London most years since the Revolution. King William went to Gravesend by coach through a flurry of gunfire and cheers, embarked on his yacht and joined his fleet for Flanders, there to re-open his annual tourney with Louis XIV. At the sessions of the Old Bailey thieves, coiners and footpads, murderers, cut-purses and stealers of bread were once more sentenced to death, burning or whipping. Lord Cutts' Regiment, in new scarlet, exercised in Hyde Park before following the King, and the nation was in-

---

* Herries also said that she was Paterson's second wife. Who was the first is unknown, unless she was the "warm widow near Oxford".

formed that there would be another day of General Fast during
which the Lord would be implored to preserve His Majesty's
person and confound those of his enemies. About the middle of
May James Chiesly called on Paterson in Denmark Street. He
was one of many Scots merchants, like David Nairne, James Reith,
Robert Douglas and James Foulis, who enjoyed greater freedom
and higher profits by trading in London rather than in Edinburgh. All of them were occasional guests at Denmark Street, and
while most of them found Paterson's garrulity tedious, and probably regretted his abstemious hospitality, they respected his
original mind and organisational skill. Chiesly had come from his
house in the City parish of Allhallows Staining, to talk of the
news from Scotland. On Thursday, May 9, the Scots Parliament
had opened its fifth session. There was, at last, to be a Commission of Inquiry into the Massacre of Glencoe, and the event of
the session promised to be an acrimonious debate upon its
Report. But what particularly excited Chiesly, and other Scots
merchants in both London and Edinburgh, was one paragraph in
the opening address given by the King's Commissioner to Parliament, the Marquis of Tweeddale. He had told the Estates that

> If they found it would tend to the advancement of trade
> that an Act be passed for the encouragement of such as
> should acquire and establish a plantation in Africa or
> America, or any other part of the world where plantations
> might lawfully be acquired, His Majesty was willing to
> declare that he would grant to his subjects in Scotland, in
> favour of their plantations, such rights and privileges as he
> was accustomed to grant to the subjects of his other do-
> minions.

It was as if a window had been opened, flooding the grey and
impoverished rooms of Scotland with the sunlight of the Indies,
promising a future prosperity as great, if not greater than that
exclusively enjoyed by the East India Company, the African Company, and other English companies trading with America and the
Levant. It was no more than was expected of the King. Though
he had accepted the Crown of Scotland, when it was brought to
him in London, he thought of the country as a recruiting centre
only, a storehouse for supplies, and was impatient with its

Parliament and its peculiar pride. For two years Scots merchants, with their friends and their bought men in the Estates and Privy Council, had been lobbying and conspiring for such an opportunity as this. In June, 1693, the Parliament of Scotland had passed a general Act which gave permission for the formation of joint-stock companies to trade with countries not at war with the Crown. It had remained on paper, and neither the King's principal servants in Scotland nor the trading companies of England wished it to become anything else.

Yet it had been one indication of a change in the spirit of the Scottish people. For six decades the nation had wasted itself in the fratricidal agony of religious and political wars, squandering its intellectual and physical resources, and covering its rags with the bright banners of the Scots Brigades when its young men went to continue these bloody quarrels in the service of France and Germany and Holland. Now it was to take its first real step away from a past of warriors and martyrs, toward a future of commerce and industry. That it would stumble and fall, and bring upon itself as sad a tragedy as any in its history, would not take its eyes from that future. What greatness the broadsword or the Bible had failed to secure for the Scots, might be found in something else. Fletcher of Saltoun, who could use a sword as well as any of his countrymen and had proved it against the Turks, recognised this new stirring of his people's imagination: "All their thoughts and inclinations, as if united and directed by a Higher Power, seemed to have turned upon trade, and to con-spire together for its advancement, which is the only means to recover us from our present miserable and despicable condition."

The misery was bitter. Scotland's trade and industry were paltry, and their disappearance would have made little difference to the commerce of Europe, and none to the rest of the world. The union of the kingdoms in 1603 had not given the parity and equality of opportunity it might have implied. Ninety years later Scotland felt herself to be the subordinate nation. As theologians once debated how many angels might comfortably stand on the head of a pin, as Spanish priests once argued whether or not an Indian was a human being in the eyes of the Church, so English jurists whetted their wits on the problem of where and when a Scot might be considered an English subject, with the rights and privileges thereof. Though there were two economies, two parliaments in the island, there was one king, and since the second Stuart he had been primarily and sometimes exclusively an English king. Nor was this all a matter of mood and emotion. Scotland had not recovered from the poverty of the Commonwealth when she had carried the heavy weight of an English army of occupation. In the earlier years of the century she had enjoyed something like free trade with England, and by the imposed union of the Commonwealth this had been legally acknowledged. Under the restored Stuarts she recovered her political independence but lost the one-nation advantages of free trade when the Navigation Acts of 1660 and 1663 were inexorably enforced.

The clauses of these Acts hung on Scotland's commerce like ignoble fetters, and increased her economic dependence upon England. No goods could be transported from the King's possessions in Africa, Asia or America except in the ships of England, Ireland, Wales and Berwick-on-Tweed, or in ships whereof the master and three-quarters of the crew were English. No foreign goods could enter England except in the bottoms of English ships, or ships of the country of origin. Scots shipping was thus limited to trade with Scotland, and the vessels themselves were largely Dutch- or German-built. No more did Scots yards create great warships and merchantmen for European kings as they had done a century before, or Scots architects work in the royal yards at Copenhagen. The Scots Parliament passed retaliatory Acts of a similar character, but this was the petulant response of a child who, rejected by his companions and having neither bat nor ball, declares that no others may play with him.

All of Scotland's meagre industries, cloth, cattle, fishing, coal, salt and lead, suffered from English competition or English legislation, and from a dispirited malaise. Her exports of grain, which in good times earned her a worthwhile income, particularly from Norway, could fall to the minimal in unpredictable, uncontrollable years of famine and drought. With no strong, reciprocal export trade she depended largely upon what England imported and sold to her across the border, paying for it in sterling. Her nobility and middle classes wore clothes made from English woollens, and equipped their kitchens with English copper and brass. Their smiths used iron from Sweden, and their coopers bought their hoops already made from England or Flanders. The best of their beer was brewed from English hops, their spices and sugars, their Levantine fruits, had come in the bottoms of English merchantmen. They rode in saddles of English leather, ate bread made from East Anglian grain when their own harvests failed, fought their quarrels with foreign muskets and Dutch powder, and treated their wounds with drugs sold to them by England.*

Since the Revolution there had been a growing feeling that these ills might be cured by a willing political union with the southern kingdom, or at least by a favourable customs union. But a wider, stronger hope, and one that answered a stubborn pride, was that Scotland might become as great a mercantile and colonial power as England. Not as a country of interloping merchants, poaching the grounds of the East India or African Companies, but as a free and independent nation, competing in ships, men and colonies.

Scotland's attempts at colonisation had so far been sad and disastrous. Sixty years before, a brave settlement on the Bay of Fundy had become a casualty in the war between England and France, and all that remained of it were the descendants of those Nova Scotia baronets who had bought their titles cheaply, each contributing six men and a thousand merks toward the colony. More recently a Quaker settlement in New England, a Covenanters' refuge in Carolina, had both failed, the one swamped by the English, the other destroyed by Spanish fire and sword. Yet there were Scots by the thousands in Africa and the New World. They had gone, roped and chained more often than not, as transported victims of lost causes. A thousand were sent to Virginia and New England after Cromwell's crowning mercy of Dunbar. After another such mercy at Worcester, fifteen hundred, many of them Highlanders, were sold on the coast of Guinea. The miserable failure of the Highland rebellion against Cromwell in 1654 gave the newly-acquired English island of Jamaica more bonded servants and plantation workers. Seventeen hundred Covenanters were transported to America after Bothwell Brig and during the Graham's furious dragonnade. And in 1685, when the Earl of

---

* A brilliant and scholarly account of the state of affairs at this time can be found in *Scottish Trade on the Eve of Union, 1660–1707*, by T. C. Smout.

Argyll made his abortive rising in support of Monmouth, his Campbell clansmen were taken to the colonies by Scots and English shipmasters who made handsome profits from the speculative gamble.

With all these, as part of a sad Diaspora that was to continue for another hundred and fifty years, went the thieves and beggars, gipsies, whores, paupers and dissolute persons whom Scotland's own government found too much of a nuisance to keep and too valuable to hang. The Scots, said the English colonists, were good and reliable servants, and the Governor of one plantation wished that he might have more, three or four thousand perhaps, promising to pay their passage and give them their freedom after a year's bondage.

Some years before the Revolution Scots merchants had become dimly aware that their counting-houses, and not the bloody banners of the Scots Brigades, could be the future glory of their nation. In December, 1681, eighty-two of them, aping the English, formed themselves into The Company of Merchants of Edinburgh. Their badge was a stock of broom, the yellow-flowered native shrub of astonishing growth, and they toasted it at every meeting. Their constitution ruled that none but those who joined the Company could conduct business in the city. Acknowledging the God of Battles in his *alter ego* as Lord of Trade, they began all their business with a supplicatory prayer: "Almighty and eternal God, the sea is Thine, and Thy hands formed the dry land. Prosper us in our present undertakings with the fruits of both."

By 1691 the Company had indeed prospered, though the same might not have been said of the country. From the legacies of dead members it had built a school for the education of the female children of those who had nothing to bequeath but orphans. For £670 Sterling it had bought Lord Oxenforde's quadrangular house by Magdalen Chapel in Cowgate (his lordship's preference for a Stuart king preventing him from disputing the sale), hung its meeting-hall with one hundred and nineteen skins of black Spanish leather stamped with gold, and turned the waste ground to the rear into a pleasant bowling-green.

It was the dogged efforts of the members of this company that secured Tweeddale's promise to the fifth session of the Scots Parliament. They had been in sympathy with Glasgow merchants in 1691 when the latter urged the need for a Scots colony upon the Convention of Royal Burghs. With the passing of the Act for Encouraging Foreign Trade in 1693, they were among the forty-eight signators to a bond which stressed "the great advantages that may redound to this nation by promoting a trade to the coast of Africa, America and other foreign parts", agreeing to work diligently for this until the Crown granted a patent for such a trading company, and each contributing three guineas toward the expense. Among those signators, too, were Paterson, Douglas, Nairne, Chiesly and other Scots merchants in London, and it is probable that these men, with their wider experience and shrewder brains, were the inspirational and organisational centre of the agitation.

For it was from them that came the first real response to the King's gracious invitation. Eight months later, standing before the bar of the Commons in Westminster Hall, and not at all sure that he might not be taken from thence to prison, Paterson made it seem a casual affair to which small thought had been given. Mr. Chiesly had called one day in May. Mr. Chiesly had said that there was talk at home of new measures to encourage trade. Mr. Paterson had given him "a scheme for erecting an East India Company", which Mr. Chiesly had carried into Scotland some days later.

There had been more to it than that. Long hours, days, months, a year or more perhaps. Coffee and chocolate in Denmark Street, or the welcome change of Hannah Chiesly's hot punch in Allhallows Staining. Discarded wigs hanging on the corners of chairs, blue smoke from long clay pipes, the squeak of a knife cutting a new quill, and Scots voices from all the Lowland shires, debating and disputing. Robert Douglas so contemptuous of Paterson's Darien dream, so ready to squash all talk of it that Paterson suspected him of treachery. David Nairne, who acted as a London banker for Scotland's nobility and their improvident sons, reporting that he had written to Lord Leven, to Lord Tarbat, entreating their support. Paterson urging that the company must be a joint venture of the two kingdoms, that its directors should include men like Cohen D'Azevedo and the Huguenot Paul Domonique, English merchants like Robert Lancashire and Thomas Skinner who were jealous of the East

India Company's monopoly, who wanted a more profitable exercise for their capital than fitting out interlopers which must wear ship and run as soon as an Indiaman's topsails broke the horizon.

The scheme was written in Paterson's good hand, and was the creation of his lucid mind and ambitious imagination. It said nothing about Darien, but it drew the framework and determined the rights and privileges of an incredibly powerful trading company with a sovereignty subordinate only to the Crown. It lay in Paterson's writing-desk against the day when good news came from the north. Chiesly took it to Edinburgh, and from it, in great haste and excitement, was drafted one of the most noble, vainglorious and disastrous Acts ever passed by the Parliament of Scotland.

"Yea the Body of the Nation longing to have a Plantation"
Edinburgh, June 1695

The Marquis of Tweeddale, an aging but conscientious man much troubled by rheums and agues, lodged in the palace of Holyroodhouse. The fine windows of his apartments looked out on the Physick Garden, the treeless park about King Arthur's Seat, and the squalid debtors who took sanctuary in St. Anne's Yard. As the King's Commissioner to Parliament he was allowed £50 a day to keep a good table, whereat most Members of the Estates dined at least once during the session. Escorted by a troop of dragoons in blue and steel, he travelled each morning to Parliament Hall in a coach drawn by six horses, another coach-and-six for his attendant gentlemen, and more for the Lord Chancellor, the Secretary for Scotland, the Lord Justice Clerk and other Officers of State. This solemn progress of patched, powdered and periwigged old men was watched by disrespectful crowds by the pillory outside the Tron Church, by the kail-wives and by women drawing water from the fountains, while the Town Guard stood to arms with drums beating. Looking up from his coach-window, the King's Commissioner could see the greystone vanity of the city's new skyline, gabled thistles, roses and fleurs-de-lys, and on the walls of older houses the sober admonitions of earlier centuries. *As you are lord of your tongue, so am I of my ears. . . .*

In Parliament Hall, forty yards long and sixteen wide, beneath the black cross-braces and hammer-beams, Tweeddale filled a lonely throne, his commission on a velvet cushion before him. Lords and Commons sat in banked tiers, sharing one chamber but preserving the distinctions of birth and privilege. Dukes, marquesses and earls were closest to God in high rows to the right of the throne, viscounts and barons to the left, and below them, descending, the knights of the shires, burgesses and commons. The fall of colour, scarlet and blue through brocade to black, ended at a long table upon which lay the Crown, the Sceptre and the Sword of Scotland, a cold fire of gold and silver, rubies, amethysts and garnets, blue enamel and pearls, diamonds, emeralds, velvet and ermine. Here, on Wednesday, June 12, 1695, before a large crowd of strangers who stood inside the doors holding the white sticks that were their tickets of entry, the Estates listened to a first reading of An Act for the Encouragement of Trade. Without debate they referred it to the Committee of Trade which, within two days, had renamed it *An Act in favour of the Scots Company Trading to Africa and the Indies.*

There was scarcely a literate man in the Lowlands who did not know what it proposed. On May 22, shortly after James Chiesly's arrival in Edinburgh, a short pamphlet appeared on the streets and in the coffee-houses and taverns. It was called *Proposals for a Fond to Cary on a Plantation*, and it is easy to believe, by deduction rather than evidence, that it was a printed version of Paterson's scheme. It was a concise, orderly plan for the creation of a joint-stock company with powers to trade, to establish colonies in America, Asia or Africa, and to hold them in the name of the Crown of Scotland, to purchase ships, and to open a bank in Edinburgh. It began without preamble, and to the point: "There is no need to take up any time in setting forth the usefulness of plantations in general to all places, or to the Kingdom of Scotland in particular, seeing now at length persons of all ranks, yea the Body of the Nation are longing to have a Plantation." The pamphlet's first condition for the establishment of the company reflects Paterson's simple idealism, his appeal to what was noblest in man. The company should be

A Body of Trading Men of the nation (not excluding either Nobility or Gentry from furnishing their shares unto) incorporated under such reasonable and lasting rules as may carry on the design, and neither leave it in the power of the Managers to misapply, nor of passionate and peevish Members either to break the company or carry off their shares.

Though this pamphlet, and the Bill before the Committee of Trade, provoked argument and enthusiasm, public interest was really excited by something much more dramatic. The Commission of Inquiry into the Massacre of Glencoe, three years before, had begun its sittings in the Long Gallery of Holyroodhouse, and at the other end of the Royal Mile the Estates were waiting for its report, declaring that they would delay all other business until they had it, though they might have no right to debate the matter before the King had given his opinion. Their impatience was due less to a respect for justice than to a realisation that here at last they might pull down and destroy the King's Secretary of State, the Master of Stair, upon whose orders the slaughter of the MacDonalds had taken place. Each day was thus another blaze of colourful pomp, the Officers of State going by gilded coaches to Parliament Hall, the members of the Inquiry coming by theirs to Abbey Close, the gates of the palace opening and closing upon scarlet and tartan. In the taverns, the broad thoroughfare of the High Street, by the coach-houses of the palace, could be seen some of the witnesses to the Inquiry: officers of John Hill's Regiment down from their garrison in Lochaber, and keeping close to their worried colonel; catlike clansmen in the tail of their chief, John MacDonald, and his brother Alasdair. And there was one riotous morning when the Earl of Breadalbane, the slippery Highland eel whose involvement in the massacre was suspected but not determined, was carried in his coach to the Castle, a prisoner by vote of the Estates.

In the noisy atmosphere of accusation and recrimination, Tweeddale required more mental and physical energy than he had shown when he changed his loyalties at Marston Moor, fifty years before. As President of the Inquiry and Commissioner to Parliament, he was sometimes needed at both ends of the Royal Mile on the same morning. A servant to both King and nation, he found it difficult to obey one without angering the other. Testy dispatches from Flanders demanded that he bring the session to an end, and from the lower tiers of Parliament Hall he was told that Members would sit until they received satisfaction. He bowed before immediate pressures and hoped for understanding from those more distant, begging the King for further time "that your service may be done with cheerfulness and alacrity."

To the merchants of Edinburgh, the responsibility for the murder of three dozen Highland savages was of small consequence at this moment. Their concern was to speed the passage of their Bill through the Committee of Trade and back to the floor of Parliament for a vote. Two of them were principally concerned in sweetening the members of the Committee, answering questions, providing information, and making promises. Both had been ardent advocates of a trading company since the 1693 Act, keeping careful note of their tavern expenses against future repayment, and both had been correspondents of Chiesly, Nairne and other London Scots. James Balfour was a solid man of business with hopes of the Caribbean trade, a decent body with a modest ancestry of Lowland lairds whose fortunes and lands had been first secured at the end of a reiver's lance. His surname was respected in Scotland for honesty and plain-dealing, and would become wider known when his descendant gave it to the hero of *Treasure Island*. Robert Blackwood was a woollen merchant, a director of the Newmills Cloth Company, jealous of the privileges of his English competitors in Africa where, it was said, a single plaid would secure many times its weight in elephants' teeth and gold.

Such men represented the emergent aristocracy of wealth in Scotland, pious supporters of the Kirk, and politically potent in the Estates. William Arbuckle, a merchant of Glasgow and one of the first to dip into his purse for the company, was able to subscribe more stock than peers whose estates spread across three shires. The Lord Provost of Edinburgh, at present a kinsman of James Chiesly, was by custom a knighted merchant who sat by right on the King's Privy Council. These trading men were as proud of their counting-houses, their factories and their town houses, as nobler men were of their castles and regiments. The Englishman, Joseph Taylor, once dined at Brandfield in the

Edinburgh suburb of Fountainbridge, the home of the leather-merchant Sir Alexander Brand whose skins of black and gold had been hung in Oxenforde's hall. Brand's daughters put aside their father's breeches, which they had been mending, offered Taylor brandy and champagne, and played the spinet for him beneath a splendid ceiling upon which the family's sturdy politics were displayed in a carving of one crown and two sceptres, and the ironic Latin motto: "This has been left us by one hundred and eight forefathers." It was Brand who offered to clean the streets, courts and turnpikes of Edinburgh, largely at his own expense, because it was "the nastiest city in the world".

For two weeks following the first reading of the Act, Balfour and Blackwood tirelessly entertained the secretary and members of the Committee of Trade, not forgetting to tip the doorkeeper of the Exchequer House where the Committee met, or to buy ale for Tweeddale's servants in return for the news they might bring from the Commissioner's table. During one exhausting evening, when the two merchants dined with Committee members at the Ship tavern, they nobly dispatched a lambshead and bowls of mutton broth, herrings and a sleeve of mutton, three ducks, three chickens with gooseberries, fruit, cheese, bread and ale, French wine and brandy, followed by tobacco and pipes. All of which, Mr. Balfour meticulously recorded, would cost the future company £33 5s Scots, including two shillings for the cook and fourteen for the serving-boys. The next evening, with heroic fortitude, Blackwood joined the secretary of the Committee at the Ship, consuming a dish of fowls with gooseberries, two lobsters, cutlets, sparagrass, bread, ale and wine, tobacco and pipes. There were also endless dishes of coffee at Maclurg's, ale at Peter Steel's, more dinners at Widow Graham's, copies of the Act to be printed and circulated, a meeting of merchants and baillies at William Ross's, and the staggering expenditure of £11 17s on "coffee and otherwise" at the Sun before Balfour and Blackwood went to give evidence before the Committee of Trade.

None of this was self-indulgence. Without relentless pressure, without liberal hospitality, the Committee might well have dallied over its business and decided nothing by the time the session ended. But by June 25, all amendments to the Act had been finally agreed and it was once more brought before the Estates.

Again it was remitted to the Committee, in order that the names of the patentees or promoters of the company—ten resident in England and ten in Scotland—might be inserted. Lord Belhaven, president of the Committee, was also advised to consult with the Lyon King of Arms upon what seal, what emblazon the company should be given. There was no doubt about this, all men agreed that nothing could better illustrate the nation's longing and its glorious future than a golden sun, rising from the waves.

Clerks worked overnight to make the amendments, and the next morning, Wednesday, June 26, the Bill was once more brought before the Estates. It was read, voted and approved, without debate and dismissed almost casually. A week before, the Glencoe Commissioners had finished their Inquiry, and their Report was already on its way to the King in his camp before Namur. Tweeddale had reluctantly submitted a copy to Parliament, and for five days Members had been hotly debating it, with no interest in, and no time for anything else. They could feel the Master of Stair's neck within their grasp, and to-day they wished to vote upon whether or not an Address should be sent to the King, demanding the punishment of those found guilty of bloody slaughter in a Highland glen. There was no objection when the Bill's supporters asked that it be given the Royal Assent that day. Tweeddale had not the strength or courage to delay this, though he must have known that implicit in the promise he had given on May 9 was the King's wish to study any act for a company before it was passed. Nor was it clear—and no argument later would satisfactorily determine this—whether or not he had the power to give the Royal Assent without royal permission. But he was old, and he too, perhaps, was caught up in the surge of patriotic emotion. The Sceptre was carried to him, a silver and gilt rod thirty-four inches in length, hexagonal, richly decorated with pearls, oak leaves and golden dolphins, enamelled images of the Virgin Mary, Saint James, and Saint Andrew in a Highland bonnet. Tweeddale took it in both hands, lowered its crystal globe, and gently touched the Act.

That evening in Michael's tavern, and for what seems an unusually cautious expenditure of £2 15s, Mr. Balfour and Mr. Blackwood, with "the Londoners and the Glasgow men", toasted The Company of Scotland Trading to Africa and the Indies.

As defined by the clauses of the Act there had never been anything like this Company, nor would there ever be anything like it again. Its promoters, its supporters in the Estates, had been like children left by an open larder door, encouraged by the imagined approval of an absent parent. For the next 31 years it had the monopoly of Scottish trade with Asia, Africa and America, and for 21 of these all goods imported by it, with the exception of sugar and tobacco, would be free of duty. For ten years it had the right to equip, freight and navigate its own or hired ships, "in warlike or other manner, to any lands, islands, countries, or places in Africa, Asia or America, and there to plant colonies, build cities, towns or forts" with the consent of the natives of such places, and provided they were not part of the possessions of any European sovereign or state. It had the right to furnish its forts and towns with magazines, stores and the weapons of war, and the powers to defend them against attack, to seek reprisals, to make treaties of peace and commerce with the native princes, governors and rulers of the lands they settled. And if injury were done to the Company, its possessions and its people by a European power, then the King and the King's men must guarantee and secure reparation.

All officers and servants of the Company in its colonies, with those of other nations who might settle with them and accept its rules, were to be free citizens of the Kingdom of Scotland, with all the rights and privileges thereof. No officer of state, civil or military, could arrest, impress or detain any member or servant of the Company, and if this were done then the Company had the right to release the men with the unquestioning assistance of the King's magistrates and officers. And all members of the Company were to be free "both in their persons, estates and goods employed in the said stock and trade, from all manner of taxes, cesses, supplies, excises, quartering of soldiers, transient or local, or levying of soldiers, or other impositions whatsoever, and that for and during the space of twenty-one years." No part of the capital stock, or of the real or personal property of the Company could be liable to confiscation or arrest, and creditors of members of the Company were to have lien over their profits only, and no rights over their stock.

Thus was the Company a nation in itself, with the right to

make governments and wage war, to grant freedoms and impose punishments, to trade where and with whom it wished. It could challenge the mercantile and colonial empires of England, Holland and Spain, fly its flag and the saltire of Scotland in any port and on any sea, and answer insults to both with fire and sword. The crystal globe of the Sceptre, catching the June sunlight from the windows of Parliament Hall, had ended a century of deprivation and despair. To the King alone did the Company own allegiance, and in token of this, and in gratitude, it promised him and his successors one hogshead of tobacco every year.

Twenty men were named in the Act as promoters and patentees, with powers to join with others, to form a Council-General and a Court of Directors, to issue stock, to determine the rules, ordinances and constitution of the Company. Ten of them were Londoners, two Englishmen, the Jew D'Azevedo, and seven resident Scots including Paterson. In Scotland there was John Hamilton, Lord Belhaven, rewarded perhaps for his noisy advocacy in the Committee of Trade, the Lord Justice Clerk Adam Cockburn of Ormiston, the Lord Provost of Edinburgh Sir Robert Chiesly, Balfour, Blackwood, two other merchants from Glasgow and Edinburgh, and three Lowland lairds who had also been members of the Committee of Trade.

That week James Balfour gathered the scraps of paper upon which he and Blackwood had kept a careful note of their expenses during the past two and a half years. He copied them out neatly on a scroll and called it "An Accompt of Mony spent in Procuring the Act of Parlement for the Afrecane Tread". The lobsters and cutlets, sparagrass and mutton broth, duck and chickens with gooseberries, cheese and ale, French wine and brandy, pipes, tobacco, coffee and tips, the charges of printers and clerks, the cost of the best Lombard paper, fees to the Lord Chancellor and the Keeper of the Seal, and a curious entry "for Mr. Robert Blackwood and my own trouble and attendance", amounted to £2,119 12s 8d Scots.

The key of the universe had been cheaply bought.

"We must not act apart in any thing, but in a united body"
London, July to December 1695

And then it was seen that the Company had two heads, each
turned to the other in suspicion. Whatever might be the intentions of the promoters in Scotland, those in England proceeded
on the assumption that the Court of Directors must be established in London, and during the next five months the childish
havering and unexplained silences of the Edinburgh promoters
persuaded them that they were right. Even Paterson had not
thought it necessary to go to Scotland to support the passage of
the Act through Parliament, though he had cannonaded Balfour
with letters of advice which were dutifully read aloud to the
Lord Provost and the Baillies of Edinburgh at the Ship ("to coffee
and otherwise, £3 15s").

For their part, Balfour and Blackwood acted as if their colleagues in London had suddenly and obligingly drowned themselves in the Thames. As soon as the Act had been touched by
the Sceptre they recruited twenty-eight of their fellow-merchants
of Glasgow and Edinburgh as members of the Company, each
contributing £3 Sterling toward immediate expenses and promising to subscribe stock to the total value of £13,600. This
placed them ahead of the Londoners who had not yet decided to
establish themselves as a Court of Directors, or opened a
Subscription Book. Nor could they, for no one in Scotland seemed
willing to send them a copy of the Act. Behind these pettish
differences lay wider antagonisms. The Scots saw the Company
as a colonising power that would release them from the political
and religious tyrannies of the past, and bring them a rich, commercial future based on the forts, towns, magazines and navies
granted them by the Act. The Londoners, with the exception of
Paterson, were less interested in plantations than in the exploita-
tion of the Spice Islands and the Indian sub-continent, too long
the jealous monopoly of the East India Company.

Paterson was accepted as the spokesman of the Londoners, or
made himself so by the sustained power of his lungs and his
indefatigable capacity for hard work. He decided that Sir Robert
Chiesly was the responsible member of the Edinburgh promoters,

and for the next three months he carried on an urgent, and usually one-sided correspondence with the Lord Provost, pleading for a copy of the Act and arguing that some of the Scots should come to London without delay. He understood his countrymen's demoralising vice of prevarication by committee, and he demanded action, action. "For if anything go not on with the first heat, the raising of a fund seldom or never succeeds, the multitude being commonly led more by example than reason."

This London summer was exceptional, the days hot and still, broken by spectacular thunderstorms which at least kept down the dust and the stench as Paterson walked or took a hackney to the City, to sup with James and Hannah Chiesly, to dine with James Foulis in St. Mary Woolnoth or Thomas Coutts in St. Dionis Backchurch. The London Scots were aware of a growing impatience among those English merchants who had been persuaded to take an interest in the Company. The traditional English contempt for the Scots, and the Scot's long envy of the English, their religious and political differences, could destroy the Company before its first whimper of life. Paterson rightly suspected that these prejudices might be stronger in Edinburgh than in London. He pleaded with Robert Chiesly to ignore them, and his letter suggests that someone had perhaps raised an eyebrow at the inclusion of the Jew D'Azevedo. "It's needful to make no distinction of parties in this noble undertaking, but that of whatever nation or religion a man be (if one of us) he ought to be looked upon to be of the same interest and inclination. For we must not act apart in any thing, but in a firm and united body, and distinct from all other interests whatsoever."

Chiesly and his colleagues probably resented the patronising tone and pedagogic style of such letters. They made irksome reading for proud men who could not see what Mr. Paterson had done in this affair, beyond the scheme he had drawn up, that he should so cock his hat and teach them their business. There had been talk of a company, and proposals for an Act, long before his voice had been heard in Denmark Street, as Mr. Balfour's account of money spent could show. And so, a copy of the Act was not sent. When it did leave Edinburgh, about mid-August, it was dispatched by news-writers and was circulating in the taverns and coffee-houses of Fleet Street before Paterson and his friends had read a word of it. "We are much surprised," he complained, "to see some of the printed Acts of Parliament in the hands of some who are not very well wishers to us, before we who are concerned can have them." The ill-wishers were the directors and stock-holders of the East India and African Companies, their friends and place-men in Whitehall. Worse still, to Paterson's tidy mind, was the deplorable mistake made in the names of the London promoters, eleven being given in the Act instead of ten, though Scots clerks and Scots printers might have been excused for turning Joseph Cohen D'Azevedo into two strangers called Joseph Cohaine and Daves Ovedo.

What letters Paterson did get from Chiesly were vague and discouraging, promising little except that one of the Scots might visit London at some unspecified date. Paterson replied that at least three should be sent, and that immediately. "Since the people here are already as much awakened as they are like to be, it becomes us to strike while the iron is hot and hasten our pace." All would go well as soon as a Court of Directors was properly established, and there should be no doubt that London was the place for it. "Because without the advice and assistance of some gentlemen here it will not be possible to lay the foundation as it ought, either to counsel or money." The best heads, the best purses; by the enlistment of these in both England and Scotland would the Company prosper.

In the end, without waiting for the Scots, the Londoners held their first formal meeting of business, on Thursday, August 29. It was a dull, cold day, with the promise of an early winter in the mists above Soho Fields. Great fires were burning in Cheapside and at Charing Cross, and the streets were noisy with drunken crowds. That morning Mr. Fry, the King's Messenger, had arrived from the Low Countries with news of the fall of Namur, a bloody affair in which three thousand of William's fusiliers had marched stubbornly on the outworks under the command of that salamander Lord Cutts, losing a third of their number by musketry and the stones which the French rolled down upon them. There were rumours that the King himself had been killed, and some days ago a mad officer of the Earl of Oxford's Horse had ridden through the City, waving sword and pistol, threatening to kill any who denied that Dutch William was dead. The mob pulled him from the saddle and took him to Newgate along with the Frenchman Pontack, who owned the fashionable eating-house in Abchurch Lane, and who had started the rumour for reasons he had so far kept to himself.

The meeting was brief and orderly, efficiently controlled by a young scrivener called Roderick Mackenzie who had been engaged as Secretary. His Highland ancestry is obscure, his Christian name common enough among his clan, but he had pretensions to gentility, sometimes sealing his private letters with a harp, and sometimes with the stag's-head of the Seaforths. He was likeable and friendly, and was quickly called Rorie by the other Scots exiles. He wrote a clear, cursive hand, kept proper minutes with the aid of two clerks, and was to be the Company's loyal and passionate servant from this day until its sordid extinction twelve years later, and would in time be so jealous of its honour that he would lie for it, take up arms for it, and see innocent men hang for it. This evening, as candles were lit against an early dusk, he wrote down the first resolutions recorded by the Company.

Resolved, that all persons who are desirous to be incorporated into this Company do give their names together with the respective sums for which they are willing to subscribe, in writing, to Roderick Mackenzie, who is to keep a list thereof.

Resolved, that the said Roderick Mackenzie do not discover the said names, or any sums, or any part thereof, to any person or persons whatsoever, without special direction of at least a majority of the members now assembled.

Resolved, that a sum be raised for defraying all necessary charges, till the constitution of the Company be settled.

There were seven members present, all of them Scots, and no reason was given in the minutes for the absence of D'Azevedo and the two Englishmen. It was agreed that each should give £25 against those necessary charges, the cost of ink, paper and candles, clerks and the Edinburgh post, wine and ale, tobacco and pipes. James Foulis was elected treasurer and was instructed to advance £20 to Mackenzie for petty cash. And then they put on their cloaks, called up their link-boys, and went home through the smoke.

Paterson sent news of the meeting to Scotland, and again asked that delegates be sent, "all the Gentlemen here do seriously press it." And again a few days later, "We find ourselves daily more and more obliged to press the coming of these persons who shall be deputed from you, the reasons still increasing for us to get our business here dispatched before the approaching Sessions of Parliament." For when William came home from his war, when Commons and Lords sat that autumn, all the trading companies of England would conspire to crush the upstart, malapert, interloping Company of Scotland.

If they were not doing so already. The East India Company, it was said, was considering a petition to the King, begging his gracious consideration of their troubles. These did not include, publicly at least, the Scots Company, but were none the less grave. French privateers, which lay off the Scilly Isles like waiting cats, and could sometimes be seen from Plymouth or Wight, had recently taken two great Indiamen, the latest of many such expensive losses to all the English companies. Great men were withdrawing their support from the East India Company, and its shares had fallen from 94 to 74. When the Londoners met on September 26, this time with D'Azevedo, they were uneasy. Tavern rumours, probably started by agents of the English companies, said that they were a conspiracy of wild men, of Jacobites even, who gathered to plot against the Crown and to slander the English people and their Government. The only business done that day was the passing of a motion upon this matter.

Whereas, upon information, it appears that some enemies to this Company do industriously spread abroad surmises, as if some of the persons concerned in this Company did openly speak reproachfully and contemptibly of the Power of the Government and People of England, in relation to this Company, *Ordered*, that Members of this Company do, upon all occasions, speak with due respect of the Power of the Government and People of England; and that they endeavour, with all imaginable candour, to obviate and satisfy the objections of any person, or persons, without heat or reflection.

Ordered, that Roderick Mackenzie do signify the contents of this resolution to absent Members.

The wording of the motion suggests that it was composed by Paterson, and its tone implies that there may have been a small truth in the rumours; that unable to hold their tempers before English jibes some of the Scots had spoken too boldly in defence of their country and its Company. It was hard for proud and ambitious men to walk softly and speak circumspectly.

Autumn, and still no assurance from Scotland, though the Lord Provost seems to have been writing more frequently. "We wonder that some of you should still be of the opinion that this matter may be transacted by correspondence," Paterson tartly told him. There was a strong feeling in Edinburgh that there should be different riders in the saddle, and a different journey undertaken. The Londoners should send a deputation to Scotland. Paterson would have none of this. The Company would fail without the strong support of English capital. "It's impossible to lay the foundation anywhere but here. We've already pressed you to hasten by our former letters more than modesty would admit, and we must now tell you that if you neglect coming up but a few days after this comes to hand, it will endanger the whole matter." The Scots should be in London by the first day of November at the latest.

Both Houses of the English Parliament had already met, and had been prorogued until the end of the month. Agents of the English companies had been seen in Westminster Hall, catching at the coats of Commons and Lords, and it was no secret that by the year's end they would have taken this Scots child by the throat and throttled it before it could be weaned. The King came home from Flanders on October 10, landing at Margate and riding in slow triumph to London with a gathering train of nobility, knights of the shires, gentlemen and merchants of the City. None could say what his humour was on matters of State and the affairs of Scotland, and since the death of his faultless Queen, nine months before, he had been more than usually aloof and withdrawn. He wore a lock of her hair, in a ring tied to a black ribbon above his left elbow, and he was happiest away from England with his army. When he came back from killing

Frenchmen he preferred to divert himself by killing a stag at Windsor, or by watching his horses run at Newmarket. He left the bonfires and the bells of London behind him, and went to his lonely palace at Kensington. There he told his Privy Council that he was satisfied with their prudent administration in his absence, and instructed them to dissolve Parliament, and to call a new one on November 22.

The Londoners could expect no interference until the new Parliament sat, and before then they must establish themselves as a Court of Directors and open a Subscription Book, with or without the presence of a deputation from Edinburgh. They gathered now at a regular meeting-place a red brick, three-storyed house in Clement's Lane belonging to a sympathetic City merchant called Nathaniel Carpenter. The ticking of his great pendulum-clock, the noise of his four young children, and the bells of St. Clement's in Eastcheap were a background to their worried anxiety. On October 22, when they met at three in the afternoon, there was the louder noise of shouting and brawling in the streets. Four members of Parliament for the City were being elected at the Guildhall. On this day, too, the King's horse won the Town Plate at Newmarket, the East India Company heard that it has lost another ship to French privateers, and its stock fell from 76 to 54.

The Directors finished their business quickly, anxious to be away home before the crowd in the streets turned to a mob, but it was the most important meeting they had held so far. Once more they agreed, in view of the growing rumours, to keep secret "all discourses and transactions passed here." And they passed two major resolutions. The Subscription Book of the Company was to be opened on November 6. The capital fund was to be set at £600,000 Sterling, one quarter of which would be taken up upon the opening of the Book.

Paterson's heart was lifted, at last something was being done. During the next few days it was resolved that the government of the Company should rest in the persons named in the Act, who could now describe themselves as its Court of Directors, with the right to increase their number to fifty. Further, there would be thirty "Proprietors" of the Company, being those who subscribed £1,000 or more in stock. In a mood of restored confidence, the ten Directors were probably pleased to hear that the East India Company's stock had reached its lowest yet. Many of its investors were making discreet inquiries about the potential of the Scots Company, and so serious had become the withdrawals from the East India Company that its Governors had called a General Court, frankly acknowledging the grave losses of ships, goods and men to the French, and declaring that only a call of £25 per cent would keep the Company in business.

The preamble to the Subscription Book of the Scots Company, written in Mackenzie's clear hand, indicated that Paterson was at this moment the most important member of the new Court of Directors. Because he, and others concerned with him, had been "at great pains and expense in making several considerable discoveries of trade and improvements, in and to both Indies, and likewise in procuring needful powers and privileges for a Company of Commerce", he was to receive two per cent of the money first subscribed, and three per cent of the profits for the next 21 years. It was an incredible gift, and it is almost impossible to understand how nine sober and experienced merchants could agree to it. In all probability Paterson himself suggested it, and it shows the mesmeric power he could sometimes exert over others, if never for long.

Mackenzie's clerks had scarcely ruled the first pages of the Subscription Book and entered the first names when unannounced, and by now unexpected, three of the Edinburgh promoters arrived in London: Balfour, Blackwood, and that patriotic rhetorician Lord Belhaven, whom the English spy, John Macky, described as "a round, fat, black, noisy man, more like a butcher than a lord." None of them was in a good humour when they attended their first meeting in Clement's Lane on November 9. They had all read the Preamble, and were all unhappy about it. They were astonished by the size of the proposed capital, and doubted whether Scotland's purse was deep enough to provide the required half of it. Paterson's simple eloquence was no match for a practised speaker like Belhaven, who tuned his oratory by printing his own speeches, and who now dominated the meeting by his rank, his presence, and his inexhaustible supply of metaphors and similes, apologues, parables and perorations. The Londoners quickly understood that the Scots regarded

Edinburgh as the proper base for the Company, and they realised that Paterson's influence there might be less than was claimed by him in London. Although they persuaded the Scots to accept the need for so large a capital subscription, they agreed that Paterson should write to Edinburgh, explaining this need, and that copies of all their journals and records should also be sent to Scotland.

Now the Court of Directors met almost every day, and usually in disharmony. Mackenzie's minutes tersely indicated the wrangling that burnt away Mr. Carpenter's candles: *Upon some objections offered... Several debates arising concerning the management... Several objections made by the persons deputed from Scotland....* The Scots' principal objection was to the terms and wording of the Preamble, arguing that some patentees in Scotland might withdraw when they realised how great was to be the capital fund. There was also one other matter which profoundly disturbed them, and although they had not yet brought it into the open it lay behind every other objection they raised. This was the rich reward granted Paterson, before the Company had begun trading and before any man could see security in its profits, and Balfour may have reflected that there had been no proposal to repay him and Blackwood for all those dinners and suppers, sealing-wax and paper, the expenses due them for their attendance and trouble.

On November 11 the East India Company took public notice of the Scots. It voted that no member of the Company could be associated with them in any way without breaking his oath. Three days later it petitioned the King at Kensington, placing before him the grave state of its affairs, its bitter losses in the war, the unfair and possibly illegal competition of the proposed Scots Company. The King accepted the petition without comment, and went off to hunt at Windsor, to attend an electoral chapter of the Garter.

The warning was clear to the Scots, though none seems to have recognised it, or acknowledged it in the minutes of their meetings. They argued on, sometimes over trivial matters, sometimes acting like sober, intelligent businessmen, and when the latter was the case it was usually due to the London merchants D'Azevedo, Nairne and Chiesly. They admitted eight new directors, all of them Englishmen and ready to subscribe stock on their own or others' behalf, and they rightly decided that a majority and quorum of the Court should not consist of the original directors but of new men, appointed directly by the stockholders and exercising their right of proxy. Now Mackenzie's minutes were nobly and properly headed "At a Court of Directors of the Company of Scotland Trading to Africa and the Indies. . . ."

Robert Douglas, the London Scot who was Paterson's sour and sceptical critic, was admitted as a Director on November 22, and Paterson was later to claim that he was an agent of some cabal in Scotland that wished him ill, and had joined the Company to destroy him. It was a day of events. The London Subscription Book was closed that morning, having reached the agreed sum of £300,000. There was also published a small pamphlet called *Some Considerations upon the Late Act of the Parliament of Scotland*, and it reads as if written by Paterson. It was the Company's only acknowledgement of English hostility, and its only attempt to ward off the disaster that threatened. It lightly argued that the English had nothing to fear from the Company, if they wished to keep their commercial superiority they should relax their own trading laws and not waste their energies in an attack upon the Scots.

That morning, too, the new Parliament of England assembled in Westminster Hall. The King went to the Lords and asked the Commons to choose a Speaker. From the Throne, at eleven o'clock the next morning, he spoke of the war, his soldiers' courage and his people's contribution in coin. It was unfortunate that he must again ask for recruits and money to continue that war, and he urged his Parliament to think of new means of raising both. He suggested that merchant shipping should be increased, and that the East India trade should be encouraged. There would, he hoped, be a speedy dispatch of all business before the House, for the French would be early in the field next Spring.

On Friday, November 29, William Paterson's influential role in the Court of Directors was abruptly ended, and that by himself. Twenty men met at Mr. Carpenter's under the presidency of Belhaven. Six of them were new English directors. Two more were Paul Domonique the Huguenot, and Daniel van Mildert a Dutchman. These, with Robert Douglas and the three delegates from Edinburgh, made a majority upon whom Paterson could rely for little sympathy or support. The business of the day began at three o'clock with the reading, by Roderick Mackenzie, of an agreed oath *De Fideli Administratione* as enjoined by the Act.

We, whose names are herunto subscribed, do severally, in the presence of Almighty God, and this Company, declare and promise, *That*, during our being jointly, or severally, concerned in the Company of Scotland Trading to Africa and the Indies, we shall not disclose any thing that, from time to time, shall by the President of the Court be given us in charge to be kept secret; but shall in our respective stations, endeavour, to the utmost of our power, to promote the Profit and Interest of the said Company.

Following business included agreement on a similar oath to be taken by the Company's servants, and a resolution to acquire a ship, or ships, that could be sent to trade in the East Indies. A Committee of Trade was elected to manage this.

When Paterson rose, asking Belhaven's leave to address the Court, it was without prompting, but stress and pressure were implicit in all he said, an awareness that the majority of those present resented the special favours granted him, and had made that resentment plain. He said that he had insisted on the royalties and profits, not doubting the justice and generosity of the Company, or his usefulness to it, but because he had had bitter experience of man's ingratitude. He had spent nearly £10,000 of his own and other men's money on this noble undertaking, though he did not say how, or where, or when. There had also been "ten years of pain and travel, six years whereof were wholly spent in promoting the design of this Company", and again he did not say where or when. The claim that he had been the suffering and impoverished creator of their Company was listened to in silence by Balfour and Blackwood, who knew that they had spent four years and more in the same service, and had their scroll of expenses to prove it, which was more evidence than Paterson was offering.

"This Court," said Paterson extravagantly, "being filled with so many excellent persons, in whose justice and gratitude I have entire confidence, I resolve to take hold of so glorious an opportunity of showing the generosity and integrity of my heart. I freely and fully renounce and resign the two per cent and three per cent mentioned in the Preamble of Subscription, back again to the Company from whom I had so brave and noble a concession."

And the Directors took it back, and thanked him for it. They gave no sign of suspecting that this bold renunciation, wrapped in flattery, might be an invitation to confirm him in the grants. Years later, when men fought over the corpse of the Company, eager to snatch up a penny where they had placed a pound, Paterson regretted his noble gesture. By then a poor teacher of mathematics in a Soho room, he said that his release "was only given in trust", that he had been prevailed upon by the lie that the two per cent had already been promised to others, to great men in Scotland who wanted payment for their support in the Estates. And this may well have been true, but again he offered no proof.

It was almost the last meeting held by the London Directors. On December 3, the Lords debated the state of the nation. "Particularly upon the Scotch East India Company," wrote Narcissus Luttrell in his annals that night, "which they think will be prejudicial to our trade; and after long debates resolved that divers English merchants trading to the East Indies, as also the Commissioners of Customs, attend them on Thursday next about it." The minutes of the Directors' meeting the next day contain no mention of this danger, although they once more warned each other that all their proceedings should be kept secret. They urged the opening of a Subscription Book in Scotland as soon as possible, and instructed Belhaven, Balfour and Blackwood to prepare a preamble. The English Directors, out of patience with the Scots' habit of arriving any time they chose at Mr. Carpenter's house, insisted that there should be strict rules on punctuality, with fines for absentees and late-comers.

On Friday, December 6, the day after officers of the East India Company and the African Company had been heard at the bar of the Lords "as to the inconveniences arising from the Scotch Company", the Directors considered a draft of the preamble to the Scots Subscription, imposed a fine of half a crown for unpunctuality or non-attendance, and agreed that the only correct time was that shown by Mr. Carpenter's pendulum-clock. They closed their business late, resolving to meet again on Friday, at ten o'clock in the forenoon.

It was the last entry in their minutes. The next morning the Lords ordered seven of them, all named in the Act, to appear before the bar.

"Impeached of the said High Crimes and Misdemeanours"
London, December 1695 to February 1696

Improvident Sawney, aping gentility while he scratched at fleas, had been a ribald jest since that clamorous train of hungry Scots came south with James I in 1603. By then England had exhausted its ridicule of the Welsh, and had not yet discovered how contemptible were the Irish. Scotland was to be its buffoon for the next two hundred years, and the joke would be kept alive by witty contributions from Johnson, Lamb and Sydney Smith, with illustrations by Hogarth, Rowlandson and Gillray.

Poverty and pretension were the usual themes, and at the end of the seventeenth century it was said that there were but Eight Commandments in Scotland, since its people had nothing to covet and nothing to steal. All Scotsmen met with abroad were men of sense, said Dean Lockier, clumsily anticipating Johnson, it was those who remained at home who lacked it. English travellers reported that the meanest Scots pedlar would have himself taken for a gentleman, wearing a sword and scattering himself with snuff. John Macky said that the park, so-called, about Holyroodhouse, was very comical, having neither trees nor deer. And the Scots were disgusting hypocrites. "As they are nasty," wrote that fastidious young barrister Joseph Taylor, "so I found them profane and vicious as other people, notwithstanding all the pretended sanctity of their kirk." Their ministers, hammering on the pulpit, were more like drummers than parsons. Though they put scolds on a Stool of Repentance, talked of branding the noses of their many whores, their washwomen were without shame or modesty as they stood in the High Street of Edinburgh, petticoats kirtled to their naked bellies, treading out clothes in a mixture of water and cow-dung. Scots lice, said Taylor, were omnipresent, and he never went to bed without wearing gloves and stockings. For all its august houses, the state of the Royal Mile was deplorable. "In a morning the scent was so offensive that we were forced to hold our noses as we passed the streets, and take care where we trod for fear of disobliging our shoes, and to walk in the middle at night for fear of an accident on our heads."

Now, as the Directors of the Scots Company were called to the bar of the Lords, here was Sawney caught up by his breeches again. London's amusement was encouraged by a two-paged, ink-smudged flyer that was sold for threepence in the Admiralty Coffee-house at Charing Cross. Called *Caveto Cavetote*, it took the usual form of a letter to a friend in the country, and was signed "by an impartial hand *Tarpallian in Querpo.*" It ironically related the rumours then current, particularly that the affair was the result of information laid against the Scots. The informer could not be an Englishman.

> Some say . . . a certain Scotch native of the tribe of Judas Iscariot, who with his natural gaiety of temper and affected humility, has stoop'd down to take up the honourable office of informer behind the curtain, with design to have the Scotch Company and the promulgators thereof impeached before no less a tribunal than King and Parliament.

Some said, also, that complaints against the Company were "only from the teeth outwards, to serve other ends", a plot to embarrass Government and Throne. Some said that the Company was a mongrel with many fathers, one of them the East India Company, since there were proprietors in the Scots Company who were also committee-men in the India Company, and conversely.

> Some say, that we have other fish to fry than to trouble our heads with any of these Companies or their fiddle faddle Indian goods, the retailers of them being generally no other than decoy ducks for alluring our nieces and daughters to the fluttering beaus of the Town, who have got such a trick of raffling that they commonly end with ruffling and rifling etc., and that when we are busy getting estates, our wives too

may be under an Indian Umbrealla purchasing Indian babies to inherit them.

But among the trading companies there was no laughter. A war prolonged beyond the limit of a fair mercantile gamble became less profitable than peace. The King's demand for more Horse, Foot and Ordnance, the theatrical re-enactments in Hyde Park of his wasteful battles, the Days of Fast and Prayer that were the prelude to yet another of his campaigns, were no encouragement when it was clear that though his regiments might win more laurels his merchants would certainly lose more ships. Before the Lords lay petitions from the Honourable East India Company, the Hamburg Company, the Royal African Company and the Levant Company, from the Associations of Merchants Trading with Jamaica, with Pennsylvania and New England, with Barbadoes and the Leeward Isles. Each was a piteous threnody against the vulgar paean for victory.

In one year the nine principal companies had lost 103 ships by storm, hurricane and shipwreck, to French warships and French privateers. The total loss was £2,262,550 in ships and cargoes, of which one million and a half had been borne by the East India Company alone. The French had taken six of its great vessels, fully laden and homeward bound from Bengal and Surat, all of them between the Scilly Isles and Ireland. The Barbadoes merchants were almost bankrupt, having lost forty small ships between September 1694 and September 1695, three-quarters of them to French privateers, and the losses to the other companies had been proportionally hard. In their petitions they gave the names, burden, crew and armament of the fine ships now gone— *Prosperity, Adventure* and *Providence. . . . Sarah, John* and *Joan. . . . Swan, Pelican* and *Phoenix. . . . Antelope, Wolf* and *Loyal Steed. . . .*

Though they asked for cruisers to protect their merchantmen, though they said that they could not defend their forts and factories without guns, their principal complaint was against the Scots. "This Scotch Act," said the Royal African Company, "is nationally so pernicious to us that when once they have colonised themselves our commerce will be utterly lost." English merchants and seamen, said the East India Company, "will remove themselves, their families and estates into the kingdom of Scotland, and thereby carry away a considerable part of the stock and hands that support the trade of this nation." The Hamburg Company said that all Englishmen, and all men resident in England, should be prohibited from association with the Scots. Some of the other companies saw that here might be an opportunity of curbing the power of the East India Company, and acquiring some of its monopolies. The Jamaica merchants said that the best way of stopping the mischievous Scots would be to make trade easier for all. And the Leeward merchants told a small parable by way of illustration. One of their association, recently in India, had bought a chicken for a halfpenny and had told the Hindu from whom he bought it that he was grateful to the man's religion, since it forbade the eating of the bird and thus made it cheap to buy. "You are mistaken, Sir, he was told, for, did we eat chickens, everybody would breed them, and they would become much cheaper."

On Monday, December 9, seven of the Directors named in the Scots Act appeared before the bar of the Lords, together with others of their Court who were called to give evidence. The day was dank, chill with mists from the river, and the House sat late beyond candle-time. Since their last meeting on Friday, the Directors had been immobilised by shock, and over the week-end many of the two hundred English subscribers to the Company had withdrawn their names in panic. Only Robert Blackwood had been alert to the probable dangers ahead. He collected the Subscription Book from Mackenzie, and sent it to Scotland by his man-servant.

Two principal questions were put to the Directors: why had they incorporated themselves into a company likely to be prejudicial to England, and who were that company's subscribers? They answered uniformly, and with innocent wonder that it should be thought they had meant any ill. They did not think it prejudicial for them to be so incorporated in Scotland, and as for the subscribers, the Book was closed. Where it was, they did not know. They were asked if they had solicited this Act before the Parliament of Scotland, or had been asked to solicit it, and James Chiesly's answer was the model for all. "I know not anybody in England that was applied to directly or indirectly. The people in

Scotland knew us, and that is the reason they put in our names. At Mr. Paterson's request it was that this Jew and another was put in it. I have heard five or six years since that Scotland had a design for such an Act."

And where was Mr. Paterson? The Lords called for him late in the afternoon, and although the Serjeant-at-Arms shouted his name down the corridors of Westminster Hall, above the heads of their lordships' footmen, and out into the courtyard where there were more footmen and coachmen, there was no answer. He had not been seen all day, and had sent no message why he would not or could not come. James Smith, his friend and fellow-director, was asked where the man lived, and replied that it was in Denmark Street by Soho. Testily, the Lords sent a messenger to summon Paterson forthwith.

Past dusk, the House was told that Mr. Paterson was at the door, and he was brought in and sworn. When he was asked the same questions he answered boldly, and with a note of truculent bitterness, a memory of hard work and ill rewards. "I have been conversant in foreign trade. I solicited abroad for a Company. In 1691 I returned to England and I had a proposal to the Bank of England, but I was not rewarded. In May I was solicited by a Scotch gentleman that if I would give my opinion as to the Scotch Act I should be rewarded. From my opinion the Act was drawn. As to the passing of it, I know nothing."

And what of the Subscription Book? It was in Scotland, he believed. And shares promised as rewards to supporters of the Company? "I know of none, but what was promised me." He was dismissed, but told to hold himself ready for further attendance.

The examinations went on through the week, the Lords looking down upon every Director and every witness above a mounting pile of papers, the depositions of witness, the petitions heavy with the black and scarlet seals of the trading companies. Had Mr. Blackwood got the Subscription Book? No, he had not. When did he last see it? "It was Friday last, and I gave it to my man to send it away. I know not whether he went on Tuesday or Wednesday. I don't know where it is, but my man is gone to Scotland." Mackenzie was asked the same question, and he agreed that the Book had left London, but when or where he could not say. But he admitted, under pressure, that he did have a list of the subscribers' names. And Balfour, when he was called, offered the Lords a copy of the Preamble to the Subscription Book.

When they were finished with the Directors, the Lords listened to the reading of a paper from the Commissioners of Customs who declared that there was no doubt that the Scots Act would have a grave effect on the trade, revenue, and navigation of England. If it could not be repealed, encouragement of a similar nature should be given to English merchants. In any case, severe penalties should be imposed upon those Englishmen, and residents of England, who persisted in an association with the Scots Company.

It was Saturday. The Lords had spent six days on this examination, longer than many of them thought it was worth. They appointed a committee to draw up an Address to the King, and they sent word to the Commons (at that moment considering the Army Estimates and voting William £2,700,000 for his next campaign) inviting the Lower House to join them in presenting it. The whole business had pushed other matters aside. One cancelled motion had been a ray of light from a not too distant future wherein the principals and the enemies of the Scots Company would be bitterly involved. "*Moved*, that a day may be appointed to receive what may be proposed in order to have a Union between England and Scotland." Nothing came of it, the Lords had had their fill of the Scots for the moment.

Until this moment the Commons had taken no formal notice of the Scots Company, but were ready to join in the pursuit of it. They elected twenty-eight of their number, led by the Attorney-General and the Solicitor-General, to meet with the Lords' committee in the Painted Chamber, and there agree upon the terms of the Address. That it was done quickly, that the written Address was before the Commons on Saturday evening, argues earlier knowledge and previous discussions. It was twice read and approved unanimously. It gave a brief but precise account of the passing of the Scots Act and the trading advantages it granted to Scotland. "When once that nation shall have settled themselves in plantations in America, our commerce in tobacco, sugar, cotton-wool, skins, masts, etc., will be utterly lost. . . . The Kingdom must be the magazine for all those commodities, and the English Plantations, and the traffic thereof, lost to us, and the exportation of our own manufactures yearly decrease." It warned William that the Act obliged him to secure restitution and reparation for any injury done to the Scots Company, to employ English men-of-war in its defence and at the public cost, which could only be to the great detriment of England. The wording sometimes slavishly copied the phrasing of the petitions presented to the Lords, and although no remedy was suggested it was none the less implicit. The Act should be repealed, and the Company crushed.

Between three and four in the afternoon of Tuesday, December 17, in fair weather for the time of the year, there was a great gathering of carriages outside Westminster Hall, a mob of shouting footmen and swearing coachmen, all waiting for the Members of both Houses to take the Bath Road to Kensington. The Commons had been sitting since nine. They had begun by giving leave to a Bill to prevent theft and rapine on the borders of England and Scotland, and they were now coming to the end of a debate on a petition from the Governor and Members of the East India Company. This reported that the Company had nineteen ships outward bound, all laden with English manufactures valued at more than a quarter of a million pounds, the trading profits of which were in danger of being lost "by reason of the great privileges granted to joint stocks of neighbouring nations". Four more Indiamen lay in the Downs awaiting a favourable wind, another four were fitting-out downriver from London Bridge, and fifteen now loading off Surat and Bengal would be home within a year. All this was in jeopardy. The Company asked "that leave may be given to bring in a Bill for establishing the Company with such privileges and immunities as the House shall think fit, and as may preserve the joint stock, and enable them to carry on the trade to the honour and advantage of the nation". Properly impressed, the Commons appointed a committee to enquire into the Scots Act, with powers to send for and examine all papers and persons connected with it. And the persons concerned were those Scots and English gentlemen who had recently spent a worrying week at the bar of the Lords.

The Commons then voted themselves into a committee of the whole House, left the Hall and joined their lordships in an undignified struggle to find their coaches in the uproar of the courtyard.

The long procession of horsemen, coaches, outriders, running footmen and clattering troopers went by way of Petty France to the frosted fields of Pimlico, and on to the Kensington Road through Hyde Park, followed by a cheering crowd. The meeting with the King was brief. The audience chamber of the Palace was airless and suffocating, a crush of silk and brocade, ringlet wigs and powder, silver buckles and scarlet heels, body sweat and pomander. Lords and Commons craned their necks to see the lonely figure at the end of the chamber, its heavy cheeks and great eagle nose, the star of the Garter on a black coat, and a mourning band on one arm. William listened politely to a reading of the Address, punctuating it with his dry, asthmatic cough, and when it was over he nodded to the bowing Speaker and said "I have been ill-served in Scotland, but I hope some remedies may be found to prevent the inconveniences which may arise from this Act." He rose and left.

Both Houses were satisfied. They had expected no passionate emotion from this reserved and grieving man, and they sensed the anger behind the shutter of his words. Though he had given no promises, though what he had said had been ambiguous enough not to offend his Scots Parliament too deeply, his impatience with it and the northern kingdom was none the less plain. By giving the Royal Assent to the Act, Tweeddale had exceeded any warrant granted him by his commission, and the arrogant assumption of rights and privileges denied his English subjects was an impudent impertinence. He had also, perhaps, more than this in mind when he spoke of being ill-served in Scotland. Five months ago, in his camp before Namur, he had received the Report of the Commission of Inquiry into the Massacre of Glencoe, and an Address from the Scots Parliament upon the same matter. Though the Report had naturally exonerated him, it blamed his favoured Secretary of State, the Master of Stair. The Address, more indignant in tone, had also accused Stair of being "the original cause of this unhappy business", implying that he should be punished, and bluntly demanding that the King send home for trial those officers and soldiers of Argyll's Regiment who had carried out the slaughter. Moreover, many outraged people in Scotland and England were encouraged by Jacobite hacks to believe that the King was in fact primarily responsible for the killing of the MacDonalds. Had he not subscribed and superscribed the original order sent by Stair?

For five months William had acknowledged neither the Report nor the Address, and had taken no action beyond regretfully accepting the resignation of Stair. But two weeks ago, in this same chamber, he had called before him all those Scots Privy Councillors then in London. He astonished them by saying that he had known nothing of the matter until eighteen months after the massacre. This shameful, and probably dishonest confession, made to the empty faces of cynical men, betrayed William's anger, his choking impatience with ministers who could not keep his honour and reputation clean. And now, here was more insufferable incompetence, bringing both Houses of the English Parliament clamouring to his throne.

He had given no promise that the Act would be repealed, even if that were possible he relied too much upon the Scots Parliament for recruits and supplies to so antagonise it, but his evident displeasure made it possible for England to crush the mushroom Company in London. Three days later the Lords, sitting as a committee of the whole House, agreed to a Bill by which all Englishmen, and all traders in England, would be prohibited from joining the Company. They agreed that all English and Irish seamen and shipwrights should be discouraged, under severe penalties, from serving in, building or repairing the ships of the Company. They agreed "to establish an East India trade in England by Act of Parliament, with such powers, privileges and immunities as may obviate the inconveniences that may arise by the late Act passed in Scotland." There was, of course, an immediate outcry from the lesser trading companies, who had not asked for the young behemoth of Scotland to be destroyed so that the East India Company might grow into a greater leviathan. The Lords grew tired of the wrangling, forgot their Bill, and passed on to other matters.

But the Commons did not forget. When Christmas was past, and January two-thirds gone, they set aside their debates on the case for reform in the sale of spices, the erection of unlawful weirs on the River Wye, the eternal need to restore a clipped coinage, and listened to a report from Colonel Granville, chairman of the Committee which had been examining the Secretary and some of the Directors of what the House called the Scotch East India Company.

Young Mackenzie had appeared first, and had been as bland, polite, and as fundamentally unhelpful as he had been before the Lords. He knew nothing of the Company's accounts, he kept the minutes only. He knew nothing about the passing of the Act, though he had heard, only heard, that the fees for it amounted to £150. Where was the Subscription Book? He did not know, he had given it to Mr. Blackwood on December 6, since all the Directors had agreed that gentleman should have it. True it was carried into Scotland, but here was a list of the subscribers' names. As for the oath, *De fideli administratione*, here was a copy of that too.

Paterson again told his story. He had been approached by Mr. Chiesly, and had given Mr. Chiesly a scheme for a company in Scotland. He had been granted a considerable royalty, "which I have since, out of my mere generosity, released." He had not solicited the Act and knew not how it was passed. He agreed that there were 200 subscribers to the Company, and that its proposed capital was £300,000 Sterling. There had been, yes, a proposal to fit out a ship of four hundred tons and send it to the Indies as an interloper, but he did not know where the vessel was to be chartered or its cargo bought. He was questioned closely about the oath, and asked if he thought it prevented him from answering questions here. By some peculiar rationalisation that may have quietened his own doubts, he said "I do not reckon myself obliged to conceal anything from this Committee." And he was dismissed, with a warning to remain in London and be answerable to the Committee.

The English Directors, and those subscribers who were called, answered all questions with an embarrassing candour that revealed their fears. Robert Lancashire said that he was a member of the East India Company as well as a Director of the Scots. He had subscribed £3,000 to the latter, because he had been told that if he did not there were many others who would. He had always thought that the royalties granted Paterson were excessive. A subscriber called Glover honestly said that he had supported the Company because "he thought it better that an Englishman should have the benefit of it than a foreigner." And another, Bateman, admitted that he had subscribed £2,000, but had loyally withdrawn from the Company when "he heard that Parliament had taken it into examination."

The Committee had been unable to question Lord Belhaven, or Blackwood and Balfour, though messengers had been sent to summon all three. Once the scare was up in Parliament, that burly lord had left for Scotland, quickly followed by the merchants.

When Granville finished the reading of his Committee's report, the Commons agreed to hear another long and pitiable petition from the East India Company. It was late, and they called for candles, while outside in the courtyard their servants huddled about braziers, blowing on their fingers. After so much reading, so much evidence of impudent conspiracy and treason, of threats to the trade and prosperity of the kingdom, the Members were savagely excited. There were shouts for a vote and cries for impeachment. The resolutions were drawn, put, and approved.

Resolved, that the Directors of the Company of Scotland Trading to Africa and the Indies, administering and taking here in this Kingdom, an Oath *De Fideli*, is a High Crime and Misdemeanour.

Resolved, that the Directors of the Company of Scotland Trading to Africa and the Indies, under colour of a Scotch Act of Parliament, styling themselves a Company, and acting as such, and raising monies in this Kingdom for carrying on the said Company, are guilty of a High Crime and Misdemeanour.

And there followed twenty-two further resolutions, each naming a Director of the Company, and each declaring that he be "impeached of the said High Crimes and Misdemeanours". One final motion resolved that a committee be appointed to prepare the impeachments, and to meet the next day for that purpose, at four in the afternoon in the Speaker's Chamber.

Yet nothing came of it. The articles of impeachment, if drawn, were never presented. The up-ended pyramid of procedure rested upon the evidence of one man, Roderick Mackenzie, and he did

not answer a summons sent him by the Committee for Impeachment. The Serjeant-at-Arms reported that his lodgings were
empty, and although a proclamation was issued for his arrest on
February 8, he was never found. He was in Edinburgh some
weeks later, with a bitter hatred of the English that was to sustain him for the rest of his life.

The failure to impeach the Directors made little difference.
There was no hope now of a joint undertaking by English and
Scots capital. The subscribers had withdrawn their names before
Christmas, and since their appearance before the Lords and
Commons the English Directors had been making peace as best
they could with the trading companies of their own country. But
a fear of the Scots remained, the risk that their pestilential
Company might re-emerge in Edinburgh and menace the pros-
perity and possessions of England.

Edward Randolph thought so. He was Surveyor-General of the
Plantations, and since he had lately returned therefrom he was
listened to with respect. In March he told the Lords that if care
were not taken the Scots would plant colonies in America to the
great mischief of England. He suggested that all proprietors,
planters and others, from French Canada to the Caribbean,
should be told that the giving of aid to the Scots would be high
treason, "the whole tract from 32° to 44° being His Majesty's
dominion and annexed to the Crown of England."

Mr. Randolph had no love for the Scots. Their merchants were
interlopers who twisted the Navigation Acts or scandalously
avoided them by pretending to be Englishmen. "They have a long
time tasted the sweetness of trade to our Plantations, they paying
no duties to His Majesty for the goods they import to the
Plantations, nor for the tobacco they carry from thence to Scotland." And he reminded the Lords, with the smug satisfaction of
a civil servant teaching legislators their business, that the Commissioners of Customs had acted sensibly in this matter weeks
before the Commons had demanded impeachment. Letters had
been sent to the Governors of all the King's colonies in America,
to New York and Jersey, Massachusetts, Pennsylvania, Maryland
and Carolina, to Jamaica, Nevis, Bermuda and the other islands
of the Caribbean. Each had been sent particulars of the Scots
Act, and each had been reminded of his obligations under exist-

ing laws for the security of the Plantations, "which will be found sufficient to prevent the inconveniences and mischiefs which may arise from this Act." But like most self-satisfied public servants, Mr. Randolph overestimated the prescience of his tidy mind.

That Spring the King gave his English Parliament their sacrificial victims. He dismissed his Commissioner to Scotland. Since Tweeddale was close to death the old man may have regarded this as a kindly release from thankless office. William also discharged his sole Secretary of State for Scotland, James Johnston. There was some irony in this. Until a few months before, Johnston had shared the office with Stair, but coveting it for himself alone he had intrigued to bring the Master down over the Glencoe business.

Abandoned by those who had once joined with him in a great and noble undertaking, William Paterson went home to Scotland.

2

The Rising Sun

"They came in shoals, from all corners of the kingdom"
Edinburgh, January to July 1696

HE DID NOT TRAVEL ALONE. There was his wife, of course, and perhaps a child or two, we cannot be sure. A manservant and a maidservant, and two Londoners who were his friends, he thought, though one was to prove himself a rogue and the other a cipher. Paterson was able to see the villainy and self-interest of men who opposed him, but was sadly blinded by flattery. Walter Herries, who had a penetrating eye for a fellow rascal, claimed to have been undeceived by both men.

He brought a couple of tutors, or nurses, along with him, who passed for partners in the project, though in effect a couple of subtle youths whose office was to put Paterson's crude and indigested notions into form. One of these was a Walloon by birth, whose native name was Le Serrurier, and his English one James Smith. He was a master of most of the European languages, and particularly of the English. He formerly acted as secretary to the famed Italian prince who put as many tricks on the Hollanders with his philosophers' stone; but at this juncture he passed for a considerable London merchant. The other's name was Daniel Lodge, born of Yorkshire parents in Leith in Scotland, per accident, bred a merchant in Holland, but cracked and turned to his shifts in England. This was a pleasant, facetious fellow, and acted his part in this tragicomedy to a miracle.

It could not have been all lies. Herries knew both men, and was writing for others who might know them too. A good carica-

ture must have a recognisable feature, a nose, an eye, a manner
of dress that is a familiar signpost to inner character. Smith had
been the first outside director accepted by the London Scots,
taking his place at their second meeting on September 26. This
was probably on Paterson's recommendation, a return for aid or
friendship during those fruitless months in Holland and Hamburg, and he continued to trust the man, even after Smith hastily
supplied the Commons with that address in Denmark Street by
Soho. Perhaps Smith had nothing to lose in coming to Scotland,
one man's coat-tails being as good as another's at that moment,
and Paterson's the closest. Edinburgh accepted him and Lodge
because they came with Paterson, and within the week all three
were made burgesses and gild-brethren of the city without payment of dues. Paterson discovered that he was the nation's
darling, the victim of English treachery, the architect of future
prosperity, larger than life when seen by eyes glazed with emotion. Men turned to smile at him in the Canongate, to call his
name, and after the bitterness of London the praise of the ballad-
writers was pleasing to his simple vanity.

> Come, rouse up your hearts, come rouse up anon!
> Think of the wisdom of old Solomon,
> And heartily join with our own Paterson,
> To fetch home the Indian treasures.

In the cooler air of their fine houses, however, the city's
merchants remembered that this Solomon had demanded a high
payment for his wisdom. Though they needed his advice, his
knowledge of the Caribbean trade, and the inspiration of his
presence in Scotland, they resented a popularity which gave him
more credit than he deserved. Letters from their friends in London encouraged this view. "I think Mr. Paterson talks too much,"
wrote David Nairne, "and people's expectations are raised too
great from him. People that did concern themselves here did
not always depend upon his management of the affair."

But Scotland needed a hero and a deliverer, for times were
hard. The Lowland fields promised a poor harvest for the second
year in succession, plague and famine seemed inevitable. "We
voted His Majesty a standing army," remembered Fletcher of
Saltoun, "though we had more need to have saved the money to

have bought bread, for thousands of our people that were starving for want afforded us the melancholy prospect of dying by shoals in our streets, and have left behind them reigning contagion, which hath swept away multitudes more, and God knows where it may end." By its gentle nettle-touch, the King's cautious complaint that he had been ill-served in Scotland brought up a rash of pride. The Scots Parliament, it was claimed, had greater powers than England's, and what it offered to the touch of the Sceptre the King could not refuse. "Have not the Scots," asked Saltoun, "ever since the Union of the Crowns been oppressed and tyrannised over by a faction in England, who will neither admit of an Union of the Nations, nor leave the Scots in possession of their own privileges, as men and Christians?" Scotland needed a hero and a deliverer. Though he was no Wallace, for a brief while there seemed to be no better man than William Paterson.

The Edinburgh promoters were probably relieved by the dismal failure of their Company in London. They had been lukewarm for a joint venture, and Belhaven's speedy retreat with his two companions had not been entirely due to a fear of the Commons. Home was best, and freed from the domineering superiority of the Londoners Scotland would now create its own Company, raise Scots money, fit out Scots ships with Scots crews and Scots cargoes, and plant good Scots shoe-leather upon whatever part of the earth a Scots Act did so permit. Great servants of the King might now draw back their ermine skirts from a venture they had once welcomed, and Tweeddale might tell his friends that he thought it his duty to stop this heat from burning up his countrymen (and would have tried had not the King dismissed him), but Balfour, Blackwood and the others decided to open a Subscription Book as soon as possible. Though they had once been alarmed by the £300,000 asked of them by the Londoners, they now called for £400,000 Sterling, an astonishing sum which was perhaps half the available capital in Scotland. The increase had been made necessary by the withdrawal of the English, but it was announced like a defiant challenge.

The Book was opened on Wednesday, February 26, at Mrs. Purdie's coffee-house, by the Cross on the north side of the High Street. The minimum amount which could be subscribed, by individuals or by associations, was £100 Sterling, and nobody who could honestly guarantee it would be turned away before the Book was closed. There was a great and immediate surge of emotion, a unity unknown since the National Covenant sixty years before. Though most of the subscribers were greedy for profit, for a share in those Indian treasures which Paterson was supposed to fetch, none was entirely free from a fevered patriotism, or unaffected by the excitement of united purpose. The uniqueness of the political, religious and social structure of the country, outside the Highlands, made it possible. The principles of the Presbytery had established the idea that men of all ranks could be equal in common dedication. The tradition of "ane band", by which Scotsmen promised to aid each other in defence of their rights, was an old one, and it was easy to see Rorie Mackenzie's Subscription Book as such a Bond. The response was national from the Tay to the Tweed, a wave flooding over the old and bloody barriers of feud, religion and politics.

It did not, however, cross the barriers between the Highlands and Lowlands. Though the promoters called it the Company of *Scotland*, it was in fact a peculiarly Lowland affair. The Highlanders, a large part if not the majority of the population, gave it little or no willing support. With a few exceptions, like MacFarlane of that Ilk and Campbell of Argyll, the clan chiefs stood arrogantly aside from this shopman's venture. No Cameron, MacDonald, Macleod or Fraser gentleman, no Appin Stewart, Chisholm, Maclean or Grant is to be found in the Subscription List. Many of them had lately been at war with William, and where they were not exiles they were subdued rebels, Jacobite in sympathy, suspicious of the Lowlands and resentful of the Government. It does not appear that the Company ever thought of support from the chiefs, apart from those who had recently fought for William. None the less, hundreds of ordinary Highlanders would share the bitter hardships of the colony to come.

"They came in shoals," said Water Herries, a grudging admiration showing through his threadbare derision, "from all corners of the kingdom, rich, poor, blind and lame, to lodge their subscriptions in the Company's house and to have a glimpse of the man Paterson."

Three women were the first to sign their names in the Book. Mrs. Purdie's little coffee-house was filled as soon as its door opened with the silk of society and the broadcloth of commerce, merchants and soldiers, the law and medicine, while the High Street was noisy with coaches, horses and a yelling crowd. Mackenzie's clerk sat on a high stool with a freshly-cut quill and wrote the first words in thin, curving strokes: *We Anne Dutches of Hamilton and Chastlerault &c doe Subscrive for Three Thousand Pounds Sterling*... He handed her the pen and she signed, and was followed by the Countess of Rothes who subscribed a thousand pounds for herself and a thousand for her son the Earl of Haddington, and by Lady Margaret Hope with a thousand pounds for herself and two thousand for her young son the Laird of Hopetoun. Sir Robert Chiesly next, for two thousand, then others, pushing back cuffs and sword-hilts, pressing close to the Book regardless of rank or precedence. Balfour and Blackwood, Fletcher of Saltoun, Cockburn of Ormiston, Baillie of Jerviswood, Belhaven and Lord Basil Hamilton. And Mr. James Byres a merchant of Edinburgh who signed for £500, and whose consequent hopes of preferment in the Company's colony were to be disastrously realised. By the end of that first day there were sixty-nine names in Rorie Mackenzie's Book, and a subscribed total of £50,400.

Throughout the Spring and Summer, in Glasgow and Edinburgh, the subscriptions continued. From lords and ladies, soldiers, sea-captains and merchants, brewers, maltsters and tailors, lawyers, surgeons, physicians and apothecaries, ministers and printers, bookbinders and glaziers, tanners, vintners, wrights, hammermen, beltmakers and weavers, farmers and Senators to the College of Justice, Writers to the Signet, goldsmiths, schoolmasters and widows, postmasters, skinners and harness-makers, gunsmiths, sword-welders and fencing-masters. Not individuals only, but associations also, the Faculty of Advocates, the Incorporated Cordiners of Edinburgh, the Coopers of Glasgow. Masons, tailors, saddlers and shipwrights, not rich enough alone, but strong in a body and able to find £100 or £300 for their joint subscription. The "good towns" of Edinburgh, Saint Andrews, Glasgow, Paisley, Selkirk, Inverness (a Highland exception), and more, subscribing in the name of their cities, so that even the poor and landless, the thieves, whores and beggars could think themselves a part of the noble undertaking.

Sensing an imminent end to the King's war, and an uncertain future on half-pay or no pay at all, officers promised their prize money, the rewards of loot, or loans from more provident relations. From Flanders honest Captain John Blackader, though sanguine enough in print about a soldier's life and always confident that the Lord stood at his side, took out insurance against a crippling ball or an unlucky sword-thrust. He wrote to his brother Adam, a merchant of Edinburgh, asking for £100 to be put down in his name. Eleven officers—two majors, six captains, two lieutenants and an ensign—all of John Hill's Regiment at Fort William, subscribed £1,900 between them. Because no other unit made so large a contribution, theirs is intriguing. They had been involved, with the Earl of Argyll's Regiment, in the Massacre of Glencoe four years before, and many of them had been in Edinburgh for the Inquiry when the Company's Act was pushed through Parliament. They may have been caught up by the enthusiasm for it, or they may have hoped that in this way they would redeem some of their honour. More probably one of them persuaded the rest, Major James Cunningham of Eickett, for like Byres he was ambitious for office in the colony, and could have argued that by bringing such support he had earned preferment.

As it had put a thousand broadswords at the service of William in 1689, Clan Campbell now offered the money they had secured and protected. Its great chief, *MacCailein Mor*, Archibald the 10th Earl of Argyll, subscribed £1,500, his brother James £700, and in their tail were twenty-two gentlemen and merchants, all of Clan Diarmaid's name and allegiance. There was Campbell of Ardkinglas the Sheriff of Argyll, and there was Campbell of Aberuchil the Senator of the College of Justice. There were Campbell lairds and tacksmen of Soutar, Monzie, Bogholt, Calder, Cesnock and Kinpoint, as well as Mungo, Matthew, Daniel, Archibald and more, who kept merchant houses in Glasgow and Edinburgh. Between them they subscribed £9,400, and this though some of them had scarcely recovered from the terrible raid which the Jacobite clans had made upon their lands and stock ten years before.

A Glasgow Subscription Book was opened on March 5 and closed on April 22. When the Edinburgh Book was also closed on August 1, the full £400,000 had been subscribed. There were over 1,400 entries in both books, but since many were for associations and incorporations, for towns and burghs, the number of people involved could be counted in tens of thousands, and all men now spoke proudly of their Company, their African Company, their India Company. When the first 25 per cent call for money was made on the subscribers in June, the response was just under £100,000 Sterling, and there were no defaulters.

Paterson was busy throughout the Spring and early Summer, writing note after note upon a proposed constitution for the Company, which he submitted to the promoters and which were politely read and set aside. The Company took shape without him. There was now a Council-General of great men, and there was a Court of Directors to which were appointed many of those whose ardent support and shrewd bargaining had carried the Act so triumphantly through the Estates. The ultimate number of Directors was set at fifty, to accommodate all who should be so rewarded and to provide enough members for the various working committees. It was a time for honouring pledges and returning favours, but Paterson had to wait until May before the Court, reluctantly almost, admitted him as a Director. Upon a promise that James Smith would subscribe the £3,000 he had underwritten in London, he became a Director too, and the Court was later to remember that the promise had been made by Paterson, and that it had been upon Paterson's recommendation that Smith was then sent to London as the Company's agent.

There was a hiring of clerks and tellers, cashiers and accountants, doormen and messengers, and no proper building as yet to house them all. Roderick Mackenzie's office was a valise of papers, quills and ink-horns which his clerk carried behind him, up the High Street to the Laigh Parliament House where the Court and Council-General occasionally sat, or down to Maclurg's coffeehouse where the Committee for Improvements gathered less formally. The five members of this Committee included Balfour, Blackwood and an intense, dedicated Perthshire laird, John Haldane of Gleneagles, who had sat in the Estates since the Revolution, which he regarded as the salvation of the Protestant faith and the promise of prosperity for Scotland. Upon these men rested the responsibility for stores, equipment and trade goods, the discovery of where ships might be bought, built and docked. Paterson fluttered like a moth about the bright flame of their work, and they treated him with good-natured tolerance, sending him once to Glasgow, to study the shores of the Clyde as far as Dumbarton, to find a good run of deep water where the ships of the Company might anchor and load. It was the first real work he had been given since he came back to Scotland, and if he submitted a report no attention was paid to it for three years.

The Committee drew up contracts that would have excited the envy of the King's Master of Ordnance or the Commissioners of Supply. Once a week they assembled in the Patern Chamber of Parliament House where tradesmen from all over the Lowlands brought examples of their work and honest estimates of their costs. The Committee ordered firelocks and cartridge-belts, powder and ball, pistols and broadswords. They signed contracts for whip-saws, cross-saws, machete knives and bill-knives, shovels, felling-axes and spades, door-nails, window-nails and tacks, for bowls, platters, spoons and smoothing-irons, candle-sticks, lanterns and hogsheads of tobacco. They ordered tartan hose and stockings, shoes at six hundred pairs a time. They bought a warehouse at Leith, and there merchants and tradesmen were told to deliver the goods ordered, every Tuesday and Thursday between eight and six. They bought second-hand stockings, seventy-nine dozen at a time, and sent them to a workman's wife, Isobel Bickerton, for darning, and from her to a dyer for colouring. They looked for Bibles at bargain prices, and found them in the store-room of Agnes Campbell, relict of Andrew Anderson, printer. They discovered that Jeremy Robertson would make them as many periwigs as they desired (and they desired an extraordinary number), and they decided that the mounting piles of serge they were buying should be dyed "one fourth part black, one fourth part blue, one fourth part of several sorts of reds, and one fourth part of several sorts of cloth colours."

By July the Company had offices fitting the solemnity of its title and the grandeur of its intentions. No longer a stool by Mrs. Purdie's window or Roderick Mackenzie's valise, the depressing

Privy Council Chamber in the Laigh House or a corner in a Leith warehouse, but a tall, grey building in Milne Square opposite the Tron Church. Paterson found it. He had been invited to arrange the purchase of a suitable property when he was appointed to the Court, and although he may have considered this a small use of his abilities he went about it diligently with the help of two other Directors. Milne Square was a large, three-sided building about a small paved court, its rear windows looking north to Leith over a fleshers' market and the green marsh of the loch. It had been built six years before by Robert Milne, whose ancestors had been Master Masons to the Crown for seven generations. It was grand, dour, and dark, and its inner windows seldom caught the sun, but it was quiet, and its narrow entrance was easily guarded by a doorman. The Company took one side only at first, paying its owner, the lawyer John Eidington, £395 17s 9½d Sterling, and later buying another side from Mackenzie of Broomhill for £455 11s. Roderick Mackenzie moved his wife and family into the upper floor, and scattered his clerks and tellers, cashiers and accountants about the rest.

Here a quorum of the Court of Directors met almost every day, resolving the general business of the Company, receiving reports from the Committee for Improvements, for Foreign Trade, and of the Treasury. Here the Council-General and the Court followed the advice given in Paterson's scheme and in the *Proposals for a Fond*, without perhaps acknowledging it. They established a Fund of Credit, which soon developed into a bank with splendidly-designed notes and agents in Glasgow, Dundee, Aberdeen and Dumfries. It was illegal from its inception. The young Bank of Scotland, now twelve months old, had been given a monopoly for twenty-one years, but if its directors resented this piratical invasion by the Company they had the good sense to hold their tongues and wait for the Fund to collapse. Which it soon did. As it sank into the morass of its colonial disasters, the Company was to have no money for Funds of Credit.

Having sent James Smith to England, to discover what trade goods were now needed in Africa and the Indies (and with the incredible hope that he might persuade some of the London subscribers to make a first payment on their subscriptions), the Court gave a warrant to two other Directors, Alexander Steven-

son and James Gibson, to "repair beyond the seas ... where you
shall inform yourselves of the best and most expeditious way of
purchasing or building five or six ships of about 600 tons each,
well and sufficiently built, and such as are fit for voyages to the
East Indies." They left for Holland and Hamburg.

All that now remained was for the Company to decide where
to plant its colony—when the ships were bought, the cargoes
loaded, the leaders chosen, and the settlers engaged.

Thus William Paterson was once more remembered. One day
in late July he and his young friend, Daniel Lodge, were appointed to the Committee for Foreign Trade, and were invited to
lay before it any schemes, any proposals which Paterson might
have for a settlement or settlements "upon some island, river, or
place in Africa or the Indies or both." Paterson's imagination,
capable of soaring beyond Europe and beyond his own age, was
impersonal, and he never dramatised himself. It is unlikely that he
felt anything more than eager satisfaction when he received this
invitation. Yet a dream had become a wondrous reality, the ten
years of pain and disappointment, of ridicule and rejection, were
now to be rewarded, the future of this noble undertaking depended upon his labours. On July 23 he came to Milne Square
with the vast paper accumulation of those ten years—manuscripts, books and journals by his own or others' hands, maps,
charts and soundings, readings by the stars and by astrolabe, the
recorded conversations with shipmasters and buccaneers, the
drawings of savage Indians and strange plants, translations from
the Spanish and from the French, the discoveries of priests and
pirates, all that was needed to turn the key of the universe and
push open the door of the seas.

The papers lay on a table before the Committee as Paterson
talked of the great *entrepôt* which should be established on
Panama, and the fact that he had never been ashore on the
Isthmus, nor could have seen it from the island of Providence
three hundred miles away, does not seem to have been important.
The evidence he had brought was overwhelming. Now and then,
by way of illustration, Daniel Lodge handed a journal to Sir
Francis Scott, a map to Mr. William Wardrop, a letter to Sir
Archibald Mure. They would have been odd men, grown strangely
far from boyhood, not to have been excited. Here they could read

of Indian kings who wore gold in their nostrils as casually as
Scots gentlemen wore lace at their cuffs. Here were descriptions
of valleys, rivers, and harbours beyond their imagination. They
could turn the pages of a journal kept by lantern-light in the
cabin of a buccaneer ship, while rare and beautiful moths danced
about its glass. They could study charts drawn beneath the compassionate shade of palm-trees, and could imagine the sailor-
artist looking up from the stiff parchment to the blue of the
Caribbean and the crystal glitter of sand. But it was the simple
logic of Paterson's proposal that convinced their counting-house
minds, a merchant colony between the Atlantic and the Pacific,
the natural hub of the world, the central point of the shortest
bridge across the seas.

When the meeting closed the Committee asked Paterson if the
Company might keep these papers, and he gave permission with
spontaneous, unconditional generosity. At the request of Sir
Francis, presiding, he gathered them into one large bundle,
securely bound and sealed. It was handed to Rorie Mackenzie
who was told that it must be further sealed by four other
Directors, and was not to be opened except by instructions from
the Court. All this was properly ordered and entered in the
minutes, and then

> Resolved, that it is the opinion of this Committee that the
> pains, expense, and damage of the said Mr. Paterson in
> promoting the said design, and the means to enable and
> encourage him freely to bestow all his pains and time hence-
> forward in prosecuting this undertaking, ought to be taken
> into consideration by the Company.

The Company duly took it all into consideration, and since
whatever was given to Paterson would, by this resolution, be re-
employed in the Company's interest, the gift was not over-
generous. He was granted £7,500 of the Company's stock.

This said design, this undertaking, was a colony on Darien. A
decision to settle there was undoubtedly made that week,
although no hint of it was allowed to appear in the minutes or
records. By such secrecy, which was to prove as useless as it was
melodramatic, the Company hoped that the English Parliament
would not be alarmed before it was too late to prevent the settle-

ment. Thus the Committee for Foreign Trade passed a vague, and deliberately misleading resolution, proposing the settlement "with all convenient speed" of some island, some river, some place in Africa, the East or West Indies. Paterson's passionate advocacy of a colony on Darien had strongly influenced the Directors, but what may have finally persuaded them was a fat manuscript among the papers he surrendered the Company. He had borrowed it from his friend William Dampier, and probably had no right to part with it, since its author did not know that he had it. It was the copy of a journal written by a young buccaneer and surgeon, lately of the *Batchelor's Delight*, and recently returned to England from the Spanish Main.

His name was Lionel Wafer, and no man in Europe, not even Dampier, had a greater knowledge of Darien.

"Valleys watered with rivers, brooks and perennial springs"
Edinburgh, July 1696

"Though there are some matters of fact that will seem strange," the Directors read, "yet I have been more especially careful in these to say nothing but what, according to the best of my knowledge, is the very truth."

Indeed, Lionel Wafer was an honest, careful man. No one, not even Herries, spoke ill of him, and when William Dampier wrote of his own voyages in the Caribbean he said little about Darien because "Mr. Wafer, who made a longer abode in it than I, is better able to do it than any man I know." Copies of Wafer's book were later carried in the baggage of many Scots who went to the Isthmus, and when they wrote home of what they found and saw they disputed nothing he had said, and occasionally used his words as if they were their own.

All that is known of him, his background and origins, is limited to what he chose to say about himself. He said that he had some knowledge of Gaelic, and that he lived in the Highlands of Scotland as a boy. He knew Ireland, too, and his father may have been one of Cromwell's buff-coats garrisoned in Ulster, and later sent with Colonel Fitch's Regiment to Lochaber. There are traditions of Huguenot descent, of a name that was originally Weaver, or Delawafer, but of this the young man said nothing, believing it, perhaps, of no importance. In 1677, when he was 16 or 17, he went to sea as a loblolly-boy, a surgeon's assistant serving that water-gruel to the ship's sick. He served on merchantmen trading in the Spice Islands, and learnt his master's business well enough to practise as a surgeon himself. And then to Jamaica, to visit a brother who worked on a sugar estate to the north-west of Spanish Town. Here he joined the buccaneers, to whom a lancet and a bleeding-cup were sometimes more important than another cutlass. He gave no reasons for choosing this dangerous, unpredictable life, but he was young, and therein is an explanation.

He sailed in the company of Cook and Lynch, Coxon and Bartholomew Sharpe, Alliston and Thomas Maggot, sharing their sea-fights, their savage raids upon the Isthmus in search of gold or Spanish throats to cut. He survived while others died from pistol-shot and sword-cut, from fever and nostalgia, from old age or impetuous youth. His companions fought and traded, drank and sang, content with a life of sudden action and quick profit, and he may have done all this too, but he also looked and remembered. His eye for detail was incredibly sharp, and the prose he used to record what it saw was simple and evocative, free from the convoluted style of men with a better education. He modestly asked his readers not to expect anything like a complete journal. "My principal design was to give what description I could of the Isthmus of Darien. . . . I was but young when I was abroad, and I kept no journal, so that I may be dispensed with as to defects and failings of less moment. Yet I have not trusted altogether to my own memory; but some things I committed to writing long before I returned to England."

The land he described lay between Latitudes 8 and 10 North, on the Caribbean side of Panama where the isthmus bends toward the shoulder of South America. Here were the numberless bays and inlets of the Darien coast, smooth shores of white sand, tiny islands like green jewels, where the buccaneers had traditionally watered and careened their ships since the days of Drake, where they planned and sometimes executed insane raids on Portobello to the west and Carthagena to the east. For three years Wafer was the shipmate of Dampier, and was one of the three hundred men who followed that excellent hydrographer but third-rate buccaneer on a march across the isthmus in May, 1681, over two mountain ranges in an abortive attack on the Spaniards at Real de Santa Maria. While drying gunpowder one night, on a silver plate over an open fire, Wafer's leg was badly scorched by a flash-ignition, and he was left behind in the care of the Indians. He lived with them for two months, admiring them and adored by them, regretting only the loss of his salves and plasters when a Negro slave ran off with his knapsack ("Yet I preserved a box of instruments, and a few medicaments wrapt up in an oil cloth"). This idyllic period gave him time for observation, reflection and discovery, and the recording, perhaps, of those notes which he later turned into a book. He had no skill at drawing like Dampier, but his pen was capable of more graphic descriptions. All about him was a thick, green-dark jungle, unexplained silences and bewildering sounds, animals to which no man had yet given a name, and others that reminded him wistfully of home. There were mountain-heads capped with mist, and "valleys watered with rivers, brooks and perennial springs", and there was the sudden, unexpected meeting of sea and land where palm-fronds idly fingered the Caribbean.

As they read the manuscript, the Directors of the Company were transported from the grey escarpment of Edinburgh, the stench of its streets and the clamour on its cobbles, to what must have seemed a paradise, a rich and compliant land awaiting rape by Scots energy and Scots industry. So heady were the hopes inspired in them by Wafer's book that none saw its implicit warnings. Certainly Darien was a land where buccaneers had beached their boats, raided the Spanish and taken to sea again, but nowhere did the young surgeon suggest that it could be planted, settled and colonised like North America. It was only in a preface to a second edition of his book, published in 1704, that he allowed his good sense to be influenced by public opinion and proposed an English settlement. Even then he was suggesting a military, strategic occupation, cutting the cord which held the Spanish American empire together.

But as the Directors read, so they saw what they chose to see, and Wafer did not disappoint them. The soil inland, he said, was generally very good, a rich, black and fruitful mould. "I believe we have nothing that grows in Jamaica but what would thrive here also, and grow very luxuriantly." Westward there were wide savannahs, dry and grassy meadows studded with conical hills, but from the sea nothing could be seen but trees, a pleated green blanket stretching away to the south and over the mountains. Inland from the tropical palms that bent to welcome the buccaneers were great glades, tall groves without undergrowth where a horseman could gallop for miles without hindrance, protected from the heat by a roof of leaves. Some of these trees were twenty or thirty feet in girth, and among them was the fabulous Nicaragua wood, exotic in fragrance and wonderful in colour, and as remote and as unattainable as El Dorado. Though he was never sure where it was to be found, and the Scots were never to discover it, Wafer later claimed that three hundred men could fell enough of this fabulous wood in six months to pay for an entire expedition to the Isthmus. This the Committee for Improvements remembered, as they ordered axes, hatchets, planes and saws by the hundred.

There were cotton-trees, their cods as big as a nutmeg and full of short wool, but their wood was useless except for canoes and the dug-out which the Spanish called a piragua and the French a pirogue. There were cedars standing like redcoat regiments, macaws with egg-shaped, scarlet fruit, and the strange bibby-tree, tall, leafless and prickly. Its wood was black and of no value, but the Indians tapped and drank its wheyish sap, and made an anointing oil from its berries. The mammee grew sixty feet toward the sun, and the sapadillo's round fruit were like sweet, russet pippins. There were calabash trees, and ash trees that burst into flame with yellow flowers, their bark so tough and stringy that it could be made into ropes and rough textiles. The lightwood was weightless, and a man could carry a whole tree upon his shoulder without strain. From it the Indians made their best canoes, and the buccaneers carved tompions for the muzzles of their guns. Nor were these all. The whitewood, thought Wafer, would be excellent for the inlaying of fine cabinets. The logwood, rich and scarlet, seemed to bleed when cut. "I tried a little of it, which upon boiling two hours in fair water turned it red as blood. I dipt therein a piece of cotton which it dyed a good red, no washing could fetch out the tincture. Twas a bright and glossy red, very lively."

By the rivers, by the shoreward swamps, bamboos grew in trembling clusters, and mangroves stood high on naked roots that were grey where the earth was dry, or red where they were washed by tidal floods. Cinnamon and tamarind, sugar-cane and prickly-pear, locusts and peppers, all were there. The Directors must have thought that a man need do no more than harvest, leaving the planting to the prodigality of God. Sweetly-flowered tobacco, and plantains that could be cut from their green and sappy stems by one blow of an axe. White and purple yams, and two kinds of cassavas, one that could be eaten like a potato, and another that gave flour for bread once its poisonous juice had been squeezed from it. Wafer had gathered pine-apples as large as a man's head, weighing six pounds or more, without stone or kernel, ripening all the year round and so joyous to the taste that he thought it was like all the most delicious fruits he could imagine mixed together.

In this waiting Eden there were also wondrous birds and beasts, many to support a man and few he need fear. The flesh of the wild hog, black and nimble on its short legs, kept well for several days, even in that climate, "and is very good, wholesome meat, nourishing and well-tasted." Timid red deer moved like shadows among the cedars, and although the Indians would not eat them, the buccaneers barbecued them at great triumphant feasts. Rabbits as large as English hares lived under the roots of trees, and their flesh was sweeter, moister than any cony Wafer had tasted in England. There were wild dogs, rough, wild-haired, snarling beasts which the Indians tamed for hunting, and coursed in packs of two or three hundreds. The tall trees were full of noisy monkeys, some white but mostly black, bearded like old men, fat with fruit and good to eat. There were snakes, but no rattle-snakes that Wafer had seen, and although the leaves, the roots and the grass swarmed with spiders none were poisonous. In the rivers were alligators and thick-tongued iguanas, both of which could be eaten, and Wafer particularly recommended the tail of the alligator. On the shore were land-crabs, larger than anything he had seen in the booths of London, and turtles that were rich, sweet and easily caught. "They have frogs and toads, and other smaller insects, but I took no particular notice of them."

The dark green of the forest groves flamed with the bright colours of incredible birds. Parrots and parakeets in Joseph coats of glistening feathers. Macaws with hook-bills and streaming tails of red and blue. They could be tamed like magpies and they called their own reveille at dawn, a hoarse, deep cry "like men who speak much in the throat." He saw pied woodpeckers climbing up and down the trees on strong claws, and although their flesh was unpleasant and earthy to the taste he had eaten it without harm when hungry. The strange chicaly-chicaly, carrying its bright tail upright like a banner, reminded him of an arrogant dung-hill cock. The quam was a fat, fruit-eating bird, as pleasing to the palate as partridge, and the black curassow had a fine comb of yellow and a sweet and delightful voice. By the sea were web-footed, grey-feathered pelicans which the buccaneers clubbed to death after a floundering chase along the shore, making tobacco-bags from their leathery pouches. Black cormorants fished from the rocks, and surprised Wafer by perching on trees and shrubs inshore. Wheeling gulls were shot in flight by the buccaneers and then buried in hot sand for eight or ten hours, to roast them and to make them palatable. So many birds, remarkable for their beauty and the good relish of their flesh.

There were bats as large as pigeons, mosquitoes, wasps, beetles, and fireflies like rising sparks in the thickets at night. Wafer marvelled at the bees, some red and fat, others that were long, black and slender. They made sweet honey and fine wax, and a man could thrust his arm into their tree-hives without any fear. "I have had many of them at a time upon my naked body without being stung; so that I have been inclined to think they have no stings, but that's a thing I never examined." The ants, however, could sting, and a wise man did not hang his hammock too close to their fortress hills.

In the sea were sharks, dogfish and barracudas, swordfish with sapphire scales, and pike with mouths like a rabbit's. On the rocks were periwinkles and limpets, and in the pools were crayfish as large as small lobsters, conch-shells shimmering with mother-of-pearl. "And many others, probably, that I have neither seen nor heard of, for 'tis a sea very well stored with fish."

The Cuna and Choco Indians who lived on the Isthmus were a dark-skinned, black-haired and friendly people, little changed in the hundred and eighty years since they were first seen by Balboa (climbing that Pacific peak upon which Keats would later place stout Cortes). Wafer admired them, respected them and, one suspects, loved them in a wistful way, though he thought them a poor and naked people too content with their lot.

The size of the men is usually about five or six foot. They are straight and clean-limbed, big-boned, full-breasted, and handsomely shaped. I never saw among them a crooked or deformed person. They are very nimble and active, running very well. But the women are very plump and fat, well-shaped, and have a brisk eye. The elder women are very ordinary; their bellies and breasts being pensile and wrinkled. Both men and women are of a round visage, with short bottle noses, their eyes large, generally grey, yet lively and sparkling when young. They have a high forehead, white even teeth, thin lips, and a mouth moderately large. Their cheeks and chin are well proportioned; and in general they are handsomely featured, but the men more than the women.

They were a clean and sober people, and if they ate noisily, all dipping their fingers into one gourd, they had their own delicacies of behaviour that were as obligatory as any European's modish manners. Everything about them was simple and expedient, their sparse clothing, their habits, their weapons and their ornaments. They were vainly proud of their lank, long hair, combing it for hours, rarely cutting that which grew on their heads but allowing their women to pluck other parts of their bodies with two sticks. Sometimes a warrior would cut off his hair, or paint himself black, as a mark of honour, and this after he had killed an enemy or a Spaniard, the two being synonymous. Wafer was entranced by the sheen of their oiled, unblemished skins, tawny orange in the sun and rich copper by firelight. Among them were a few albinos who were sluggish and dull during the day, but at nights they would run in the woods like wild bucks. They were not pink, but "rather a milk-white, and much like that of a white horse." These sad, ostracised mutations were ridiculed by the buccaneers, and regarded as monsters by other Indians.

Both these and the copper-coloured Indians use painting their bodies, even of the sucking children sometimes. They make figures of birds, beasts, men, trees or the like, up and down in every part of the body, more especially the face, but the figures are not extraordinary like what they represent, and are of differing dimensions, as their fancies lead them. The women are the painters, and take a great delight in it. The colours they like and use most are red, yellow and blue, very bright and lovely. They temper them with some kind of oil, and keep them in calabashes for use; and ordinarily lay them on the surface of the skin with pencils of wood, gnaw'd at the end to the softness of a brush. So laid on, they will last some weeks, and are renewed constantly.

Wafer idly indulged his own vanity, and pleased the Indians, by sitting cross-legged and patient while his body was so painted. The women wore aprons of cloth or leaves, tied about the waist and hanging to their knees or ankles. The cloth they got from the buccaneers or Spaniards, and they were childishly excited by fine colours. Wafer and Dampier once "prevailed with a morose Indian" by giving his wife a sky-blue petticoat. The men, too, were delighted by an old coat or a discarded shirt, but they were usually naked except for one extravagant ornament which amused all Europeans who had forgotten the cod-pieces of their own ancestors. This was a curving cone like a candle-extinguisher, worn over the penis and held to the waist by a cord, and no man removed it without first turning his back. It was cunningly made from leaves, or from gold and silver if the wearer was rich and important.

Both metals were rare, and obviously prized by the Indians. They hammered out thin, crescent plates and hung them from their nostrils over their mouths. "Such a one I wore among them," said Wafer proudly, "was of gold". Each man might have several, varying the size of them according to the importance of the day or the event, a council, a hunt, or a war-party. The women wore circular rings in their noses, the thickness of a goose quill. "Neither the plates nor rings hinder much their speaking, tho' they lie bobbing upon their lips." But when they ate, the Indians removed both plates and rings, polishing the metal before restoring it to their noses. They also hung themselves with necklaces of shells and beads, sometimes three or four hundred strings, and it was a poor woman who did not carry twenty pounds weight in this manner, the men much more.

The Indian kings and captains, as Europeans called the tribal leaders and village headmen, wore gold at their mouths and ears, heart-shaped plates of gold, richly painted, on their chests and backs. Wafer thought that one called Lacenta was the most powerful on the Isthmus, and remembered how he once came to a great council in the forest. In addition to his nose-plate, his ear-rings and his cuirass of gold, he wore a diadem of the same metal, eight or nine inches broad and mounted on a framework of cane. His armed bodyguard also wore crowns, but of cane only, painted scarlet and decorated with the feathers of parrots, parakeets and macaws.

Their villages were simple, the huts no more than roofs of plantain leaves. In the centre of each village was a long war-house where young and unmarried men were trained in the use of weapons and the duties of manhood. More than a hundred feet long, ten high, and twenty-five broad, this house was also the defensive fort of every village, its walls pierced for arrows, its doors held by club and lance. Though an armoured man could have pushed his way through the plaintain leaves, the Spaniards never attacked a long-house by assault. They set fire to it. And they shot down the Indians who ran from the flames.

The round, bright-eyed faces of the Cunas peered at the Directors from the simple framework of Wafer's prose, their guttural voices clacked in the words and sentences he wrote down phonetically. He said that his knowledge of Gaelic had helped him to learn the language. *Pa poonah eetah caupah?* Woman, have you got the hammock? . . . *Cotcha caupah?* Will you go sleep in the hammock? . . . *Aupah eenah?* What do you call this? . . . As well as painting his body and wearing a nose-plate, he got drunk at their weddings, filled his lungs with the smoke of their great cigars, danced with them, and sang their strange songs. After their feasts he lay helpless in his hammock like other men, while women sprinkled him with water to cool his over-indulged body. He respected their uncomplicated religion. He said that although the women were drudges, he never

knew an Indian to beat his wife, or speak harshly to her. Even
when drunk and quarrelling, the men were always gentle to their
women and their children. He admired their love of noise, the
music they made by humming or by fingering slender flutes made
from reeds. They were able to dance from dawn until sunset, and
would then plunge into a river to wash the dust and sweat from
their bodies. They walked from the water with naked dignity,
drying their hair and skins by long, caressing strokes of their
hands.

They gave directions by the simple method of pointing, the
height of the hand indicating the time of day a man might
expect to reach his destination. They kept no hours of the clock,
made no particular distinction of days and weeks, and took their
months from the moon. They could count up to a hundred and
no further, for numbers beyond that they shook a lock of their
hair. Their laws were short and expedient. They killed adulterers
and thieves, and recognised no other crimes. They swore upon
their eye-teeth, and were faithful to the oath. They indulged
their children until the age of puberty, when a girl put on the
clout and a boy the funnel and both began the long training to
be an adult.

They hated and feared the Spaniards, though many of them
had worked in the mines or served as native levies of Spain
against other tribes. But they rarely opposed the buccaneers and
repaid the rough kindnesses of these men with love and loyalty.
When one of Lacenta's wives was ill, Wafer was allowed to
bleed her, drawing off twelve ounces until the fever was gone.
Lacenta bent on his knee and kissed the surgeon's hand.

> Then the rest came thick about me, and some kissed my
> hand, others my knee, and some my foot, after which I was
> taken up into a hammock and carried on men's shoulders ...
> and lived in great splendour and repute, administering physic
> and phlebotomy to those that wanted.

The Directors of the Company did not ask themselves why, if
Darien were such a paradise, Spain had not already settled there,
having occupied and planted lands to the east, west and south of
it for nearly two centuries. They chose, instead, to regard this as
a stupid oversight by the Dons, and to believe that the country

could be rightfully claimed by any nation. They had heard of
Pope Borgia's bull, of course, but it had been ignored by Pro-
testants and Catholics alike for two hundred years, and was
only taken seriously by the Spanish and the Portuguese. Wafer
did not dispute that Darien was a province of Spain, though he
could not see why someone should not take it from her if possible. The Spaniards had garrisons, forts, towns and villges all
along the Isthmus of Panama, but they were wise enough, and
had been in America long enough not to waste time and men on
the swamps of Darien. There were three thousand men, said
Wafer, in the forts above the narrow streets and fine harbour of
Portobello, with outposts at Nombre de Dios. To the east, on the
coast of South America, was the powerful garrison and naval
base of Carthagena. On the southern side of the isthmus the
stockaded town of Santa Maria was held by two hundred
infantrymen, and thousands more were stationed in the great
city of Panama, the seat of the provincial governor. Since 1671,
when Henry Morgan's bloody cut-throats sacked and burnt the
old city of Panama, taking gold, silver, slaves and women, the
Spaniards had built a new one, and made it virtually impregnable. Northward from its white walls ran the road to Portobello,
the jugular vein of the Spanish empire, the mountain track for
mule-trains loaded with the wealth of Peru, and for this reason
alone Spain could tolerate no other European nation on the
Isthmus. She kept two fleets of warships in American waters, one
off the Main and the other in the South Sea, and there was not a
bay or an inlet on the Darien coast that had not been visited and
named by a galleon or pinnace from the northern fleet. The
Indians of Darien were the reluctant vassals of His Catholic
Majesty, their chiefs were given Spanish names, were forced to
supply levies or mine-workers when needed, and were paid for
their loyalty with an old musket or a rusty hauberk.

If the Scots did not understand this, and if they did not see
that there was more to Darien than rich meat and sweet honey,
it was not Wafer's fault, for he was honest about the risks, the
dangers and the discomforts. But they were blinded by the
startling colours of his narrative, and excited by their own greed.
They heard the sound of axes in groves of fragrant wood, they
saw strong forts and green plantations, great merchantmen

anchored in broad bays. What they should have read again, and again, and yet again, was what Wafer had to say about the weather. So much rich vegetation, so many forests, swamps and marshes, bright brooks and rivers, so abundant a life growing on its own putrefaction, could mean one thing only. The land wept more than it smiled.

It rained. Wafer remembered how it rained, how he had lain in an Indian hut with a burning knee and listened to the unending sound of water. The rains began in April or May and continued with increasing violence until September. "It is very hot also about this time, wherever the sun breaks out of a cloud, for the air is then very sultry, because then usually there are no breezes to fan and cool it, but 'tis all glowing hot." In October the storms slackened, but it was sometimes January before they stopped, and thus a third of the year, perhaps only a quarter, was entirely free from rain. The season began with brief and sudden showers that reminded Wafer of Spring in England, a cooling rustle on leather leaves and the earth running with singing streams. Then, in one day, there would be two or three violent storms, a rolling cannonade of thunder, a black sky stabbed with lightning and a smell of sulphur beneath the trees.

After this variable weather, for about four or six weeks, there will be settled, continued rains of several days or nights, without thunder or lightning but exceeding vehement considering the length of them. Yet at certain intervals between these, even in the wettest of the season, there will be several fair days intermixed, with only tornadoes or thunder-showers; and that sometimes for a week together. These thunder-showers cause usually a sensible wind, by the clouds pressing the atmosphere, which is very refreshing and moderates the heat.

Cooling though these powerful winds were, they also pulled down trees, dammed rivers, and turned the swamps and westward savannahs into green and stinking lakes. In the brief intervals between the storms there was no compassionate silence. "You shall hear for a great way together the croaking of frogs and toads, the humming of mosquitoes or gnats, and the hissing or shrieking of snakes and other insects, loud and unpleasant;

some like the quacking of ducks." Fairer weather came with Christmas, but from the swamps at night, the rotting shores of the floodwater, there rose throbbing clouds of newly-hatched mosquitoes. Wafer called them "uneasy vermin". That they were also lethal would be unsuspected for another two hundred years.

"'Tis a very wet country," said Wafer. Yet there is no indication—in the minutes of their meetings, the inventories of their ships, their lists of clothing, equipment and trade goods—that the Directors gave serious thought to his warning that Darien was one of the wettest parts of the torrid zone, or concluded from it that Europeans who settled there might suffer terribly from fevers, ague, and the rotting of the spirit that comes from wretched idleness.

"I must bear these as I have done the rest of my troubles"
Edinburgh and Hamburg, July 1696 to June 1697

Wise Paterson, the ballads were now calling him, judicious Paterson, creator of wholesome laws and the architect of Patersonian Government. Men would have found it hard to define this government, or name one of the healthy statutes it might enact, but all agreed with the ballads: where it was established, upon some future colony in Asia or America, there would be no cause for discontent, no factious brawling and complaints. Within three years the savage Indians would cry "God bless the Scottish Company!", their souls uplifted by trade, their bodies liberated, and their simple hearts full of gratitude. Extravagant though the street-songs were, they did reflect the selfless emotion which gave the Company much of its early impetus.

> To Scotland's just and never-dying fame,
> We'll in Asia, Africa and America proclaim
> Liberty! Liberty!—nay, to the shame
> Of all that went before us.

And now, it seemed, the Company could not do enough for Paterson. Within a fortnight of his appointment to the Committee for Foreign Trade, and a week of the generous surrender of his papers, it was agreed that he and two other Directors should leave as soon as possible for Amsterdam and Germany. There they were to "engage such foreign merchants and others as may be needful to be concerned in this Company, as also to make and conclude such negotiations and agreements as may be found beneficial to the trade thereof." It was a belated acknowledgment of his stubborn belief that the Company could not survive without "the best heads and purses for trade in Europe", and it was a wise employment of his peculiar talent for persuasion. He should have been reassured, but he was not. Ten years of disappointments had worn his armour thin, and he was hypersensitive to criticism. He became suspicious and petulant. He saw malice behind every compliment, and spite behind every smile. In London he had believed that a cabal in Edinburgh was intent on ruining him, and now in Scotland he suspected the London Scots, who had once been his friends, of plotting his disgrace. He was convinced of this when Robert Douglas arrived in Edinburgh, at the request, it would appear, of some cautious Scots who wanted his experienced judgment on the Company's proposals for a colony.

Paterson remembered the candle-lit bickering in Mr. Carpenter's house, and that terrible afternoon when the envy and distrust of his colleagues had compelled him to renounce his royalties. He became almost hysterical with indignation, and appealed for the sympathy and aid of great men on the Council-General of the Company. Douglas had come to slander him, he told the Earl of Annandale, and not only him but the Company and the country as well, just as in London he had tried to "turn out me and my party, as he calls them, and set up himself and his own", and this though Paterson had always treated him with patience and civility. Now there was vicious gossip, accusing Paterson of seeking office and profit. If the Council-General truly believed this it was free to cast him out and put another in his place, perhaps one of those gentlemen who vilified him. Did he not put the Company's good before his own, he would gladly make room for such a man.

This I must say, that in all the course of my life my reputation was never called so much in question as about this matter, and it is no very easy matter to me, reputation being the only thing I am nicest in; and no doubt but malicious stories of me will fly like wildfire in England at this time; since I, in a special manner, lie under a national hatred. But patience; I must bear these as I have done all the rest of my troubles. I doubt not but your lordship and all my friends will discountenance malicious stories behind a man's back.

It was a sad and childish letter, and it probably wearied Lord Annandale, who spent much of his public life in the service of his own interest, and would accordingly believe that a man who made such a noise about his own unselfishness ran the risk of being thought a fool or a liar.

Douglas went south to his home in Surrey, sending his friends in Edinburgh a long and reasoned disapproval of what he rightly concluded were the Company's plans for a colony. Nobody had openly admitted that this was to be planted on Darien, but he had found the nation besotted with Mr. Paterson, and he remembered the fellow's coffee-house prattle in Amsterdam nine years before. "I heard accounts of his design, which was to erect a commonwealth and free port in the Emperor of Darien's country, as he was pleased to call that poor miserable prince, and whose protection he pretended to be assured of from all who would engage in that design." Douglas was shocked by the innocence of his countrymen, by their stupidity in abandoning all thought of the East India trade and committing the Company's resources to a ridiculous Fund and a Caribbean adventure that could only end in disaster.

My friends give themselves up blindfold to another at his pleasure.... He deceives the Company, and imposes upon them (and, indeed, the nation, which is generally concerned in it) that he puts them upon attempting so hazardous and costly an undertaking with their little stock. Whereas it is reasonable to believe that if they were able at last to accomplish it, after a long war with the Spaniards, and to make themselves masters of both seas—without which it would be no ways profitable—it may cost more millions than they have hundreds of thousands.

This prescient, and tragically accurate warning was undoubtedly circulated privately in Edinburgh, but while it may have caused some men to temper their enthusiasm, and others to thank God they had ventured no silver in the Company, the Directors ignored it. As they had ignored the implicit warnings of Wafer's narrative. They were busy, and being busy were far too involved with plans, schemes, contracts and agreements to concern themselves with the sour opinions of one envious merchant.

The Committee for Foreign Trade had taken into the Company's employ—as Supervisor-General of Medicaments and Provisions (such as might be needed by 1,500 men for two years)—a Highlandman from the far north, Dr. John Munro of Coul. Though he was later to be accused of peculation by some of those who survived the lack of proper medicines in Darien, he was a resolute and active worker. He was also a tireless traveller. He was here, there and everywhere that summer, in Dundee, Montrose, Aberdeen, Inverness and Wick, buying salt beef and dried cod, ordering pistols and firelocks, Cheshire cheese and butter, instructing four surgeon-apothecaries of Edinburgh to prepare vast quantities of powders, potions, salves and plasters. What he was not doing, or had no time to do, was being done by others. Biscuit was ordered, baked, bought and casked (James Balfour was told to find 300 tuns of it). Two hundred oxen were driven to Leith and there slaughtered in one bloody day, and barrelled within the week. Ten tuns of black and yellow rum, five of crimson claret, four hogsheads of musket flints, suet and pork by the oaken cask, spades, mattocks and hoes, horn-spoons and white-iron candlesticks, fish-hooks and plaiding hose, thus was the Leith warehouse being slowly filled.

On September 30 the Committee was clearly gifted with cynical foresight. Two thousand reams of paper were ordered for the colony, and the Scots in Darien were to use much of it in libellous complaints against each other.

In Holland and Germany the Company's ships were already bought or building. James Gibson had early acquired a 46-gun trader from an Amsterdam merchant, a gilded, broad-beamed vessel called *Saint Francis*, gentle to the helm and sweet to handle. In a rush of British rather than Scots patriotism, which would not be shared later by the Directors, he renamed her the *Union*. A rough and brutal man, he had spent a lifetime at sea as mate and master aboard the ships of his brother Walter, the Provost of Glasgow. The money they made, often by the transportation of bonded servants and prisoners to the Plantations, had enabled them to become rich and influential, subscribers and directors of the Company, and James Gibson's ambitions now included office and profit in the colony. On September 29, in the red-brick, canalside house of a Scots merchant in Amsterdam, over pipes and glasses of Hollands, he signed a contract for a second ship, larger than the *Union*. When built by Willem Direcksone, shipwright, she would be as stout and as seaworthy as any Dutch Indiaman, with an upcurving beak, clinker-laid bulwarks of scarlet and green, a great whipstaff on her quarterdeck, and a baroque stern heavy with lanterns, cupids, caryatids and the golden orb of the name already chosen for her, the *Rising Sun*.

In Lübeck to the north of Hamburg, Alexander Stevenson had placed orders for the building of four more ships, and the rounded ribs of one had already risen above the Baltic. Though both men were empowered to commission the ships, the completion of the contracts, the final payments, were the responsibility of Paterson and his colleagues.

And it was mid-October before any of them left for Amsterdam. Colonel John Erskine of Carnock, the Governor of Stirling Castle, and Haldane of Gleneagles had been appointed as Paterson's companions, and James Smith had been instructed to join them from London. Like Haldane, Erskine was sternly dedicated to the political and religious principles of the Revolution, jealous of the honour and prosperity of his country. In his youth he had been a law student, but had abandoned advocacy for a buff-coat and sword when Argyll rose in the West against James II. He escaped from this pathetic disaster with little more than his life, lying in the bilge of a ship off Bo'ness until a fair wind took him to Holland. He returned four years later with William of Orange, to that preferment and favour guaranteed by exile. He had a particular and personal interest in the success of a colony. In 1684 his brother, Lord Cardross, had led a mixed company of transported Covenanters and free colonists to a miserably unsuccessful plantation in Carolina (aboard a ship owned by Walter Gibson and commanded by James Gibson). Erskine went to Gourock to say good-bye to his brother and his friends, and he never forgot the sweet sound of the ship's trumpet, calling farewell across the Firth of Clyde.

He and Paterson left Leith together for Amsterdam, it being agreed that Haldane should follow later by way of London, bringing Smith with him. Paterson was glad to be gone from Edinburgh, although the trust the Company now placed in him was absolute. He had been given £25,000—a quarter of the first call on the subscribers—for the purchase of ships and stores, and upon his own responsibility he had sent £17,000 of this to James Smith in London, with instructions that it be used to honour all drafts issued by himself or others abroad. He was anxious to open books in Amsterdam and Hamburg, and had assured everybody that his friends there, merchants, senators and princes, were waiting to subscribe. Gossips still troubled him, particularly the retelling of Douglas's sneer that he had been bribed by the East India Company to ruin the London venture, but he had now decided that the reason for such malice was envy, as he explained in a valedictory letter to Annandale.

> Envy usually attends the prosperity of any man, and my own natural defects, as well as those of some of my country-men, will doubtless lay me open, as well as others, to the usual treatment in such cases, and as I have always found, so I find now, that the best remedy for these things is patience. I hope this Company, like Hercules in the cradle, shall strangle all these snakes.

Once he was gone, this Hercules instructed Roderick Mackenzie's clerks to employ their spare time in making fair copies of all the manuscripts, journals and papers which Paterson had lent to the Court.

In Amsterdam the Commissioners found that James Gibson had prepared some of the ground for them. The Company's Act had been translated into Dutch, printed and bound, and dis-tributed among the independent merchants of Holland. In the beginning the Dutch were attracted by the thought of joining

with the Scots in the Indies trade, but their warmth did not last
long. It was first chilled by a tavern rumour claiming that
Paterson had privately boasted that the Company was empowered
to give favourable commissions to anybody, provided they sailed
under Scots colours, made a token call at a Scots port, and gave
the Company three per cent of the twenty they could thus earn
by underselling the English and Dutch Companies. The Commissioners hotly denied the rumour, and might have been believed had not the powerful Dutch East and West India
Companies awoken to the sharp danger of this thistle that had
appeared in their orderly tulip bed. Less spectacularly than the
English East India Company and without any public show, by
the whispered threat of their displeasure they squashed all
interest in the subscription book. Still Paterson and Erskine
remained in Amsterdam, reluctant to leave lest their miserable
failure to be too obvious, and give too much satisfaction to the
enemies of the Company. As winter came on, canals froze over
and windmills turned swiftly before the fierce gales that blew in
from the polders, they got what comfort they could from the
Rising Sun, the final contracts for its equipment and stores. They
visited Direcksone's frosted yard, heard the encouraging noise of
hammer and saw, smelt oil, resin and turpentine, and watched
the argosy of their dreams take shape in a fine round hull and
carved sterncastle.

Haldane came to Holland in December, and with him a
strangely furtive and hangdog Smith who was protesting innocence and shame in one breath. He behaved like a prisoner, and
in a sense that is what he was. When Haldane had arrived in
London he had been first uneasy, then suspicious of Smith's
conduct of affairs, and finally alarmed by the discovery that £8,000
was missing from the money Paterson had sent to London. Smith
had a ready explanation. The deficit, he said, was covered by
bills which Paterson had drawn, and seemed unconcerned by the
fact that he was thereby accusing his friend and patron of
embezzlement. Haldane was an honourable man, and he was
reluctant to think ill of Paterson before he had been given an
opportunity to explain. In the presence of two of the Company's
London agents, Smith's papers were bound and sealed, and were
then carried to Holland in Haldane's baggage. By some unknown

means, it may have been the threat of arrest, Smith was persuaded to accompany Haldane.

Paterson was shocked by the news. Erskine and Haldane later described "how much he was surprised and afflicted when he heard of this disappointment, and how earnest and careful he was to get Smith to make a discovery of his effects, to the end the Company might be secured therein." They also believed in Paterson's innocence. A dishonest man they said, with more generosity than logic, would certainly have deserted them and the Company at that moment.

Throughout December and January, in their lodgings close to Direcksone's shipyard, the three Commissioners sat in melancholy examination of Smith, confused by his changing moods of defiance and abject submission. His guilt, which he seems to have finally acknowledged, was the least of their difficulties, the recovery of the money, or some of it, was primarily important. They also believed that if the affair were made public, so soon after their failure to open a book in Amsterdam, it would do irreparable damage to their hopes of success in Hamburg. It is not clear when they informed Edinburgh, but the Directors also agreed that any public action the Company took against Smith, or Paterson or both, should be postponed until the Commissioners returned to Scotland. They did, however, pass one curious resolution, declaring that "without the help of considerable foreign subscriptions this Company is not at present in a condition to put Mr. Paterson's said design in execution." The said design, of course, was still Darien, and the intent of the resolution may have been to confuse the English, as it must have confused everybody, since a second resolution paradoxically re-affirmed the Company's determination to found a colony in America. More probably it was an oblique warning to Paterson. His future share in the credit for a colony, as much as his present reputation, depended on his success with the Hanseatic merchants.

In February he and Erskine left by ship for Hamburg, Haldane remaining in Amsterdam to watch the building of the *Rising Sun* and to subject the wretched Smith to closer and closer examination. What had he done with the money? What were his assets in London and the West Indies? How soon could they be realised and surrendered to the Company? Were there other incriminating papers in the trunk he had left behind at his London lodgings?

The Hamburg venture was also a failure, more disastrous than Amsterdam because it promised well at the beginning. This time England stretched an arm across the North Sea and snuffed out Paterson's hopes. The inexorable hand at the end of this arm was Sir Paul Rycaut, English Resident at Hamburg, a dry, dull man, a willing civil servant whose letters reveal the spiteful pleasure he got from obeying his master's voice. Since August he had been sending reports about "a certain crew of Scotchmen" who had come to buy and build ships for the India trade. He had not met them, he said, nor did he desire their company. Their leader was an "active and cunning person", and when he and Stevenson came face to face in the house of a mutual acquaintance, the Scot was exquisitely snubbed. Rycaut was delighted to hear—from William Blathwayt, Commissioner of Trade, and Sir William Trumbull, Secretary of State—that the King would be displeased if the Scots established themselves in the Hanseatic ports. With God's help and grace, he said, they would get no footing in his province.

> I have been, and shall be very watchful over all their motions and am very sure and confident that the business is yet gone no farther than to the building of ships. . . . I do not believe as yet that there have been any motions, the which in all probability may be reserved until the coming over of the Scotch Commissioners, who can never conceal themselves here without my knowledge, nor any of their negotiations without my particular inspection.

He sent pompous letters to all the Hanseatic towns, threatening them with England's disapproval and King William's anger. He summoned the members of the Hamburg Senate before him to say the same thing in sharper words, and to make trebly sure he ordered his secretary to write another letter, in Latin this time, which was delivered with proper solemnity to the Magnificent and Noble Lords, Great Men and Citizens of Hamburg, Bremen and Lübeck, warning them against any treaties or agreements with the Company. All this "to leave no stone unturned which may defeat the Scotch design."

He waited like a cat for the arrival of the Commissioners. One of them, he said with thin-nosed contempt, was "the son of a lord, or at least a laird", and the other, Mr. Paterson, was a poor liar who had failed to dupe the Dutch with his promises of riches and a golden age. On Monday, February 13, he was astonished, and probably annoyed, to be told that Erskine and Paterson were at his door, within two days of their arrival in Hamburg. Instead of hiding from him, as he had said they would, they had called to let "me know that out of duty and respect to His Majesty they were come to pay their civilities to me who am his Minister." He turned an ill day into some good by asking them searching questions about their intentions. Paterson declared that he was well affected toward England, and had always believed that Scots and English should be one nation under the name of Britain. He frankly admitted that they intended to open a subscription book for the Company as soon as possible. Rycaut told Trumbull that he did not think they would get far with that, "the merchants not seeming fond of so dark and doubtful a design."

But, to make sure, he reminded the Hamburg Senators of the warning he had given in October, and he was childishly pleased, three days later, when they sent one of their syndics to assure him that they would permit no treaties or agreements with the Scots without the consent of the King of England.

In fact, however, the Hansa merchants were willing to listen to Paterson, giving profit its proper priority, and his hopes rose. He and Erskine had told Rycaut that they would not open their subscription book before some of their ships were launched, and now, despite the worst Baltic winter within memory, the Lübeck shipwrights finished two of them on time. They were launched in the second week of March, when there was still snow on the roofs and ice on the shores of Lübeck Bight. Saint Andrew's cross and the rising sun of the Company snapped in the wind above the yard, evergreen boughs hung from the golden galleries of the ships, casks of Canary were broached, and hired trumpeters splintered the frosty air with bright calls of joy. The vessels were called *Caledonia* and *Instauration*. Fine names, said Rycaut sarcastically, by which the Scots hoped to seduce the Hamburg merchants into parting with their money.

The Resident was depressed for some days after this small
Scots triumph, and then was cheered by news from Amsterdam.
One of the Scots Company called Smith, wrote his correspondent
there, had been arrested for embezzlement, and Paterson was
rumoured to have been his confederate. "Though there were
nothing more to it than a report," Rycaut told Blathwayt, "yet it
is sufficient to break the whole credit of the Company in these
parts." By which he no doubt meant that he would make it his
business to give the rumour the widest circulation.

And then he was depressed again, alarmed to hear that
Paterson was holding "several conferences with the most rich and
monied merchants of this city, at which several articles were
agreed which as yet are not made public." He was writing this to
Trumbull when his secretary informed him that the Scots were at
his door again. There were three of them this time, a Mr.
Haldane (whose name Rycaut could never spell) having just
arrived from Amsterdam. There was a fourth, too, Mr. Smith,
but he was wearied from his journey and begged leave to call on
the Resident some other day. Rycaut swallowed his curiosity, and
did not trouble to explain to Trumbull how a man who was said
to be in an Amsterdam gaol one day could the next be asking for
an audience with him in Hamburg. He was much more upset by
what these troublesome, straight-faced Scots had to tell him.
They had finished the articles for the Company's subscription
book, and intended to publish them in Bremen, Hamburg, Leip-
sic, Dresden and Frankfort, as well as other great cities, and that
they would employ men there to take up subscriptions. Moreover,
they were confident of the support of such eminent men as the
Dukes of Cell, Brunswick and Wolfenbüttel.

Rycaut did not believe a word of that. He was assured by Mr.
Cresset, English Envoy to the Court of Lüneburg, that it was all
lies and quite contrary to ducal humour, but he decided that this
might be the moment for another warning blast from an English
trumpet. He told his secretary, Mr. Orth, to write, print and
distribute a pamphlet in High Dutch, warning the Germans that
investments in the Scots Company would be a hazardous venture,
with little or no hope of profit. And when Mr. Orth had done
that, he was told to do it again, this time in French. For a day or
so Paterson thought of writing an answer, but rejected the idea as

a waste of time. Instead, the Scots announced that they would open their Subscription Book on Thursday, April 8, in a room above the Hamburg Exchange, and they asked the Senate for permission to place a bold sign above its door: *This is the House of the Scots Company*. Rycaut was indignant. "I applied myself to the chief Burgomaster, giving him to understand that such a concession would be a downright owning of this Company, against which I have by the order of the King my master given them so many cautions." For once the Senate, tired of his arrogant bullying, refused to say whether the Scots would or would not be allowed to put up their sign.

On the evening of April 5 Paterson called on Rycaut, apparently expecting dinner, and that without invitation. The Resident received him civilly, or said he did—"as I do all other strangers who come to me"—doubtless thinking that though this way of obtaining information was an irritating embarrassment, it was perhaps cheaper and more reliable than his spies. It is probable that Paterson was making a sincere, albeit naïve attempt to enlist the Resident's sympathy, and to assure him that the Scots had no wish to prejudice the interests of the English trading companies in the Baltic. Rycaut reported only the information which Paterson honestly gave him. Erskine, Smith and Haldane (whom Rycaut was now calling Walden of Coneguy) were gone to secure support for the Company's book in Lübeck, Gluckstadt and Tormingen. Whatever was laid on the table, the dinner cannot have improved the Resident's digestion.

On April 7 he decided that it was time to finish with the Scots. He and Cresset summoned deputies from the Hamburg Senate and bluntly ordered them "not only not to bestow on this new Company any privileges in this city, but not so much as to grant them licence to write over the door any motto for the house." The meeting was followed that afternoon by a memorial to the Senate, written in French and signed by the Resident and the Envoy. It said that the presence of the Scots in Hamburg, the encouragement given to their Company, was an affront to the King of England which he could not fail to resent. The Senate was asked to remedy this unhappy state of affairs before it disturbed the good relations which should exist between the City of Hamburg and the Kingdom of England.

The arrogant threat was successful. Paterson opened the book but nobody came. A few bolder merchants did subscribe later, but for small sums, and without a wide and generous response their names were a mockery. The Scots remained in Hamburg for another fortnight, watched the launching of two more ships at Lübeck, published a sadly ineffectual reply to Rycaut's pamphlet, and then accepted defeat. Erskine, Smith and Haldane left for Holland on Friday, April 23, followed the next day by Paterson. "I am glad we are quit of 'em," said Rycaut. He heard that they intended to lodge a complaint before the King, against the obedient Mr. Orth, "For writing the German paper ... of which they cannot prove him to be the author, yet if they could, he and I are too well satisfied in having done this duty that we are both without fear of having gained His Majesty's displeasure thereby."

In Amsterdam there was no need now to keep up the degrading pretence that Smith was a trusted member of the Commission. How the others had prevented him from escaping is a mystery, unless he had chosen to be a willing prisoner, hoping to earn some remission. Haldane had him committed to a Dutch gaol, for greater security, and against the day when he could be carried to another prison in London or Scotland. Smith broke down, writing tearful letters to Haldane in which he threatened to kill himself if it were not believed that he had had no intention of cheating the Company. He offered to repay £5,000 over eighteen months, offering his shares in the Hampstead Waterworks as part security, and saying that the rest might be got by fitting out a merchantman for a running adventure in the Caribbean or the eastern seas. But if it were known in London that he was in prison now, he would have no hope of raising a penny. "If you do upon these terms release me, and it should afterwards be disapproved of by those concerned with you, or the Company, I do solemnly promise you to deliver myself up as your prisoner where you shall require, until they are satisfied." Haldane's generous heart relented, and he let the man go to London, to raise what money he could.

Paterson went home to Scotland with a heavy heart. All things that he had touched, the London Company, Amsterdam and Hamburg, had turned to sour failure. A new ballad, welcoming him from the walls of Edinburgh's coffee-houses, was a bitter irony.

Amongst the many visiting everywhere,
Judicious Paterson, with many more,
Fraught with experience, back again do come,
Striving to propagate their skill at home.

He waited throughout summer and autumn for an opportunity to clear himself from the suspicion of fraud. He was rejected and ostracised, and street-rumours soon stopped the flattering tongues of the ballad-writers. Though Haldane had recovered some of the money by a sale of Smith's property, the greater balance of the default was still outstanding. Had all of it been returned it would not have cleared Paterson. In November the Company finally appointed a committee to examine him. It consisted of two Directors only, Robert Blackwood and William Dunlop, the Principal of Glasgow College. Both were reasonable and compassionate men, anxious to help him without dishonouring their obligations. They asked him if he could repay the money, and he said he had no funds at all. He was almost destitute. By leaving his business affairs in London he had lost more than was now owing to the Company. If the Court would release him from service he would endeavour to raise the money in some commercial venture. If he could not be released, then perhaps the Company would take what was owing from the profits of his work. Though he had not himself cheated the Company, he took responsibility for the thief whom he had so highly recommended.

In their report, Blackwood and Dunlop exonerated him of anything more than stupidity, and they reminded the Council-General of the time when "Mr. Paterson did merit very well at the Company's hands." They generously urged the Company to keep him in its employ, to allow him to go to the colony when it was founded and there work off the debt he had taken upon himself. His knowledge and reputation, his skill and arts should not be foolishly thrown away.

The Council-General wanted no more of him. He was expelled from the Court of Directors. Though his papers and journals were not returned to him, his share in the Company's stock was withdrawn, and the committee's recommendation that he should be allowed to go to the colony was rejected. He became a shadowy figure on the periphery of great events, and had he turned his back on Scotland few men would have blamed him and many might have been relieved.

But he stayed.

"Scotch hats, a great quantity; English bibles, 1500 . . ."
Edinburgh and London, July 1697 to July 1698

Summer came, sunless, once more a blighted harvest and bitter hunger. It was the second of seven terrible years. What was now harsh privation would soon be bitter famine. Each year snow would come early and linger late, summer rains would rot the feet of sheep and cattle, blacken the hopeless fields of young grain. Men would sell some of their children to the plantations so that they might buy bread for those who remained. Before the century was out it would be impossible to count those who had died of starvation. Already the diseased and dying, begging in the streets, filled more fortunate men with anger, not against misfortune but against the English from whom they must buy meal to keep alive. In the streets, too, along the highways, were other reminders of a payment made to England and a debt owed in return. The King's war was ended, his Scots regiments disbanded, and home had come the survivors of Strathnaver's Foot, of Leven's, Mackay's and Argyll's. In coffee-houses and taverns, junior officers quarrelled over points of honour and bragged of their conduct in worthless battles. Their men became beggars and thieves, or clung to their coat-tails asking for bread and employment. Fletcher of Saltoun would remind his countrymen of a great imbalance, of the contribution their sons had made to King William's long war: ten or eleven thousand seamen in the English and Dutch navies, twenty battalions of Foot, and six squadrons of Dragoons. Every fifth man in the King's armies at home or abroad had been a Scot or Scots-Irish. And yet, he said, the English "vilify us as an inconsiderable people, and set a mean value on the share we have borne."*

* For one hundred and fifty years England fought her wars with armies that were increasingly recruited in Scotland and Ireland. By 1840, according to Sir William Butler (*A Plea for the Peasant*, 1878), nearly 60 per cent of the

As they filled the courtyard of Milne Square, offering their idle swords, the returned soldiers gave a renewed impetus to the Company. In the face of famine, destitution, unemployment and an emptying purse, the Noble Undertaking now seems like a sick man's delirium. To the people then it was hope, it represented their fevered longing for freedom and prosperity, and it symbolised their defiance of England. Roderick Mackenzie fed this feeling with his own hatred of the English, secretly publishing a copy of Rycaut's memorial to the Hamburg Senate, that Scots might know how inexorable was England's determination to destroy their one hope of bread, trade and glory. The King's aging Chancellor, Lord Marchmont, was so incensed by this impudence that he had the printer laid by the heels, and would have sent young Mackenzie to the Tolbooth too, had he dared.

All the King's principal servants in Scotland were alarmed by the growing anger against their master, fearing the loss of his favour as much as they expected riot and burning. It was a time for great men in great office to choose between King and country, and they hastily made that choice known to William Carstares, the fat, smiling Presbyterian minister who was the King's secretary and adviser on Scots affairs. Since he was always at William's side, in camp or court, a letter to him was the same as nudging the King's attention, and his unpriced sympathy was more valuable than the services of a bought man.

From Holyroodhouse the young Duke of Queensberry wrote anxiously to Carstares. A genteel, black-haired Douglas, he held the office of Commissioner vacated by Tweeddale, and although he usually preferred to face trouble by turning his back on it, he now found it all about him. The Councillors of the Company, he said, intended to address the King in protest against the Hamburg Memorial. "I wish that something may be done to quieten the people who make a great noise about it and other prejudices they think are imposed on them by England." He admitted that he was deeply involved in the Company, but would do only what was pleasing to the King, if someone would be good enough to tell him what that might be. The Lord Advocate, Sir James

infantry rank and file were Scots and Irish. As late as the Crimean War it was still 44 per cent. There was probably no fair balance until the introduction of conscription in World War I.

Stewart, an affable old man who was never certain of the King's trust, was badly frightened by a rumour that he had given a licence for the printing of the Memorial. He wordily denied it. It was a malicious lie started by the printer's boy. And being more of a lawyer than a moralist he saw no sin in proving his loyalty by acknowledging his countrymen's hatred. "My relief is to be attacked where all see my innocence, for I have no dealing with our African Company, and many of them reckon me an unfriend." Sir James Ogilvy, whose services to the Throne as Secretary of State would soon be rewarded with the viscountcy of Seafield, also told Carstares that he had put no money into the Company, neither had any member of his family. His fellow Secretary was Lord Tullibardine, a young man of choking passion who had deserted his family and King James at the Revolution, had been given an earldom taken from his Jacobite father, and who was never sure that he was doing the right thing. He had subscribed £500 to the Company, but explained to Carstares that this was a trick whereby "I shall have the more influence to hinder any designs that may prove uneasy to His Majesty." When the Company appealed to the Privy Council for support in their Address to William, both Ogilvy and Tullibardine argued against it, carrying the Council with them by a narrow majority of four.

The Company sent its protest to the King. Now that the matter was of no real consequence, William replied (in his own time) that he would order his Resident at Hamburg not to use his name or authority for obstructing the Company in the prosecution of its trade with the inhabitants of that city.

The Directors kept up the façade of secrecy, deluding themselves with the belief that England did not know where they intended to settle their colony. And the English Government, which knew very well that it was to be Darien, pretended that it did not. The slow dance of ignorance and counter-ignorance was performed with comic gravity. When the Lords Justices of England wished to ask Ogilvy's advice on the Directors' plans, William Blathwayt persuaded them against it, and the Secretary —loyally declaring his non-involvement with Milne Square— would not have been pleased to know why. "It might be expected," said Blathwayt cynically, "he would own no knowledge of what the Company intended, and underhand intimate to them to forward their expedition so much the more, since notice of it was begun to be taken here."

Blathwayt's information about Darien had come from Rycaut and Orth in Hamburg, whose spies had got it from the loose-tongued sailors whom the Company had sent to bring their ships to Leith. "I was informed," reported Orth, "that the two Scotch East India Company's ships now lying in this river were designed for the south coast of America, at the Isthmus of Darien." He had been to see the ships, and reported that each carried 56 guns, 12-pounders and 8-pounders on their lower and upper decks, and he had heard that they would be loaded with fine linen, lace and other goods for the Spanish and Indian trade. Hamburg merchants were also admitting that Paterson and Erskine had talked frankly of the intended colony on Darien. "It is in my opinion," said Orth, "not to be doubted but that this is their real design."

He wrote so much that his imagination took over his pen. He said that the Scots were recruiting pirates from John Avery's ship, lately returned to Ireland. Some person had told him, and this person had also said that the Scots would be willing to try a little piracy themselves if they saw a profit in it. A handful of Avery's men were accordingly dragged out of ale-houses in Dublin and Cork, imprisoned and interrogated, and since some of them were later pardoned they may have had the wit to lie in support of Orth's person, once they realised the purpose of their examination.

The Lords Justices and the Commissioners for Trade were particularly concerned with the steps which should be taken to make the Scots colony impossible, or at least untenable, but they were also anxious that everything should be done within the law, English law that is. They were greatly helped by Mr. James Vernon. He was the middle-aged Member for Penryn, a scholar of Oxford and Cambridge, a onetime political agent in Holland, now an assistant in the Secretary of State's office and soon to be Principal Secretary. A tall, thin man with a brown face and a hanging lip, untidy in dress and brusque in manner, he was a superb and dedicated civil servant who lived and died an untitled gentleman, having been particularly unfortunate in his choice of patrons. John Macky said he was a drudge to office, no man ever wrote so many letters. His habit of working all day and half the night at his desk, Macky explained, was due to an ill-tempered wife whose company he desperately avoided.

He gave the Lords Justices and the Commissioners their ruling in what came to be known as "Mr. Vernon's Line". It was based on four questions put to the Attorney-General and the Solicitor-General. Both gentleman declared that the Scots colony would be against the laws of England, and the King had thus the right to prohibit his English subjects from giving it aid and assistance. All magistrates and officers, in England or the Plantations, would have the right to search any Scots ship going to the colony, and to take from it any English subjects they found aboard. There was no doubt that the colony would be prejudicial to His Majesty's allies and to the trade of England. When Vernon became Principal Secretary a few months later, he used this minute as the legal justification for the Royal Proclamation which he composed and sent to the Governors of all English Plantations, warning them against giving so much as a cask of pure water to any ship flying the sunburst standard of the Company of Scotland.

He also listened patiently to anyone who could give him information about the Caribbean and the Main. Thus Captain Richard Long of Jamaica found a welcome in his office and before the Lords Justices. This leathery seaman was said to be a Quaker, but one without a troublesome conscience, no doubt, since he was a hard master and a foul-mouthed roisterer. He wanted £200 and a vessel, he told their lordships, and if given both he would bring the King £1,500,000 in gold plate salvaged from Spanish-American wrecks. They debated his petition, considered his further request for a sixteenth of the treasure, and took no action. But they did not forget him.

Toward the end of November London heard from Orth that the Scots ships had left the Baltic, and on the day that Secretary Trumbull endorsed his letter "Recd Read 22nd Nov. 1697", the *Caledonia* was sailing up the Forth. In clear, winter's light she anchored off Burntisland and took in all sail. Her beak and stern were a glory of gold and scarlet and blue, and as pennants flew from her main-top and mizzen her bow-chaser fired a signal salute to the cheering crowds on both sides of the firth. It was joyously answered by a white thunder from the walls of Edinburgh Castle. She had been brought from the Baltic by seamen of

H.M.S. Royal William, the flagship of Scotland's little Navy, although there is no record of anyone asking the permission of royal William himself. A week later the second Lübeck ship, *Instauration*, came bravely by the Bass Rock and into the firth, firing her signal gun as she dropped anchor a cable's length from the *Caledonia*. Before sunset she had lost her equivocal name, the Directors toasting another in their panelled chamber at Milne Square, and resolving "that from henceforward it shall be called *Saint Andrew*, and that the usual ceremony be executed to-morrow, it being Saint Andrew's Day." Both were clinker-built, 56-gun Indiamen of 350 tons, three-masted and rigged with stay-sails on fore and main, a lateen on the mizzen, and a steep, square-sailed sprit above a golden prow. When the *Union* came over from Amsterdam the distasteful implications of her name, too, were quickly rejected, in favour of *Unicorn* and in honour of Scotland's ancient heraldic beasts. Though a silver unicorn now supported one side of King William's arms, every nursery child knew that it was in spirited and relentless defiance of the English lion opposite.

Two smaller ships also arrived before the year was out, both of them to be tenders for the others, and neither of them much more than a coastal vessel. The *Dolphin* was a two-masted, snub-nosed snow, a French prize which James Gibson had bought from her captors in Holland. In strong seas she would stub-bornly bury her head in the waves and run with water from stem to waist. Her companion, the *Endeavour*, was a pink which the busy Dr. Munro purchased at Newcastle, which indicates that one English ship-owner, at least, was indifferent to the wishes of his government. She was high-sterned, with a great rudder and a round hull that bellied out from the water-line and in again to her narrow deck. Seaworthy enough, she was quixotic and hard to handle, rolling with sickening rhythm as she dipped her yard-arms to the sea.

The Company had its fleet. The *Rising Sun* should also have come, but without topmasts and rigging she was locked in the ice at Amsterdam, where Peter the Great took wine in her cabin with Direcksone and Gibson. Yet she, too, would come. The pro-mise that she must come was already there in five splendid ships, etched in beauty against the white hills of Fife.

All winter, when tide and weather permitted, ferries bounced across the Forth from Leith to Burntisland, emptying the warehouse and filling the ships' holds. There was now a Committee for Equipping Ships, which met under William Arbuckle at the coffee-house owned by the nieces of James Maclurg, a merchant member of the Committee. It loaded hogsheads of beer from Thomas Whyte the brewer of Leith, bread from Ninian Hay the baker, clay pipes from David Montgomery, and dye from Ephraim Roberts. In one day, packed in dry water-casks, there were loaded 380 Bibles, 51 New Testaments, 200 Confessions of Faith and 2,808 Catechisms, all printed by Widow Anderson and all intended to sustain the settlers and inspire the Indians, if the latter could be taught English. Three Edinburgh hatters, as the first instalment of their contracts, delivered 1,440 hats (at two shillings each), and Jeremy Robertson sent boxes of his bob-wigs, periwigs and campaign wigs. With derisive hindsight, Walter Herries would find these very amusing, though his humour grossly exaggerated the number.

Scotch hats, a great quantity; English bibles, 1500; periwigs, 4000, some long, some short; campaigns, Spanish bobs and natural ones. And truly they were all natural, for being made of Highlanders' hair, which is blanched with the rain and sun, when they came to be opened in the West Indies they looked like so many of Samson's fireships that he sent among the Philistines, and could be of no use to the Colony, if it were not to mix with their lime when they plastered the walls of their houses.*

The total value of the goods loaded on all five ships was £18,413 5s 0½d Sterling. The *Caledonia* and the *Saint Andrew* carried the largest cargoes, as they were to transport the greatest number of settlers. There were axes, knives, mattocks and hammers, tools for coopers, carpenters and smiths, and

---

* Macaulay, later, was equally derisive, accepting Herries as a reliable authority and jeering at men who carried wigs to the Tropics as trade goods, forgetting that they were probably intended for use by the settlers. But Fletcher of Saltoun, answering Herries, attempted to justify their trading value. "The cargo of cloth, stuffs, shoes, stockings, slippers and wigs must needs be proper for a country where the Natives go naked for want of apparel, and fit to be exchanged for other commodities, either in the English, Dutch, French or Spanish Plantations."

enough nails in oiled boxes to hold together the doors and windows of a city. Fuses, grenades, cannon and cannon-shell, lead shot and powder, blunderbusses and muskets, pistols and broadswords, cutlasses and pikes, and a thousand cartridge-pouches of good black leather. For parley or triumph, when these had been used, there were brass trumpets and drums. There were men's hose and women's stockings, and more than 25,000 pairs of shoes, pumps and slippers. There was "cloth in great bulk", bales and bolts of ticking, canvas, linen, serge, muslin, glazed calico, tartan plaiding, hodden-grey and harn. Coloured crepe for flags and bunting, striped muslin for neckcloths, and Holland duck for seamen. Fourteen thousand needles, balls of twine and thread in black and grey and white. Iron frying-pans and pots, basins and jugs of English pewter, a thousand precious drinking-cups of glass, horn spoons and wooden trenchers. Twenty-nine barrels of tobacco pipes in Mr. Montgomery's best white clay. Printing-tools, parchment for treaties with princes, ink and quills, sealing-wax and scarlet ribbon of watered silk. Flints for guns and tinder-boxes, candles uncountable and three thous-and candle-sticks. Buttons of wood, brass, horn and pewter, looking-glasses and two thousand pounds of pure white soap.

And combs. Remembering Lionel Wafer's idyllic picture of the Cuna Indians, combing long hair with their fingers, the Directors ordered and loaded tens of thousands, large and small, made from lightwood, boxwood and horn. Such small vanities as a wooden comb, inlaid with beads of mother-of-pearl, could buy an imperial foothold.

Three hundred tons of biscuit—coarse, middle, and fine—seventy of stalled beef, twenty of prunes and fifteen of pork, casks of suet, flour and unmilled wheat. Twelve hundred gallons of strong claret, seventeen hundred of rum, five thousand of vinegar and five thousand more of brandy. All carefully tasted. Once a week the Committee for Equipping went down to Leith with the ships' captains and there dined and "particularly tried the state and condition of both the grass-fed and stall-fed beef, as also of the pork and other provisions, and found the same in extraordinary case and well-cured to their own and the said captains' great contentment."

There were also men. On March 12, 1698, a single folio sheet was posted at the entry to Milne Square, and on the walls of every coffee-house in Edinburgh, Leith and Glasgow.

The Court of Directors of the Indian and African Company of Scotland, having now in readiness ships and tenders in very good order, with provisions and all manner of things needful for their intended expedition to settle a colony in the Indies; *give Notice*, that for the general encouragement of all such as are willing to go upon the said expedition:

Everyone who goes on the first expedition shall receive and possess fifty acres of plantable land, and 50 foot square of ground at least in the chief city or town, and an ordinary house built thereupon by the colony at the end of 3 years.

Every Councillor shall have double. If anyone shall die, the profit shall descend to his wife and nearest relations. The family and blood relations shall be transported at the expense of the Company.

The Government shall bestow rewards for special service.

By Order of the Court,

RODERICK MACKENZIE, *Secy.*

The Proclamation carried the Company's device, lately approved by the Lord Lyon King of Arms: Saint Andrew's white saltire on a blue field, cantoned with a ship in full sail, two Peruvian llamas burdened, and a towered elephant, the whole supported by an Indian and a Blackamoor holding goat's-horns of abundant fruit. The crest was a rising sun, upon the tilted human face of which was an expression of peering incredulity.

The political and social structure of the Colony had been determined. Although there were plans for a parliament ultimately, it would be ruled at first by a Council, each member taking his weekly turn as President (and the proposer of that astonishingly inept suggestion is unknown, to the benefit of his memory). Below the Council, and subject to it entirely, the majority of the settlers were divided into Overseers, Assistant or Sub-Overseers, and Planters. They were all soldiers, the first being field-officers and captains, the second subalterns, and the third, despite the noble promise of the name, were private sentinels enlisted at threepence a day and mustered in companies of forty. The deception was thin, and all called themselves and were referred to by their military rank, but the Company's Act forbade the employment of soldiers as such without the permission of the King's Privy Council, and nobody would ask for that.

There were also to be ministers, surgeons, physicians and apothecaries, clerks and craftsmen, and while military rank cut clear divisions horizontally the expedition was also split vertically, into Landsmen and Seamen. In time these definitions would become bitter pejoratives.

There was no lack of volunteers, and few had waited for Mackenzie's proclamation. Every young and disbanded officer was eager for the venture, and in his tail were a dozen or more hungry men whom he had led in Flanders and the Highlands, and who now saw in him their only hope of bread and employment. Edinburgh blazed with scarlet coats and facings of buff, green and blue. There was a swing of swords above the cobbles, and a high-spirited clamour in the taverns. A forlorn hope well-led before Namur might count as much as an uncle's preferment, and a wound well-healed provide a testament of courage in the scar. James Ogilvy, now Lord Seafield, was in Edinburgh and was embarrassed by men who thought he could secure them service with the Company. "I have multitudes of broken officers lying about my doors," he complained to Carstares, "and I know not what to say to them." All Directors were plagued with petitions on behalf of this captain and that ensign, of this son or that nephew, of a good sergeant or a brave drummer. No family could claim respect if it had not one young man who was hot to serve the African Company.

Twelve hundred were finally accepted, and three hundred of these were Gentlemen Volunteers, the heirs or cadet sons of good families, with the same rank and duties as Planters but with social precedence over them. A third or more of the Planters were Highlanders, discharged soldiers from Argyll's, Strathnaver's, Hill's or Mackay's, following their officers and answering the same pull of clan loyalties that had taken them into the regiments. Many of them could speak nothing but Gaelic.

The sixty officers selected were chosen with care, twelve captains, twenty-four lieutenants and twenty-four ensigns. Though influence may have brought them before the Directors, all had then to be passed by a special committee which met to "discourse with them pretty freely concerning the encouragement which they are to expect, and report accordingly concerning their sentiments thereof." This encouragement was considerable to a young man hoping to restore a family fortune or make one for himself: £150 in the Company's stock to every captain, £100 to a lieutenant and £5 to an ensign. Many of them were Highland too, captains like Lachlan Maclean, William Fraser, John Campbell and Colin Campbell, lieutenants Hugh Munro, Patrick MacDowall, and Colin Campbell, ensigns Alexander Mackenzie, Duncan Campbell and William Campbell. Eight of them were from Clan Campbell, lately officers of Argyll's, and the valour of their regiment, the influence of their chief the Earl, and the loyalty of their clan to the Revolution guaranteed their selection.

Dr. John Munro recruited surgeons and physicians for the expedition, interviewing applicants at Milne Square, and putting them through small examinations in anatomy, surgery and the practice of medicine. He was helped by two doctors already chosen, Hector Mackenzie and Walter Herries. When Haldane of Gleneagles went to London in November, 1696, he had unmasked one rogue in James Smith and had been duped by another in Herries. He met this plausible Dumbarton man at Moncrieff's coffee-house, and was so impressed that he took him into the Company's employ and on to Holland. He thought that he was doing an unfortunate fellow-countryman a service by saving him from unjust extinction at the end of an English rope.

Until the year before this, Herries had been a surgeon in the English Navy, having secured the appointment, said Fletcher of Saltoun, by becoming a convert to Catholicism and by pimping for the King's officers. He smartly abandoned this faith a few months later when the Papist on the throne was replaced by a Protestant, but he continued to prosper as a pander. He was hot-tempered, jealous of his imagined honour, and gifted with a corrosive and perceptive wit. His career as a naval surgeon ended one day in Portsmouth when, upon some real or imagined slight, he drew his sword and lunged at his commanding officer Captain John Graydon of the *Vanguard*, the hero of Beachy Head and Barfleur. Graydon recovered from the wound and would have had Herries brought out of irons, before a Council of War, and from thence to a yardarm, had not the influence of a Scots officer enabled the surgeon to escape. Though pricked as an outlaw by Graydon, he was still skulking in London, and protected by other Scots, when he was introduced to Haldane. For the next eighteen months, in Holland and Scotland, he worked for the Company as a supervisor of provisions and medical stores, and now he enjoyed Munro's total trust and respect. He would repay both later by accusing the doctor (perhaps not unjustly) of filling his own purse at the expense of the Company's. "Save a rogue from the gallows," said Andrew Fletcher, quoting the old proverb, "and he shall be the first that will cut your throat."

In February two brothers, Robert and Thomas Drummond, offered their services to the Company, the one a sailor and the other a soldier. Hard and self-seeking, contemptuous of weakness and stubbornly brave, loyal to their own code and kind but without compassion for others', they were among the few men of decisive action to whom the Company gave responsible office, and they would be principals in its final, melodramatic tragedy. They were sons of an impoverished branch of the Drummonds of Borland and of Concraig, Strathearn lairds who claimed descent from Malcolm Beg, Thane of Lennox, and through their mother they had blood ties with the powerful Hamiltons. Robert was a discharged naval lieutenant when he walked into Milne Square, boldly asking for the command of a ship, and bringing with him enough family influence to be given the *Dolphin* and £5 10s Sterling a month. Ship and pay were less than he believed he merited, and he argued the thought persuasively enough, for he was later given the *Caledonia* and five shillings more. He was a good seaman and a stern shipmaster.

Thomas Drummond needed no recommendation, his name was known to all Scotland. As a captain of grenadiers in the Earl of Argyll's Regiment he had served with courage in the Low Countries, leading his company in the van of Ramsay's Scots Brigade when it attacked the French redoubts at Dottignies. But it was not for this bloody slaughter, in which he lost most of his company, that he was well-known. He and his grenadiers had also been in Glencoe on the morning of the Massacre, under the command of Robert Campbell of Glenlyon, and to Drummond the duty seemed to be no more than the extermination of a nest of rats. When the sickened Campbell hesitated to kill the last of nine bound MacDonalds, Drummond pushed him aside and shouted "Why is he still alive? What of our orders? Kill him!" He pistolled the young man himself, and then shot a boy of twelve who was crying for mercy at Glenlyon's feet. After the Commission of Inquiry in 1695, the Scots Parliament demanded his recall from Flanders, for trial and punishment, but he and his regiment were then prisoners of the French. When he did come home, two years later after the Peace of Ryswick, the King had made it plain that he wished to hear no more of Glencoe.

If the Court of Directors debated the shadowed past of this rough and inexorable man they did not make their doubts public. They gave him a commission as an Overseer. He was not, in any case, the only soldier they employed who had been involved in the Glencoe affair. There were private sentinels from Hill's and Argyll's Regiments, and at least two officers from Hill's—Captain Charles Forbes, to whom they gave a company, and Major James Cunningham of Eickett whom they were to make a Councillor. Such men, and others who had had nothing to do with the Massacre, formed Drummond's party during the bitter quarrelling on Darien, and their enemies called them the "Glencoe Gang".

Thus the colonists were engaged, by major appointments and small. Mr. Hugh Rose to be Clerk to the Colony, on the enthusiastic recommendation of his patron, the Lord President. Alexander Hamilton, a none too successful merchant, offered his services as an Accountant, and was no more successful when he was made Keeper of Merchandise and Goods. The Reverend Mr. Adam Scott gladly agreed to go as Minister, with the blessing of the Presbytery, £100 in stock from the Company and £10 for the purchase of necessary books. A similar offer made to the Reverend Mr. Thomas James was sadly refused. He was a warm admirer of Paterson, and he could not serve the Company while it so unjustly rejected his friend. Roger Oswald was one of the eager and romantic young men who clamoured to be taken as Gentlemen Volunteers. His father, Sir James Oswald of Singleton, was a Lanarkshire laird, an officer of the Lord Treasurer's department who had recently been in prison for some innocent default in his accounts, and a stern, unforgiving parent who left his son in no doubt that family as much as national honour depended on the boy's conduct in the Colony. John Eison, a Highlandman of Clan Mackay whose name was a clerk's mauling of the Gaelic, was also taken as a Volunteer after he had extravagantly claimed to be an "absolute master of the several species of mathematics, particularly fortification, navigation, etc." Though in theory only, he added. James Lindsay, sitting on a stool in Mackenzie's office, grew tired of making ledger entries for broadswords and pistols, hodden-grey and tartan, his elbow brushed by luckier men in scarlet coats and tarpaulin jackets. He was no Gentleman, by social reckoning, but he asked leave to go as a clerk, and was accepted. William Simpson, printer of Edinburgh, offered to work the press that had been loaded aboard the *Unicorn*, and was engaged at forty shillings a month, ten of which were to be paid to his wife at home.

And Benjamin Spense, a Jew, was taken as an interpreter. He said that he could read, write and speak six languages, and was particularly fluent in Spanish and Portuguese, qualifications that were to help him more than the Company. He would be a prisoner of the Spaniards for fifteen months.

Among the lower-deck seamen waiting aboard the ships at Burntisland there was little enthusiasm for the Company or the Colony. Since the end of the war the ports had been full of workless and hungry sailors, and any berth was better than none. The Committee for Equipping Ships had paid off the crews that brought the Company's fleet from Holland and Germany, and had taken on others from the idle men on the quays. This was good business sense, not compassion. Peace had brought lower wages, since supply now exceeded demand, and the first crews had been receiving wartime rates. The seamen accepted this hard bargain silently for some weeks, and then they rebelled. At the beginning of April the ring-leaders of a mutiny aboard the *Caledonia*, John Bowrie and Robert MacAlexander, were brought before the Committee. They were charged with "going in a tumultous manner to their captain to represent their pretended grievance", with desertion, and with threatening to knock down any who would not desert with them. The Committee wasted no time on the pretended grievance. Between a file of musketeers both men were sent to the Tolbooth, there to stay at the Committee's pleasure, together with a warehouseman, William Turnbull, who had been solving his particular problems by embezzling the Company's stores.

Perhaps as a result of the trouble aboard the *Caledonia*, and realising that a mutiny at sea would certainly be worse than one in port, the Directors decided to improve the shipboard conditions of the sailors. They did not raise pay or improve rations, but they ordered that for every five seamen there should be one chest for the stowing of their meagre property. Lest this be jealously resented by the young Gentlemen aboard, it was further resolved that every Volunteer should be given room in the hold for one barrel, in which to keep his personal effects or any trade goods he wished to take to the Colony.

The Company also had trouble with James Smith again. It had finally, and incredibly late it would seem, struck his name from the roll of Directors "for his villainous violation of the trust reposed in him". He had been in London a year and had been insufferably slow in realising his assets and repaying the money. Dr. Munro was sent south to encourage him. Smith endured a few days of Munro's nagging, and then put his wife, his family, his relations and his luggage in a coach and set off for Dover and France. Munro pursued him by horse, with officers and a special warrant, caught him on the quayside and took him back to London and prison. The Directors sent Munro £400 to pay for the wretched man's prosecution.

They also sent him orders to seek out Lionel Wafer in London and sound him on the matter of employment with the Company. It was the second attempt to engage the young buccaneer. A few weeks earlier he had dined at Pontack's and discussed the proposal with Andrew Fletcher and Captain Robert Pennecuik, the recently-appointed master of the *Saint Andrew* and Commodore of the Company's fleet. They reported that he was open to persuasion and they advised the Directors to pursue him further. Fletcher held no office in the Company and he acted throughout with disinterested good faith, honestly believing that the Directors wished to employ the surgeon, but their intentions were in fact more subtle, and were motivated by an almost hysterical fear that Wafer was about to place their whole undertaking in jeopardy.

A year before, Wafer and Dampier had been closely examined in London by the Commissioners of Trade, and had been asked whether the Scots, or anyone else, could settle and hold a plantation on Darien. They said that two hundred and fifty good fighting-men, with the help of the Indians, could secure and maintain a foothold against anything the Spanish might muster by sea or land. Five hundred could settle the country and keep it. Although they were probably thinking of buccaneers, not sluggish Flanders veterans and green boys from English or Scots shires, their confidence was impressive. The Commissioners advised the Lords Justices that a ship should be sent to take possession of Golden Island off the coast of Darien. But nothing came of the suggestion.

Now the Directors heard that Wafer had placed his narrative in the hands of a printer, and they believed that once it was published, once its account of that waiting paradise was common knowledge, the English would order Admiral Benbow's West Indian Fleet to claim Darien before their own ships could leave the Forth.

Munro called at Wafer's lodgings in early June with James Campbell, the Company's London agent. They discovered that the young man was no ingenuous tarpaulin, that he was a shrewd bargainer and well advised by an Irish merchant called Fitzgerald. When he was offered twenty guineas to postpone his book for a month, he said that for £1,000 he would give the Company all the information it wished. Munro did not tell him that the Directors already had most of that, in the copy of his manuscript which Paterson had given them. He made a counter-offer of considerably less, and they haggled until the articles of a contract were agreed, composed by Campbell and written down by Fitzgerald. Wafer was to withhold publication for a month and leave immediately for further discussions with the Directors and Council-General in Edinburgh. He was to receive £50 for the expenses of this journey and the settling of his affairs in London, and if he entered the Company's service for two years he would suppress the book entirely and receive £700. If no agreement were reached in Edinburgh, he would be free to leave and publish at the end of one month. Wafer signed, and took post-horse for Scotland within the week.

The affair then became a comic farce. He travelled as "Mr. Brown", Munro insisting that secrecy was all. Wafer tolerantly agreed to this, though he may have wondered who could not be in the secret, since the English knew of the Scots' interest in him and Darien. He crossed the Border and rode toward Edinburgh by way of Haddington. At the post-house there, he said in a Memorial he wrote later, he was met by Pennecuik

.... who told me that he was sent express from the secret committee of the Company to acquaint me it was not convenient I should be seen or known at Edinburgh for some private reasons, that he was to lodge me at a house about a mile wide of the road.

The house was Saltoun Hall, Andrew Fletcher's home, and the great patriot was there to make him welcome. The next day a coach brought five great men of the Company, the Earl of Panmure and the new Marquis of Tweeddale, both Councillors, and three Directors, Haldane, Blackwood and Sir Francis Scott. They asked him if he had so ordered his affairs that there was no need for him to return to London, and he told them that he was able to go aboard at a day's notice. This, they said, was good news, for their fleet would be ready to sail in eight or ten days. They left, and returned the next day with Pennecuik.

The subject of this day's conference, as likewise for the next two or three meetings, was to inform themselves of the country of Darien, which I performed faithfully, not suspecting any private design upon me by persons of so great honour, and having unbosomed myself of all the secrets of that country of Darien, as likewise of a treasure of Nicaragua wood unknown to any person in Europe but to myself, they insisted most on this treasure, where it grows, if it were near the sea, or easily shipped aboard. I satisfied them particularly of all and in every question they asked me.

There was too much talk of that fabulous red-wood, too little of his duties with the expedition, too many notes taken by Pennecuik about harbours, soundings, and pilotage. And when the Directors spoke of Darien they used words and phrases that may have reminded Wafer curiously of his own manuscript. He was being treated as a child, he thought, and likely to be dismissed

as a child at any moment, with no more than a worthless rattle
for his trouble. But the Company had not yet finished with him.
Walter Herries was now sent to bring him by night and in secret
again to Edinburgh, where he was privately lodged off the High
Street and told to keep to the house, "less their enterprise should
take air in England, which they said must inevitably happen if I
were known to be in Scotland." High in this smoke-grained
building he saw nobody but Pennecuik and Herries, and had no
diversion but what he could see from its greasy windows, until
one day he was at last visited by the Committee for Equipping
Ships. He was told that since England now knew about the
Company's plans for Darien that site for its Colony had been
rejected in favour of another. Did he perhaps know something of
the River Plate? He did not. Of the Amazon? No. A pity, yet he
need not be too disappointed, the Company would think of a fit
gratuity for his pains. That evening Captain Pennecuik brought
him twenty guineas and the Directors' good wishes for a safe
return to England.

Walter Herries, who took Wafer out of Edinburgh and some
way down the post-road, was amused by the whole affair, particularly the night-rides, the lonely rooms at a quiet stair-head.
He thought the Directors' last warning that the visit should still
be kept secret was unnecessary, since the bitter young man
could scarcely talk about it without being laughed at. "He hath
acquired so little knowledge of Edinburgh that if he were to
return to that city he could no more find the way to his lodging
than the Company could to the Nicaragua wood."

In one matter the Directors had been honest with Wafer.
Their fleet was ready to sail. It would be at sea before the printer
had set the first page of his book.

"A brave and generous band, inspired with thirst of fame"
Edinburgh, July 1698

There were fine ships in the firth, but against the broad hills and
the wide water they seemed absurdly small to carry a nation's
desperate hope of survival. The sun which shone brilliantly, day

following day, was a cruel mockery of the emblem the Company had chosen for itself. For every ton of meal or cask of beef taken aboard the fleet there were dry fields and empty byres that promised little in replacement. "The main difficulty and discouragement," Lord Marchmont wrote to Carstares, "is from the bad appearance of the crops on the ground. The drouth has continued long, and the corns are very short and look ill... Truly the country is in a hardened and straitened condition, and all people are very sensible of it." What harvest there might be would certainly be late, and this was dangerous in a country where snow could fall on high ground before summer flowers had turned to seed. In the worst year of scarcity yet known, Scotland had stripped its larder to provision the fleet, and was left with nothing to supply the Colony when needed, and little to help itself through the certainty of a more bitter famine next year.

The Company was aware of the heavy obligations upon it and to it. "Whereas," it declared to the newly-appointed Councillors of the Colony, "the Company has laid out, expended, and bestowed the most considerable part of their whole stock toward the settling of their intended Colony, the charge thereof ought in all reason and gratitude to be refunded in due time by the Colony to the Company, with a valuable consideration during the non-payment thereof." The seven men who were thus bluntly told that the purpose of the Colony was profit had been chosen by a special committee, set up at the beginning of the year to determine the type of man most needed as a Councillor. In view of the contentious, jealous band finally selected, it is hard to know what qualities the committee particularly admired.

Major James Cunningham of Eickett was the first to be accepted by the Directors, and would be the first officer to desert. He had served in Hill's Regiment at Fort William, and as a company commander he had marched into Glencoe with that battalion on the morning of the massacre, later carrying Hill's account of it to Edinburgh. He was stiff-necked, egocentric and insolently proud, and his first thought as Councillor was to secure the appointment of his brother William as his secretary. He had never been out of Scotland in his life, had seen no action in the field, and knew nothing of ships or trade. Walter Herries said that he was "a Pillar of the Kirk", and this may explain his appointment, for by now the Company was doing little without the approval and the prayers of the Presbytery.

Daniel Mackay, who was selected on the same day, was a hot-tempered but conscientious young Highlander from Lord Reay's country, and a hard man to like for he intrigued as busily as he worked. According to Herries he was "a scrivener's or writer's clerk, newly come out of his apprenticeship", but he was in fact already a practising lawyer, though the Directors might have found one more experienced. The third Councillor, James Montgomerie, was another of Hill's disbanded officers. He had been an ensign in the Scots Guards, said Herries, "but not liking that office, left it, and carried a brown musket in another regiment." He was a brave soldier, and if he could make no intellectual or political contribution to the government of the Colony he served it in the best way he knew, against the Spaniards in the field. Even so, his appointment can only be explained by the fact that his grandfather was the Earl of Eglinton, his father a Major-General, and his uncle a Privy Councillor and a Lord of the Treasury.

William Vetch, the fourth appointment, had accepted the office only after several representations, and even now he was sick and doubted whether he would ever be able to get up from his bed. Herries said that he was a man of no trade, "but was advanced to this post on account of his father who was a godly minister and a glorifier of God." The father was certainly a legendary member of the Scots hagiarchy, a Lanarkshire preacher who had led a troop of horse against the Episcopacy, been a spy for the Covenanters in Edinburgh, and suffered more than most from persecution and exile. The Privy Council had condemned him to death *in absentia*, and only since the Revolution had he and his family known private peace and security. He had intended that both his sons should follow him into the ministry, and had educated them at Utrecht to this end, but with the accession of William III they became soldiers instead. William joined the Scots Greys, and Samuel became a lieutenant in the Cameronians, sharing their first bloody fight when they drove the clans from the burning streets of Dunkeld. Both young men later served in Flanders, and it was a nagging wound got at Steinkirk that still kept the elder brother to his bed. They were resolute veterans,

and loyal friends of Thomas Drummond whom they called their
"entire comrade". Samuel Vetch,* who had inherited little of his
father's piety and unselfishness, was now an Overseer, commanding a "mixed lot" which included the young volunteer
Roger Oswald.

The three remaining Councillors chosen were seamen. Robert
Jolly, however, had not commanded a ship for a dozen years or
more, having left the sea to become a merchant in Hamburg. His
proposal for a Scots company with the monopoly of trade between
that city and the Shetland Isles (and with a certain net gain, he
was sure, of 30 or 40 per cent on every voyage) never got much
further than the paper on which it was written, but such unin-
hibited visions of profit, and the help he gave the Company's
Commission in Hamburg, probably impressed the Committee for
Selection. Labouring the inevitable pun, Herries said that he was
"a jolly Scotch overgrown Hamburger", but in truth he was a sad
and ineffectual man who would have been happier had he kept to
his house on the Elbe.

Robert Pincarton, the second seaman Councillor, was of a
different warp and weft, and even Herries grudgingly admired
him, describing him as "a good, downright, rough-spun tar, never
known before by any designation or state office save that of
boatswain." Boatswain or not, he was the Company's best sea-
officer, courageous and uncomplaining, esteemed by his men and
respected by the Landsmen. He took pride in his command, the
Unicorn, in his simple, lonely cabin with its folding-table and
linen cloths, its cushions and copper candle-sticks, peppermill
and looking-glass. As if he were commanding a man-of-war he
dressed his boat's-crew in smart uniforms, every man wearing a
velvet cap embroidered with a silver unicorn. He was to have too
little time to prove himself as a Councillor, and the Colony was
to be the worse for that.

Finally there was Captain Robert Pennecuik, commander of
the *Saint Andrew* and commodore of the fleet, and by his own
reckoning the only man on the Council with the wisdom and
experience to justify the office. He was pig-headed and domineering, suspicious of all but other seamen, and of those too if they

* The father spelt his name Veitch. I have used the spelling used by both
brothers and by the Company.

challenged his judgment. He had been twenty-one years away from Scotland, and his qualifications for a sea command were that throughout the war he had served, consecutively, as a surgeon, lieutenant, and captain of a bomb-ketch in the English Navy. He was appointed to the Council, said Herries, "by the interest of the Kirk party, the better to balance that of the Church, and to keep out Dr. M——, a reputed Atheist who would certainly have debauched both." This anonymous doctor was undoubtedly Munro, who sulked and pouted like a thwarted child, and found excuses for refusing when he was later ordered away to the Colony. Pennecuik's conditions for accepting office were almost despotic, but appear to have been granted by the Directors without argument. He insisted that those placed in authority over him, if ever he were to suffer that ignominy, should at least be men who had seen action afloat. He asked for, and was given, fifteen shillings a day plus allowances for each of his five servants, half-pay when not at sea, and half-pay for life if disabled. He also demanded, and received, "as much privilege in trade as any commander in the English East India Company."

These were the strange, ill-assorted men chosen to govern Scotland's noble undertaking. With the exception of Robert Pincarton, and possibly Vetch, none of them had qualities that promised a wise and selfless administration. It is impossible to believe that the country could not find a more experienced lawyer than Daniel Mackay, a nobler spirit than Cunningham, a more skilful soldier than Montgomerie, a less foolish merchant than Jolly, or a more humane commander than Robert Pennecuik. If they had been chosen by lot they might have been more representative of what was best in the nation, but interest and preferment had appointed them, and the method cannot be judged by hindsight since it was the custom of the age, and Scotland has always had more than her tragic share of place-men and committee-men. They were chosen, and at the beginning of July six of them took the oath, William Vetch sending word that he was still "under the physic". They took the oath at Leith, and within sight of the fleet.

We do solemnly promise and swear, in the presence of Almighty God, that we shall be faithful and just to the trust reposed in us by the said Company, and shall to the best of our knowledge and skill endeavour to promote the benefit of the said Company and interest of the said Colony, as we shall answer to God.

Men and ships had been ready since early June, five good vessels, twelve hundred men, and a year's provisions. On the eighth day of that month the first eighty Landsmen were sent aboard the *Caledonia, Unicorn* and *Saint Andrew*. During the next few weeks there were delays and havering, few men being willing, while there was no sign of an immediate sailing, to exchange their quarters ashore for hot and foetid 'tween-decks afloat. At the end of the month the Directors whipped up those laggard officers who had not yet mustered their companies, promising them fourteen-and-a-half pence "for every man raised here in town, and half a dollar for every man they brought in from the country", providing they went aboard at once. Roderick Mackenzie issued a coffee-house proclamation on Wednesday, June 29, "ordaining that all officers and others who are resolved to proceed on the voyage be on board of the several ships allotted for them before or upon Monday next, at twelve a clock in order to sail." So the streets of Edinburgh and Leith rattled with drums, the tap and paradiddle of a company call, and the long roll of assembly. Ferries took the men across the firth, and in the three great ships they waited for another two weeks.

Much had not yet been done. There were still quarrels and disputes over the payment promised the laggards, which the Directors now seemed reluctant to make. Unusually low tides made loading difficult. The water aboard the *Saint Andrew* was found to be brackish, and long-boats from the *Unicorn* and the *Caledonia* were sent away to bring fresh casks. Captains for the pink and the snow had still to be appointed, and Pennecuik was confusing everybody with his own preferences. There were small matters, like the petition of Marion Smyth, asking for charity because her only support and her only son, a ship's boy, had been drowned. She was sent twenty shillings. From their miserable cell in the Tolbooth, Bowrie and MacAlexander and Turnbull pleaded for mercy, promising to go with the expedition if they were released. They were sent aboard under guard. William

Vetch had not yet taken the oath, though he was still eager to go "if his health serve him at that time." The Court of Directors was meeting daily now, in Milne Square and at Leith. Even the Council-General, which had rarely met and usually without a quorum, now managed to assemble, determining the government of the Colony and issuing instructions to its Council. They were published on July 8, and if the site of the Colony was still not identified it was at last given a name.

> Know all men by these presents, that in pursuance of the powers and privileges granted by the 32nd Act of the 4th Session, and the 8th Act of the 5th Session of this current Parliament, as well as by His Majesty's Letters Patent under the Great Seal of this Kingdom, to the Company of Scotland Trading to Africa and the Indies, the Council-General of the said Company have upon mature deliberation, *Resolved* (God willing) to settle and plant a colony in some place or other not inhabited in America, or in or upon some other place by consent of the natives thereof, and not possessed by any European Sovereign, Potentate, Prince or State, to be called by the name *CALEDONIA. . . .*

All powers of government, military and civil, would rest in the Councillors of the Colony, who would have the right to increase their number by not more than six once they had landed and settled the plantation. They were to divide the land into districts of not less than fifty, and not more than sixty free men, "who shall yearly elect any one Freeman Inhabitant whom they shall think fit to represent them in a Parliament or Council-General of the Colony." This Parliament, to be called or adjourned at the discretion of the Council, was to make and enact all rules, ordinances and constitutions, and to impose what taxes might be necessary for the good of the Colony. A free man of any nation could trade with and from the Colony, enjoying equal rights and privileges with the Scots if he made it his home, and the conditional word in these splendid declarations was "Freeman". Although it was not directly stated, it was clearly understood by the Company and its supporters that this Colony, like all others, could not prosper without the ultimate employment of slave-labour.

All exports from the Colony would be subject to a two per cent levy, payable to the Company in money or goods. The Company also reserved to itself one twentieth of all the lands, and one twentieth of all gold, silver, jewels, gems or stones, pearls, wrecks, ambergris and precious woods, the remaining nineteen parts belonging to the Colony in return for one hogshead of tobacco yearly (which presumably the Company then intended to give to the King). From January 1, 1702, all goods imported by the Colony from Europe, Asia, and Africa, and in the ships of the Colony or Scotland, would also be subject to a two per cent levy.

Less publicly, the Councillors received their particular instructions. They were to direct the fleet to the land named in their secret sailing orders. There they were to build, plant and fortify, to employ men and ships in the best interests of the Colony. They were to be jealous of the Company's honour, to accept no insults to its flag, and to defend both by force of arms. They were to keep an exact journal of the voyage and the landing, and to send this home by the first ship leaving. They were also to maintain proper accounts, to insist upon fair trading, and to ensure that the land was justly divided. The original and egalitarian promise of fifty acres to every man had, not surprisingly, been changed. Officers were now to receive a hundred, and Councillors one hundred and fifty. Given this much, they were warned to take no more, and to grant no more to others, "to the end that what is taken up may be the better cultivated, and may not be engrossed by a few to the discouragement of other industrious people."

The Councillors signed an acknowledgement of their instructions at Leith on Tuesday, July 12. That morning the ships came over from Burntisland and anchored off the southern shore of the Forth. Among the white saltires and the rising suns that flew from sprit and top-mast, a commodore's red pennant was run up to the fore-peak of the *Saint Andrew*, a vice-admiral's snapped above Pincarton's *Unicorn*. It was another day of yellow sunshine, bright on white canvas and red gun-ports, the refurnished gold of stem and stern. The little tenders now had their captains, Thomas Fullarton on the *Dolphin*, and John Malloch on the *Endeavour*, both being men whom Pennecuik had known in the English Navy and who had now been given these commands by his preferment. Great crowds on the Leith shore watched and cheered the ships until late dusk passed into night, and there was nothing to be seen but the orange glow of stern-lanterns, nothing to be heard but the creak of the yards and lone voices calling the hours of the watch. Ballad-writers had been alert to the pleasing ambiguity of the ships' names, and the author of *Caledonia Triumphans* made good use of them.

> Saint Andrew, our first Tutelar was he,
> The Unicorn must next supporter be,
> The Caledonia doth bring up the rear
> Fraught with brave hardy lads devoid of fear;
> All splendidly equipt, and to the three,
> The Endeavour and the Dolphin handmaids be.

All the Directors were now in Leith, in cramped and crowded quarters, conducting the final business as best they could. For three years there had been a great expenditure of ink and paper that was to enrich the archives of Scotland with both trivia and tragedy, and among the busy writers now the most tireless was Captain Pennecuik. He had not been aboard a day before he sent his clerk ashore for more pens, more ink, more paper. Three miles away, Lord Seafield was also writing, to Carstares, and confessing himself much fatigued by the excitement, viewing the expedition with lacklustre eyes. "I believe, and so does most people here, that it will not succeed so well as expected; but yet no man that desires to be well esteemed of in his own country will be persuaded to oppose what is for the interest of the Company." The paradox contained its own untruth, for the country was in fact afire, convinced that the expedition could not fail. Edinburgh was full of visitors, the inns and houses of Leith crowded with men and women who had come to say good-bye to a son, a brother, or a husband, to pay valedictory honour to their glorious fleet. The Colony could not fail, not when it was served by such noble young men. *Caledonia Triumphans* spoke out against the scattered faint-hearts, the English traducers.

> Nor are these youths the scum of this our land,
> But, in effect, a brave and generous band,
> Inspired with thirst of fame and soon to have
> Titles upon the marbles of their graves.

Twelve hundred men, some boys, a few women. Graves most of them would certainly have within the year, on land and at sea, but no marble headstones. A wooden marker for the more fortunate, and that quickly eaten by ants.

The fleet sailed on the morning tide of Thursday, July 14, the fiction of its secret destination still maintained. Though few men did not know that it was to be Darien, it could not be acknowledged until Pennecuik and his captains broke open their sealed orders. Three packets wrapped in oiled sailcloth, one to be unfastened when the fleet had cleared the firth, the second to be read at such a time and place indicated in the first, and the third to be opened "when at the place of settlement".

There were crowds on Castle Hill and Caltoun Craigs, white faces and waving hands at every window on the northern cliff of the city. At Leith, men and women pressed forward to the water's edge, crying, calling, singing. Some knelt to pray, exhorted by the inspired voices of their ministers. A few were bitter with disappointment. At dawn, officers had gone through each ship from stem to stern, from truck to keel, turning out stowaways, wrenching their hands free from rigging and timber, ignoring their imploring voices. Now these unhappy men stood on the quay and the dunes, watching the ships they would willingly have joined without payment or reward. As top-sails cracked and bellied, there was a bray of trumpets from the decks, a rolling of drums, and a great cry from Leith Sands to Castle Hill. The ships passed through the smoke of the *Saint Andrew's* signal gun and turned their golden stern-castles to the shore.

But that day they sailed no more than ten miles, northward to Kirkcaldy where they took up moorings again. There they remained for five days more, while Robert Blackwood and his clerk came over from Leith to check the last of the invoices and bills of lading. He also brought word that William Vetch was still too ill to leave his bed, and the expedition must sail without him. Aboard the *Dolphin* young David Dalrymple, seaman, stared at the windows and chimneys of Kirkcaldy, trying to pick out his own house. When he could endure his homesickness no longer, he slipped over the tender's stern and into a dory with another deserter, John Wilson the boatswain of the *Dolphin*. They went ashore in the dark.

On the evening of Monday, July 18, the ships cast off their moorings, lay by all night, and were finally gone in the morning. They sailed on an early tide and into the rising sun.

They did not go without William Paterson. At the beginning of July the Company had asked the Presbytery to order prayers for a fair wind, and to persuade the Reverend Mr. Thomas James to change his mind. After a week of emotional argument and equivalent meditation, he agreed to go with the expedition, providing, he said, "that Mr. Paterson did go, believing him to be a propagator of virtue and a discourager of vice, and would be exemplary to others." The Directors did not see Paterson in this light, or any light at all nowadays. They would rather have done without the man, and they havered for another week. But Mr. James was insistent, and so was the Presbytery. Paterson was called before the Directors and asked if he wished to go. He said yes, without hesitation, and was told that the Company therefore accepted him as an ordinary member of the expedition, without office and without authority. When he asked permission to take with him his wife and his clerk, Thomas Fenner, it was grudgingly granted.

On Saturday afternoon they were rowed across to Kirkcaldy, where Pincarton generously found the Patersons a small cabin board the *Unicorn*. Sudden good fortune, the warm welcome he received from other colonists, went to Paterson's head. Within the hour he boarded the *Saint Andrew* and told the astonished Commodore that there should be an immediate inspection of all stores, so that any deficiencies might be reported to the Directors and made good before the fleet sailed.

Captain Pennecuik wasted no words. He told Paterson to mind his own business.

❦ 3 ❦

The Door of the Seas

"Yet we had patience, hoping things would mend ashore"
The First Voyage, July to November 1698

IT BEGAN WELL. There was a strong and favourable wind, blowing so hard that the larger ships sailed with their main canvas reefed. For most of the first day the fleet kept in to the Fife coast, passing between it and the Isle of May. Horsemen from Kirkcaldy had brought news of its departure and there were crowds on the shore at Elie and Saint Monans, Anstruther and Crail, fluttering hands and unheard cries. Before dusk, with Fife Ness on their larboard quarter, the ships were sailing north-east by north toward Bell Rock, spritsails curtseying to the open sea. Hull down by nightfall, their stern-lanterns were unseen by the last crowd on Saint Andrews' sands.

Captains and Councillors had opened the first of their sealed orders long before the fleet cleared Largo Bay. They were to make for the Orkneys and the Atlantic west of Ireland, thus avoiding the curious watch of English cruisers in the North Sea and Channel. At the Orkneys they could take aboard what provisions might be necessary, and from thence they were to make all sail to Madeira. Here the second orders were to be opened, but if wind and weather made this landfall impossible the papers were to be broken out as soon as the fleet reached Latitude 32° North.

On the fourth day and north of Aberdeen the ships were becalmed, the sunlit air so still that the captains' pennants scarcely moved at the topmast heads. At noon the wind rose and blew gently from the south, carrying the fleet gallantly past Peterhead where the townsfolk fired three guns in salute. The compliment was ignored by Pennecuik. He was in his cabin, presiding over a bitter meeting of all sea-captains and Councillors whom he had called aboard the *Saint Andrew* during the calm. They had brought with them, at his request, a list of their provisions and stores as drawn up by their pursers, and the reading of these produced at first a state of speechless shock and then violent argument. The Directors of the Company had assured the Council that the provisions would be more than enough for nine months, but now the pursers reported that they would not last above six. A great deal had been consumed during the weeks the ships lay at Burntisland, and much of the bread that remained had become damnified, beef and pork had been spoilt by bad stowing. Walter Herries, who presented himself as the originator of all wise decisions and the steadfast critic of all that were bad, later claimed that the reports had been called for at his suggestion. He made his own inspection and said that he "could not make above five months and a half of any provisions except stockfish, of which there was a full eleven months and that at four days of the week, but (we) had not above four months butter and oil."

The squabbling and bickering in Pennecuik's great cabin lasted until nightfall, by which time a heavy fog had come down and the *Caledonia* was lost in it, despite Pennecuik's orders that all ships were to close in to his stern-lights at dusk. Robert Drummond and the two Councillors who sailed with him, Montgomerie and Jolly, were grudgingly allowed to stay aboard the Commodore's ship until the dawn look-out sighted the *Caledonia*'s topsails above the sunbright mist. They went away to her in an ill-humour, and with Drummond convinced that Pennecuik was an ignorant fool. The first meeting of the Council had set the pattern of acrimony and suspicion of all that were to follow. Factions were already forming, jealousy and vanity marking the division between landsmen and seamen. "Our Marine Chancellors," said William Paterson, in his report to the Directors more than a year later, "did not only take all upon them, but likewise browbeat and discouraged everybody else, yet we had patience, hoping things would mend when we came ashore." He had not been present at the meeting, and could have got little comfort from the thought that had Pennecuik taken his advice at Kirkcaldy the shortages might have been discovered in time.

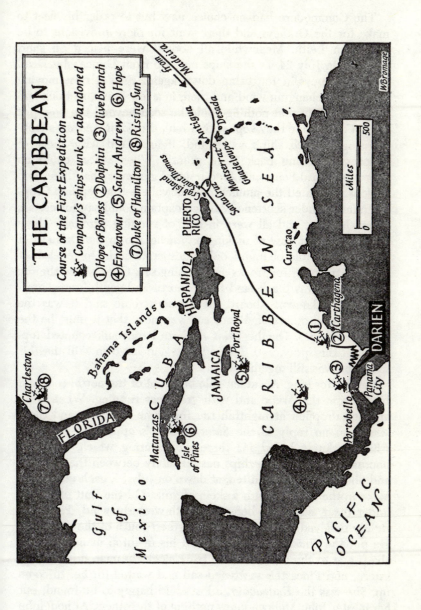

THE CARIBBEAN

Course of the First Expedition
xxx Company's ships sunk or abandoned

① Hope of Boness ② Dolphin ③ Olive Branch
④ Endeavour ⑤ Saint Andrew ⑥ Hope
⑦ Duke of Hamilton ⑧ Rising Sun

from Madeira

Gulf of Mexico

PACIFIC OCEAN

CARIBBEAN SEA

Charleston ⑧

FLORIDA

Bahama Islands

CUBA

Matanzas

Isle of Pines ⑥

JAMAICA

Port Royal ⑤

HISPANIOLA

PUERTO RICO

Crab Island (Saint Thomas)

Santa Cruz

Montserrat

Guadeloupe

Antigua

Desada

Curaçao

Carthagena ②

① ③

④

Portobello

Panama City

DARIEN

Miles
0   500

W.Bromage

The Commodore had no choice now but to order his fleet to make for the Orkneys and there wait for more provisions to be sent from Leith. Meanwhile all aboard were placed on short rations. On July 24, as the ships beat up from Duncansby Head to the Orkneys, a fog came down again. First a mist moving gently on a changing wind and then, in a few hours, so thick and white a curtain that nothing could be seen beyond the bowsprit head. For a while they kept within hail, the *Saint Andrew*'s lookout singing each ship's name and, if answered with a cry of "Success!", calling back "God grant!" When voices could no longer be heard Pennecuik fired a signal gun every half hour, and anxiously counted the muffled musket volleys that replied. Groping blindly under shortened sail, no captain could say for certain where he was, and all were in fear of running aground. There was no thought now of making an anchorage in the Orkneys, if indeed they could be found, only a desperate desire to get clear of this nightmare of fog, rocks and a rising sea. Once, when the fog lifted, there was black land to the north and south, unrecognisable and unknown. Aboard the *Unicorn* some said it was the Orkneys, and others Shetland, and yet more that it must be the Outer Hebrides. On the *Saint Andrew* Pennecuik counted topmasts in the spray, and thanked God and his own skill that his squadron was still together.

But not for long. A sudden gale blew out of the north, cold and bitter from the Arctic and with grey seas running. When wind and sea dropped at nightfall the fog came on again and there was soon no reply to the *Saint Andrew*'s appealing gun. The white darkness lasted for three days during which, by some impossible miracle, the ships passed safely between the Orkneys and Shetland. When it lifted, at dawn on July 31, each vessel was alone in the Atlantic with a skein of gulls. Off the Butt of Lewis, under clear skies and before a north-westerly wind, Pincarton rightly believed himself to be the furthest south of the squadron. He put the *Unicorn* about and told his maintop man to keep a sharp eye to the north. Before ten o'clock the man cried a ship astern, and Pincarton shortened sail and waited for her to come up. She was the *Endeavour*, a lost child happy to be found, but her master John Malloch knew nothing of the others. Although he would willingly have waited, Pincarton could not ignore a favourable wind, and with the pink to starboard he set course for Madeira. The next day they passed the cloud-head of Saint Kilda, and the sick and miserable landsmen aboard the *Unicorn* stared at the black wall of rock until it was gone and there was nothing about them but the sea.

On August 2, tacking across the mouth of the Minch between Cape Wrath and Lewis, the *Saint Andrew* found the little *Dolphin*, and later the *Caledonia*. Together they sailed south-west and south, believing the others lost.

Little was left now of the high spirits in which the settlers had left the Forth. Some of them were to remember the miseries of that northern voyage more vividly than the horrors they were still to suffer. "For God's sake," William Paterson would write to the Directors, "be sure to send the next fleet from the Clyde, for the passage north about is worse than the whole voyage to the Indies." Kept below decks by the unsympathetic seamen, sick with the stench of their own bodies and the rolling of the ship, maddened by incessant noise and choked by the fog that seeped through the hatches, angered by short rations and foul water, never clean, never alone, never told where they were or where they might be to-morrow, never seeing the sun and rarely the sky, most of them had lost all heart for the venture long before the ships broke out of the fog. What strength they had they wasted in pettish quarrels, resenting the small privileges of those above them and jealously preserving theirs against those below. During the gales they clutched each other in fear, or closed their eyes and wished for death. No one left any record of how Mrs. Paterson and the few other women aboard endured this wret-chedness. Only the very young kept their courage. Colin Camp-bell, whose family had sent him aboard the *Unicorn* under Pincarton's protection in the hope that he might learn enough to make the sea his trade, somehow managed to make daily entries in the journal he was writing for his brother. Nothing a seaman would admire, he modestly admitted, for there was no man aboard who was ready or willing to give him the simplest lessons in navigation. Patiently he recorded the winds and the weather, the changing latitude, the sight of a distant and unspoken ship, the day when the *Unicorn* lay becalmed and her foretop-men went aloft to repair a trestle-tree that had been broken in the

Orkney gales. On August 15, west of Cape St. Vincent, there came to the ship two white pigeons, lifting the hearts of all aboard.

Days behind Pincarton, the other three ships made slower sailing, and at night the *Caledonia* frequently lost sight of the *Saint Andrew*'s light. The dawn hours were thus wasted in frustrating delays until Drummond's topsails came over the horizon. Pennecuik believed that Robert Drummond was deliberately dropping behind at night out of wilful spite, and the tempers of both men were not improved by the indignant signals that passed between their ships before they got under way again. Off the coast of Portugal there were frequent calms during which the squadron was idle enough for the land officers on one ship to visit their friends and kinsmen on another. They drank too much brandy, and indulged in too many intrigues. When the Drummond brothers came aboard the *Saint Andrew*, Robert in his blue coat and Thomas in scarlet, they boasted that the entertainment they gave aboard their ship was more generous than the niggardly hospitality a man might expect on the *Saint Andrew*. Pennecuik resented the arrogant contempt and secret smiles of the idling gentlemen who stood on his main-deck in red coats and campaign-wigs, talking of such exclusive matters as family, rank, battles and sieges. He readily believed the gossip brought him by Captain Lachlan Maclean, commander of a land company. This Highlander, who had his own dark reasons for disliking the Drummonds (one of which might well have been a clansman's memory of Glencoe), said that the brothers were forming a cabal and plotting against the Commodore. Pennecuik was hot for court-martialling them at once, but Mackay and Montgomerie persuaded him to wait until the fleet reached Madeira. There, they said, a full Council should debate the affair.

On August 20, at three in the afternoon and sailing due west, the *Unicorn* and the *Endeavour* sighted Madeira ahead, but a brisk gale that blew up suddenly kept them beating about for two more days. When they finally came in to Funchal roadstead, below a white castle and green and lemon hills, a Genoese ship at anchor there ran out her guns with trumpets braying. Pincarton went ashore, his boat's-crew smart in their silvered caps badged with unicorns. The Governor said that the Scots had been taken for Algerian pirates, and although he could now see that Pincarton was no rogue he had been told by the English that Scotland was too poor a country to possess such splendid ships. By patient courtesy, by producing a copy of the Company's Act, and by a 12-gun salute providentially fired from the *Unicorn* at the most awkward moment of this interview, Pincarton convinced the Governor that the Scots were what they claimed to be. Twelve guns were fired in reply from the castle, and the islanders came down from their vinyards and their houses with shouts of welcome.

There had been good reason for caution. Aboard the Genoese ship were tempting prizes for a corsair: a bishop worthy of ransom, a bride who was to marry a gentleman of Madeira, and her dowry of £15,000 Sterling. "Yet the woman," wrote a Scot whose respect for this vast sum had led him curiously to her cabin, "was no beauty for all that." To his amusement, a second Genoese arrived a day or so later with another bride from Lisbon, "but cheaper and better favoured than the first."

Pennecuik's laggard ships arrived on August 26. As soon as they were sighed John Malloch went out to them in the *Unicorn's* pinnace, piloting them into the roadstead and telling the Commodore that despite some early suspicion the Scots were now welcome to water and victual their ships. There was another thunder of salutes from ships and shore, and then Pennecuik turned to matters uppermost in his mind. He called a full meeting of the Council aboard the *Saint Andrew*. The behaviour of the Drummonds since leaving the Forth, he said, had "smelled of mutiny", and he moved that they be stripped of their commands and set ashore. Young Mackay and Montgomerie, weak from seasickness, weary of Pennecuik's quarter-deck manner, and aware that they must endure more of both before the voyage ended, were inclined to humour him. But Robert Jolly and James Cunningham, the uneasy traveller of the middle road and the committed member of the Glencoe Gang, argued forbearance. They promised to secure the Drummonds' submission to Pennecuik's authority while at sea, and upon this assurance the Commodore's motion was defeated.

The Scots swarmed ashore, seeking wine, food and entertainment. They ate unripe fruit and were ill. Some officers sold their scarlet coats and plumed hats, their swords or their shoe-buckles to buy meat. They marvelled at the number of lizards they saw, thought the Portuguese were no better than thieves, and observed that in the general poverty of the island a few English merchants seemed to be living remarkably well. Paterson, however, was pleasantly surprised by the kindness of these Englishmen, and he concluded from this that there must be more goodwill toward the Company than the Scots imagined.

He was in a rare and warm state of euphoria, having been elected to the Council in place of the absent William Vetch. Which of the warring factions supported his election, hoping for an ally, is unknown, but they were undoubtedly disappointed for he refused to take part in their childish squabbles. "I must confess," he wrote later, "it troubled me exceedingly to see our affairs thus turmoiled and disordered by tempers and dispositions as boisterous and turbulent as the elements they are used to struggle with." He was thinking of Pennecuik's jealous feud with Robert Drummond, and of Pincarton's lack of sympathy for both. The mad proposal that the Council should elect a new President each week had been further complicated by the Commodore's noisy claim that until a landing was made he was the supreme and only authority. Paterson said that a weekly presidency was "a mere May-game of government", and he proposed that each Councillor should hold the office for a month, and that when the colony was reached the Land Councillors should take their turn before the Seamen. They would thus have four months in which to make proper rules and ordinanances, to secure a firm government that could not be upset by Pennecuik's irascibility or Pincarton's ignorance. But he got no support from the other Land Councillors. "They, like wise men, had begun to make their court, and had agreed beforehand with those of the sea that the presidency should last but a week."

Though the Scots were able, at a price, to fill their watercasks, the impoverished island had no great quantities of bread or meat to sell. The cargo of the *Endeavour* was exchanged for 27 pipes of wine, nearly three thousand gallons which, it was innocently hoped, could be traded in the Indies. Under threat of severe penalties, the Scots had been told not to discuss their venture with the islanders, or at most to pretend that they were bound for the Guinea Coast. The kindly English merchants were not deceived by this, they deluded themselves instead, and told London that in their opinion the squadron was certainly making for the East Indies.

At noon on September 2, Pennecuik loosed his fore topsail and fired his bow-chaser. It was the signal to weigh anchor and sail, and as the ships moved out they filled the roadstead with the smoke of thirty-nine saluting guns. Pennecuik was disappointed when the Governor replied with thirty-seven only, but he smugly logged the fact that even these were more than the Portuguese would give to King William's warships.

The *Saint Andrew* was already out of the bay when the Commodore looked back over his stern-rail and saw that the *Caledonia* had shortened sail and put about. When Drummond's pinnace was then seen rowing ashore, Pennecuik fired another gun, hoisted his mizzen topsail and brought the fleet to anchor again. The Council was summoned to his cabin, and Drummond was ordered to attend it with an explanation. He came aboard with his redcoat brother and said that his second mate had offended him, and had accordingly been discharged and put ashore. He out-blustered the infuriated Pennecuik, saying that his commission gave him the right to accept or refuse any of his crew, but the Council told him to behave himself, and to take the officer aboard again. He did so with ill grace, and once more the fleet put to sea.

There was no longer any pretence about its destination. The second packet of sealed orders had been opened, and its contents made known to all.

You are hereby ordered in pursuance of your voyage to make the Crab Island, and if you find it free to take possession thereof in name of the Company; and from thence you are to proceed to the Bay of Darien and make the isle called the Golden Island, in and about eight degrees of north latitude; and there make a settlement on the mainland as well as the said island, if proper (as we believe) and unpossessed by an European nation or state in amity with his Majesty.

If the land were indeed found to be occupied by such a nation, the fleet was to make to leeward until it came to some other part of the mainland that was not claimed or possessed. Except by the Indians, of course.

The fleet was four weeks at sea before it made a landfall in the West Indies. Six days out from Madeira it got in to the Trade Winds, and had fair sailing by day and by night. Four men were dead of the flux before the ships left Funchal, and thirty-six more were to die before Darien was reached. Yet death was a commonplace expected and accepted by all sea-captains on long sea voyages, and by washing their decks regularly with vinegar, by smoking the holds, they believed that they kept sickness to a minimum. The landsmen were less sanguine, and many were unnerved by the suddenness of death. They could take no comfort in their own good health when they saw others, seemingly as well as they, heaved overboard within hours of the first spasm of black vomit. Even so, spirits were generally high, tempers cooled and old quarrels were temporarily mended. There was still hunger, however. Though the Commodore, his captains, and the Councillors dined well, at tables set with English pewter and white linen, the lower the rank the hungrier the man, and at bottom there was harsh privation. When a Dutchman on the *Saint Andrew* broke open another's chest to steal bread he was forced to run the gauntlet, angry men pressing forward to strike a blow as he staggered along the ship's waist.

There were less brutal entertainments. "This day," wrote Colin Campbell on September 10, "we supposed ourselves to have passed the Tropic of Cancer, and so designed to make merry according to the English custom." Pennecuik ran up his pennant to the mizzen peak, fired a gun, and as the ships scarcely moved under shortened sail "every officer and gentleman who had not passed over the Tropic were ordered to pay a bottle of brandy, or three of Madeira wine, otherwise to be thrice ducked, which some obeyed, others not." Captains and Councillors came aboard the *Saint Andrew*, dined at one o'clock, drank punch until five, and by six all but Paterson were drunk and asleep aboard their own ships.

The celebration had not been a success. "The heat of the weather and the punch," remembered Robert Jolly, "began to alter the humour of some commanders." As was usual, drink distorted Pennecuik's judgement and reason, and after the second or third bowl he took some fancied objection to both Mackay and Montgomerie. Having treated them most unkindly, said Jolly in cautious reproach, he proceeded to abuse his first, second and third mate, and then all the redcoat officers aboard his ship. Walter Herries, who had earlier attached himself to Pennecuik and was now thinking he might have made a mistake thereby, took the man aside by the sleeve and told him to remember that he was no longer aboard a King's ship, that these soldiers were gentlemen with influence at home. The word influence always had a sobering effect on Pennecuik, and he at last held his tongue.

The Drummonds and Samuel Vetch watched this childish performance with sour satisfaction. Hating Pennecuik, and pleased to see him making enemies, they also had no respect for the Council or its authority. Jolly said that they began their intrigues again, asking him and Cunningham to insist that the Council be enlarged to include one or more Land Officers, meaning, no doubt, Thomas Drummond and Vetch. If this were done, they said, and "if any mutiny or disorder should occur (for want of provisions) it might easily be crushed by the command they had over their companies." It was sound advice perhaps, but Robert Jolly was shocked. He and Cunningham fell back on their authority as Councillors, loftily ordering that no more be said of the matter. The Drummonds and Vetch marked down both men as weaklings, as indeed they were.

And westward again, the wind veering east-south-east to east-north-east, until there came a week of sickly calm during which the air was hot and motionless, thick to breathe and foul to taste. Pitch bubbled between the ships' timbers, and there were sometimes two or three deaths a day. Officers and Volunteers, Planters and Seamen, a surgeon's mate and a midshipman, a cooper and a carpenter's boy, quickly ill, quickly dead, and quickly turned overboard with a short prayer. The Councillors were alarmed and ordered an issue of wine as a prophylactic, but it was of little use. The diarists briefly recorded each sad departure. *About 2 a clock in the afternoon one of our seamen called Alexander Alder died of a consumption, and thrown over ... this day Robert Hardy, a gentleman in Captain Dalyell's company ... John Stewart, gentleman ... Smith, a seaman ... a Sergeant of Captain*

Colin Campbell's ... died of a fever ... of a flux ... heaved overboard...

In the forenoon of September 28 one of the leading tenders hoisted a jack and an ensign, the long-desired signal, and soon the look-outs on all the ships were crying land, land ahead. There had been hope of it for days, started by the flying-fish that hung above a bow-wave, by a man-of-war bird lazily circling. "We saw in head of us," wrote an anonymous diarist aboard the *Saint Andrew*, "the island of Dezada, in English the Land of Desire, so called by Columbus being the first land that he did see when he came to these seas." It was passed to larboard in the late afternoon, and beyond it the island of Guadaloupe was a purple shadow dissolving into the night. To its waters was committed the body of Andrew Baird, seaman, dead of the bloody flux that day.

The fleet made little way during the night but at dawn, sailing west by north before a freshening wind, it passed between Antigua and Montserrat. At noon it was abreast of the tiny isle of Redonda which reminded Pennecuik, in a moment of uncharacteristic sentiment, of the Bass Rock in the Firth of Forth. Homesickness was endemic. Surrounded by the Leeward Isles, green jewels bright in the sun, the Scots searched for a rock, the prow of a hill, a curving bay or a cluster of trees that could warm them with the memory of home. At three in the afternoon they passed Nevis, hoisting their ensigns in an answering salute to an unknown vessel anchored offshore, and with more imagination than truth they told each other that the wedge-shaped island was like Castle Rock in Edinburgh when seen from the Roads of Leith. That night the body of Walter Johnson, surgeon's mate, was slipped overboard. Sick of a fever, he tried his own skill upon himself, "got his hands on *laudanum liquidum*, took too large a dose thereof, and so he slept till death."

By noon the next day the fleet was seven leagues to the southeast of Santa Cruz, a windless day and the sails bleached white against a deep blue sky. As the Landsmen leant idly on the ships' rails, watching the gannets that flew suicidally into the rigging, the Councillors and the Captains came aboard the *Saint Andrew*. They met in Pennecuik's stifling cabin, its stern windows opened wide to catch the faintest movement of the listless air outside, the reflected sunlight rippling across their tired faces. The Commodore grumbled again about the Drummonds and would have forced a vote in favour of setting them ashore as soon as possible, but once more Jolly and Cunningham persuaded the rest of the Council to leave this unhappy matter until the colony was reached. There was a more important decision to make. By their second sailing orders they should now steer for Crab Island*, but they had also to find a pilot who could take them to Darien. Since Paterson was the only man there who had been in these waters, and since it was hoped that he would know and find such a man, his advice may have influenced the proposal finally accepted. It was agreed that the fleet should separate, the *Dolphin* and the *Unicorn* (with Paterson aboard) sailing north and east about Santa Cruz for the Danish island of Saint Thomas, and the others making north and west about for Crab Island. The ships parted after sunset, each firing a farewell gun, the smoke of it white and luminous in the indigo dusk.

On October 1 the *Unicorn* and the tender anchored in seven fathoms off Saint Thomas, and were still being saluted by the guns of the fort when Pincarton and Paterson were rowed ashore. The lonely Danes made the Scots welcome, giving them sugar-cane, pineapples and rum, but Pincarton was uneasy. Four English sloops from Jamaica were lying off the island, and one of them came up to take a closer look at the *Unicorn*, making no signal and sending no boat until the second day when her captain himself came aboard. He said that he was Richard Moon, bound from New York to Curacao with a cargo of provisions, and Paterson immediately recognised him as a man he had known many years before. They embraced each other warmly, and Moon agreed that since Crab Island was nearer than Curacao it would be plain good sense for him to go there and exchange his provisions for any goods the Scots had.

Ashore in a tavern Paterson also found a pilot, the buccaneer Robert Alliston, now sadly old, white-haired and garrulous. He still had a good conceit of himself, however, confident that he could set the Scots down on any part of the Main they wished. He drank a lot in Pincarton's cabin, talked with maudlin regret of the old days, of the bitter changes that had taken place. Did

* Ile de Vieques, between Puerto Rico and the Virgin Islands.

Paterson know that Captain Sharpe—Batt Sharpe who sacked Portobello and who crossed the Isthmus with Dampier and Wafer—did Paterson know that after escaping a hanging in England Captain Sharpe had now been taken by the Danes and thrown in prison for 99 years? And where was it they wished to settle, Darien? He remembered it well.

Still uneasy about those other Jamaican sloops, Pincarton weighed anchor after four days, sailing out to a roar of seventy guns from his own ships and the walls of the fort.

Pennecuik's squadron had sighted Crab Island on October 1, tacking about it for twenty-four hours before dropping anchor. It was almost entirely covered with rich green trees, and uninhabited except for the monstrous crabs that gave it its name, but when Robert Drummond took the *Caledonia* on a cruise about it he found a Danish sloop hidden in a narrow bay. Despite his liberal hospitality to Pincarton, the Governor of Saint Thomas had quietly sent this ship to enforce Denmark's claim to Crab Island, her captain further emphasising the point by setting up a tent ashore and unfurling his country's flag. Pennecuik answered this by pitching his own tent beneath the trees on the opposite side of the island and by flying his pennant, the Company's standard, and the saltire of Scotland. According to his journal the Danish protest was more of a formality than a threat, "they were obliged so to do to please their Court, but wished with all their hearts we would settle there, for then they would have a bulwark betwixt them and the Spaniards of Porto Rico who are very troublesome neighbours." Whether he believed this or not, to impress the Danes and to flatter his own vanity he also landed a redcoat guard of sixty men, their arrogant drums beating against the hills at dawn and dusk.

On October 5, a day of thunder, lightning and great rain, Pincarton's ships arrived with the Jamaican sloop. Richard Moon took a hard look at the loading-lists and the displayed samples of wigs and stockings, shoes and slippers, plaiding and hodden grey, needles, nails and horn-spoons, Bibles and Catechisms, and decided that he wanted none of them, certainly not at the ridiculous prices the Scots were asking. Nor would he part with any of his provisions for drafts on the Company's agents in New England. He would sail on to Curacao, he said, and there exchange his cargo for slaves. Paterson saw the danger, and he told the Council that if Moon spread a report that the Scots were over-pricing their goods it would not encourage other traders to visit the Colony. It would be better to sell at a loss and avoid the risk. "To all this I was answered that they were not obliged to take notice of any particular man's assertion as to the over-valuing or ill-buying the goods, but rather to believe the prime cost was as in the Company's invoice; and that they would not be so imposed on by Captain Moon."

Moon shrugged his shoulders and made ready to sail. It was of small consequence to him what these madmen thought or did, but before he left, and upon Paterson's earnest appeal, he promised to bring or send provisions to the Colony when once it was settled. If the Scots had not found a friend, Paterson had at least saved them from making an enemy.

Pennecuik's high-handed contempt for Richard Moon had turned the Council against the trader. Sitting in his tent, a glass in his hand, his wig on the back of his chair, and a scarlet sentry at his door, the Commodore was the same loud-mouthed bully he had been afloat, convinced that he and those sea-captains of his party knew what was best for all. Paterson realised that his earlier hope that things would mend ashore had been mistaken. "Though our Masters at sea had sufficiently taught us that we fresh-water men knew nothing of their salt-water business, yet when at land they were so far from letting us turn the chase that they took upon them to know everything better than we." Pennecuik had now been abandoned by Herries who was exercising his talent for intrigue and malicious gossip on the Drummonds and Vetch. Again the Commodore demanded a court-martial, insisting that the brothers and their friend be set ashore on Saint Thomas, and again Cunningham and Jolly turned the vote against him. Paterson's respect for the Drummonds (though these hard men had only contempt for him) also persuaded the Council that it could ill-afford to lose them, insufferable though their conceit might sometimes be.

The water-casks were full and it was time to leave. Though their sailing-orders had given the Scots leave to settle the island if it were found to be unoccupied, no one thought the point worth disputing with the bold Dane, his tiny sloop and his fourteen armed men. The fleet sailed in the forenoon of Friday, October 7, after heaving overboard the bodies of James Paterson, gentleman, and Thomas Dalrymple, planter, both dead of the flux. Above the noise of water, wind, and singing ropes, the Scots heard the sad crying of sea-fowl, the excited chattering of monkeys in the retreating trees. One man was left behind. Michael Pearson had stood guard ashore with Captain Maclean's company, and had thought of what had so far happened and what yet might come when the fleet sailed. He was seduced by the gentle beauty of the island and he ran away to the woods with his musket.

For three weeks the fleet sailed south-west across the Caribbean toward the Isthmus. It was a bitter time of foetid calms and violent gales. None of the seamen had known such storms, winds that blew up suddenly out of the heat, seas that heaved above the topsail yards, and lightning so bright and sustained at night that it all but blinded the boatswain of the *Saint Andrew* when he looked up to it in wonder. Twenty-five lives were lost to fever, flux and despair, and among them was the young wife of John Hay, a lieutenant in Captain Charles Forbes's company. She was turned overboard from the *Unicorn* in the early morning as another gale was rising, and her valediction was a rending report as the main-topgallant sail parted from its yard. On all the ships the sick lay below in their own filth, tormented by the pitching of the deck and the endless noise of the wind. There was little water to ease their burning thirst, for that taken aboard at Crab Island had soon turned foul, and whether they lived or died seemed of little importance when all aboard expected to be drowned at any moment. They had come to the edge of the world and there was no land, though old Alliston, standing by the helmsman of the *Saint Andrew*, swore that it was near, very near. And then suddenly, dramatically, it was there.

"About two a clock this morning," wrote a diarist on Monday, October 17, "we saw with the lightning black, high stones like land. We lowered most of our sails till break of day, at which time we found it to be really land, so prodigiously high. . . ." A dark escarpment rose out of the spray, a menacing wall from sea to sky, and the water that broke over the sprit-sail heads was strangely yellow. Alliston recognised this inhospitable coast, naming it to Pennecuik who wrote the words down phonetically in his journal, *Nostra Segniora della Popa*. It was Spanish land, said the buccaneer with unhappy memories of the times he had walked through Spanish blood, and close by Carthagena. That afternoon, as the fleet turned westward seeking Darien by elimination rather than by good pilotage, the wind dropped and the sea was calm. Still golden yellow, the water rolled like rich cream in the wake of the ships, and Alliston said that it came from some great river to which he gave no name. But it was the colour of hope, of gold, of rich promise.

Two more weeks passed. The winds that carried the ships westward during the day turned against them at night. There were long hours of dispiriting calm, minutes of wild squalls during one of which the *Dolphin* lost her main-topmast and almost foundered. Sometimes there was land to larboard, high cliffs, the startling green of distant forests, a white fort, the long roll of dangerous surf. And the dying continued. Three midshipmen of a fever, soldiers of the flux, a young Volunteer of "a decay". There died Adam Bennet, son to Sir William Bennet of Grubbet, and Adam Cunningham, brother to Sir William Cunningham of Caprington, both young men of eager ambition who had pressed their families to secure them service with the Company. There died Henry Charters, a cheerful young Volunteer, and there died an English seaman called Malbin. But the death which moved men to tears, particularly Paterson, was that of the Reverend Mr. Thomas James, who had refused to sail without his friend. Four guns were fired over his body as it slipped into the sea.

Toward the end of the month the ships were able to make little way. A great current, which may have been a movement of the sea or the outflow of another river, dragged them eastward and they were forced to tack wearily against it. At last, on October 26, they dropped anchor in ten fathoms with a green ribbon of land to starboard. Alliston would not, or could not say what it was, but he plainly hoped it might be Darien. A boat was sent away from the *Unicorn* in search of fresh water. When it returned, its casks were still empty, the crew having found no stream, but they brought instead a great pelican, a hundred dead gannets and a live lizard with a licking tongue.

The fleet moved westward again for two days. The smell of land was thick on the air, and there were distant sounds at night. By day dolphins escorted the ships, arching their iridescent backs, but no one had the strength to catch them. A strange malaise fell upon all. Sickness increased, seven more young men died, though the decks were frequently washed with vinegar and the holds purified with smoke. Alliston stubbornly insisted that they must soon come upon the Gulf of Darien and Golden Island, but few believed him. And then, at eight o'clock in the evening of Friday, October 28, he swore that they were there. Off the larboard bow of the *Saint Andrew* was a bar of dark trees, a line of surf or crystal sand. The *Caledonia* and the *Endeavour* stood out to sea as sentinels, but the other ships dropped anchor where they were.

Before dark two canoes came out from the shore, and almost before the Scots were aware of them several painted Indians had came boldly up the flagship's side to her waist. They were friendly and unafraid, their bows unstrung in their hands and their lances lowered, but at first they said nothing, staring shyly at the Scots with gentle eyes. "We gave them victuals and drink," wrote Pennecuik, "which they used very freely, especially the last." More accurately the Scots deliberately made the Indians drunk, although this was unnecessary, for they were anxious to talk once their shyness passed. They had a few words of English and some indifferent Spanish which Benjamin Spense was called up to interpret. They had seen the Commodore's red pennant flying from the *Saint Andrew*'s fore-peak and had taken it for the English flag, which they had seen many times above the ships of their buccaneer friends. It is doubtful whether they understood the difference between an Englishman and a Scot, if Spense attempted the explanation, for they said that they had been expecting the ships for two years and were happy to see them now that their people were at war with the Spaniards. By midnight they were in a drunken stupor, and were left lying in the scuppers until morning when they were sent away with some old felt hats, knives, and a few twopenny looking-glasses. "With which," wrote Pennecuik, "they seemed extremely pleased."

By morning, too, Alliston had changed his mind. The ships were not in the Gulf but two leagues eastward of Caret Bay, which was itself some miles from Golden Island. The Commodore sent three of his boats to the Bay where their crews found the same Indians they had entertained the night before, offering gifts of cocks, hens and a wild turkey. More valuable even than these was the Indians' assurance that Golden Island was three or four leagues to the west. After turning over two gentlemen who had died of the flux, the ships weighed anchor, joined the *Caledonia* and *Endeavour* out to sea and sailed westward in fair weather.

At four o'clock in the afternoon of Monday, October 31, as the bodies of David Hay and John Lucason were turned over from the *Unicorn* and the *Saint Andrew*, the blue cap of Golden Island was cried ahead. By dusk the ships had come within a league of it, dropping anchor in 25 fathoms. That night another young Volunteer died, and although there was a rank smell of death aboard the ships there was also a great feeling of relief, a lightening of the heart, as if all believed that the sickness and the dying were now ended.

The fleet moved in to the island at dawn, anchoring again within half a mile of it. The sea-fowl in the sky were as thick as windblown leaves. The great rock, rising above the five small ships, was topped with glistening trees, and the only break in its black cliffs, the only landing-place was a narrow inlet of sand. Alliston remembered it well. Here had been the rendezvous of the buccaneers before their overland raid on Santa Maria in 1680. Here gathered sun-browned men from many ships, his own among them. Captain Sharpe had tied green and white ribbons to his rallying flag, Cook had drawn a hand and sword on his, and Sawkins had painted his scarlet banner with yellow bars. There had been great fires, the sound of sword on stone, dreams of blood and gold long since ended by old age or a hangman's rope. If Alliston remembered all this with regret, he kept the thought to himself. His work, for what it had been worth, was now done. By luck rather than skill he had brought the Scots where they had wished to come.

That afternoon Pennecuik called the Councillors to his cabin. Whether there was, or was not, a great Gulf of Darien as they had been told, Golden Island was certainly a reality. The lifting of the morning haze had shown the mainland some miles off, and this was undoubtedly theirs to settle. To the south-east could be seen what might be the entrance to a natural harbour, and since there was no safe anchorage off the island it was agreed that it should be immediately explored.

Pennecuik went away to it in his pinnace. He discovered that it was a wide bay formed by a narrow peninsula of high ground that cut it off from the sea, and on either side of its entrance were tall hills which even his limited knowledge could recognise as excellent sites for defensive batteries. The blue water of the bay was still, scarcely moving on its shore of sand, and beyond the mangroves that bordered it was an unbroken forest, rising and falling, rolling toward the emerald ridge of distant mountains. The pinnace went in past a sentinel rock at the entrance and shipped oars. The Scots looked at the green trees, the grey-legged mangroves, listened to the strange calls of unseen birds, and marvelled at the wonder of the land.

When Pennecuik saw a white flag waving on the far shore he ordered the pinnace in toward it, and then shipped oars again as twenty Indians came out of the trees with bows and lances in their hands. Scots and Indians stared at each other, until the latter unstrung their bows and threw down their lances, beckoning to the pinnace. Pennecuik told one of his seamen to swim ashore, which the man did reluctantly no doubt, and when he came back he said that the Indians wished to be friends, that one of their great captains would visit the ships the next day.

That night, before dawn, there died Thomas Fenner who had been Paterson's good and faithful clerk.

"This harbour ... capable of containing a thousand sail"
Caledonia, November 1698

The great captain who came over the side of the *Saint Andrew* on the morning of Wednesday, November 2, was a sturdy little Indian with an unsmiling face. His name was Andreas, or so he was called by the Spaniards from whom he had also acquired his clothes and the hidalgo gravity of his expression. His painted chest was covered with a loose red jacket, his thighs by white drawers from which jutted the silver cone of his manhood, and his golden nose-disc gleamed in the shadow of an old, wide-brimmed hat. He was accompanied by a bodyguard of twelve men who stood boldly about him in the ship's waist, their brown eyes looking back into the curious stares of the Scots. They were all stark naked, wrote Hugh Rose in his journal that night, "only a thread tied round their middles, to make fast another that kept on a small piece of plate upon the end of their yards."

Benjamin Spense greeted them with Castilian compliments. Andreas looked at the scarlet coats and blue, the white faces framed by monstrous curls of false hair, the dark sheen of muskets and the glitter of steel, bleached canvas, tarred ropes and decks reeking of vinegar. What did the strangers want? "We answered," said Pennecuik, "our design was to settle among them, if they pleased to receive us as friends: that our business was chiefly trade, and that we would supply them from time to time with such commodities as they wanted, at much more reasonable rates than either the Spaniards or others can do." Were they friends of the Spanish? Not friends, said the Commodore, nor yet at war with them, but ready to resist them by force of arms if any affront were given. Andreas was pleased by this. He decided that the Scots were privateers, and he chattered about his two good friends, the buccaneer captains Swan and Davies, at whose side he had fought long ago in the overland raid on Santa Maria. Mr. Spense's translation kept up with these nostalgic reminiscences as best it could until Pennecuik coldly cut them short. The Scots, he said, were not rogues but traders. Andreas took the rebuke with good humour, since it was soon followed by gifts. He went away with the Scots flag flying from the prow of his canoe, and upon his head a fine new beaver hat, richly embroidered with golden galloon.

Relieved by the Indians' assurances of friendship, though he would never believe that they were not idle thieves, Pennecuik sent the *Saint Andrew*'s boats away to explore and make soundings of the harbour. The next day he wrote a full account of their discoveries in his log and ordered Hugh Rose to copy it faithfully in his journal, since this was to be sent to the Directors as soon as possible.

The green bay was almost two miles in length, shelving from six to three and a half fathoms, a mile or so across at the most, and with a narrow entrance no wider than a random cannon-shot. In the middle of this sea-gate was a black rock, three feet above water on a still day but hidden by breaking waves when the wind blew hard. "This looks terrible to those who know not the place well, but on both sides is a very good and wide channel." There was a second rock further in and for most of the time it was under water, a constant hazard to ships and boats. The narrow peninsula forming the northern side of the bay was covered with trees, tall cedars, manchineels and sapadilloes through which the wind sang with such gentle sweetness that a sentimental Landsman, dreaming in the sunlight, immediately called them The Shades of Love. For most of its length to sea-ward the peninsula was a high and unscalable escarpment, plunging into deep water. No European fortress had such a defence. On the bayside it rose less steeply, with level ground, and with a small promontory of sand where boats might be safely beached. "This harbour," said Pennecuik, with insane exaggeration that can only be explained by his desire to impress an ignorant Court of Directors, "is capable of containing a thousand sail of the best ships in the world. And without great trouble wharves may be run out, to which ships of the greatest burthen may lay their sides and unload."

The southern shore of the bay was bordered with red-legged mangroves, thick and impenetrable, and beyond them, almost immediately it seemed in that hazy heat, rose the blue and green mountains of the continental divide. There appears to have been no argument, no dispute about the proper site of the Colony. The land about the bay, as far as their feet might take the Scots and for as long as their swords could hold it, was to be Caledonia, but here on the peninsula would be built the town of New Edin-burgh, here above its sandy promontory would be Fort Saint Andrew. The choice of this crooked finger of land, for strategic reasons at least, was a wise one. A single ship might hold the sea-gate against a fleet, helped by land-batteries on both points. The peninsula was well-watered by streams that sprang in bub-bling joy from the feet of the cedars, whereas across the bay, according to Pennecuik, there were dry riverbeds only. At its eastern end the peninsula narrowed to a strip of land little more than 130 paces wide. If this slender neck were cut by a rampart

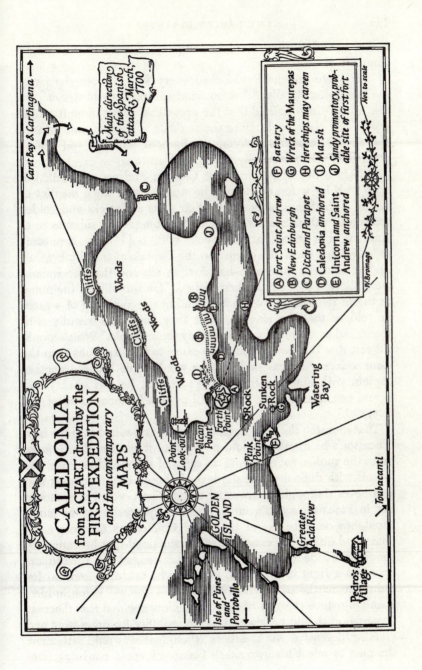

CALEDONIA
from a CHART drawn by the
FIRST EXPEDITION
and from contemporary
MAPS

Caret bay & Carthagena

Main direction of the Spanish attack, March, 1700

Cliffs
Woods
Woods
Cliffs
Cliffs
Woods
Woods
Cliffs

Point Look-out
Pelican Point
Forth Point
Rock
Sunken Rock
Watering Bay

Pink Point

GOLDEN ISLAND

Isle of Pines and Portobello

Greater Acla River

Pedro's Village

Toubacanti

A Fort Saint Andrew
B New Edinburgh
C Ditch and Parapet
D Caledonia anchored
E Unicorn and Saint Andrew anchored

F Battery
G Wreck of the Maurepas
H Here ships may careen
I Marsh
J Sandy promontory, probable site of first fort

W. Bromage

Not to scale

and a sea-filled ditch a single company of resolute men might stand off an army.

"And here you lie land-locked every way," wrote the Commodore optimistically, "that no wind can possibly hurt you." No one at this time realised that the prevailing winds blew from the north, that they might close the sea-gate for weeks and prevent the clumsy ships from leaving the harbour. The bay was a trap, created by and quixotically sprung by Nature.

Within a day of his first visit Captain Andreas returned, this time with his wife and sister. The women wore linen mantles of white, with strings of beads on their arms and necks and golden crescents in their nostrils. They said nothing, were submissive to Andreas, but stared at the Scots with bold eyes. Pennecuik reported that the first woman was the Captain's "travelling wife", adding that the little man had four in all, and that the Indians were allowed as many as they wished. "He was still on the pump as to our designs, but when he found our accounts all of a piece he told us that the English, after they had been friendly with them, had several times carried away their people." Which would suggest that the Indian had more cause to be suspicious than the Commodore. Andreas said that he would have brought another captain with him, a man called Pedro, but he was uneasy and would not approach the Scots "till he was better assured of our integrity."

That morning the fleet weighed anchor and sailed into the bay. Pincarton's helmsman made a poor job of it and ran the *Unicorn* on to the sunken rock, tearing off some of her sheathing. She was got off with difficulty, but she leaked abominably thereafter and was never thoroughly seaworthy again. The Council met aboard her in Pincarton's cabin under the uneasy presidency of James Montgomerie, the first of the Land Councillors to occupy the chair, and although Pennecuik still maintained that his authority should over-ride all he grudgingly acknowledged that the soldiers now had a right to be heard. For once he made no demand for the court-martial of the Drummonds and Samuel Vetch, understandably since the rest of the Councillors decided that Thomas Drummond should be given the responsibility for organising and erecting defensive works ashore (though they would not allow the man to select his own sites). Pennecuik could not bring himself to write Drummond's name in his log however. "All the Land Captains being consulted," he said, "it was resolved to build a battery on the west side of the entrance to the harbour."

Forty men from each ship were put ashore on the peninsula, to clear the ground for New Edinburgh, to cut down trees from the Shades of Love, and to build huts for the sick. Another party was set to digging graves, above the high water mark and out of the sun. Death had not abandoned the expedition. Lieutenant Inglis died of a fever as he lay on deck listening to the strange sounds of a new world. The gunner's boy of the *Caledonia* was drowned unseen as he swam in the blue water below her stern. The bloody flux killed an Englishman named Jenner, Henrique Ghaup a musician, and James Clerk a Volunteer. And William Simpson, the printer, lost his devoted boy to a fever that was at least mercifully quick in dispatch.

William Paterson's loss was sudden and heartbreaking, though he never referred to it in the report he wrote for the Directors. Within a few days of the death of his clerk, his wife died of the flux and was buried on the peninsula to a dropping salute from the *Unicorn*'s guns. Thus, with no record of what she might have thought or felt, passed this loyal woman whom Walter Herries described as "a red-faced coffee-woman". His report of her death was even crueller. Paterson had carried her to Darien, he said, and "at her first landing thrust her about seven feet underground to make the possession, *de facto*, of New Caledonia more authentic."

Paterson hid his grief, turning to the business of the Colony. He had lost his fight to extend the presidency to a month, and now he tried to get the settlement and the fort moved to a more sensible place. "The sea Councillors," he said, "were for a mere morass, neither fit to be fortified nor planted, nor indeed for men to lie upon. I know no reason they had for it, unless it might be to save one of their boats the trouble, once in two or three days, to bestow three or four hours to supply the Landmen with water." It was two months before experience, the schoolmaster of fools he said, taught the Councillors that they had made a mistake, and the fort was re-sited on other ground.

From the first day the boats went ashore with the working-parties it was clear that the men were almost too weak for the prodigious task of building a town and a fort. The want of enough food was bitter, and the privations of a long and sickly voyage had affected all. Their rations, that "scrimp allowance" as Paterson called them, had been meagre enough aboard ship, but then, at least, there had been no obligation to work long hours in damp and exhausting heat. There was no fresh meat, the barrelled beef and pork were green and malodorous. Some men caught fish in the bay, shot wild-fowl and monkeys, bought plantains and fruit from the Indians, but most of them had no more than what they were sparingly given. "And this," said Walter Herries, "was not fit for dogs to eat, but it was a mercy we had a good many Highlanders in our legion who were not used to feed on much of God's creatures that's hallowed." Upon Pennecuik's orders the provisions were kept aboard the ships and landed when necessary, or when he thought necessary. "Our marine masters," complained Paterson, "continually pretended other urgent business, and so could hardly spare their boats to bring the provisions ashore, and many of the most needful things that I know were only designed for the shore were detained on board under pretence they belonged to the ships."

The old division between Seamen and Landsmen was thus further widened by anger and envy. Aboard their ships, away from the poison of noxious mists and rotting vegetation, better supplied with provisions and drawing their water from those southern rivers Pennecuik had said were dry, the sailors avoided the worst of the fevers and fluxes that harassed the men ashore. Sixteen more Landsmen died in November, including the remaining minister Adam Scott. His spiritual influence over his dismayed congregation had become increasingly tenuous as men turned from his arid exhorations to a more stimulating comfort. Drunkenness was common, the only escape from hunger, from weariness, and from bewildered anger. Brandy was freely given to the sick, as much to cheer their departure as to help their recovery. In one evening the Planters drank all the beer issued to them for a week, and all they could win on a throw of dice or the turn of a card, passing happily into a stupor that shut out the cries of the sick, the whispering of the surf, and the unnerving night-sounds of the forests. Once a week they were also given a quart of wine to be shared among each mess of five men, and this too was gambled for and quickly drunk by the winner. The officers, with more liberal rations, were more frequently drunk. Captains received two quarts of wine a week, said Herries, and on the day of issue "went as merry to bed as if they had been in their winter quarters at Ghent or Brussels."

Drink also brought more Indian captains to the peninsula and the ships, for the Scots were generous with their hospitality. They sometimes pressed brandy upon these simple people as men will indulge an appealing child with sweets, and sometimes made them drunk in the malicious hope that they would fall into the water as they stumbled overside to their canoes. Andreas came again and dined with the Councillors, his new hat on his head and his travelling wife at his side, her brown arms and neck heavy with rosy beads. On a fourth occasion he came with a fleet of canoes that were decked in leaves and feathers, bringing a chief called Ambrosio to whom he showed great respect and whom he obviously expected the Scots to honour likewise. This Ambrosio was a strong and vigorous man of sixty who controlled the Darien coastline from the River of Pines to the San Blas Islands. He had been fighting the Spaniards all his life, and he said that if Pennecuik gave him a hundred men, with arms for two thousand of his own, he would drive the Spanish "not only out of the mines, which are but three days journey, but even out of Panama itself." He had good reason for hoping that the Scots would join him in his absorbing life's work. A week or so before the fleet's arrival he had attacked a small settlement of priests on Golden Island, slaughtering them all. He did not tell Pennecuik this himself; the Commodore heard it from a wandering Frenchman whom Ambrosio brought with him. Pennecuik gave no promise of help, and he privately thanked God that the massacre had taken place before the Scots' arrival, otherwise Spain would undoubtedly have held them responsible.

With Ambrosio was his son-in-law and sub-chief Pedro, a brisk young man who was as gay as Andreas was grave. French gaiety, Pennecuik called it disapprovingly, understanding the reason for it when he heard that Pedro frequently entertained French privateers in his village. He had once been a slave in Panama City, had not forgotten that harrowing experience or forgiven it, and was as hot for cutting Spanish throats with Scottish swords as his father-in-law. He spoke French well, and was thus able to talk to many of the Scots officers without the aid of Mr. Spense's Spanish. He quickly made a friend of Lieutenant Robert Turnbull, a bright-hearted, courageous young man who, alone among the Scots, took the trouble to learn something of the Indians' language. Pennecuik did not know what to make of Pedro. Polygamy was one thing, understandable if not commendable, but the man was not only married to Ambrosio's daughter but also to his own daughters by her, "which is allowed here, yet it seems it's believed a crime, since if they have any children during the life of their mother they are burnt alive, the children, I mean."

From these captains the Scots learned that there was no great King or Emperor of Darien, no Golden One such as Paterson had once believed, though there was a legend of a barbarous tyrant who beheaded men for pleasure and allowed no one but himself to have more than one wife. He was murdered one night by a group of his followers who resented the pleasure and envied the privilege, and since then the land had been divided unequally among a number of chiefs, great and small, whose power and influence seemed to depend on their success in the field against the Spaniards. Captain Diego, who held the coast eastward from Caledonia to Caret Bay, commanded three thousand warriors and was more esteemed than Ambrosio. He had been at war with Spain since he and some of his clan broke out of the mines where they had been working as slaves. Pousigo, the brother-in-law of Andreas, was a powerful shaman, a "clergyman" Pennecuik called him, and although he possessed little land his influence was great. Corbet, whom the settlers never met, was an ally of the French and had joined them in their recent attack on Carthagena, but the other captains thought little of him. Nicola might have been a valuable ally had the Scots taken the trouble to send him gifts and seek him out. He was Ambrosio's rival, a wise, brave, and good-natured man who could not only speak Spanish but read and write it as well. He also had a surprising knowledge of European affairs. He had once been a pet of the Spaniards, but had broken with them when the Governor of Portobello stole his prized musket. Since then he had wasted his talents in fruitless raids, in the killing of Spaniards whenever and wherever he found them.

At the sea-gate end of the peninsula were three promontories. The largest, which the Scots called Forth Point, was a sandy thumb of land and a few feet only above sea-level. To the north of it, across a small bay, was another which was named Pelican Point. The third was the highest, the end of the northern escarpment of the peninsula, and this was called Point Look-out. Here a wooden tower was built, wherein a watchman was posted by day and night. Two week's after the fleet's arrival he reported a strange ship standing to westward, and the following day she dropped anchor off the Isle of Pines to the north-west of the harbour mouth. It was another twenty-four hours before her captain was rowed into Caledonia Bay. He came up on the *Saint Andrew*'s quarter and boarded her, giving his ship's name as the *Rupert*, a French vessel taken as a prize during the war, and his own as Richard Long with the King's commission to search for sunken treasure in these waters. Mr. Secretary Vernon had found a use for the man, though exactly what that was neither of them was ever indiscreet enough to put to paper. The Scots greeted him cordially, although they were not pleased by the visit of an English ship so soon. She was not unexpected, however. Some days before, the Indians had reported her furtive presence off the coast.

Long dined aboard the flagship and the *Unicorn*, and proved that he had a greater capacity for brandy and Madeira than Andreas, Pedro or Ambrosio. He sat late with Pennecuik and Pincarton, explaining that he had cruised along the coast but had made no landing, and had no wish to claim any part of it for England. He asked questions about the settlement, its strength and intentions, and he did not think it necessary to tell Pennecuik and Pincarton that he was obliged to inform James Vernon of all that he learned from them. Also understandably, he did not admit that while down the coast he had told the Indians that if they were attacked by these Scots privateers the King of England would protect them.

Pennecuik decided that he did not like the man, and that night in his journal he wrote a judgment upon Long that other men might well have used about himself. "We could by no means find him the conjuror he gives himself for."

On the evening of November 17, with Long drunk and asleep

aboard the *Unicorn*, the Council decided to accept Ambrosio's invitation to visit his village, and the next day, after the Quaker had returned to his ship, there was a squabbling argument over who should go. Pennecuik of course, there was no debate on that. Jolly was elected, but was sick and proposed Cunningham, Vetch, and Thomas Drummond. Pennecuik objected strenuously, and won his point by the strength of his voice rather than the power of his argument. It was finally agreed that the mission should consist of the Commodore, Pincarton, Cunningham and Mackay. They left at eight o'clock in the morning of November 19, four ship's boats, a strong force of armed men, the Company's banner and the flag of Scotland. They got no further than the Isle of Pines that day, for the wind turned north to a stiff gale and they were glad to run in to the lee of the *Rupert* and board her.

The English Quaker liberally returned Pennecuik's hospitality, but the Scots found him even less attractive aboard his own ship than he had been aboard theirs. "Whatever the King or Government of England may have found in Captain Long," wrote Pennecuik, "we know not, but to us in all his conversations he appeared a most ridiculous, shallow-pated fellow, laughed at and despised to his very face by his own officers, and continually drunk." The questioning and the answering were now reversed, but the Scots were unable to discover the real purpose of Long's commission. Indeed, from his stumbling letters to London it is plain that he was not sure himself, whether he was truly to search for treasure, whether he was merely to report on the Scots settlement, or whether he was to claim the country for England and turn the Indians against the Caledonians. James Vernon got little in return for the ship and money that had at last been given to the importunate man.

When the gale dropped the next morning, Pedro arrived in a piragua, happy to guide the Scots to his father-in-law. They left in the forenoon, making frequent soundings along the coast westward until they came to a broad bay which Pennecuik, with his customary flair for exaggeration, thought might easily harbour ten thousand sail, with deep-water keys alongside which the greatest vessel in the English Navy might safely moor. It was an old meeting-place of the buccaneers, and there were marks ashore where they had once careened their ships. For a moment he thought of uprooting the settlement from Caledonia Bay and transferring it here, but he decided that it would be an ill place to defend, having no sea-gate and no high ground for batteries.

A guard was left on the boats, and the rest of the party marched inland for a league to Ambrosio's village. It stood on the bank of a river, ten or twelve small huts dominated by the captain's house—a great building of cane and plantain leaves, ninety feet long, thirty-five broad, and thirty high. Ambrosio was waiting fifty paces from its door, smiling, and surrounded by a bodyguard of twenty men all wearing fringed cloaks of white linen and carrying feathered lances. In the background a band of musicians played sweetly on reed pipes, while others hummed, and still more danced about the Councillors in a manner that reminded them of the graceful movements of their own Highlanders. "Ambrosio saluted us kindly," said Pennecuik, "and gave us a calabash of liquor almost like lamb's-wool, which they call Mislow: it's made of Indian corn and potatoes." They were taken into the cool shade of the great house where Ambrosio and Pedro lived with their wives, their children and forty dependants. Pedro proudly introduced Ambrosio's grandmother and communal cook, a surprisingly young-looking woman for the 120 years she was said to have lived. The Scots politely doubted her age, whereupon Ambrosio called up representatives of the six generations from her body, himself among them, and added that her age was nothing, it was common enough for his people to live thirty or forty years longer. "Yet it is observed," said Pennecuik naïvely, "those who converse often with Europeans and drink our strong liquors are but short-lived."

The Scots spent the night at the village, sleeping in the great house which, for some reason, reminded them of a church. In the morning they broke their fast with plantains, potatoes and wild hog, after which Ambrosio and Pedro went in to the forests and shot the largest partridges the Scots had ever seen, pressing them upon their guests with disarming promises of love and friendship.

The Councillors returned to the settlement on November 23. The *Rupert* had weighed anchor three days before, which infuriated Pennecuik for he had hoped to send dispatches home with her. He soon had other matters to anger him. His report that there was no better place than Caledonia Bay for the settlement brought both Vetch and the Drummonds into open opposition. In as many words they said that he was a fool. The ground chosen for the town and the fort was dangerous and unsuitable, and the work already done, little though it was, had been wasted. Pennecuik refused to listen to them, and bullied all the Councillors but Paterson into agreeing that the building should continue as originally planned.

And then there was the problem of Major James Cunningham of Eickett. Behind his stiff-necked arrogance and punctilious manner he was an ineffectual member of the Council, uncertain which faction his duty and his interest inclined him to, now a member of the Glencoe Gang and now cannily neutral, and usually declaring for that party which could cause him the least inconvenience. He had finally decided that the best interest was his own, and that lay as far away from Caledonia as he could place it. "He became so uneasy," wrote Paterson, "and so possessed (as we thought) by unaccountable conceits and notions that he gave us no small trouble, and at last would needs forsake not only his post but the Colony." He wanted to go home, and he was determined to go home with the first ship. Pincarton and others thought that he ought to be placed in irons, or at least disciplined until he came to a proper recognition of his duty, but even upon this the Council could not agree. He continued to nag and complain on the edge of all debates.

He was not alone in his desperate wish to be quit of this wretched land. At the end of November, on the eve of Saint Andrew's Day to make the crime more disgraceful, ten Planters broke open the magazine aboard the *Unicorn* and deserted with all the weapons they could carry. A captain and four subalterns were sent after them in one of the flagship's boats to Caret Bay, where it was assumed they had gone. The incident spoiled the flavour of the Saint Andrew's Day supper which Pennecuik held for the Council, although Captain Andreas enjoyed it. He had been invited with intent, the Scots now suspecting him of correspondence with the Spanish at Portobello. "We taxed him home with it," said Pennecuik, by which he meant that the Indian was given all the brandy he wished and then questioned. He agreed that he had been friendly with the Spaniards and that they had made him a captain of their native levies, but he had accepted the friendship and the office because he was afraid of them. They had recently told him that the Scots were privateers "who had no design to settle but to plunder both Spaniards and Indians, and be gone in two or three months." Pennecuik assured him that they were there to stay, that they would protect him and his people and give him a commission in their service, and that all they wanted from him in return was "all his right to this part of the country." He gave it to them with drunken generosity, and went happily home in his canoe.

On December 1 the deserters were brought back. They were put in irons and given nothing but bread and water.

"From henceforward . . . we do call ourselves CALEDONIANS"
Caledonia, December 1698

Where was the fine weather which Lionel Wafer had said should now be favouring this promised land? There were days when Hugh Rose had no spirit to record anything more in his journal than the miserable fact that it was still raining. *Much thunder, lightning and rain. . . . Great showers of rain with much wind. . . . The weather very bad which hinders the work. . . . These twenty-four hours there has fallen a prodigious quantity of rain. . . . Much wind and rain. . . . Wind and rain as above. . . .*

Weak from fever and flux, depressed by a heavy melancholy, exhausted by daytime heat and shivering at night beneath the dripping palmetto roofs of their huts, the Landsmen looked bitterly through this slanting rain to the ships. The sea-captains were jealous of the health of their crews, and wisely allowed no man ashore except under close watch. Even so, the sailors were frequently ill, although their chances of recovery were higher. Aboard the *Unicorn* young Colin Campbell survived a severe fever, blessed be God, but it had left his hands weak, as his brother could no doubt see from the unsteadiness of his writing. Shipboard life was dull, and there were times when he envied his namesake and clansman "Captain Colin", an officer of Argyll's who commanded one of the companies ashore. Yet he had no real wish to leave his friend Henry Erskine and land on the peninsula.

"There is nothing to be had there, and besides, if I did then Captain Pincarton would never own me nor speak to me any more, as he did to another gentleman who was recommended to his care."

Many men were writing such letters, and keeping journals against the day—pray God let it be soon—when a ship left for Scotland.

The Council at last agreed that the site chosen for the fort was unsatisfactory, and ordered another to be built on the sandy promontory of Forth Point. Although he was no engineer, Thomas Drummond was again the only fit man to organise the work, and he, said Paterson, "according to the tools he had, did beyond what could be reasonably expected from him, for our men, though for the most part in health, were generally weak for want of sufficient allowance of provisions and liquors and the irregular serving of their scrimp allowances." Drummond was remorseless in the iron discipline he imposed upon his men, and spared his own body less than he did theirs. He was a hard man to like, having no compassion, but there were few who did not respect his ability and strength, and what talk there was about his dark service in Glencoe was kept to a guarded whisper. Indeed, what had been deplored in his behaviour at home might here have been regarded as evidence of resolute leadership. The fort he started to build was to be as simple and as effective as he could make it with the tools, labour and materials available, and large enough to hold a garrison of a thousand men—a star-shaped, palisaded wall made from a double row of wooden stakes packed with earth, cut with embrasures for the forty guns that would be brought ashore from the ships. The earth for the palisades would come from a wide moat, open to the bay and flooded by the tide. On the landward side, and beyond the moat, would be a *chevaux de frise* of sloping planks spiked with iron. All this, it was hoped—with the ditch that was being dug across the neck, with the land-batteries on the sea-gate and with the ships in the bay—should be strong enough to protect the Colony against anything but a formal siege-train, and it was not likely that the Spanish would have such ordnance.

On December 3 the uncertain friendship of Captain Andreas was cemented by a treaty. He came aboard the *Saint Andrew* in

the forenoon, with a wife or two and a bodyguard in sodden
white smocks. A platoon of soldiers, equally drenched, saluted
him from the ship's waist, and beneath an awning on the poop-
deck the Councillors sweated in their heavy clothes and itching
wigs. The treaty, written fairly on parchment by Mr. Rose and
decorated with gold-striped ribbon and the Company's seal, was
read aloud by the Clerk and translated into Spanish by Benjamin
Spense. It commissioned Andreas as a captain in the service of
Scotland, and promised him the protection of the Colony against
all his enemies. It was then handed to him, together with a
basket-hilted broadsword and a brace of pistols. He accepted
them with the grave bow he had learnt from the Spanish, swore
that he would use the weapons in defence of the Scots, and presented in return a sheaf of brightly-feathered arrows. The
flagship's seven waist-deck guns fired a salute, and everyone
retired hurriedly to the roundhouse for a glass of wine. According to Herries, one glass led to another, and another. "Captain
Andreas went ashore with his flag flying and the other designs of
his honour, except the Commission which I found the day following crammed into a locker of the roundhouse where empty
bottles lay."

A week later, a smartly-manned longboat came through the sea-
gate just as the watchman on Point Look-out was reporting a
ship, or perhaps two, at anchor in the haze of rain by Golden
Island. A French lieutenant climbed aboard the *Saint Andrew* with
a flourish and told Pennecuik that he was from the *Maurepas*, a
merchantman of 42 guns, commanded by Captain Duvivier
Thomas who had King Louis' commission to sail and trade in
these seas. The other ship, he said, was a 22-gun Dutchman. The
news he brought of the Spanish was alarming. Their Windward
Fleet, the Barliavento, was fitting out at Carthagena for an attack
on all European privateers, and its cruisers had already snapped
up two English turtling sloops which bad weather had blown
within range of their guns. The *Maurepas* and the Dutchman
would be grateful for the protection of the Scots' ships and
harbour until the Barliavento had sailed by to Portobello. The
Council gave it willingly, and the next day Captain Thomas came
in by longboat. He was as hearty a drinker as Richard Long, but
carried himself better, and was able to tell the Scots "all the news

of the coast, and that the President of Panama had given an account to the Governors of Carthagena and Portobello of our arrival." Wildly over-estimating the strength of the Scots, they believed that the settlement was a bridgehead for an intended attack across the Gulf of Mexico to the mouth of the Mississippi. "This obliges us," wrote Pennecuik that night, "to make all possible haste in our battery, and to get our ships in line of battle across the mouth of the harbour."

Despite the rain, the sickness and the exhaustion, the Scots were heartened by the news the Frenchmen brought. Even Hugh Rose, normally a cautious body, was moved to vainglory. "Our men are very hearty, and seem to long for a visit from Jaque, that they might have a just pretence to their gold mines not far off." The thought of gold, the hope of gold, of great fortunes to be won by the sword, excited the Scots more than a wretched life growing plantains or trading hodden grey. The greater the risk of fever and death, the stronger their desire to be quickly rich and quickly away. When the *Maurepas* and the Dutchman came into the bay, dropping anchor behind the Scots' line of battle, a rumour spread that the Frenchman's hold was full of treasure taken in the raid on Carthagena. The Frenchmen did not deny it, or confirm it, they were too busy drinking and feasting.

The day their ships came in, the *Rupert* was once more sighted to the north-west. Long sent a boat with news that the Barlia-vento, now at sea, consisted of seven great sail and a number of tenders full of soldiers. He was soon gone again, apparently in fright and not waiting for his longboat to return. When questioned by Pennecuik, its crew revealed that the Quaker had been behaving very oddly. He had put a landing-party ashore and joined the Indians in a senseless attack on a trading-post east of Portobello, killing seven Spaniards. He had then sent messages to all the Indian villages, "to tell them we were a pack of thieves and robbers, being only a parcel of disbanded officers and soldiers, and that nobody would protect us." The Commodore was glad that the battery on Forth Point was completed, with sixteen 12-pounders mounted. "We are now in such a condition," he said, with an arrogance that wearied Drummond and Vetch, "that we wished nothing more than that the Spaniards would attack us." This braggart self-confidence, which most of the Scots shared, was increased when Ambrosio came with a warning that the Spaniards were mustering 600 veteran soldiers and 200 Indian levies at Santa Maria and Panama City for a landward attack across the Isthmus. "It's feared with us," wrote Hugh Rose, "that they will not come, but whatever be in it, the work goes well on, the men working with much vigour and resolution."

The Council met in dissension and argument. Each new President spent much of his week's office undoing the work of his predecessor, or hampering what he believed would be the intentions of the next. Paterson was less worried by the thought of a Spanish attack than by the shortage of provisions, the urgent need to secure fresh supplies from Jamaica. They were, he said, in a prison for want of sloops or brigantines, coastal vessels for trade, and he was delighted when an English sloop slipped into the harbour on December 20. Captain Moon had kept his promise to an old friend and had sent a colleague, Edward Sands, with a cargo of beef and flour. The Council's gratitude was shortly phrased and shortly given, it then began to argue about the proper value of the goods to be traded for Moon's supplies.

At least there was now a real chance of sending letters and journals back to Scotland. An earlier hope that the *Maurepas* might take them as far as Jamaica had been soon destroyed by her captain's plain reluctance to leave either the harbour or the pleasant drinking-companions he had found among the Scots. Edward Sands said that he would take the papers to Jamaica, and any messenger the Council appointed to carry them. The question now was: who shall go? The decision would be important, the choice involved inevitable risks for all the Councillors remaining. The first man from the Colony to reach Edinburgh would have an uninterrupted audience with the Council-General and the Court of Directors. His prejudices, the complaints of his faction, his account of the settlement would be accepted by virtue of his office, despite what might be written in Hugh Rose's journal or the Commodore's letters. Daniel Mackay was anxious to go, and was lobbying for the election. Cunningham, whose conceits and notions had now become unbearable, thought that he should go, that he would go whether chosen or not. Walter Herries had tired of the Colony, as everybody had tired of him, and he had already transferred himself; his servant, his baggage and a purse of gold-dust aboard the *Maurepas*, but nobody thought seriously of his candidature. Paterson, with the interested support of Cunningham, proposed Samuel Vetch and two other Land Officers, but Pennecuik noisily quashed that. He would not have one of Thomas Drummond's friends at large in Milne Square, and to prevent it he decided to support Mackay, having no reason to believe the young lawyer bore him any ill-will. For the next two or three days both of them spent as much time as they could aboard the *Unicorn* appealing for the support of Pincarton and Robert Jolly.

Inevitably, the man finally chosen belonged to no faction. If he could not be trusted to favour one party before another, he might at least report impartially upon all. Alexander Hamilton, the Accountant-General of the Colony, was a sober, sensible man who had kept apart from the more acrimonious disputes of the settlement. He was still accepted reluctantly by some of the leaders within the Council and out. Paterson thought they could ill afford to lose the man's knowledge of the cargoes and stores, and said that his departure would cause even more disorder and confusion. The Drummonds and Vetch objected to him because they believed him to be a friend of Robert Jolly, whose weak, vacillating humours they now detested.

Cunningham was also told that he might go with the sloop. The other Councillors had given in to his nagging, as men agree to the extraction of an incisor, considering the relief from pain against the loss to their appearance. "After weighing his temper," said Paterson, "they consented to his going, but thought it were prudent to part with him in friendship than otherwise, lest any that might espouse his humour in Scotland should prove a means of retarding or frustrating our needful supplies." He was given a letter of recommendation, but it was made clear to him that Hamilton, not he, was the emissary.

Now there was a great writing of letters throughout the Colony, a parcelling of journals and small gifts—an arrow, a silver disc, the wing-feathers of a parakeet, a wondrous sea-shell, a pressed flower. Though many were homesick, disillusioned, despairing, at the least full of doubt, there was an almost unanimous desire to reassure their friends and families, to pretend that New Edinburgh was not a mean huddle of palmetto huts, that Fort St.

Andrew was not an unfinished palisade, that sickness and death were not commonplace. "Being in haste," wrote Colin Campbell to his brother, "else I would have writ to my mother, and other friends, but let me be remembered to all." Surgeon Mackenzie's letter to Haldane of Gleneagles said nothing of his distressing failure to check the fever and flux, it glowed with praise of the abundant land, and only at the end betrayed the colonists' fear that Scotland would forget them and abandon them. "I very heartily wish that a mistaken notion . . . may not occasion the old mother to obliviate her new-born babe before it is fit for weaning and in a condition of doing for itself." One phrase occurred again and again in many of the letters, in Hugh Rose's journal and Pennecuik's log, as if there had been some agreement to use it and it alone. Mackay used it when he wrote to the Earl of Leven. Darien, he said, was "one of the fruitfullest spots of ground on the face of the earth" And being a Highlander, with an ability to confuse hope with certainty, he added that "it will make the Scots nation more considerable in the balance of Europe than ever, and you'll have such a settlement in the Indies in a few years as scarce any European nation could brag of."

Writing to the Earl of Panmure, one of the Councillors-General, Pennecuik blithely said that all things had succeeded beyond expectation, and that nothing could go wrong if the Company's friends in Scotland did as much for the Colony as Heaven had already done. To another Councillor he wrote of gold mines within three days' march, of a country that was "one of the most fruitful and healthy upon earth." He sent them trinkets for their wives, nose-plates and rings which Ambrosio had given him. And also "a little instrument of silver which I beg your Lordship will not expose to the view of the fair sex, for if they measure the country by the magnitude of that instrument I am sure they'll have no inclination to visit these parts."

All members of the Council signed a brief letter to the Court of Directors which was to go as a cover for the journals and dispatches. Although it declared that God Almighty must have preserved the country for their occupation, that its "fruitfulness" was unequalled anywhere, it ended on a note of uneasy urgency. Supplies were needed, provisions and stores, and it was hoped that they would be sent with the least delay. "But however it be, by the help of God we shall not fail to do our utmost. . . ."

As the year ended, bad weather delayed the departure of the sloop. Obstinate winds closed the harbour, and although Edward Sands could have warped her out he was unwilling to risk his ship in the gales beyond. The *Maurepas* had been forgotten by all except Herries, who was still aboard her. On the evening of December 23 there was not a sober man among her officers and crew, and most of them were still drunk the next morning when Captain Thomas unaccountably weighed anchor, set his topsails and mainsail and moved toward the sea-gate. Great rollers were coming through it, but by fool's luck his helmsman managed to ride them well until the wind dropped abruptly. The ship swung to leeward and on to the sunken rock.

Pennecuik, who had been watching in astonishment from the *Saint Andrew*, ordered his longboat away and was rowed across to the *Maurepas*. He took command with a rare decisiveness, calling for more boats and hauling the Frenchman off the rock. Little serious damage had been done, and when the ship had weathered the point he advised Thomas to drop his bow and stern anchors and wait for a gentler sea. Forty-five minutes later both cables broke, which was what Pennecuik should have foreseen, the ship spun about and back on to the rock, this time tearing a great hole in her hull. She sank slowly, her timbers parting and her masts snapping, but Pennecuik bravely stayed aboard until he had seen Thomas lashed to a raft. He then stripped off his clothes and walked from the deck into the water. "Naked as I was born, with much ado I swam ashore. The seas broke over me, under each of which I was at least twenty seconds, and indeed two such more had done my business." He found Thomas along the beach, half-drowned, and ordered him to be hung up by the heels until the water had run out of his lungs. Nearly half the crew of the *Maurepas* had been lost, including all her officers with the exception of Thomas and a lieutenant, and the angry survivors would have cut the throats of both had not Pennecuik sent them aboard the *Saint Andrew*.

There they were to remain for the next two months, and never, thought the Scots, were men "more ungrateful, unreasonable, and uneasy." They had good reason to be. According to Pennecuik, there had been 60,000 pieces of eight in gold and silver aboard their ship, and 30,000 more in trading goods, and the thought of this, lying out there in the bay, would plague the greed of the Scots for weeks. Thomas made some attempts to dive for the treasure, without success, and gave up when Pennecuik promised him that all that came ashore from the wreck would be his. He was cheerfully unconcerned when a package of letters was washed up on the beach. Some were for delivery to the Indian captains, threatening them with the anger of France and Spain if they continued to support the Scots. Others were from Spaniards of Carthagena and Portobello, promising the support of the Indies for the Dauphin's claim to the throne of Spain when His Catholic Majesty, who had been making a long business of dying, finally expired.

Walter Herries also escaped from the wreck. Though he lost his baggage, and his unfortunate servant, the purse of gold-dust was in his pocket when he swam ashore.

Christmas was a day of rest, and was celebrated by a great feast aboard the *Saint Andrew*. Andreas and Ambrosio were both invited, nobody realising or caring that each had a hearty dislike of the other. They were civil enough at first, but as the bottles passed they began to quarrel. Herries was there again, and his story may perhaps be believed against the indignant denials of others who were not. From a wordy quarrel the Indians went on to brawl, until they were separated by Pennecuik. Drunk himself, he was still jealous of his own dignity and the solemnity of the day. The next morning no one could remember much of what had happened, and it was assumed that both Indians had gone happily away in their canoes some time before dawn. And then Andreas was found in the hold below the main hatchway, unconscious and with a bloodied head. Little was done for the man. He was hauled up to the waist and left on deck until his wives and his bodyguard came to collect him.

Once the desperate, self-indulgent carousal of Christmas was over, the year ended on a high and noble note. Edward Sands said that he would sail on Thursday, December 29, and on Wednesday the Council hurriedly published a declaration constituting the settlement as a Colony of the Company of Scotland. Drawn up and written by Hugh Rose, it repeated the substance of the Act and the Company's right to the land. It established that all who were then, or who might thereafter come to be associated with the Colony were free men, with equal privileges, immunities, and rights of Government. It declared "a full and free liberty of conscience in matter of Religion, so as the same be not understood to allow, connive at, or indulge the blaspheming of God's holy name." Freedom and liberty of conscience are words that always have the inherent and expedient qualifications of the age which uses them, and in this case no one took the first to mean that the Colony would not buy or employ slaves, or that the second included the toleration of Papists.

The declaration was read to all as they stood on the wet earth about New Edinburgh, to tired men and sick men in stained scarlet, yellow duck and rusty broadcloth. They were told that not only were they here in "one of the most healthful, rich and fruitful countries upon earth", but that they were also to live by reason, by the Scriptures, and by the example of the most wise and just among nations. From truth and righteousness would come the blessing or prosperity.

And now, by virtue of the before-mentioned powers to us given, we do here settle and in the name of God establish ourselves; and in honour and for the memory of that most ancient and renowned name of our Mother Country, we do, and will from henceforward call this country by the name of Caledonia; and ourselves, successors, and associates, by the name of CALEDONIANS.

There was little but this to show for the first two months. An uncertain foothold on an exposed peninsula, a ragged village of huts and an uncompleted fort. The price paid so far had been high, though it seems to have been accepted stoically. For dispatch to Edinburgh, Mr. Rose had drawn up a list of those who had died, seventy-six between July 23 and Christmas Day. The greatest number in one group were Planters, men with little stake in the Colony except the obligation to defend it and the hope of fifty acres when the land was broken. For many of these the venture had been no more than an alternative to a beggarly life as a disbanded soldier. Few of them, certainly not the Highlanders who were cut off from the rest of the settlers by their knowledge of no language but Gaelic, shared the youthful zest of the Volunteers. Both ministers had died, and since November 20 the Colony had thus had no one to intercede on its behalf with a quixotic Almighty. There had died the trumpeter whose music had been a solace, two surgeon's mates from exposure to their patients, five young midshipmen and the junior mate of the *Saint Andrew*, whose splendid name was Recompense Standburgh. The last name on the list was Thomas Fullarton, captain of the *Dolphin*, who "died suddenly after warm walking." He had eaten and drunk well at the Christmas feast, taken a stroll to clear his fuddled mind, and was dead of the flux before nightfall.

"No doubt," wrote Roderick Mackenzie when he published the list later in Edinburgh, "everyone will justly regret the loss of his own nearest friend. . . . As even a greater number of so many as went might have died by this time, had they all remained at home, so it may be some satisfaction to the nearest friends of the deceased that their names shall stand upon record as being among the first brave adventurers that went upon the most noble, most honourable, and most promising undertaking that Scotland ever took in hand."

The sloop sailed, taking with her Hamilton, Cunningham, and Walter Herries. The decks and yards of the ships, the high ground of the peninsula were crowded to watch her going. The watchman on Point Look-out was the last to see her as her sail went down over the horizon to the north.

"An Address to His Majesty in such terms as shall please him"
Edinburgh, August to December 1698

When Robert Blackwood returned to Edinburgh from Kirkcaldy on the afternoon the expedition sailed, he brought the shocking news of the desertion of young David Dalrymple and John Wilson, both of the *Dolphin*. The Directors were incensed, and particularly noted that the boy had gone with two months' advance pay in his pocket. Before the Court resolved anything else it ordered that the deserters be pursued, arrested, and prosecuted with the utmost severity. The incident was a clashing note, and spoilt the harmony of the fleet's departure. The Company's affairs were at stake in the arena of Parliament House, and it would have been a comfort to know that its ships had sailed without fainthearts and cowards. There was also John Dickson, the clerk who had gone with Blackwood to Kirkcaldy, and whose deplorable book-keeping had caused the delay in sailing. He was told to bring his accounts to order before the end of October or forfeit half of his year's salary.

The seventh session of Parliament had assembled. The King's servants had come to town from London or their estates, deter-mined to defend their paymaster against the Company's adher-ents who wished to send him an angry Address of protest, one which complained most bitterly of the behaviour of his Agent in Hamburg. His Majesty's Commissioner, the Earl of Marchmont, was especially concerned for the honour of the king he had served with devotion and loyalty. He had once been "handsome and lovely", but tireless service had aged him prematurely and much of the work of bribery, corruption and oratorical persua-sion would necessarily fall upon Seafield as President of Parlia-ment. When this Ogilvy came to Edinburgh he looked anxiously from the window of his coach, doubtful of the welcome he might receive. He was relieved, he told Carstares, to see "many coaches and horsemen ... most of the nobility and parliament men .. and a very great confluence of the common sort", all, apparently, greeting him with joy. He was thus hopeful that things would go well for the King. Reason and persuasion, of course, would not be enough. "We do treat and caress the members, and have our friends at work doing all they can with them."

Softer than silk would be that caress of gold. This Parliament was a paradox. Though it introduced legislation of the most humane and enlightened nature, it was also one of the most corrupt in Scotland's history. Eight years before, William had told his Scots Secretary, Lord Melville, that he was to be generous to those who would favour the King's cause, that "what employ-ment or other gratification you think fit to promise them in our name we shall fulfill the same." Few public men resisted such bribes, and fewer still protested against them or saw that the nation suffered by them. The sickness was endemic. "Let no man say," Fletcher would write, "that it cannot be proved that the

English court has ever bestowed any bribe in this country. For they bestow all offices and pensions; they bribe us, and are masters of us at our own cost."

But within a parliamentary government it was still necessary to bargain with the as yet unbribed, to persuade or corrupt the honest men. The Address before the Estates boldly asked the King to give the Company of Scotland that support and protection the Act demanded. Seafield and Marchmont, Argyll and Queensberry, could not hope to see it voted out of Parliament Hall, but they could soften its language—take out its sting, as Argyll proposed—and delay its dispatch. This they had to do without loss of reputation, for although the King was their master he could not save their windows from being broken. "God knows what trouble this matter is to me," Seafield told Carstares, "and what anxiety is upon my spirit to get fairly out of it, which I am hopeful I shall."

The debate opened on August 1 with long speeches on behalf of the Address as drafted. One was made by Tweeddale, and another by Tullibardine who was still trying to ride two horses and in opposite directions, to be the King's faithful servant in London and the Company's supporter in Edinburgh. Seafield listened to him without alarm, knowing just how far the young man might run when his pockets were filled with the right metal, or his ambition diverted by brighter promises. To the President this debate was tiresome, but not greatly to be feared. A month before the fleet sailed he had shaken the support of many peers in the Company's party by letting them know of the King's resolve that "no man who opposed him should enjoy either place or pension." He had since been buying others on the lower benches of the Estates, taking a boyish pleasure in outwitting or outbidding the Company. "I have gained the Commissioner for the town of Brechin, under my Lord Panmure's nose." Argyll also boasted of having won over some purse-greedy members of the Hamilton clan. "All the heads of the opposite party are broke," Seafield reassured Carstares, "except the Earl of Tullibardine, and I believe his wings are clipped."

The case for the Address was presented with passion and urgency. The country had subscribed a great sum of money. Fine ships, brave men, and rich cargoes were already on their way to found a Colony. If the Company did not get the support and encouragement it deserved from Parliament, if its privileges and immunities were not confirmed by the Throne, if the King did not protect his Scottish subjects then the noble undertaking would be ruined.

For a week the supporters of the Address spoke without serious opposition. The King's men, from whom Seafield had expected an early return on the payments made them, were silent. Many of them were probably waiting for a lead from him or Argyll, but others were uneasy, uncertain of the volatile passions outside Parliament Hall. The anger of the people, their resentment of English arrogance and English contempt, their joyous pride in their Company, separated them from their time-serving representatives. A few months later, Andrew Fletcher would put his people's defiance of the English into angry words.

They must not think that we have so far degenerated from the courage and honour of our ancestors as tamely to submit to become their vassals, when for two thousand years we have maintained our freedom, and therefore it is not in their interest to oppress us too much. If they consult their histories they will find that we always broke their yoke at the long run.

"I waited a considerable time," Seafield wrote to Carstares, "but none of the King's servants speaking anything, I thought it needful to speak my mind freely; and yet I did it so as that my enemies could catch no advantage of what I said." He blandly acknowledged that of course it was important for the Company and the nation to prosper jointly. If he had any quarrel at all with the undertaking it was upon the matter of the assistance which should, or should not be given to it. The demands for an extension of the Company's monopolies, for a new Act confirming its privileges, for the gift of ships by the King, were extravagant and foolish. Let the Colony be properly settled, let it then be seen how things marched. It had been unwise to give the King's Secretary and the King's Commissioner no foreknowledge of what they were now being asked to place before him, for "there might be many proposals made of greater advantage to the Company than these, and it would be cross and contrary to press a vote." He further disarmed the major complaint of the Address by explaining at length how he and others had persuaded the King to restrain his Resident in Hamburg from putting obstacles in the way of the Company. "I think that since His Majesty has done so much in this matter you would not offer to give him further trouble concerning it."

A motion by the Company's friends to put the Address to a special committee was hotly debated for three hours, during which, said Seafield, "I did not so much as sit down." He intervened persistently, with adroit argument and soft threats, persuading the uncommitted and subtly reminding the bought men of their obligations. He did not oppose a committee, believing it would be more manageable than the whole house, and persuaded the Members to pass the matter to the existing Committee of Security rather than elect a new one. He was pleased when the Directors appeared before it to press their demands. "I hope it shall turn to our advantage," he told Carstares, "for this does plainly make appear that (they) proceed by way of humour, and have no regard either to the honour of the King or the satisfaction of his servants."

When the Committee reported to Parliament the debate became a formality. There would still be an Address, a sop to the self-respect of the Estates and the pride of the nation, but it was now easy to turn it from a protest into a declaration of loyalty. The resistance of the Company's party had been broken by the bribes and threats of the King's servants, and Seafield retired exhausted from the battle, leaving the rout to the light cavalry of Argyll and Marchmont. The Address was rephrased and accepted unanimously. The sting had been removed and there was now what Marchmont called "an Address to His Majesty in such terms as shall please him." It thanked William for his gracious assurance that the kingdom's trade would be suitably encouraged, and it humbly recommended the Company to his favour, without suggesting how he might bestow it. Argyll sent copies of the original and final version to Carstares in Flanders. "You'll see it clipped as much as possible of what might choke," he said. "It is now in the King's power to establish his servants who have always been faithful to him." And that, in the opinion of those servants perhaps, was all that really mattered.

Throughout autumn and into early winter the Company's

committees were engaged, in a desultory manner, with preparations for a second great expedition to Darien, and they were in no
haste to send a ship with those supplies the Council had so
urgently demanded in letters from Madeira. In September the
Rising Sun arrived from Amsterdam, dropping anchor by Greenock on the Firth of Clyde. There she would stay for months,
her bare yards black against the water of the Gair Loch and the
snow-hills of Dunbarton. At one time it had seemed as if Scotland
would never see this fine ship with the emotive name, upon
which Willem Direcksone had expended such skill and art. When
the ice melted and released her from his dock, the Company's
Dutch creditors had detained her against the money owing them.
The Company had sent Stevenson orders to sell her and realise
what he could, but she had been saved by generous advances
from some of the richer stockholders and by the prospect of a
second call on the subscribers at Martinmas.

In Edinburgh it was as if the great orgasm of the fleet's
departure had left the Directors listless and benignly unconcerned. They were late for meetings at Milne Square, if they
attended at all, and it became necessary to fine them sevenpence
if they were not there promptly at nine, and to withhold their
sederunt fee of twenty shillings entirely if they could not arrive
before a quarter past. There were other distressing matters.
James Smith, thought to be safe in the King's Bench Prison,
London, escaped therefrom one night with the aid of his gaoler
and was never to be seen again. Dr. John Munro was troublesome, complaining that although he had worked two years for
the Company, and had brought his family from Caithness to
Edinburgh at great expense, he had received no salary at all. The
Directors may have been unimpressed by his protestations of
loyal and diligent service when they discovered that the apothecaries who had supplied medicines for the expedition, and whose
accounts he should surely have settled, were now clamouring for
their money. Erskine and Gleneagles also wanted to be paid for
their expenses in Hamburg. And finally there were English and
French ships lying in the Forth and Clyde, taking on bonded
servants and provisions for their own plantations, to "the manifest prejudice of the Company".

There was no news of the fleet, no reason for hope or despair, no encouragement and no dismay. But the spirit of the nation was high. At his print-shop in Parliament Close, James Wardlaw published *A Poem upon the Undertaking of the Royal Company of Scotland*.

> Admire the steady soul of Paterson;
> It is no common genius can persuade
> A Nation bred in war to think of trade.

"I represented how sad and scandalous our condition was"
Caledonia, January and February 1699

Don Andrés de Pez, General Commanding the Windward Fleet of His Most Catholic Majesty, was troubled by wild rumours from Spain, by the indecision of the Council of the Indies in Madrid, and by the failure of the provincial governors to realise that his splendidly-styled squadron was in a lamentable condition. Apart from the tenders, he had four warships only, and when they finally sailed from Carthagena at the beginning of January they could limp no further than Portobello. There, he said, they would have to stay. His flagship, and one other, leaked so badly that they would have to be careened before he would take them to sea again, and this work could not be completed before April. The maintenance of the fleet, which was Spain's only defensive force on the Main, was costing 8,000 pesos a month, and this did not include the pay of the soldiers in the tenders. Don Andrés had been given no exact account of the strength of the Scots in Caledonia, and he was alarmed to hear from Spain that a second expedition had already sailed to reinforce them.

Since it would be madness to take his tenders and his two sound ships out of Portobello for an attack by sea, he proposed a sensible alternative to the Conde de Canillas, President of Panama. He would bring 500 of his soldiers over the Isthmus to Panama City, and they, together with all the men the President might gather, could attack the settlement from the south. The Conde accepted the proposal, not because he believed it would be possible to destroy the Scots, but because, as he later explained to his King, "we should alarm them, and let them know that in this kingdom there was force and inclination to oppose them." Having thus excused failure before trying for success, he mustered two companies of gentlemen volunteers and waited for de Pez.

The expedition was miserable, wretched and useless. The soldiers and the volunteers were carried eastward by boat along the southern coast of the Isthmus until they reached the Gulf of San Miguel. There, at the mouth of the River Savana, was waiting a cloud of Indian levies in whose canoes the Spaniards were to travel into the heart of the Isthmus. Once the stores were loaded, however, there was no room for men, and the soldiers had to march along the bank, sweating in the moist heat, hacking desperately at the thick undergrowth. Leaving the river they entered the jungle, moving northward and climbing. In the foothills of the continental divide, with tall, green mountains rising before them, they reached Toubacanti. This was an outpost which the President had established three months before upon the first news of the Scots' arrival. A crude, palisaded fort, it was manned by four companies of militia under Campmaster Don Luis Carrizoli, and they now brought the strength of the expedition to fifteen hundred men. Still not sure that he was strong enough to engage the Scots, the President decided to advance over the mountains. Each man was to carry a basket containing rations for ten days, as well as his arms and ammunition. Though he thanked God for the fine weather, de Canillas remembered the nightmare misery of that march.

We had first to cross a river shut in between cliffs and full of boulders. We could not avoid it, and had to march through the actual bed of the stream. It took two days and the men were much knocked-up, because of the weight of the supplies to which was added that of muskets, arquebuses and rifles, bags of shot and fifty balls which the soldiers carried loose. The most lamentable part of it was the men fell frequently, which wet the food they carried. . . . We came to the end of the river, which is at the foot of the southern slope, and despite the fact that the men were much exhausted, lest the subsistence give out entirely at dawn next day we began to ascend the range, which is extremely impenetrable. We mastered it in that day's march and reached a very marshy place, only two leagues distant from the enemy's settlement.

The Divine favour, which the President believed had sent them good weather, now deserted them. That night it began to rain, and the river which fed the marsh turned it to flood, washing away the shelters which the soldiers had built. It rained for three days without ceasing. A party of Negro slaves who arrived on the second day from Toubacanti, with baskets of sodden biscuits and cheese, were half-drowned and terrified by the loss of their lances. There was now no spirit in the soldiers. They had marched fifty leagues from the Gulf of San Miguel and the country frightened them. Most of the men brought by Don Andrés were lately come from Spain, and the memory of the dry, red earth of their homes was an exquisite torment in this green ocean of leaves. The Indian levies, who may have been enjoying the misery of their masters, told them that the Scots had laid cunning ambuscades ahead. At night, from vespers until dawn, they heard the regular thumping of a gun from the settlement, and believed that at any moment there might be a volley of musketry from the dark trees. By day they crouched on the earth, unable to dry their arms and ammunition, staring at the rain-cloaked mountain heads, and praying for the order to be gone. Their officers passed the time in fruitless councils of war. The President had lost his voice from exposure and exhaustion, and the others could talk of nothing but how they might save both their lives and their honour.

At Caledonia, since the departure of Edward Sands' sloop, little had been done to finish the town and the fort, and nothing at all to break the land. In the irritation of the heat and the persistent rain, the Council was still quarrelling childishly. With Cunningham gone, said Paterson, there was now a need to elect a new member, or even more. "I represented to them separately how sad and scandalous our conditions was." Without a powerful majority, which would be possible if the Council were enlarged, there could be no hope of authoritative government, an end to factional bickering and a beginning to their proper business. He won Jolly and Montgomerie to this point of view, and they agreed to support his motion. But both were weak men. Montgomerie had a young and inexperienced soldier's admiration

for Thomas Drummond, and he may have been reluctant to provoke the man's dislike if the new member were not one of the
Glencoe Gang. He was also influenced by Mackay who, cur-
rently in Pennecuik's favour, was inclined to do what pleased the
Commodore. Montgomerie withdrew his support from Paterson,
whereupon Jolly, who was President that week, lost his courage
too and quashed Paterson's motion before it could be put, there
being no seconder.

Robert Jolly had his troubles. Like all the Councillors, except
the self-sacrificing Paterson, he lived aboard ship, having comfortable quarters on the *Caledonia.* He liked to think he was an
honest, plain-spoken man, and certainly he was frank enough
about his own importance. He sometimes thought that he was in
command of the ship, or that at least his office empowered him
to give orders to her captain. Robert Drummond endured this for
the length of his patience, which was invariably short, and then
told Jolly that since he was master of his own ship the Councillor
could take himself, his baggage, and his servant ashore. Jolly
lordly refused, and went off to a meeting of the Council. While he
was away, he later complained in a pathetic memorial, "Captain
Drummond caused to break down all his apartments, so therefore
Captain Jolly was obliged to go aboard the *Unicorn.*"

The Council was angered by this affront to the dignity of one
of its members, although Pennecuik maliciously reminded Jolly
that his soft-headed intercession had prevented the Drummonds
from being put ashore at Crab Island. He was advised to lay a
formal complaint against Robert Drummond but he refused, lest it
be thought, he said self-righteously, that he desired the command
of the *Caledonia* for himself. His quarrel with Drummond was
further embittered by a dispute over an invoice for the goods
aboard the ship, in which each appeared to be accusing the other
of theft. It was a complicated, confused squabble of which the
details are not important, only the sadness that men with such
responsibility should have been concerned with such trivialities.

Paterson's great dream of a trading *entrepôt* had come to this,
and what opportunities there might have been at the beginning
were now lost. Wafer and others, perhaps even Paterson, had
warned the Company that the Colony would need weatherly
ships for coastal trade, but the Scots ships were of little use to

windward and were thus idle in the harbour when they were not actually imprisoned in it by the northerly gales. The few North American ships and the Jamaican sloops that came curiously to the Colony had provisions to sell and goods to trade, but none of them, as the Council ought to have realised from its experience with Moon at Saint Thomas, wanted anything from the fleet's bizarre cargoes, certainly not at the rate of exchange the Scots were still asking. They preferred money. Gold was something the Company had not thought of sending, nor could have sent.

At the beginning of February, when the gales began to moderate, it was decided to send the *Dolphin* on a cruise to Curaçao and Saint Thomas, to trade for a sloop, rum, sugar and provisions. Paterson opposed the decision. On the voyage out, he said, the snow had proved to be the worst of all to windward. It was also unwise to send, as was proposed, both Pincarton and John Malloch, the new captain of the *Dolphin*. What could be done by both could be equally well done by one, and the Colony had few good sea-officers. Finally, their present circumstances were bad enough without sending so much valuable cargo to sea on a hazardous adventure. "But to all this I was answered in the usual form, that I did not understand." The *Dolphin* sailed, with Pincarton and Malloch, a good crew and a cargo of trade goods worth £1,400 Sterling.

A few days later Richard Moon's sloop came into the bay. With him was his partner Peter Wilmot, and neither of them wished to sell or trade. They had come to recover the provisions bought from Sands, declaring that the goods given him in exchange could be bought at less the price in Jamaica. Moon said little, perhaps being ashamed of the matter, but Wilmot insisted that the Scots had over-valued their goods by forty per cent, and that if they would not make the balance good he would take back the provisions. After some clamours, said Paterson, the Council offered thirty per cent, which Wilmot accepted. "He would not let us have any more of his provisions at that rate, but parted with us, complaining that he should be a loser. It vexed me not only to see us part with such a parcel of provisions, but also for the effect it might have to discourage others."

Any rise there had been in the Colony's morale was lowered by this, and it dropped still further when Captain Pedro sent word that the Spaniards were about to attack the settlement. It had been known for some days that they were in the timbered hills to the south, and the gun which had been fired at regular intervals during the night from the battery on Forth Point had been designed to keep up the Scots' courage as much as to frighten the attackers. Now Pedro said that they were within two leagues of the bay. There was an immediate alarm, drums beating the Assembly inside the fort, trumpets sounding aboard the ships. The Council met, and for once wasted no time in quarrelsome debate. James Montgomerie was elected to lead one hundred soldiers to Pedro's village, and Robert Drummond was ordered to muster sixty fit men from the crews of the *Saint Andrew*, *Unicorn* and *Caledonia* and to follow Montgomerie as soon as possible. "If you shall be attacked by an enemy before you join him," he was told, "you are hereby ordered to take or kill such as wrongfully attack you." The small force of soldiers, and the use of sailors as a reserve, suggest that fever and sickness had seriously weakened the military strength of the settlement. Neither Thomas Drummond nor Samuel Vetch was given command of the expedition, and though this may have been due to Pennecuik's stubborn hatred of both, more probably the Council decided that they would be better used in the defence of the peninsula if Montgomerie were overwhelmed.

Montgomerie left at dusk on February 5 and reached Pedro's village before midnight, his men exhausted by the weight of their arms and ammunition, their thick uniforms, the marshy ground beneath their feet and the tangle of branches before their faces. On their way they met two frightened Indians who said that the Spanish had already taken possession of the village. Montgomerie halted, and sent the Indians to make certain. When they did not return he pressed on valiantly, and found the village deserted except for a group of wailing women. An hour later Pedro came in, happy to see the Scots in arms at last, and said that about 26 Spanish soldiers, with fifteen or more Indians and Negroes, were camped in a plantain grove a few miles off. He made no apology, nor explained why he had earlier reported that there were three hundred of them. These were frightening enough, and the courage of Captain Diego, who arrived shortly afterwards, was no bolder. When he was told that the Spanish had posted no sentinels

Montgomerie detached forty men to guard the village, and advanced cautiously on the grove with the rest of the company and a large party of Indians. He arrived on its outskirts toward five in the morning, and although the sun was rising it was still dark beneath the thick roof of leaves. He drew up his sixty men in an extended line with bayonets fixed and muskets cocked, intending a sudden, surprise attack. This resolute action restored the courage of the Indians on the flanks and to the rear of the Scots, and they hooted in defiance. Surprise was lost. Montgomerie ordered his drummer to beat, and led his men in a threshing advance. The Spaniards were gone when they reached the clearing, their fires still burning, their meagre provisions abandoned. Montgomerie ordered his hungry men to take what they wanted, and wondered what next he could or should do. A decision was made for him by a spatter of musketry ahead where Pedro's screaming warriors had come up with the Spaniards' stubborn rearguard. Montgomerie's drummer again beat the advance and the Scots went forward. They saw no enemies in the mist, in the slanting columns of sunlight, only the flash of muskets. And then there was silence. The Spaniards were gone.

In the growing light, young Montgomerie calmed his Indian allies and counted his dead and wounded. In the mud he found the bodies of Ensign Alexander Swinton and a private soldier called Andrew Jaffrey. Two more officers were wounded, a sergeant and nine men, including Drummer James Forbes who had beaten the advance in the confusion of the plantain grove. That night in Pedro's village, Montgomerie wrote a proud report to the Council. He did not put his own name among the list of wounded, but admitted that "I'm a little hurt myself in the thigh." The Spaniards had taken to the hills and he did not think it safe to pursue them, for there was a larger force there which, he was told by the Indians, was intended for an attack on the settlement. He was impatient to know what to do, "not doubting but your care and speedy measures will prevent any danger we may be in by the smallness of number." The council recalled him to the Peninsula, and he went back in triumph.

In fact the Conde de Canillas had abandoned any design he may have had for an attack, and the Spaniards whom Montgomerie had routed had been a thin rearguard with orders to watch rather than fight. High on the green ridge of the cordillera, drenched by mists and rain, their stomachs knotted by wet bread and rotting cheese, the Conde's dispirited men could scarcely stand. At the interminable councils of war his officers quarrelled and protested, accepting the inevitability of retreat but delicately jealous of their honour. The confusion was at last resolved by a company commander from the Panama garrison, Don Juan Martinez Retes de la Vega. Thirty-one years of campaigning in Flanders as soldier, sergeant and officer, from the siege of Charleroi to the withering crossfire in the breach at Maastricht, had proved his courage and honour and taught him a simple lesson: the wisest soldier, the best soldier was he who knew when to retreat. Moreover, His Majesty would be well served by a withdrawal, for if they remained the Conde would lose an army and thus be robbed of future victories it would undoubtedly win. "And that this is his feeling," wrote the clerk who was taking down Don Juan's words for later dispatch to Madrid, "and what he offers as his opinion, he declares and swears by God our Lord, and the sign of the Cross which he made with his own right hand." Other officers, including Carrizoli, hurriedly supported de la Vega, and the Conde gratefully ordered a retreat to Toubacanti, to the coast and Panama City. When he sent his report to the Council of the Indies he wisely said nothing of the skirmish with Montgomerie's men.

Cheered by their small victory, the Scots still lived in fear that one morning the blue and yellow of Spanish uniforms would appear out of the trees to the south. It was partly this fear, and partly their naïve belief that no one could contest their presence once their right to Darien had been reasonably explained, that persuaded the Councillors to make a civil approach to the Spanish. They sent formal letters by the Indians to the Conde de Canillas and the Governor of Santa Maria, informing both of the nature of their settlement and its proper establishment by Act of the Parliament of Scotland. They enclosed safe-conducts for any Spanish officers who might come to treat, and asked for the return of similar courtesies. They said that they had a Spanish prisoner, Domingo de Bada who had been taken by Montgomerie on his return to the peninsula, and "whom we have and will continue to treat with all kindness and civility." De Bada was no soldier, a frightened merchant who had been trading with the Indians, and from fear or simple conviction he had told the Council that all the people of the Spanish colonies were delighted by the arrival of the Scots. He did not say why.

With the letters on their way, the Colony was certain that it was safe from attack, at least until a reply was received. The long rainy season was now slackening, though the ground was still sodden and life ashore still wretched. But the sun was bright, and sometimes shone for a whole day without a single cloud. Four days after Montgomerie's fight, the watchman on Point Look-out cried two ships to the north-west. They were Jamaican sloops, one commanded by Edward Sands and the other by his friend Ephraim Pilkington. Despite the orders of their owner Wilmot, or perhaps in defiance of them, they had brought a small quantity of provisions which they were willing to sell. Beyond this, they were ready to put their ships at the service of the Colony, Pilkington to trade along the coast and Sands to go turtling. Paterson was delighted, aware that both men were doing this more out of regard for him than respect for the Council. Two days later, two more Jamaicans arrived, and their masters were less obliging. One of them had a cargo of provisions consigned to Paterson, and the other had beef and flour to sell. They were "purse-proud fellows", said Paterson, and when the Council havered over the price they said that they would sell for money only. They broke off the bargaining and turned their attention to what Paterson believed had been their main purpose in coming, the salvaging of treasure from the *Maurepas*. They were ordered away, and they sailed with the provisions still in their holds.

Pilkington was gone on his commission, and his departure encouraged the Council to send out the *Endeavour*. She sailed with John Anderson as Master, Alliston as supercargo, trade goods worth £100 Sterling, and ambitious orders to touch at Jamaica and New York for provisions. Gales and storms drove her leaking hull back to Caledonia.

There was a listlessness over all the settlement, sometimes too heavy for despair. Thomas Drummond drove his men hard to their work, but got no more energy from them than damnified bread and rotting meat could supply. Paterson was unwell, a steel spirit that had been bent by the death of his wife was now bending further under sickness, but he would not spare himself. "I had then some fits of intermittent fever; but, however, I put force upon myself as much as possible to be present in the Councils, lest some rash act be committed or an innocent man suffer." His mind, reaching the point of collapse, was bewildered by the squabbling of the other Councillors, and since he still would not drink he could not join them on the occasions their carousing gave them a brief and obscene unanimity. They met ashore more frequently now that it was dry, beneath the palmetto roof of the largest hut, sitting with comic dignity in their embroidered clothes, their swords and baldricks, sweat on their unshaven cheeks. There had been a great quarrel between Pennecuik and Mackay over some forgotten issue, and the others moved to and from each other in the macabre dance of their factional disputes. There were only five of them, and they still would not accept Paterson's urgent advice to increase the number.

Though the Indians brought welcome gifts of fruit, plantains and fowl—which were eaten by the Council and officers—Andreas and Pedro no longer came to the peninsula, and there were rumours that both were dead. Ambrosio sent occasional messages of continuing goodwill, but would not leave his village. Diego was persuaded to come, late in February, for gifts and the signing of a treaty that had been written by Hugh Rose, sealed with bright red wax, and tied with ribbon of watered silk.

TREATY OF FRIENDSHIP, UNION, AND PERPETUAL CONFEDERATION, agreed and entered into between the Right Honourable the Council of Caledonia, and the EXCELLENT DIEGO TUCUAPANTOS and ESTRARA, Chief and Supreme Leader of the Indians, Inhabitants of the lands and possessions in and about the rivers of Darieno and Matoleme. . . .

It promised freedom of trade, mutual assistance in danger, succour in distress, courts of justice, and an explanation of all its clauses should they be in future doubt. It also invited the other chiefs of the Isthmus to apply for membership of the alliance. It was read aloud, interpreted and explained to Diego, and then signed by the Council. Diego put his mark to it happily, and went away with a copy in Spanish. He left with a warning. "He advises us," Pennecuik wrote to a friend in Scotland, "to prepare for the worst, believing that the Barliavento Fleet, as soon as they are in a condition, will be upon us. But this we do not fear, being assured that their General, who is said to be a man of no courage, had positively denied to attack us, his master the King of Spain having no war with the Scots."

Apart from being a natural braggart, the Commodore had also been reassured by a dispatch the Council had just received from Don Luis Carrizoli, the militia commander at Toubacanti. With elegant politeness it thanked the Scots for their letters which he would forward to the Governor and the President. Until he heard from them he would naturally suspend his activities against the Colony, and would not molest its emissaries. The Scots could dispose of Domingo de Bada as they thought fit, and thus "God preserve you, Illustrious Council, whose hands I kiss. . . ."

Warmed by the courtesy of the letter, the Council did not see that it was a mere acknowledgement from a postmaster, a franking of their own letters. Nor could it be known that, far to the north in Mexico, Don Joseph Sarmiento de Valladares, Conde Moctezuma, Viceroy and Captain-General, the most powerful man in the hemisphere, had recently received news of the settlement and had made up his mind what to do about it for the glory of Spain and the salvation of the Church. "These orders, unless something new changes them," he would soon write to his commanders, "will be to exterminate the Scottish pirates for the reasons which have dictated my resolution, the greatest one being to destroy the heresies which the Scots may introduce amongst the ignorant people." Sarmiento was less confident than this breath of fire might indicate. The Isthmus was the unguarded heel of the empire, and the past of Drake and Morgan had shown how few men were needed to cut the tendon of its rivers and roads. He had been told that there were already four thousand Scots on Darien, and that six thousand more were at sea to reinforce them. In a wild moment of alarm he believed that even the Philippines might be in danger.

Still waiting for his ships to be careened at Portobello, Don Andrés de Pez might have wondered what he was expected to do about that.

The Scots' hope of an amicable settlement with the Spanish was not only worthless, it was also short-lived. On February 26 Ephraim Pilkington came back with his sloop, the *Maidstone*. He had not sold a bolt of cloth, a wig, or a pair of darned hose along the coast, and this was not the worst of what he had to report. The *Dolphin* had been taken by the Spaniards, he had seen her in Carthagena Bay.

Paterson had been right in his warning. The snow was clumsy to windward and impossible to handle. Within twenty-four hours of leaving Caledonia a strong gale drove her eastward to Carthagena, and despite Malloch's efforts to turn her out to sea she would not respond. She struck a rock in the lee of Pointa de Canao, throwing Pincarton against the helm and breaking one of his ribs. Badly holed and leaking quickly, there was nothing that could be done with her but take her in to the shore and under the guns of the fort. As she went aground and heeled over, her crew knew what was now awaiting them. A shouting crowd gathered on the esplanade below the white city, and soon the Governor came down in a gold and varnished coach. He sent out a boat to the crippled ship, and Pincarton went ashore first, his ribs strapped and his mouth bitter with humiliation. He asked the Governor if his men might return to the *Dolphin* to save her cargo, and Don Diego de los Rios Quesada, who was probably still shocked by her sudden and unexpected arrival, gave him that permission.

"But before we could get to the boats," said Pincarton two years later, reporting to the Directors whom he had never expected to see again, "we was hindered from going on board, and sent up to the town with a strong guard, and separately put in a dungeon and in irons."

"If a man were sick, no victuals for him that day..."
Caledonia, March and April 1699

The Councillors' reaction to the loss of the *Dolphin* was both splendid and ridiculous. As if they were the government of a powerful nation, with a fleet and ready battalions to enforce their will, they demanded the immediate release of the ship and crew under pain of their terrible displeasure.

Lieutenant Alexander Maghie, because he was a smart young fellow said Pennecuik, was sent to Carthagena with this demand. He left aboard the *Maidstone* on March 11 (his departure being delayed by the usual argument in Council) with a drummer, a guard of honour, and a flag of truce. In the letter he carried, the Spanish Governor was reminded of the treaties signed by Great Britain and Spain in March and July 1670, by which each was bound to respect the rights and subjects of the other. If the *Dolphin* and her crew were not released, if Mr. Maghie suffered any indignity whatsoever, then Caledonia would "by force of arms, both by sea and land, set upon, take and apprehend any of the men, ships goods, moneys and merchandise of His Catholic Majesty."

Maghie was ordered to wait twenty-four hours for a reply, and then to leave with or without it. He returned to the Colony ten days later, his Highland blood inflamed by several affronts to his country's honour and his own pride. He had gone ashore at Carthagena in a canoe, his drummer beating at his side and his flag of truce in the prow. A file of soldiers marched him through the sun to the Governor's house, and there he was kept in an ante-room until the Governor and his council found the time and inclination to receive him. Don Diego broke open the letter, read it quickly, scowled at its threats of reprisal and bloodshed, and threw it to the floor. It was joined, unread, by a copy of the Act which Maghie next gave him, and by copies of the Letters Patent granted to the Company. The Scots, said Don Diego when he could find his voice, were rogues, pirates and cuckolds, and he called for a guard to throw this one into prison. The soldiers were at the door when Don Martino de Saballe, commander of the Spanish forces at Carthagena, gently interceded for Maghie, asking the Govenor's leave to lodge the boy that night at his own home. Don Diego grudgingly agreed.

De Saballe was a kindly man, or perhaps more subtle than the Governor. He was impressed by Maghie's spirited courage, and reasoned with him in Latin, their only common language. He suggested that if the Scots did not insist upon the return of the *Dolphin*'s cargo (which he would not admit the Spanish had salvaged) he might persuade the Governor to release her crew. In the morning, however, Don Diego's humour was no better, and was worsened by Maghie's loyal but tactless demand to see Pincarton and his men. Not only could they not be seen, shouted the Governor, they would stay in prison for as long as the King's Majesty pleased. Moreover, had his soldiers been in a better condition—and this, no doubt, with a resentful eye on De Saballe —he would long ago have driven the Scots from Darien. But let them not take too much comfort from their present security. He was fully resolved, Maghie reported, "to gather such a force by sea and land as would quickly, at one blow, root us all out of this place."

At least the young Highlander was allowed to leave, and for that he probably had De Saballe to thank. In Carthagena harbour were the flagship and three others of Benbow's West Indian Fleet, and before the *Maidstone* sailed Maghie paid a courtesy call on the Admiral. John Benbow had as yet received no orders from London about the Scots, and saw no reason why he should ruffle the Spaniards' feathers, particularly since he was at this moment selling them a cargo of Negro slaves. Yet he was civil to his angry visitor, politely read the Company's Act which Maghie carried like a talisman, and generously wished the Company well. He said that he would press none of its servants into his ships, and would do what he could for the *Dolphin's* crew. "At my going over the side he said we had a great opportunity before us, and bid us remember that fortune always favours the bold." All of which could only have confused Maghie. He had been told by De Saballe that Benbow had assured the Governor that the King of England disapproved of the Scots settlement, and would not support or protect it.

The Councillors now had the choice of stomaching the Governor's insults or honouring the threats they had made. To his surprise, Ephraim Pilkington was invited to take the *Maidstone* out on a reprisal raid against Spanish shipping. The Letters of Mark, signed by Jolly as President, were attractive enough: twelve full shares of all booty for the hire of his sloop, and two and a half for himself, 600 pieces of eight or six slaves for any of his crew seriously disabled, and the choice of one in three of all the prizes taken. Though no man of war, there was little profit for

Pilkington in Caledonia Bay, and he accepted. He left on the next favourable wind, captured nothing, sank nothing, saw nothing, and was back in the harbour within a few days.

The only comfort in Maghie's return had been that the *Maidstone* brought with her a New England brigantine she had sighted off the coast, east of Caret Bay. This was *The Three Sisters* which Scots sympathisers in New York had fitted out and loaded with salt mackerel, butter and flour for their countrymen on Darien. This scanty cargo would not last more than a few days, but the realisation that they had not been forgotten raised the settlers' spirits for a short while. There were now several trading-sloops in the Bay or at anchor off Golden Island. Moon and Wilmot had returned in one called the *Neptune*, and with them another commanded by a Matthias Maltman. They still demanded money only for their provisions, but sober, reasonable men might have persuaded them to accept goods. There were no such men on the Council now: even Paterson was fretful, captious and disillusioned. Pennecuik was fighting a nagging illness with brandy, his temper ragged, his mind dark with suspicion. He quarrelled with Moon almost immediately, accusing him of carrying off one of the colonists on his last visit, a homesick boy called Skelton. He arrested one of Moon's boats, declaring that he would hold it and its crew until the boy was returned. There then followed a heated wrangle, boats going to and fro across the Bay with ultimatums like emissaries between warring camps. Ashore, the Planters watched this tragi-comedy with bewildered apathy, their skins yellow and scabrous for want of the good food in the ships' holds. Paterson called upon some inner reserve of strength, persuaded Moon to give up the boy and Pennecuik to be content with an apology. It all ended, he said, "in a little hector and Billingsgate".

But it had not ended. Daniel Mackay, who had been ill with a fever for some days, now returned hot-faced to the Council for his week as President. Still delirious, he said that Maltman's sloop was sailing under a Spanish commission, and that there were three Spanish merchants aboard her at this moment. He demanded the Councillors' signatures to an order authorising Robert Drummond to arrest the ship, her master and her crew, as a reprisal for the imprisonment of Pincarton and the insufferable insults to young Maghie. When Paterson protested, Mackay turned on him in fury. "I'll warrant you'll not meddle," he shouted, "because your friend Wilmot is concerned!" Paterson surrendered and reluctantly signed the order. Away went Drummond's boats from the *Caledonia*, with a great show of swords, muskets and pistols. They found no Spanish commission, only papers that plainly indicated that the sloop was truly a Jamaican. Hiding in her hold, however, were two frightened Spanish passengers whom Maltman was carrying to Portobello. Drummond brought them off in triumph, together with £100 in pieces of eight which he found in Maltman's cabin. The Council appropriated the money, using it to pay the master of *The Three Sisters* for his mackerel and butter, but Paterson was miserably unhappy.

"I said that I would write home about this matter, and then left them. God knows, my concern was not upon my own account, or any humour of my own, but the true love of justice and the good of the Colony."

Recognising that an excuse might be needed for this little act of piracy, Pennecuik said that Maltman's crew were a "parcel of barbarous fellows". They had recently raided a Spanish island to the leeward of Carthagena, captured a rich friar in his cell, whipped him, and hung him up by the heels until the blood was black in his face. Which may have been true, but scarcely supported the claim that Maltman was sailing under a Spanish commission.

Ashore in the rotting huts of New Edinburgh there was increasing horror. "Our men did not only continue daily to grow more weakly and sickly," said Paterson, "but more, without hopes of recovery." By the beginning of March there were two hundred graves in the cemetery, and now ten or twelve new ones were sometimes dug in a day. In Samuel Vetch's company there had been twenty-three Gentlemen Volunteers of whom one only, Roger Oswald, was still alive. The survivors, yellow skeletons in torn scarlet, stared at each sunrise with surprise, unable to explain their hold on life or understand their comrades' loss of it. One surgeon, Herries, had left with Hamilton. Another, Andrew Livingstone, had been captured with the *Dolphin*, and a man could now fall sick and die before Hector Mackenzie or his over-

worked assistants could be told that he was ill. The best a man
might hope for was that his friends would be strong enough to
dig him a grave, that he would not be left unmourned, his body
thrown into the bay when the water-boats went back to their
ships. There is now no way of knowing which of many tropical
fevers it was that daily weakened and reduced the demoralised
settlement. Patrick MacDowall, who would bring a ship to the
relief of the second expedition next year, wrote a clinical account
of the illness he survived.

It was a very severe spotted fever, my whole body being
entirely pale red. My extremes was worst and some places
about my wrists and ankles altogether red. But all was
without either itching or inflammation or any sort of exturb-
ance above my skin. I had an hellish, vicious, bad, intoler-
able taste, so that everything I took was with the greatest
reluctance imaginable. I had, in the beginning, an extraordinary desire of vomitting, and accordingly drunk warm
water which did make me vomit up some base, yellowish,
bitter, unpleasant choleric sort of stuff of which I found great
ease. I continued very ill for four or five days. I took with it
a great headache, soreness of my eyes, and weariness of all
my joints and bones, which continued all the time with me. I
was very inclined to fainting all the while of my sickness, and
a considerable time afterwards it brought me so extraordinary weak that I am not yet able to walk alone now. I
had blistering plasters applied to my neck at the time of my
sickness, and other plasters to my temples, of both of which
I found very much good, but our Doctor would neither bleed
nor vomit me, though I was still very pressing to have both
or either done.

A few men remained loyal to the hope and enthusiasm they
had brought with them from Scotland. Lieutenant Robert Turnbull had fallen in love with this land, with a devotion that
neither hunger nor despair could destroy. As late as April he
wrote to his friend, Erskine of Carnock, in language of extravagant hyperbole. Darien was a green paradise where fruit fell
from the trees without the pain of plucking them, where magnificent forests ran with gentle deer, where the songs of bright-

feathered birds sweetened the evening air above rivers of silver-scaled fish. He believed in this Colony. He longed for "honest Councillors" who would make it a success, men such as his friends Thomas Drummond and Samuel Vetch. He was not just a dreamer. He urged Carnock to tell the Company to send nets for fishing, sensible working-tools, more kettles, coarse harn for tropical clothing, and good shoes, many shoes "for this country burns them". And if women must come, let them be those who knew how to cook, to launder, to nurse the sick.

But most of the settlers had long ago lost any interest they might have had in the land or the Colony. Like Roger Oswald, they wished only to survive, to be gone, to return home. Afraid of his stern father in Lanarkshire, Oswald could not tell him of this misery and despair. He wrote instead to his cousin Thomas Aikman, a Writer in Edinburgh, hoping that he would explain to an unrelenting parent. He was penniless, he said, and like most of the others was thus without the means or influence to buy more food. The salt mackerel brought by *The Three Sisters*, the turtles caught by Edward Sands and sold at five pieces of eight for every hundred pounds, may have come in a "happy hour" for Penne-cuik, but it would seem that few of the ordinary Planters and Volunteers shared in this happiness. They lived on two pounds of flour a week. Two pounds by the Company's weighing, said Oswald, which meant one pound only, and "if it had been well-sifted you would have got a quarter of a pound of mouldy maggots, worms and other such beasts out of the same." Beef, on the rare occasions it was issued, was "as black as the sole of my foot and as rotten as the stump of a rotten boot." Sometimes a handful of dried peas was shared amongst five men for their daily allowance. "When boiled with a little water, without anything else, big maggots and worms must be skimmed off the top of the broth as ever scum is taken off a pot."

In short, Sir, a man might easily have destroyed his whole week's allowance in one day and have but one ordinary stomach neither. . . . Yet for all this short allowance we were every man (let him never be so weak) daily turned out to work by daylight, whether with the hatchet, wheelbarrow, pick-axe, shovel, fore-hammer, or any other instrument the

case required, and so continued until 12 a clock, and out at 2
again and stayed till night, sometimes working all day up to
the headbands of the breeches in water at the trenches. My
shoulders have been so wore with carrying burdens that
the skin has come off them and grew full of boils. If a man
were sick and so was obliged to stay within, no victuals for
him that day. Our Councillors all the time lying at their ease,
sometimes divided into factions and, being swayed by particular interest, ruined the public.

At least Thomas Drummond, driving half-starved and sickly
men to work in this fashion, could claim that their labour was not
wasted. By the beginning of April, the palisades of the fort were
finished and thirty guns were mounted in its embrasures. Twenty
more had been dragged up to the land batteries on the points.
Across the neck of the peninsula had been dug a great ditch,
twenty feet deep and twenty-five wide. Yet this was all that had
been done in five months. There was no land broken, no
plantations sown, no trade established, no goods sold, no town of
consequence built, no parliament elected, no government but the
meddlesome rule of five quarrelling men. The Councillors no
longer had the respect and confidence of the settlement. Oswald
called them "superlative Doges", and was probably repeating
the general gibe. When he left Edinburgh he had been placed
under the protection of Robert Jolly, but "I was never a straw
obliged to him, though he promised great things to my father."
Worse than this neglect, Jolly had taken from him a sow and four
sucklings, the loss of which he remembered bitterly in his hunger.
Oswald did not know why the Almighty should grant him his
life and yet take it from others, but he praised and thanked God
for this mercy. "Though I preserved my life, yet I kept not my
health. I was troubled with fever and ague that I raved almost
every day and it rendered me so weak that my legs were not able
to support me.... Our bodies pined away and grew so macerated
with such allowance and hard work that we were like so many
skeletons."
Drunkenness increased, there was no shortage of spirits or
wine, and a cunning man could get all that he wished. A little
was medicine, enough was solace, and excess was suicide. The

Council issued brandy as a bribe, and sometimes as the only reward it could give. Toward the end of March a bearded, exhausted white man was brought into the settlement by a party of Indians, and it was some time before the Scots realised that this horrifying caricature of their own form was Andrew Livingstone, the surgeon who had sailed with the *Dolphin*. How he had escaped and travelled from Carthagena no one recorded, and perhaps his bewildered mind could not remember, but in recognition of the courage he had shown he was given four gallons of brandy "for his own proper use, over and above the common allowance". Since wine and brandy assured the oblivion of temporary stupor, and for some a peaceful slide into death, Paterson had little success in his efforts to persuade the colonists to abstain altogether. He promised them that the price of the allowance would be placed to their credit in the Company's accounts, but only one man—an officer called Gordon—accepted the offer. He was still petitioning for the money many years later.

Faced by the smouldering hostility of the settlement, and aware that it must be placated before it burst into a flame of mutiny, the Councillors finally decided to increase their numbers. Even this decision was not made without dispute and sulks. Since his recovery from a fever which all but he had thought would kill him, Daniel Mackay had been noisily active in Council, and it was during his week as President that he persuaded Paterson (who needed little persuasion) and Pennecuik (who must have needed a great deal) to move and second a motion to appoint four new members to the Council. Mackay's suggestion was not disinterested. It had been decided earlier that *The Three Sisters* should leave as soon as possible with letters for Scotland, and Mackay was anxious to carry them, but while there were so few of them it would have been unwise for one of the Councillors to go. When the motion to increase was put by Paterson, James Montgomerie protested without explanation and withdrew in a huff. Robert Jolly also objected, arguing with obscure logic that the smaller the number the greater the ease of government and the wiser its rule. Moreover, since no Councillor would receive a salary until the Colony was well established and thriving, it would be improper to involve the Company in extra expense. Receiving no support for this paradox, he also withdrew. "Although we sent our Secretary several times," said Paterson, "entreating them in a friendly and respectful manner to give their attendance and assistance in Council, yet they refused, and altogether forsook us." They were both tired of the Colony and wished to go home.

With doubtful legality, the remaining three voted on the motion themselves. The new men were probably suggested by Paterson, accepted by Mackay who knew that they would be happy to see the last of him, and hopelessly opposed by Pennecuik. They were all officers—Thomas Drummond, Charles Forbes, Colin Campbell, and Samuel Vetch. The Glencoe Gang now dominated the Council, and although Montgomerie had once been their comrade-in-arms at Fort William and one of their faction in the Colony, he still would not come to the Council. He was perhaps jealous of them, and resented the fading of his little battle-honour before the blaze of their red coats.

The increase in numbers brought no harmony to the Council. Supported by Vetch, Thomas Drummond did not hide his contempt for Paterson, and was the instrument of his brother's hatred of Pennecuik. Though they were bitterly concerned for the condition of their starving men, Forbes and Campbell had no skill in debate or government, and their only value to the Council was that their presence restored a little of the Planters' respect. Not sure that he could survive an open breach with the Drummonds, Pennecuik began to quarrel with Mackay. The Commodore divided all men into "brave boys and lads" or "lubberly rogues and rascals", and he had recently moved the Highlander from the first to the second category. He remembered that Mackay had once taken Pincarton's part against him in some childish dispute, that on another galling occasion he had persuaded him to apologise to Jolly and invite the lubberly rogue to dinner. When Ephraim Pilkington brought the *Maidstone* back from her fruitless cruise against the Spaniards, Pennecuik reminded the Council that he had opposed the idea of reprisals and that Mackay had hotly supported it. He badgered the sick man at every meeting, wasting hours in abuse and recrimination. He opposed the motion that Mackay should carry dispatches to the Company and then, realising that the vote must go against him and that he would thus have a vengeful enemy abroad in Edinburgh, he shamelessly put about and came up on another tack. He visited Mackay's sick-bed with blustering good cheer, pressing upon him a letter of recommendation to the Directors in which he asked that Mackay be given a guinea a day should he travel home through England, and that they bear all his expenses while he was in Scotland. Mackay cynically accepted the letter, and their uneasy friendship was restored. There were suspicions later of a darker compact between them.

The Councillors now met regularly ashore, in Paterson's hut or one shared by the officers. They could be seen through its open walls, wigs removed and coats loosened, the air thick with tobacco smoke to fight off clouds of insects, Mr. Rose's pen scratching at paper, and the noise of shouting voices. No longer separated from the colonists by the water of the bay and the closed door of a ship's cabin, they lost some of their august superiority, and were seen and heard to be what they were—jealous, contentious and human. This, as much as a growing discontent in the Colony, led to the first of several seemingly unrelated incidents that took the settlers and the seamen to the end of their ragged patience and a sad and abortive mutiny.

Encouraged by the presence of their officers on the Council, some of the Planters went hopefully to the door of the hut and asked for more food. If their miserable rations could not be increased, they said, then the Colony should be abandoned. Pennecuik blandly told them that there was not a month's supply left in the ships, and therefore not enough to provision them for a withdrawal. He refused to accept the proposal, which was supported by other Councillors, that the stores should be brought ashore from the *Saint Andrew* and lodged in the fort, confident that Robert Drummond would allow none to be unloaded from the *Caledonia*. The Planters went away confused by what sounded like a sentence of death, and they were further angered when Robert Jolly, hearing of the Commodore's reply, came out of his sulky retirement and said that there were enough provisions for three months at the present allowance, not including the oatmeal set aside for the sick.

The Commodore denied it, and no one could persuade him to release an inventory of the stores aboard his ship. He was acting altogether strangely. His seamen were filling the water-casks of the *Saint Andrew*, and a rumour quickly spread that he intended to weigh anchor and leave the settlement to starve. Robert Drummond believed it, and with the same concern for his own safety ordered the *Caledonia*'s casks to be filled and the ship put in trim for sailing. When both vessels began to take ballast aboard, John Anderson of the *Endeavour* hurriedly did the same. Ashore, the Planters watched in stupefied amazement, and the Council did nothing.

"About this time," wrote Jolly in his memorial, "Captain Pennecuik invited aboard several of his best and trustiest friends to whom, after dinner, he proposed that, seeing victuals were like to be expended and ships destroyed, he thought it most expedient that the *Saint Andrew* and the *Caledonia*, well-manned and provided with provisions, should be fitted out for a design." This design, it was implied, would be a privateering cruise, but to those best and trustiest friends—and to the rest of the colonists when they heard of it—it sounded like desertion and cowardice. Pennecuik hurriedly withdrew the suggestion, protesting that he was thinking only of the good of the settlement. The affair had a paradoxical effect on morale. "The greatest number of the Colony," said Jolly, "were positively inclined that rather than forsake the place before they have recruits, or hear from Scotland, that they will be satisfied with the quarter or third, yea rather than sail, half abatement of their ordinary allowance of provisions." It was a noble declaration of faith, but it made hunger no easier to endure.

The only sea-captain who showed any concern for the sick and the starving was William Murdoch, Pincarton's first mate, who now commanded the *Unicorn*. When the others were taking on water and ballast, he ordered his yards to be stripped and the ship prepared for careening, hoping that the men ashore would understand that he did not intend to desert them. He and his crew also volunteered to take their boats out in search of turtles, and invited the other ships to join them, but they, said Jolly, "busied in fishing the French wreck and catching of small fishes with their twined nets, appropriated all they took for themselves." The *Unicorn*'s boats had extraordinary luck, sometimes returning at sunset with a dozen or more great turtles, one alone being enough to feed a hundred men on the peninsula.

Murdoch had a rough integrity, and a stubborn wish to do what his "honest Captain Pincarton" would think was best for his ship and the Colony. "I stood in defence of the ungrateful Company's interest," he would write with pride seven months later, "and in support of the Colony against their Glencoe Council when few of their men of honour had the soul to do it." He sympathised with Jolly, now aboard the *Unicorn*, and with Montgomerie, and when both were formally expelled from the Council he bluntly declared, with more generosity than justification, that they had been unfairly treated. He detested Pennecuik whose sole ambition, he thought, was that "the world might hear of his grandeur". He had called Cunningham a "greeting beast", and now, when he heard of Mackay's wish to carry the dispatches home he made no secret of his contempt for the Highlander's "vain stomach". Understandably, he was popular with his own crew only, and the grateful Planters ashore. His innocent involvement in the mutiny was a disaster for him, and ended his loyal service to the Colony.

He heard of it one evening when he returned with his turtling boats. Going aboard the *Endeavour* to take a glass of wine with John Anderson, he found the master alarmed and troubled. One of Pennecuik's officers, said Anderson, had that day approached him with a scheme to take over the *Saint Andrew* with drawn swords and bent pistols, and to sail her out on a buccaneering cruise. Though Anderson had refused to join the plot and had reprimanded the officer (whom he would not name), he was reluctant to inform the Council, thinking, perhaps, that Pennecuik might somehow be involved. "I told him that it was dangerous to conceal it," wrote Murdoch, "and that I going aboard presently should have the opportunity to declare it to Captain Jolly, which I did." Jolly advised him to keep a good watch, and that if any of the other ships attempted to clear the bay he should open fire on them with the *Unicorn*'s guns. According to his own memorial, Jolly then told Montgomerie and Paterson of the plot, but the Council's report, which Paterson signed, said that he kept the information to himself. Probably he did, in the machiavellian hope that Pennecuik would be brought down and disgraced when the mutiny failed.

A few days later, the Council ordered Murdoch to beach the

Unicorn for careening and to put all his crew ashore in the fort. Though he had intended careening her himself, he decided that this must be an attempt to prevent him from opposing the *Saint Andrew*'s departure. His stern sense of duty, his respect for the only government of the Colony, albeit the Glencoe Gang, would not permit him to refuse an order. He resigned his command instead and told the Council that he would serve it no longer. He asked permission to go aboard the *Maidstone* or *The Three Sisters*, and to leave for Scotland with whichever sailed first. Jolly and Montgomerie, fearful of their safety ashore, were already aboard Pilkington's ship.

The President of the week, Daniel Mackay, invited Murdoch to Sunday breakfast, which he refused. There followed an invitation to dine, which he again refused when he saw that the other guests were all members of the Highlander's clan. He lost his temper with Mackay and told him that neither flattery nor bullying would change his mind. "On Monday the Council sent for me and flattered me which I took little notice of, upon which Mackay produced my saucy note, as he termed it, and called me a hundred rogues, rascals and villains. I was remanded about and told they would force me to serve them." At ten in the evening of the next day he was again called before the Council, accused of disobedience, and placed under guard in the fort. Jolly, who had also been summoned, wisely pleaded illness, but it did not save him. A file of musketeers took him out of the *Maidstone* and across the bay to the *Caledonia* where Robert Drummond "used him like a dog" and locked him in the surgeon's cabin. He was accused of taking aboard the *Maidstone*, as his own property, half a hogshead and two ankers of brandy, as well as a cask of Madeira, all the rightful property of the Colony.

In the confusion of evidence, the deliberate obscurantism of its reporters, the truth of this miserable comedy cannot now be discovered, for each man recorded only what he thought to be true, or what he wished the Company and his countrymen at home to believe. Yet it is possible that Murdoch came closest to understanding when he said that he was kept a prisoner until Mackay sailed for Scotland "lest I should force a passage with him and spoil his embassy."

On April 11, still weak from another attack of fever, Mackay went aboard *The Three Sisters* and left with her before sunset. The dispatches he carried from the Council, the sad letters home, had one common theme—an appeal for help, for food, for reinforcements. Those that were private were also bitter with complaint against the Council, the idle Lords, the Doges, the Glencoe Gang. Murdoch, who knew something of these complaints, and who would be in Scotland when the letters should have been delivered, later hinted at that compact made between Mackay and Pennecuik at the moment of their reconciliation. He said that Mackay opened many of the letters on the long voyage home, and destroyed those "that gave account of the truth." But by the time of writing this his hatred of Mackay was venomous, and it may have clouded his good sense. "Wherever I meet him, if he was guarded by the ghost of the great Mackay, and all the Macraws and Mackays in the Highlands, it shall not save his carcass."

Throughout it all William Paterson had been weakly acquiescent. Sick, tired, closer still to losing his reason and unmercifully bullied by Pennecuik and Thomas Drummond, he signed all that was placed before him. But his conscience was troubled. When Murdoch was released from the fort, five days after the sailing of *The Three Sisters*, Paterson went to him and wept. "He hoped I would not take in ill part his pronouncing that unjust sentence against me," said Murdoch, "the Council had obliged him to do it to please Pennecuik." He begged Murdoch to reconsider his resignation, and to take service with the Colony again, but the seaman refused.

On April 17, Jolly was also released, and he joined Montgomerie and Murdoch aboard the *Maidstone*. Jolly said that seamen from the *Caledonia* came aboard the ship at night, asking Pilkington for rum and sugar, offering salt-blackened coins which they had fished from the French wreck. The *Maidstone* sailed in the afternoon of April 20, but the wind fell once she was clear of the harbour and she was forced to drop anchor. Before sunset, the *Caledonia*'s pinnace came up under the sloop's stern, demanding Murdoch's presence at a Council meeting aboard the flagship. He went with reluctance, and upon an assurance that Pilkington would wait for his return.

He discovered that the plot he had long ago reported to Jolly had now been betrayed to the Council by one of the conspirators, a midshipman. He and three others—the boatswain, gunner and gunner's mate of the *Saint Andrew*—were in irons and accused of resolving "in a most barbarous manner and with cocked pistols to attack the officers thereunto belonging, as likewise for nailing up the guns on the battery and other mischievous and horrid designs tending no less than the ruin of the Colony."

When he appeared before them, the Councillors told Murdoch that they had but discovered the plot that evening, yet were disturbed to learn that he had known of it for some time and had not laid information against it. He stared at them with astonishment. "I could not forbear laughing to see a heap of rogues sitting magistrate-like to examine about that which they themselves had hatched." He meant Pennecuik, who he was blindly sure had been responsible for the conspiracy, but remembering the *Maidstone* waiting for him beyond the harbour he controlled his anger and his amusement and told the Councillors all he knew. Mr. Rose took down his deposition, and Murdoch insisted that the secretary sign each page, "that I might not be tricked." When Murdoch, growing bold, began to accuse them of making ill use of the information he had given Jolly, they dismissed him, saying they had no complaint against him.

At the ship's side, Pennecuik plucked at Murdoch's sleeve and invited him to take a valedictory bowl of punch, believing no doubt that here was another departing enemy whom drink might transmute into a friend, or at least a submissive servant. They were joined by Robert Drummond, who offered the use of his cabin and could thus be present to hear all that was said. By the fourth bowl, Murdoch was angry and disgusted with them both. He said that he believed Pennecuik to be at the bottom of the mutiny, and he asked Drummond for a boat to carry him back to the *Maidstone*.

She sailed at dawn, the guns on Forth Point firing a salute as she cleared the headland. The sound was muffled by the heavy air. The rainy season had begun again.

"There was none of us but would afterwards be ashamed. . ."
Caledonia, April to June 1699

A Parliament was at last elected and called. It was too late to be
effective, and most of the Council had long been cynical about its
value. "We found the inconvenience of calling a Parliament,"
Mackay had written to Roderick Mackenzie, "and of telling the
inhabitants that they were freemen so soon. The thought of it
made them insolent and ruined command." But it was that
insolence and insubordination which finally made a parliament
necessary, if only as a token to stiffen the spirit of the colonists
and persuade them that they were not servants but partners in
the noble undertaking. The election was held toward the end of
April, eight representatives chosen in the rain from eight ill-
defined districts of New Edinburgh. Watching under guard from
the palisades of the fort, Murdoch had been delighted by the
open annoyance of the Council when the Caledonians rejected its
nominees and elected "an honest subaltern or soldier rather than
a knavish captain". Admirable though this was as an expression
of political enlightenment, it would before long be fatal to the
Colony.

The delegates were called on April 24, and met beneath the
dripping roof of the largest hut in New Edinburgh. Under the
guidance of the Council and the presidency of Captain Colin
Campbell, they enacted thirty-four Rules and Ordinances for the
government of the Colony, the establishment and execution of
justice. Those settlers who were not working crowded about the
hut, drenched by the rain, listening to the reading of each clause
and the voting upon it. The Preamble, as read by Hugh Rose,
gave "the Council and Deputees assembled in Parliament" the
right to appoint its president, clerk and officers, and to govern
under the following ordinances and rules which had "the full
force and effect of laws within this Colony and its dependencies
by land and sea."

It was clearly affirmed that such laws were based on the
precepts, examples, commands and prohibitions of the Holy
Scriptures, and the Caledonians were warned that blasphemy,
profanity and disrespect toward the Colony's officers would be

punished by hard labour and a diet of bread and water. Hard labour at the public works would also be the punishment for slander, quarrelling and brawling. Death was the penalty for murder, rape, robbery, house-breaking, treason and correspondence with the Colony's enemies. It was also the just punishment for mutiny and sedition, disobedience and the violation of the Council's safe-conducts, for duelling and assault (be that only the striking of another with a stick, whip or sheathed sword), for kidnapping and the abuse of a freeman's liberty. More constructively—and here Paterson's liberal mind can be detected at work —the civil rights of the Caledonians were defined and protected, proper justiciary courts and juries ordained, their duties laid down. No man could be imprisoned for more than three months without trial. The property of a freeman could not be restrained for debt unless there were proof of intent to defraud. No judge or juryman could sit upon a case in which he was in any way interested. Corruption, bribery and the perversion of justice were to be punished as theft, but "benefits received, good services done, shall always be generously and thankfully compensated."

The first act of the eight Members reflected the mood of the men who had elected them. They appointed a committee to search all the ships for provisions, to make a correct inventory of them, and to organise their transfer to the fort. Both the *Caledonia* and the *Saint Andrew* were found to be well-supplied, and their fortunate crews living above the meagre rations of the Landsmen. Pennecuik and Robert Drummond were outraged by the search, declaring that their word alone should have been enough, and although the masters of the *Unicorn* and the *Endeavour* obediently sent their provisions ashore, the Commodore and his truculent Vice-Admiral delayed and finally did nothing.

The food supplies (though "spoiled and rotten" said Paterson) proved to be more than the worst that had been feared, but what there was could not last long. Few men were strong enough for the arduous boat-work of turtling, and the Indians rarely came now with gifts of fowl and plantains. When the *Maidstone* sailed, Pilkington had promised to direct any merchantman he sighted to the Colony, and to return himself as quickly as he could with beef and flour. But the days passed and no one came.

In the bay was a sloop which had come with the *Maidstone* on her first visit, and which Pilkington had left behind in the Colony's commission, without crew or master. The Council and Parliament now decided to send it to Jamaica with what money there was. It would also carry letters. Lying in his hut, sick and desperate with fever, Paterson asked the surgeon to bleed him and so give him the strength and clear mind to write to Roderick Mackenzie.

> I hope ere this comes to hand that Scotland will be suffi-ciently concerned and busy to support us who are now at the head of the best and greatest undertaking that ever was to the Indies. I assure you that if they do supply us powerfully and speedily we shall in a few months be able to reimburse them all and make the Company the best fund of any in Europe, but if through poorness of spirit, and little humour and jealousies, as well as delays, this little thing should be neglected, then what we have sown others will reap the fruit of, which I hope not to live to see.

In the clear mind that wrote this there was perhaps more delirium than the fever into which it once more relapsed.

The sloop left on May 3 under the command of Henry Paton, second mate of the *Unicorn*. He was told to buy what food he could with the money given him, and to return with all haste. There followed days of spiritless lethargy, of unending rain that washed the earth from the palisades of the fort and turned the mean streets of New Edinburgh into runnels of mud. The Council quarrelled with Pennecuik, and gave no advice or direc-tion to its despised Parliament. A French sloop came, with orders from the Governor of Petit Guaves to examine the wreck of the *Maurepas*. Her master did this indifferently, sold the Colony a few provisions, and then left. When he was gone the Caledonians must have asked themselves if the man were a fool, or had been amusing himself maliciously at their expense. He had told them that he admired this country for its riches and benign climate, that he would come and live among them, and so would five hundred other Frenchmen.

About the middle of the month, desperate for information and food, the Council sent out a piragua. It went eastward along the coast and was back within the week with news that stunned the Colony. It had spoken with a Jamaican sloop and begged her master to sail to the Colony. He would not, and why he would not was plain in the printed sheet which the piragua brought back to the Council. On Sunday, April 9, Sir William Beeston the Governor of Jamaica had published a Proclamation he had signed the day before.

IN HIS MAJESTY'S NAME and by command, strictly to command His Majesty's subjects, whatsoever, that they do not presume, on any pretence whatsoever, to hold any correspondence with the said Scots, nor to give them any assistance of arms, ammunition, provisions, or any other necessaries whatsoever, either by themselves or any other for them, or by any of their vessels, or of the English nation, as they will answer the contempt of His Majesty's command, at their utmost peril.

The unprecedented publication of such a proclamation on the Sabbath was explained on Monday. Two sloops, freighted with provisions and about to sail for Darien, were stopped before they could clear Port Royal.

Throughout all the English colonies, from the border of French Canada to the Caribbean, Governors and Lieutenant-Governors had issued the same Proclamation in obedience to orders sent them by James Vernon. The reasons given by the Secretary were that His Majesty had been unaware of the true intentions of the Scots, that the colony of Caledonia was contrary to the spirit and the word of the treaties he had signed with his allies, that Darien was possessed by His Most Catholic Majesty and therefore the settlement was a breach of the Company's Act and of England's friendly relations with Spain. The phrasing of such fine-edged, diplomatic hypocrisy was one of Mr. Vernon's most adroit exercises in clerking. He and his royal master were well aware that in September, 1697, the English Commissioners for Trade had advised the King that Darien was not possessed by Spain, that it ought to be seized by the Crown of England "with all possible dispatch lest the Scotch Company be there before us, which is of utmost importance to the trade of England."

The news of the Proclamation destroyed what was left of the colonists' morale. They could now expect no supplies, no food, no relief. They believed that England's unequivocal hostility explained their countrymen's failure to reinforce them. "That the long silence," said Paterson, "proceeded from no other cause but that they were brow-beaten out of it, and durst not so much send word to us to shift for ourselves." Their miserable failure and hopeless future were now plain even to the most optimistic. They were weak and hungry, and only a few had escaped fever and flux. Of the twelve hundred who had left the Forth ten months before, between three and four hundred were now dead. Forty more lay in the dungeons of Carthagena, or might well be dead too for all the Colony knew. There was nothing to show for their work but a ridiculous huddle of huts and an uncompleted fort. They were ruled by quarrelsome men who wasted their time in ignoble intrigues. It was raining, and would rain for another six months. Their shoes were rotten, their clothes ragged, their skins itched with inflamed sores, they could scarcely swallow their maggot-ridden food. For weeks they had wished to be gone, and now this Proclamation persuaded them that they might go without dishonour. Through their honest subalterns and soldiers in Parliament they demanded to be taken away.

So properly expressed, the demand could not be dismissed as insubordinate and mutinous, and on the Council there was none but Paterson to oppose it. Thomas Drummond had been suffering from an intermittent fever since March, and before his election he had asked for, and been refused, leave to return to Scotland for the good of his health. Though his self-respect was injured by the thought of surrender, his family pride wounded by his brother's belief that the Colony should be abandoned entirely, he was now contemptuous of the wretched colonists and agreed that the settlement should be deserted, if only temporarily. The other soldiers on the Council accepted his leadership. Paterson again had himself bled, and came bravely from his bed to fight the motion.

When I saw there was no talking against our leaving the place, I persuaded them what I could, that first rumours of things of this nature was always most terrifying and that happily our native country knew nothing of all this; and if they did not, but remained firm to the design, there was none of us but would afterwards be ashamed of our precipitant forwardness in going away upon this occasion.

He was told that the Landsmen were too ill and weak to defend the ditch or the fort, that if there were a Spanish attack they would be over-run. He agreed, but suggested instead that the colonists should be taken aboard the ships, which might then lie off the coast until help arrived from Scotland. The Council seemed to agree with him, and issued orders for the loading of the ships. Not unnaturally, a rumour spread that the settlement was to be abandoned and that the fleet would return to Scotland. Paterson protested, demanding a public denial, but the Council said nothing, and it is probable that Pennecuik and Robert Drummond intended to make all sail for home once their ships were clear of the bay. By the beginning of June the Colony was demoralised and disordered, without proper leadership or clear decision. Paterson struggled to prevent the general unease from becoming panic, putting "lets and stumbling-blocks" to the obvious preparations før departure. He said that when Henry Paton returned from Jamaica the sloop should be manned by thirty of the fittest men, cruise off the coast, "and live upon turtling and fishing till we should see if any recruits or news came from Scotland." He volunteered to remain with it. Thomas Drummond supported the proposal, but said that he would stay. Paterson should go home and tell the Company how matters stood with its noble undertaking.

And then, on June 5, Paterson's weakened body collapsed, his mind fled into the wildest delirium yet. The next day a French ship came into the harbour, and her captain brought terrifying news. He had come from Carthagena, he said, where a new Governor had recently arrived from Spain. This man had placed his predecessor, Don Diego, under arrest and was mounting a great force of ships and soldiers against the Colony. Now the last of the Scots' resistance crumbled into panic, officers and men fighting for a place in the boats on the shore. By June 10 most of the company commanders, and all of the Councillors with the exception of Paterson and Drummond, were aboard the ships with their servants and baggage. Little attempt was made to organise the evacuation, and it took a week of mounting fear and confusion. The Planters boarded what ships they could, angrily demanding that they set sail at once. The guns which had been mounted in the fort would have been abandoned but for Thomas Drummond. Gathering a few men by force and threat, he tore a breach in the palisades that had cost so much in labour and death, and dragged the guns down to the boats, standing by with an armed guard until they were ferried out to the flagship.

Ashore in his hut, in a delirium for most of the time, soaked by the rain that ran through the roof, Paterson was ignored. "None visited me except Captain Thomas Drummond, who, with me, still lamented our thoughts of leaving the place, and praying God that we might but hear from our country before we left." Though Drummond had little respect for Paterson, and was usually scornfully impatient with him, he recognised the sick man's courage at this moment and honoured it with his loyal attention. In one of Paterson's rare periods of consciousness, the grenadier captain brought him news of a disquietening rumour aboard the *Saint Andrew*. Pennecuik, it was said, had no intention of sailing to Scotland. He proposed a cruise along the coast as buccaneers, saying that since the Scots had been called pirates and were certain to be hanged as such if caught by the English or Spanish, they should take what profit they could and be damned. Moreover, if the ships went home to Scotland the seamen need not expect an ungrateful Company to pay the wages owing them. Paterson sent a desperate message to the other Councillors, imploring them to meet him ashore and to place Pennecuik under guard if the report were true. None came, and those who troubled to reply said that they were too ill to leave the ships.

Paterson remembered little of the last two or three days. On June 16 he was hurriedly carried aboard the *Unicorn*, probably by Drummond or Turnbull. His few articles of clothing, the sad relics of his wife's possessions, were brought out that night, "almost all of them damnified and wet, which afterwards rotted most of them." Like a thwarted child, he vainly asked for several brass kettles and sixteen iron pots, loaned to him by a friend in

Jamaica and now left behind in the ruins of his hut. He became angry in his fever, demanding the immediate payment of £72 Sterling which he had spent on sugar, tobacco and resin for the Colony. In such a mood of sick petulance did he leave his great dream for ever.

On the morning of June 18, a northerly wind making it impossible for them to sail through the sea-gate, the *Caledonia*, *Unicorn* and *Endeavour* were warped out of the bay. They lay by off Forth Point and Thomas Drummond was rowed across to the *Unicorn* from his brother's ship. He brought papers which he was anxious for Paterson to sign. "I was very ill and not willing to meddle," remembered Paterson, "but he pressed it, saying there could be no quorum without me. Upon this I signed." He could recall little of what the papers said, but he thought there were orders for the ships to sail to Boston or Salem in New England, for the Councillors aboard to sell what goods they could for provisions, and to carry the remainder to Scotland. Pennecuik's bold scheme for a buccaneering venture, if indeed he had truly proposed it, was forgotten. They were going home.

When Drummond got back to the *Caledonia* a sunset gale blew her and the *Endeavour* out of sight to sea. Ineptly handled by her weary crew, the *Unicorn* was struck broadside by a wave that smashed her long-boat in the waist and tore her away from her bow anchor. She ran in to the lee of Golden Island where she dropped another from the stern and rode out the night in danger and fear. The next morning the *Saint Andrew* was sighted to the east, under full sail and making for the open sea. She ignored the *Unicorn*'s signal and was soon hull down. Without the strength to weigh anchor, the *Unicorn* cut her stern cable and followed.

Behind in Caledonia Bay were left decaying huts, muddy tracks, the slipping palisades of Fort Saint Andrew, and six men. Too exhausted to fight their way to the boats, they had been left to die at their own request. "Poor silly fellows," Roger Oswald called them, having crawled to the shore himself, "who being so weak did not dare adventure themselves to sea." The Indians, who had watched the departure of the ships with sad incomprehension, came out of the trees and offered them shelter. These six men would have been surprised to know that they, alone of all the colonists, would later be admired and respected by their countrymen.

Some weeks later a Spanish brigantine slipped cautiously into the bay. Her captain, Juan Delgado, went ashore and wandered among the ruins of a hundred empty huts. He counted the twenty-four embrasures of the fort and a dribble of cannon-balls by the breach in its palisade. He counted the graves too, four hundred in battalion ranks and two inside the fort. He sent an armed party into the forest. It came back with four frightened Indians and a white man, one of the abandoned Scots. Delgado treated him with gentle kindness.

Before they left, the Spaniards destroyed what they could of Fort Saint Andrew and burnt the huts of New Edinburgh.

"Most of them dead, the rest in so lamentable a condition"
Jamaica and New York, July to October 1699

Robert Drummond's orders, as signed by a quorum of the Council on June 18, had been to make the best way he could "in company with the rest of the ships". He waited for none of them. Yet the little *Endeavour* was able to keep the *Caledonia's* top-sails in sight for twelve days, and sometimes come within a cable's length of her stern, despite a dying crew and timbers that threatened to split under every wave on her larboard quarter. On July 1, her master, John Richard, made desperate signals to Drummond, asking for help. The pink's mainmast was sprung and she was taking in water forward. Without waiting for a reply, Richard ordered his crew and his frightened passengers into the boats. As the *Endeavour* went down by the head, Drummond reluctantly put his ship about and picked up the survivors. Most of them would soon wish that they had been mercifully drowned.

Two hundred and fifty Planters had crowded aboard the *Unicorn*, lying below decks on the rotting mockery of useless trade goods. Before she left the lee of Golden Island her water had turned sour. Her provisions, the smell of which made starv-ing men retch, would scarcely support half the numbers aboard, though death would soon balance that accounting. Waiting in the bay, her crew had caught the fever and the flux brought aboard by the Landsmen, and now she could muster no more than half a dozen seamen to a watch. John Anderson, who had been given command of the ship when Murdoch left, put the fittest Landsmen to work aloft and below, and crowded on as much sail as

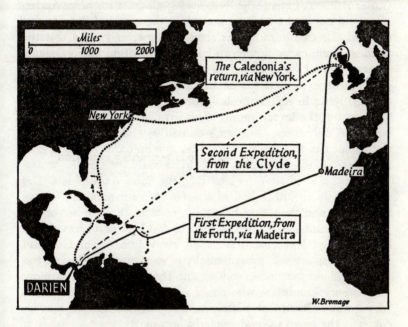

the weather would allow. That weather was bad, skies of awful thunder-heads, sudden squalls, changing winds that could send men into the shrouds three or four times within an hour. South of Jamaica the *Unicorn* came up with Henry Paton's sloop, on its return voyage to Caledonia. The two ships lay close, their masters shouting across the heaving seas. The *Unicorn*'s news was plain by her presence, by the white faces of the haggard men at her rail, and Paton reported no more than had been expected. Because of Beeston's proclamation, he had left Port Royal without provisions. The weather parted them, but the sloop put about and followed the *Unicorn* like an uneasy dog.

That night a violent gale struck both ships. The sloop weathered it, but the *Unicorn* lost her foremast and mizzen top and sprang so many leaks that her waist was awash. Anderson ordered all but the unconscious and the dying to the pumps. By dawn the sea was calm, the wind soft, and in the pellucid light of a fine day the *Unicorn* was astonished to see the *Saint Andrew* two leagues off, her mainsails set and the sun golden on her stern. Closer still was Paton, silently ignoring all cries for help. Anderson could not haul up his main courses, the signal of distress, but he fired the two guns which should follow, and upon this the *Saint Andrew* came slowly up and lay by within half a league. Anderson went away to her in his boat, hoping that she would give him men to clear his decks and rig a jury-mast. Pennecuik was ill, lying in his cabin and peevishly indifferent to all misfortunes but the impertinence of his own sickness. He refused to help, and only after Anderson's entreaties and the insistence of Councillor Colin Campbell would he sign an order to Paton, telling him to stand by and give what aid he could.

When the wind rose the next day, the *Saint Andrew* left. The sloop remained within hail of the *Unicorn* for another twenty-four hours, and then, said Paterson, "notwithstanding her orders in writing, and Paton's repeated oaths to Captain Anderson that he would not leave us, they sailed away from us at fair daylight." It was a week, providentially of calm weather, before the *Unicorn* could get under way again. There were now not more than twenty Landsmen who could stand on their feet, Anderson having driven them mercilessly to the pumps while his seamen cut away the wreckage and erected a jury-mast.

It is possible that the *Saint Andrew* could have given no help even had her commander been willing. Her seamen were as weak as, if not weaker than the *Unicorn*'s. All her sea-officers were dead or dying, and she was soon commanded by Colin Campbell. Resolute soldier though he was, he knew more about picquet-guards and enfilade fire than he did about binnacles and whip-staffs. Shadowed by a wary cruiser from the Barliavento Fleet, she was seven terrible weeks at sea before she came in to the lee of Jamaica and dropped anchor off Blewfields. The fever brought aboard in Caledonia Bay had burnt furiously below her stinking decks. One hundred and forty men had died in the passage. Somewhere, some day or night, Robert Pennecuik had joined them, carried from his fine cabin in a canvas shroud, thrown overboard with the minimum respect and ceremony due to a member of the Council and Parliament of Caledonia, a Commodore of the Fleet of the Company of Scotland. In none of the letters and journals of the survivors is there any regret for his death.

"I know not in all the world what to do," Campbell wrote to his friend Rorie Mackenzie, "for I am certain the seamen will mutiny and play the devil, for they have not a week's bread, and besides they expect to have their wages here... They are the damnedest crew that I ever saw, for such of them as are not lazy are most confoundedly mutinous."

Uncharitable though his opinion was of these sick and starving men who had brought him to a safe landfall, Campbell did his best to find them food. He went ashore and took horse to Port Royal where, in a fine white house above the fort, Sir William Beeston welcomed him cordially. A glass of wine, a pipe of tobacco and an exchange of courtesies, however, were all he was prepared to give the Scot. "He could by no means suffer me to dispose of any goods for supplying my men, although they should starve." Apart from the orders he had received, Beeston was also afraid of the Spaniards who had been taking reprisals against Jamaican merchantmen, in the outrageous belief that there was no difference between an Englishman and a Scot. They had attacked a sloop off Crab Island, blowing away her master's jaw-bone as he swam from his ship, detained two more in Carthagena, and robbed another of her cargo of slaves. Beeston knew that the angry shipmasters of his island would not tolerate any help being given to the *Saint Andrew*. But he was not without sympathy. "The Scotch are quite removed from Caledonia," he reported to London, having carefully questioned Campbell, "most of them dead and the rest in so lamentable a condition that deserves great compassion."

Stifling his bitter pride, Campbell then called on John Benbow whose fleet was at anchor in the harbour. The Admiral would give him no provisions and no help in bringing the *Saint Andrew* to a safer anchorage at Port Royal. The Company's agent in Jamaica, Doctor Blair, was a frightened man and pleaded illness as an excuse for not receiving Campbell.

Thus the Scots were forced to beg or steal. Their ship rotted where they had brought her to anchor, the sick without attention and the daily dead pushed hurriedly into the bay. Many of the crew deserted, taking ship with merchantmen or the bitter alternative of Benbow's fleet. For want of bread to eat, the Landsmen who could struggle ashore signed themselves away as bonded servants to the plantations. Few, if any, would return home again. Campbell lived out the summer aboard the ship, rejecting advice to lay her up in harbour while he still had men to handle her, hoping for relief from Scotland. That autumn there was a virulent epidemic throughout the Caribbean, and no island escaped it. On Jamaica it was the worst the English had known, and the thin and yellow skeletons aboard the *Saint Andrew* were helpless before it. "The Scotch that came from Caledonia," reported Beeston, "are so many dead that at last they are forced to lay up the ship for want of men to carry her away." Campbell went ashore, living on charity and on drafts which Blair finally honoured. He still believed that relief would come.

The *Caledonia* reached New England in seven weeks, dropping anchor at Sandy Hook on August 8. She had lost one hundred and five men on the voyage, and eleven more died before she came up to New York two days later, foul with the smell of death, vomit and excrement. Of the hundred and fifty still alive, a third were sick, including the Drummonds and Samuel Vetch, and the remainder weak from exhaustion. Until he went down with fever, Robert Drummond and his officers had driven their crew and passengers with a pitiless brutality which the survivors remembered more vividly than the endless gales, the groans of the dying, and the prayers that were cried in the night. Three Scots merchants of New York, who went aboard the ship when she arrived, met afterwards in shocked horror and wrote a passionate letter of protest to Scotland.

Was there ever a more horrid barbarity than in the passage they exercised toward their poor men, who no sooner fell sick but were turned out on deck, there exposed to most violent rains; and though the most of their provisions consisted in flour, yet they whose distemper was the flux must have nothing but a little sour oatmeal and a little water, nor their share of that neither. When they complain, to condole or comfort them—sweet Christian-like consolation!—"Dogs! It's too good for you!" Their visits from officers and surgeons were, in the morning, questioning, how many are to be thrown overboard? Answer 4, or perhaps 5. "Why," reply they, "what, no more?"

Aboard the *Unicorn* conditions were worse, though from sickness and over-crowding, not brutality, for Anderson was a compassionate man. Making little way under her jury-mast, and leaking badly, she was driven westward of Cuba and then beat to windward along the coast until she found shelter by the port of Matanzas. Anderson took his pinnace ashore in a green bay to look for water. He found instead a Spanish fort, with twenty-four guns gaping from its walls. He managed to escape under a spatter of musketry, but left behind Benjamin Spense who had had little opportunity to exercise his skill in languages and now stepped forward to greet the Spaniards in their own tongue. Anderson got the ship out of the bay with great difficulty, pursued by an armed piragua and the rolling fire of the fort's guns.

Northward went the *Unicorn*, past the Florida Keys and up the coast of Virginia, running ashore several times and hauling off by some miraculous strength of will and body. On August 13 she reached Sandy Hook, and the next day came in to New York. "Under God," said Paterson, "owing the safety of the ship and our lives to the care and industry of our commander, Captain John Anderson." With a leaking, dismasted ship he had indeed served the Company well, but at a high cost. Sixty of the hundred men left aboard were sick or dying. Councillor Charles Forbes had been turned over in Matanzas Bay, out of range of the Spanish guns. There was not a captain, lieutenant or subaltern left, and few of their soldiers. "We lost near 150, most of them for want of looking after and means to recover them, in which condition we had no small loss and inconvenience by the death of Mr. Hector Mackenzie, our chief surgeon." He had died, said Paterson who loved him, as a result of "his unwearied pains and industry among the people on shore as well as on board, for many weeks together."

But these things Paterson would not write for months yet. He was now gravely ill and could do nothing for himself, nor be removed from the little cabin built for him. From the moment he had been carried away from Caledonia he had slowly relinquished his interest in life. All had gone—his wife, a dream, his friends and companions, and it is possible that he felt so deep a responsibility for the omnipresence of death that he fled from it into silly regret for the loss of some brass kettles and iron pots. In a little while even these were of no importance. His spirit was still, his eyes clouded, his mind gone. The same three Scots who had visited Drummond's ship later came aboard the *Unicorn*. "The grief has broke Mr. Paterson's heart and brain," they said, "and now he's a child."

Recovering from fever and writing to his brother William, Samuel Vetch had no sympathy for Paterson. He said that all misfortune and disaster might be blamed on the man's "knavery or folly or both". Robert Drummond, also recovered and writing his first report to the Directors, blamed no one by name and Providence only by implication. The responsibility for any future calamities, he further implied, might well be the Company's. "I am afraid I shall have a hard pull to get the ship home, for my people are still dying, being all weak: and men is very scarce here to be had.... With God's help, fourteen days or three weeks hence I design to put to sea. I am not capable by writing to give you an account of the miserable condition we have undergone, first before we came off Caledonia, being starved and abandoned by the world, as also the great difficulty of getting the ship to this place."

The claim that he might put the ships to sea within three weeks was insanely optimistic, and perhaps he did not believe it himself. He could scarcely muster enough seamen to make one crew for the Atlantic passage, even should he be able to provision the ship. And the matter of provisions was his greatest problem. There was a strong Scots settlement in New England. The principal traders of East and West Jersey, Pennsylvania and New York were Scots, and there were more of them to the south in Maryland and Virginia, but although they were rich, influential, and a growing political power, they were watched with intense suspicion. The Proclamations had frightened them, and had effectively choked any more practical sympathy like the dispatch of *The Three Sisters* to Darien. The Navigation Acts had always been strictly enforced against them—one of their ships had recently been arrested in the Thames—and they were often accused of treason and Jacobite plots. Governor Jeremiah Basse of Jersey, a bigoted Anabaptist minister who sometimes behaved as if he were still fighting the Civil War, believed (with some justice) that many of them were in collusion with pirates. He spoke of the Scots as if they were a creeping disease in the colonies, "their numbers yearly increasing whilst the interest of our nation seems so much declining."

The Governor of New York, Massachusetts and New Hampshire was Richard Coote, Earl of Bellamont, a high-spirited, impulsive Anglo-Irishman in his early sixties, rightly regarded by his friend the King as "honest and intrepid". He hated corruption and bribery, and had an aristocrat's fine contempt for most of the colonials who attempted to influence his government. The practice of Law in New York, he said, was in the hands of scandalous characters, one of them a dancing-master, another a glover, and the third a Scot who should have been hanged for blasphemy in Edinburgh. He suffered badly from the gout, and was sometimes sorry for his lack of charity when in pain. He worked from five in the morning until ten at night, and preferred the company of his *valet de chambre* to that of his lazy officers. He was sorry for the Caledonians, but his orders were to give no assistance and he was determined to obey. In any case, he had other things on his mind at this moment. He was away from town, concluding a successful treaty with the Iroquois, and when he returned he would have to deal with the pirate William Kidd. This unfortunate, pock-marked Scot had once been given the Governor's commission as a privateer, had interpreted it as a licence for piracy, and had come back to New England with £1,000 in gold, several ingots of silver, and a handsome enamelled box of jewels which he boldly sent to Lady Bellamont. The Governor impounded the gift and threw its presumptuous donor into prison. He was further outraged when he heard that Kidd had once intended to join his fellow-countrymen in Caledonia. There was no doubt what the Governor's enemies in London would make of that. The Commissioners for Trade had recently censured him for allowing five New England ships to carry provisions to Darien, and they had yet to receive his tart reply that the five were in fact one brigantine, *The Three Sisters*, and she had sailed before he had taken up his appointment here. From the savage lodges of the Iroquois on Lake Cayuga, he sternly reminded Lieutenant-Governor Nanfan of the Proclamation against the Scots and his obligations thereunder.

John Nanfan, a kinsman of Lady Bellamont and no doubt owing his office to her husband, was a fussy, indecisive man who would have been happier had the Earl left his Indian friends and returned to deal with the Scots. Though he loyally disapproved of the Caledonians, and knew that he should be firm with them, he was moved by their deplorable state. "They are so weak from pure fatigue and famine," he wrote to Bellamont, "They have no money, so I desire you will let me know how far the law will allow the barter of stores. Their miserable condition is enough to raise compassion." The Governor was not a hard man, and his gout had been improved by the less indulgent diet his surgeon had advised, and by the astringent air of Massachusetts Bay where he was now in gubernatorial residence. "You know how strict my orders are against furnishing the Caledonians with provisions," he wrote, "Yet if you can be well assured these ships will go directly for Scotland you may furnish them with just provisions enough for their voyage."

Unfortunately, Nanfan could be well assured of nothing. Until he heard from Bellamont he had allowed the Scots to buy immediate necessities on credit, and this had emboldened them to ask leave to provision their ships entirely, offering trade goods in exchange. Robert Drummond, it was true, swore that he intended to return to Scotland, but his brother Thomas was said to be seeking a sloop or a brigantine which he proposed to sail back to Darien. He and other officers, particularly Vetch and Turnbull, also offended Nanfan by their insolent pride. They had been lodged ashore by sympathisers who were delighted to embarrass the Governor, and they walked arrogantly abroad in ragged scarlet, touching their swords at every smirking glance.

Most of the Caledonians aboard the ships could no longer afford pride. Day by day one or more of them died from the fever or the flux. Except for a few gentlemen, and those who were certain of obtaining credit, they were not allowed to land. Roger

Oswald went ashore on his hands and knees to find a merchant who was willing to lend him money against his father's name. "I drew the bill sore against my will, but one of them I was obliged to do—either to lose my life or draw that bill." Others less fortunate still ate the sour meal that had kept them alive for so long, or now died for want of better. The August days were hot and airless. Across the East River, New York was neat and sunlit like a canalside town in Holland, tall houses of many-coloured bricks, gabled roofs of crimson tiles. The smell of food. The sound of wheels on cobbles, the cries of children. The sight of women walking. Some men slipped down the bow cable at night and swam or rowed ashore, disappearing into the Colony, swearing that they would never go to sea again in the Company's ships, never return to Darien, nor yet to Scotland if that must be.

Paterson was carried from the *Unicorn* to friendly lodgings. As he slowly recovered from what men called his "craziness", he asked Nanfan for permission to bring ashore his "wearing clothes and linen, household linen and goods, with some books", and was allowed to have them upon his promise that he would not leave New York except for Scotland. Other gentlemen were also given their small baggage, upon the same assurance and once it had passed through the Customs House. Like the men who had deserted the ships at night, some of them had decided that they were done with Scotland and its Company.

Robert Drummond's three weeks passed, and two weeks more. Neither ship was provisioned, nor her crew fit to take her out into the autumn gales of the Atlantic. Thomas Drummond was restless, not for the voyage home but for a bolder venture. His sense of duty urged him to return to Darien. As it had once compelled him to pistol a Glencoe child without remorse, to cry on murder with a shout of "What of our orders?", so now it drove him to an act of piracy. He persuaded his brother and Samuel Vetch to agree to the seizure of one of the merchantmen lying in the East River. He would then sail it to Caledonia and hold the settlement until relief arrived.

The ship they selected was appropriately named *Adventure*. Her master, John Howell, had brought her up the East River on September 9 with half her crew dead of the fever, and now, with a pilot aboard, he was awaiting Nanfan's permission to take her further up for provisioning. She was also Scots, and this may have persuaded the Drummonds that there was some legality in what they proposed, that the Company's Act gave them the power to take, hold, and possess any ship of Scotland they desired. Howell was invited to dine aboard the *Caledonia*, and when he came he was given a glass of wine and asked to what port he belonged. To Glasgow, he said. "Then you belong to us," said Robert Drummond, "we seize you and you are our prize." Too astonished to answer or protest, Howell listened silently to the reading of an order, signed by the Council of Caledonia, declaring his ship taken and under the command of the *Caledonia's* guns.

A boat's-crew, armed with cutlasses, went away to the *Adventure* where the Dutch pilot, Peter Wessel, was told to bring her under the lee of the *Caledonia*. Despite the pistol at his temple, he refused, and the Scots weighed anchor and brought the ship up themselves. They then set Wessel ashore, and he was soon hammering on Nanfan's door. Howell was taken aboard his ship by Robert Drummond and locked in his cabin, guarded by two soldiers with drawn swords. And then, at dawn, the Drummonds and Vetch lost some of their courage, sending for Howell and asking him what he thought of the situation. Would he go ashore with them and declare that he had willingly surrendered his ship to the Company of Scotland? Willingly, he said, but once ashore he too was appealing for Nanfan's protection.

At ten o'clock in the morning of September 14 the Drummonds and Vetch were summoned before the Lieutenant-Governor and the Council of New York at Fort William Henry, where they denied the charges laid against them by Howell and Wessel. Samuel Vetch wrote a deposition for all, having the most plausible pen. It was all a misunderstanding. Upon their honour, there had been no intention of seizing the ship. They had taken command of the *Adventure* because her master and pilot were drunk, and there was a risk of her running afoul of the *Caledonia* in the night. "We extremely regret that there should ever have happened anything that should have given the least umbrage to a misunderstanding betwixt us and the Government for which (as our duty is) we have all the respectful deference imaginable." If there had been any rudeness to Howell and Wessel, any indiscreet behaviour, it had been committed by the common seamen of the *Caledonia,* not by the gentlemen who signed themselves in truth and sincerity.

William Paterson was persuaded to write a brief postscript to this disarmingly ingenuous fiction. It sadly indicated the weakness of his will, the anguish of his spirit, and the desperation of his wish to save the Company from further disgrace. "Although I was not present upon the occasion, yet I fully consent and agree to the submission."

Nanfan believed none of it. He wanted to make an example of Robert Drummond, but he was not encouraged by the colony's Attorney. By an exasperating coincidence, the man was also a Scot. "All he would say," Nanfan later complained to Bellamont, "was that it was no better than felony, and he was sorry his countrymen should be so imprudent, but no advice how to act or what to do, although I pressed him as earnestly as I could." He reluctantly accepted the Scots' deposition, promising himself that he would arrest Robert Drummond at once should the rogue ever come ashore from the *Caledonia* again. Drummond wisely kept to his ship.

Defeated in their attempt to seize one vessel by force, the Drummonds decided to acquire another more circumspectly. They were helped by two rich merchants of New York, Stephen Delancey and Thomas Wenham, who may have been particularly amused by the raid on the *Adventure,* the foundations of their now-respectable fortunes having been laid by the Madagascar pirates they had once financed. They were willing to supply the Scots with a sloop, the *Anna,* and to fit her out with stores and provisions for a return to Caledonia, although her destination could not, of course, be made public in New York. In return, the Scots agreed to put ashore a large part of their trade goods as security. As long as these did not change hands, but remained in a warehouse under the care of a Company's servant, it would be difficult for Nanfan to prove that Delancey and Wenham were giving aid in breach of the Proclamation. The only illegal act would be the departure of the *Anna* without proper clearance.

She quietly slipped her moorings after sunset on Friday, September 20, and under her new name, *Ann of Caledonia,* was gone from the East River before the Crown officers were aware of it. Her commission had been in Thomas Drummond's pocket for more than a week, and had been signed by Vetch and the weakly acquiescent Paterson while Robert Drummond's boarding-party was rowing away to the *Adventure*. He was to sail south, to find the relief expedition which must surely have left Scotland, and to inform it "of our circumstances, of the nature and situation both of the harbour and landing." The sloop's master was Alexander Stewart, and he was ordered "exactly and punctually to obey the said Thomas Drummond in everything as you shall be answerable."

The few Landsmen whom Drummond had chosen to go with him were all young, resolute, and free from sickness. Some of them had served with him in Argyll's and were enthusiastically loyal to his leadership. They burned with the humiliation of their retreat, anxious to restore their country's honour and their own self-respect. Robert Turnbull, whose love for the green land of Darien had grown more intense in his absence from it, had been hot for the venture since it was first proposed, but he was almost left behind. He was staying with friends on Staten Island when the sloop sailed, and he pursued her stern-lantern through the night in a small boat until he came up with her. In his lodgings he had left a small nugget of gold, a nose-piece once worn by an Indian woman, and a fine parrot which he had somehow kept alive during the terrible voyage from Caledonia. He hoped that Robert Drummond would carry these small gifts safely to Scotland, and deliver them to Erskine of Carnock.

When Nanfan heard of the sloop's departure, he wrote to Bellamont in fear and frustration. "The Caledonians, by and with the advice and assistance of their countrymen, have played us not fair." This was all he could say, lacking the courage to tell the Earl about the *Adventure* or the *Anna*. Bellamont was angered by the prevarication and demanded a full account of all the Caledonians had done, pointing out that this was surely ten times more important than what Nanfan usually wrote in his dispatches. The Governor would be glad when all these troublesome Scots were gone, but he had no sympathy for his whining subordinate. "I wish you had not burnt your fingers with them, and broke the instructions I sent you from the Secretary of State."

Robert Drummond was ready to leave for home. He was daily losing men by death and desertion, and although Vetch had petitioned Nanfan for aid in arresting the deserters, the Lieutenant-Governor had been churlishly unhelpful. It was hopeless now to think that both ships could make the Atlantic crossing, and at the end of September the *Unicorn* was warped across to Perth Amboy on the Jersey shore. There she was abandoned and would slowly rot, stripped by looters, her timbers splitting in the frost and sun. Once the miserable survivors of her crew and passengers were aboard the *Caledonia*, Drummond prepared his ship as best he could for departure. By Bellamont's instructions, Nanfan had allowed him to acquire provisions for ten weeks, and he hoped that these would be enough to bring him to the Clyde.

The survivors now began to think of the welcome they might receive in Scotland, and it gave none of them any comfort. Roger Oswald found the courage at last to write to his father. Perhaps Sir James now knew of that bill he had drawn for £21 Sterling in New York, but, as God was his witness, it had been necessary. The surgeon had given him no more than two days to live if he did not find food. When he reached Scotland he would not come home. He would lodge with the Widow Finlay by the Stable Green Port in Glasgow, and there wait in hope for his father's forgiveness. "I know that you have good reason to be angry with me, but Sir, if you knew what hardships I have endured since I parted with you, you would excuse me in some part. . . ."

A few days before the *Caledonia* left, Samuel Vetch told Paterson that he would stay in New York. "He acquainted me that he designed to stay there this winter, and that in the meantime he would look after the effects put ashore to satisfy Messers Wenham and Delancey, and that by that means he would be in readiness to go back to the Colony." Paterson disapproved of the proposal, but since they were the only Councillors left he had no power to influence the man's decision.

Piety was the best policy, Vetch had written to his brother William, and sincere honesty the surest way to honour. He could have added that opportunity boldly seized, and wisely exploited, was the surest way to prosperity. It is probable, even at this moment, that he had no intention of returning to Caledonia, though he was prepared to serve the Company while its interests served him. He had looked upon New England and liked what he had seen, both in general and in particular. That particular was his cousin by marriage, Margaret Livingstone. Her father, Robert Livingstone, was one of the most powerful Scots in New York, with a great estate on the east bank of the Hudson and a merchant-house connected by marriage and contract with such influential families as the Van Cortlands, Van Rensselaers and Delanceys. It was Livingstone who had given the Scots credit when their ships arrived, and had provisioned the *Caledonia* for its departure. Though he had done this for profit, he also considered it his duty as a political opponent of Bellamont, and a moral obligation to those kinsmen who had served on Darien. One of them, a nephew, was Andrew Livingstone, the surgeon of the *Dolphin*.

When Vetch married his plain-featured, sharp-nosed cousin, her father gave them a house and a lot on Pearl Street, a fine residence with a high roof and two stacks of chimneys said to be worth £1,000. Vetch set himself up as a merchant, and since the Company never discovered what happened to the goods left in his charge it was assumed that he had converted them to his own use with the assistance of Wenham and Delancey. The detestation and contempt of his countrymen at home, the hatred of those who had sailed with him from Caledonia, the shocked pain of his family, did not trouble him, at least openly. He prospered, became rich and influential, a Colonel of Militia and the Governor of Nova Scotia, until his ambition over-reached his talents and he was ruined by political enemies who had once been his friends. He fled to England. Thirty-three years after he had deserted the Company and his comrades he died a lonely debtor in the King's Bench Prison.

The *Caledonia* sailed on October 12. Of the five ships that had left the Forth fifteen months before, only she returned to Scotland. She carried no more than three hundred men, and some of those would die before she reached the Clyde.

The Key of the Universe

"It will be wonderful to see the Sun rise in the West"
Edinburgh and London, January to August 1699

IN LONDON THE ATTORNEY-GENERAL was considering his answer
to a question put to him on behalf of certain interested subjects
of East New Jersey, where a Scot had recently been appointed
Governor. Could a Scotchman hold such office in the Plantations,
or was he disqualified therefrom by the Act regulating frauds and
abuses? It was three weeks before Sir Thomas Trevor gave his
opinion: "That a Scotchman born is by Law capable of being
appointed Governor of any of the Plantations, he being a
natural-born subject of England in judgement and construction
of Law, as much as if he had been born in England."

In Edinburgh that last week of January, the Directors of the
Company (who would have been as angry as the rest of their
countrymen to hear that they were subjects of *England*) were
giving their final instructions to Captain Andrew Gibson of the
brigantine *Dispatch*. Three months after receiving the Council's
letters from Madeira, urgently appealing for provisions, they
were at last sending a small cargo of biscuits, flour, pork, stockfish, oil and brandy. Gibson's orders were to sail his little ship by
the most expeditious route to Darien, to take no insults from the
men-of-war of any nation, and to defend himself by force of arms
if necessary. With him sailed William Vetch, now recovered from
his sickness, anxious to join his brother, and eager to take his seat
on the Council of Caledonia. The brigantine weathered the
northern passage, but was hit by gales as she came down the
Hebrides and was finally wrecked on the isle of Texa, two miles
off the coast of Islay. All she carried was lost, and her crew swam
ashore with nothing but what they wore.

For the next month the Company was leisurely engaged in the purchase of another small ship, the *Marion of Leith*. She was renamed the *Olive Branch* when her owner was at last persuaded to part with her—or with fifteen-sixteenths of her, though his prudent foresight in retaining the last fraction for himself was to be a misjudgement. She was soon joined in Leith Road by a chartered ship, the *Hopeful Binning*. As the weather improved, deep-laden lighters began to fill their holds with casks of biscuit, barrels of ale, meal, tobacco, raisins and sugar, bolts of cloth and cases of hardware.

Though much of the delay in reinforcing the Colony was due to the astonishing complacency of the committees for this and for that, there were less controllable causes and the Directors had referred to them in the letters carried by the *Dispatch*. "We have had a scarcity of corn and provisions here since your departure, even to a dearth, and poverty of course occasioned thereby." Scotland had moved closer still to famine, to privation and epidemic disease. It had little enough for itself, and was reluctant to spare some of it for those distant adventurers who must now be enjoying the fruitful pleasures described in Mr. Wafer's book, lately off the press. The stockholders were loyal to the Company, if not disinterested, and with few exceptions they had answered the Company's third call on the subscriptions at Candlemas. In their turn, to reward such faith, the Directors declared a small dividend on the first call.

A stronger encouragement to any doubters was that physical manifestation of the Company's glory, the *Rising Sun*. Still moored off the mouth of the Gair Loch, her splendid lines and gilded hull were noble in the sun of an early spring. The sight of her, and the thought of others soon to sail with her, moved a modestly anonymous Lady of Honour to compose some romping stanzas which she called *The Golden Island or the Darien Song, in Commendation of All Concerned in that Noble Enterprise of the Valiant Scots*.

> We have another Fleet to sail,
>   the Lord will reik* them fast;
> It will be wonderful to see
>   the Sun rise in the West.

* blow.

>Some are noble, all are great,
>Lord bless your company,
>And let your fame, in Scotland's name,
>o'er spread both land and sea.

The friends and relations of the great and noble already gone, however, were wondering what had happened to them, and their growing anxiety burst into extravagant joy on March 25 when Alexander Hamilton arrived by express from England. He carried a large sealed packet of letters and dispatches from the Colony, and a crying, shouting mob of men and women waited at the entrance to Milne Square for a glimpse of his fever-yellow face. He had travelled in haste from Bristol, where a West Indian ship had brought him, as eager to outstrip Major Cunningham of Eickett as he was to bring the good news. He was greeted warmly by the relieved Directors, who questioned him closely and then made public as much of the dispatches as they thought politic. *Resolved*, wrote Roderick Mackenzie in the minutes

> ... that this Court shall order a compliment to the said Mr.
> Alexander Hamilton as being the first person who has
> brought the welcome news.
> *Resolved*, that the Ministers of this city and suburbs thereof
> be acquainted with the good news to the end that they may
> in their discretion return public and hearty thanks to Almighty
> God upon this occasion.

The compliment given to Hamilton was a purse of one hundred guineas, and he was further granted two guineas a week during his stay in Edinburgh. In token of its gratitude and pleasure, the City Corporation made him a burgess and a gild-brother. Two days later, after the dispatches had been thoroughly studied, the Directors sent deputations to the Lord Chancellor, Lord Provost, the Governor of the Castle, humbly asking for public demonstrations of joy. The guns of the Half Moon Battery were fired across the North Loch and the Grassmarket, bells rang above a *feu de joie* from the muskets of the Town Guard, bonfires were lit by Holyroodhouse and the Netherbow Port, and at night all the windows of the Royal Mile glowed with happy candles.

Riders were sent to every city in the kingdom, ordering more gunfire, more bells, more candles.

Major Cunningham arrived in the midst of the riot and celebration, having travelled home by way of London. He was in an ill humour, and resented the rewards given Hamilton, who was no member of the Council after all. He caught at the sleeves of the Directors with his tale of misfortune, of his "considerable travelling charges and expenses in coming hither by way of Jamaica and England." He was perhaps an embarrassment to them. If the Colony had been successfully established what was one of its Council doing in Scotland? He had persuaded the City to elect him a burgess and a gild-brother too, and this made it impossible for the Directors to ignore him or censure him for desertion. Upon his assurance that he intended to return to Caledonia, they gave him £200 Sterling. He then retired to his estate and never went back to the Colony.

Hamilton's news had lifted the wave-top of the nation's enthusiasm, and Milne Square was once more crowded with eager volunteers. The King's servants were alarmed by the passion of the people, its undercurrent of hostility to England and the Throne, though none of them could see what should be done about it. "It is an unaccountable thing," Lord Marchmont wrote to Carstares, "to find so great a disposition in people to go thither as there is. God knows what shall come of it."

Six weeks after Hamilton's arrival, and three after the Company heard of the loss of Gibson's brigantine, the *Olive Branch* and the *Hopeful Binning* sailed from Leith with provisions, stores, and 300 men and women to reinforce the settlers. The Directors had been sending letters of advice and admonition by every ship they thought might touch at Jamaica, and with the *Olive Branch* they now sent the promise of spiritual encouragement. "There is so general an inclination to supply you with whatever is needful that you need not doubt but suitable care will be taken to provide good ministers for you." In the meantime, since the Colony was without clergy, it was hoped that the Councillors would do what they could to discourage all manner of vice, and to inspire the colonists by their own sober, discreet and religious behaviour. At that moment the Caledonians, having just heard of the English Proclamations, were encouraged and inspired by their Council's plain intention to be gone from the Colony as soon as possible.

As a cool spring moved into a wet summer, once more with no promise of a good harvest, preparations for the second expedition were increased. "Question not," the Directors wrote to the Council, "but the *Rising Sun*, and four ships more of considerable burden, will sail from the Clyde with a greater number of men than went along with yourselves." In the meantime, remembering Hamilton's unhappy report of squabbles and dissension, they implored the Councillors "to be one in interest and affection, and to have a watchful eye over any that may be of such clattering, mutinous, and pernicious temper as Herries has proved to be." For Surgeon Herries, having made his own way to London from Jamaica, was now reported to be writing a scurrilous attack on the Colony, for his English paymasters no doubt. The man's abominable impertinence went beyond honour and imagination, and the Directors were astonished to hear that he had committed Haldane of Gleneagles to gaol in London, holding him responsible for wages allegedly owing by the Company. Gleneagles was released on his own bail, left England at once for Edinburgh, and asked the Directors to indemnify him. They did so with reluctance.

None of the news from England was good. The settlement of the Colony had openly angered the Government there, and the King's continued silence was alarming, though that naïve Lady of Honour had declared that "he did encourage us against the English will." It was rumoured in London that some of the Councillors-General, notably the Earl of Annandale, were bought and employed by the English for "undoing the African Company." James Johnston, out of office since his dismissal from the Secretaryship in 1696 but still in William's favour, warned his "dear Chief" the Earl to be more circumspect. "Whatever becomes of the Company, any Scotchman that shall have a hand in undoing it will be detested by all mankind." Though he had once believed the undertaking to be an act of Providence, Johnston now thought that its failure might be for the best, ultimately producing "a union of trade betwixt the kingdoms".

Scratching away by night, secure in his office from a nagging wife, James Vernon had been waiting impatiently for some formal protest from Spain, knowing that this would allow him to declare England's innocence and Scotland's guilt. When envoys to the Spanish dominions complained of snubs and insults he told them to reply boldly, to say that the Colony was no responsibility of England. "I don't know but we have taken more care to render it ineffectual than they have done, while their silence encourages the undertakers." On May 3 he got his wish. The Spanish Ambassador called upon him and delivered a wordy memorial of protest. His Most Catholic Majesty, Charles the Sufferer—that victim of inherited syphilis, dropsy and epilepsy, now mercifully approaching his last year of dying—declared that the Colony of Caledonia was an insult to his kingdom, an invasion of his domains in America, and a violation of the treaties between himself and his cousin of England. After such a scowling start, the memorial ended amiably with the hope that William would take such measures as he found convenient to put an end to the settlement. Vernon accepted it politely, explained the difference between an Englishman and a Scot, and assured the Ambassador of His Majesty's continuing affection and friendship for the King of Spain.

Some token action was taken. Vernon advised the Lord Justice of Ireland to be vigilant in preventing the departure of any ship to Darien, and in Madrid the English envoy, Alexander Stanhope, patiently told a sceptical Royal Council that Scotland was independent of England under the Crown, "and for this reason must be handled with much prudence and circumspection." Vernon was relieved that the Spanish protest had been so mild, and he thought he knew why. Spain might soon need England's help. Upon his desk where he laid the memorial was a dispatch from Dover, written by the spy John Macky. Couriers from France had reported that Charles was already dead and that Louis XIV would soon claim the vacant throne for his grandson. "We should be glad to hear something to the contrary," Vernon told the English envoy in Brussels, "for the 50,000 men that lie ready in Flanders look to us as if they smelt a carcass and are ready to enter upon the inheritance."

In Scotland the Spanish protest aroused a flurry of anger and contempt quickly lost in the greater surge of enthusiasm for the second expedition. Enclosed with the dispatches from the Colony had been a chart of Caledonia Bay, and this was now copied, printed and circulated as a crudely inaccurate map. It gave a wondrous reality to what had been until now a misty conjecture, and the wording of its imaginative legend excited envy and cupidity. *"Place where upon digging for stones to make an oven, a considerable mixture of gold was found in them. . . ."* Men were eager to advise the Company, though they might get no closer to the Colony than this map and the paper on which they wrote their earnest contributions. The Duke of Hamilton, that popular friend of the undertaking, was sent a cure for those colonists who might eat poisoned fish. The bones of the fish itself, said the recipe, should be burnt, ground to a powder, and then drunk in a glass of wine. The Duke was also pleased to submit some of his own thoughts on the construction of New Edinburgh.

It must be observed on the building of the town that all the principal streets must go from north to south, and that those you are obliged to make which cross east to west must be as narrow as possible, because the sun looks plumb on them all day long. . . . There must be wells or cisterns in three or four different places, lest the enemy should poison the water by a bomb when but in one place.

This was sound advice, but when it was being written, in the Duke's great home by Holyroodhouse, Captain Juan Delgado was burning what was left of New Edinburgh.

August came, and the Court of Directors moved westward and took up lodgings in Greenock and Glasgow so that they might be near the Company's fleet. Their confidence had been momentarily shaken by the news of the English Proclamations, which reached them at the beginning of the month, but they had quickly recovered. The nation, too, when its anger subsided, took the Proclamations as a challenge. The Lord Advocate, Sir James Stewart, watched the excitement with a sour eye. "You cannot believe," he told Carstares, "how great an edge is upon persons of all degrees here for that plantation." A week later, when the Directors went to the Clyde, he was more depressed. "I am truly grieved at this matter. The nation is bent one way, and the King is of another persuasion; and whether it succeed or not it is like to have ill consequences." Unless matters took another turn, by which he meant that unless the Company met with a crippling setback, the King's servants and the King's cause in Scotland could not prosper.

Four ships now waited in the Clyde. Direckstone's handsome flagship had been joined by the *Duke of Hamilton* and the *Hope of Bo'ness*, both of 300 tons or more and both chartered. The fourth vessel, the *Hope*, was smaller and owned by the Company. It was the *Rising Sun* that attracted most of the people who came down the firth to see the fleet. Made of good Berlin oak and 450 tons in burden, she was more than 150 feet long from her forecastle head to the carved caryatids on her stern. She was armed like an Indiaman with 38 guns, twelve, eight, and four-pounders, their ports painted red and encircled with golden laurels on the after-deck. She glowed with the gold of her name. One rising sun burst into gilded rays beneath her sprit, and another below her stern. All her golden carving was rich and elaborate, curling leaves, convolutes and whorls twined about her windows, poop-deck rail, roundhouse and captain's barge. Her yellow-panelled cabin was luxuriously furnished—bed-curtains of Bengal cloth, fringed, canopied and tasselled with gold, gilded handles to the doors, five tablecloths of yellow damask in a chest of orange wood, eighteen ells of linen napery, two large looking-glasses framed in gold, dark red earthenware, blue cups of polished pewter, and spoons of yellow horn.

The man chosen to enjoy the lonely splendour of the cabin, to command the ship and to be commodore of the fleet, was James Gibson. The sea-going partner of a rich merchant-house he owned with his brother, he was a Director of the Company, a large holder of its stock, and until recently its agent in Amsterdam. He had seen the ship's keel laid in Direckstone's yard, watched her grow, taken wine aboard her with Peter the Great, and sailed with her to the Clyde. From her beginning he had been certain that he would and should be her commander. Others were less sure that he merited it. "Some good people in Scotland," wrote the Reverend Mr. Francis Borland, "took occasion to remember and reflect upon his former cruel and inhuman carriage toward those poor prisoners whom he transported to Carolina in 1684."

The minister of Glassford in the Covenanting parish of Avondale, Borland had himself been chosen to go to the Colony. In July, the Commission of the General Assembly of the Church of Scotland had met in Glasgow, listened to an inspiring and relevant sermon (upon the text Hebrews 11:8, *By faith Abraham, being called of God, obeyed, and went out, not knowing whither he went*), chosen four ministers for Caledonia, and given them their instructions. In addition to Borland, they were Alexander Shields, Archibald Stobo and Alexander Dalgleish, all good men in the faith and of proven worth. Upon arrival, they were told, they should immediately set a day apart for public thanksgiving, and should then constitute themselves as a Presbytery by electing a Moderator and a Clerk. Thereafter, with all speed and the consent of the people, they should select the most pious, prudent and judicious among the settlers to be Elders and Overseers of the community, holding parochial sessions and Diets of the Presbytery as often as occasion required. "And thus we commit you, and our Lord's great and glorious work in your hands, unto His own powerful, wise and gracious conduct and blessing."

Of the four ministers only Borland would return to Scotland, and it is history's good fortune that he was a tireless scribbler. He was also a bigot, a prig, and an intolerant critic of human frailty, convinced that the Almighty guided him in righteousness and damned those who did not follow. If Gibson had transported Papists and Episcopalians, instead of Covenanters, Borland might not have deplored his inhumanity toward them. He had been particularly chosen because he had spent some time in the Dutch colony of Surinam, though this had given him little sympathy for other men and no understanding of the peculiar temptations they suffered in such remote places. His dear friend and mentor was his companion Alexander Shields, minister of the second charge of Saint Andrews, and a strong man in the service of the Lord. Shields was still young, but for most of his life he had been persecuted for his beliefs, and had at one time been a prisoner on the Bass Rock in the Firth of Forth. His physical courage was exceptional: as chaplain to the Cameronians he had sung psalms with them in their advance at Steinkirk, and sustained them with prayers in the trenches before Namur. He had been a field preacher with James Renwick and had vindicated that ardent Covenanter's work in *The Hind Let Loose*. In his study at Saint

Andrews he left behind a manuscript life of Renwick, and would never live to see its publication.

The last of the supplies were being loaded by gabbards from Glasgow and wherries from Greenock, the same diverse cargoes of hardware and haberdashery that had been sent with the first expedition. And bayonets and powder. Raisins and sugar. Brandy and beer. All entered in his ledger by Peter Murdoch, the Company's agent in Glasgow, with a neat index so that the Committee for Equipping might know at a glance how many pounds of bees-wax or casks of brimstone, firkins of black soap or kegs of nails were aboard the ships. The Directors worked industriously, rose early, and consumed prodigious quantities of claret when they entertained each other at dusk. Their euphoric self-satisfaction was disturbed only momentarily by some unpleasant news from London. Montgomerie and Jolly, back from Caledonia by way of Jamaica and Bristol, had arrived there and had as yet sent no word that they were coming north. Writing to Paterson, the Marquis of Tweeddale said that he could not think what the villains would have to say for themselves. They were reported to be preparing a petition for presentation to the Duke of Hamilton, but His Grace, having had notice of their behaviour in letters from the Colony, would be on his guard against it. The arrival of both men in England reminded the Directors of the sad lack of unity in Caledonia, and they wrote long letters to the now extinct Council, recalling earlier admonitions against "jealousies, animosities, factions, heart-burnings and disagreements." Such evils the colonists should zealously renounce with the help of their new ministers, even though they were "penned up in a corner close together, in a state of lazy idleness."

And let them be of good cheer, a great number of reinforcements was coming with these letters, including men whom the Company understood were desperately needed. For the defence of the fort there was John Jaffray to be Fire-master and Bombardier. Captain John Wallace and Thomas Kerr were engineers of renown from Flanders, and the former something of an artillerist as well. He had recently examined and fired 36 leather guns, the gift of Lord Elcho, and declared them in good condition. For the proper management of the precious metals that would seem to be found in every stone upturned, the Company was sending a goldsmith, Robert Keil, and also John Hunter who was "perfectly versed in the art of coining money and the making of mills for the edging of money." David Dovale was coming to help his friend and co-religionist Benjamin Spense, having a remarkable fluency in Spanish, Portuguese, French, Dutch and English, as well as some of the Indian tongues of the Darien coast. Upon the recommendation of the Duke of Hamilton Robert Johnson had been appointed to employ his new method of teaching the Indians both English and Scots. And George Winram had gone aboard the *Hope* with his "stills and other necessaries, for the distilling and fermenting of several sorts of liquors."

A hundred women were sailing with the expedition at the Company's expense, and as many more were willing to pay £4 to a private speculator who was proposing to charter a sloop or brigantine for the purpose. Most of them were loyal wives, and all but a few of them are now nameless. There was Mrs. Stobo, wife of the minister. There was Mrs. Jaffray, sailing with the Fire-master and their daughter Mary, Mrs. Johnson and her son. There was Mrs. Bell and there was Mrs. Merston who did not know that they were in fact widows, for the husbands they hoped to join in Caledonia, like the men of other wives aboard, were long since dead in their water-logged graves.

The captains, lieutenants, ensigns and soldiers were again discharged men of the disbanded regiments of Leven and Strathnaver, Mackay, Hill and Argyll. Many of them had been waiting impatiently about Milne Square since the Company refused their services a year ago. More than a third of the common men, according to Francis Borland, were from the mountains, Highlanders whose lack of English and scandalous contempt for the discipline of the Presbytery were to fill him with disgust and pity, the pity being reserved for himself. William Dunlop, Principal of the University of Glasgow, asked the Company to take as volunteers "some young men who passed their course at the college and are desirous to go to Caledonia." They were accepted, on condition that one of their masters accompanied them, and that Dunlop advanced them £10 for the purchase of small necessities.

The cadet sons of twenty-two leading families were given commissions as lieutenants or ensigns. Others, of no eminence but proud lineage, asked to go as Planters or Volunteers until their valour and industry won them a commission. One of these was Lauchlan Bain, whose father was a tacksman in the Mackay country, and his promotion would be as rapid as his following disgrace was irrevocable. Among the company commanders was another Colin Campbell from Argyll's, and two more of his clan were lieutenants. Another overseer was Lord Mungo Murray, a brave and selfless member of the house of Atholl. Captain Andrew Stewart was the landless brother of the Earl of Galloway, but carried with his commission the Company's promise that if he purchased "some considerable share of the stock this Court shall for his further encouragement assume him to the number of Directors." Among all the officers of the companies there was once more a scattering of splendid names, predominantly Highland—Carmichael and Campbell, Farquhar and Grant, Ramsay, Colquhoun, Mackay and Urquhart, Murray, Gordon, Menzies and Ross. At least one father was inflamed by the fire of his son's enthusiasm and went with him. Alexander Kinnard of Culbin had once been a Jacobite, an officer in the Highland army that had risen against William ten years before. Although he had been pardoned in 1693, his estate on the Moray Firth had since been engulfed by tidal sand. When his son was appointed an ensign in Captain John Telfer's company, he secured an overseer's commission for himself, and it may be that in addition to sharing the boy's life he hoped to restore a tarnished name and a broken fortune.

Another father concerned with family honour, if not his own obligations thereto, was Sir James Oswald. He plagued the Directors during these last days with petitions on behalf of his luckless heir. It had been understood that Roger Oswald would serve the Colony as a clerk, but the only letter Sir James had received—by Mr. Hamilton's hand and addressed to Thomas Aikman—suggested that he was not so employed. Would the Directors once more recommend the young man to the Council? Wearily, they resolved that they would.

Four new Councillors, described as "men of special trust", were being sent with the expedition. Firstly William Vetch of course, though his uneasy health had again been affected by the wreck of the *Dispatch* and his struggle to reach the Islay shore.

From his sick-bed, he promised the Directors that should he be able to stand on his feet he would most certainly go aboard the *Rising Sun* at the time appointed. As Commodore and captain of the flagship, and in acknowledgement of the assistance he and his brother had given to the Company, James Gibson was also elected. He was a rough man and little liked, and it is easy to see him as another Pennecuik, though he was the better seaman. The third was James Byres, the Edinburgh merchant who had been among the first to sign his name in Mrs. Purdie's coffee-house, subscribing £500 in the hope of a preferment now abundantly realised. If a contentious nature and an arrogant conceit were the principal qualifications for the Council—as they seem to have been—then Byres was an excellent choice. Upon his appointment he asked for a certificate declaring his right to the office, a passage for his brother-in-law and his apprentice, and a guarantee that he, his dependants and his baggage would be given fitting accommodation aboard the *Rising Sun*. The fourth man was Major John Lindsay, so self-effacing, unquarrelsome and obliging that little has survived of his existence but his signature, boldly penned below those of his colleagues.*

Lindsay was a late appointment, almost an afterthought. It had been intended that he and Dr. John Munro of Coul should go as "persons of special trust", without office or authority clearly defined. Remembering that he had lost his hoped-for place on the first Council when the Company followed the Kirk's advice and chose Pennecuik, Munro said that he could not accept unless he were made a Councillor and member of the Court of Directors. Refused these offices, he sulkily declined to go, and was thus saved the embarrassment of explaining to the other surgeons why the medical supplies he had ordered were so inadequate.

Drummers beat along the Renfrew shore on Wednesday, August 16, with a proclamation calling "all Overseers, Assistants, Sub-Assistants, Gentlemen Volunteers, Tradesmen, Planters and Others" to the boats. At once, lest they forfeit their passage. By

---

* He may have been one of the disbanded officers of the Earl of Argyll's Regiment. A disproportionate number of them served in the Colony, as a result, no doubt, of the Earl's efforts on their behalf. A John Lindsay took part in the Massacre of Glencoe as a lieutenant in Campbell of Glenlyon's battalion-company, but the Councillor could have been the John Lindsay who was Aide-Major to the Earl.

ten o'clock the next day nearly thirteen hundred men, women and children were aboard, crowding the decks and lower shrouds, cheering and waving as a dozen Directors were rowed by in a last review. In Gibson's yellow cabin later, the ships' captains and the four Councillors—William Vetch having come despite his febrile health—took wine and meat with the Court and were given their final instructions.

They were to go jointly and with all speed to their ships and make ready to sail. Once at sea, and westward of Ireland, they were to make for Golden Island by the shortest route and without landing a man, except for watering-parties, until Caledonia was reached. There they would stand off the harbour mouth, fire a gun, and wait for a pilot. During the voyage they would keep good order among their crews and passengers, insist that the surgeons took diligent care of the sick, and exercise the Landsmen regularly in the use of arms. A strict eye would also be kept on the ships' stewards, who might otherwise sell the Company's provisions to the colonists "under pretence of goods belonging to them". The daily allowance of brandy was that laid down in the Bill of Fare, but since some thought the ration too large it could be left to each captain's discretion. They were to fight if attacked at sea, fly the Company's standard and no other if sighted by an English man-of-war, and to send word of their progress by any homeward ship they believed to be a friend to the Company. "And so, wishing you a happy voyage and a safe return, we bid you a hearty farewell. . . ."

The fleet left with the ebb-tide on Friday. By dusk it was sailing south, with Loch Long astern and the heather-red hills of Cowal turning black on the starboard beam.

"Repossess yourselves thereof by force of arms. . ."
Glasgow and Edinburgh, August to October 1699

The four ships sailed no further than the Isle of Bute. As they came up to Rothesay Bay the wind changed against them. Liking none of the weather signs, Gibson hoisted a white flag to his ensign-staff and fired one gun. Upon this signal the others drew in to his flagship and dropped anchor in the bay. There they remained for a month, waiting for a fair wind, wasting their provisions, watching the days pass in wondrous colours across the mountains to the north. They were visited every forenoon by anxious message-boats from Greenock. From Glasgow the Directors impatiently urged Gibson to sail, but he stubbornly refused to move until he could be sure of a wind that would carry him down the firth and about the Mull of Kintyre.

Daniel Mackay arrived from Darien in the middle of September. The different tone of the letters he brought, the worrying reports of death, disease, hunger and despair, alarmed the Directors, and they sent an express to Gibson, ordering him to remain in Rothesay Bay until Mackay joined him with fresh dispatches for the Colony. He acknowledged the order, but his master at this moment was the weather and he was determined to obey that before all else.

Montgomerie and Jolly had come to Edinburgh at last. Jolly had presented his long, exculpatory memorial to the Duke of Hamilton, and both men were ready to answer any questions the Directors might wish to put, to refute all charges made against them. The Court had no time for them, and refused to see them. They waited miserably in their lodgings, or went abroad to defend themselves passionately before any man with the time or inclination to listen. And it can have been no comfort to see young Mr. Mackay going in and out of Milne Square daily.

Toward the end of the month an express from London brought news of a disturbing rumour. It was said there that the Colony had been entirely abandoned, that the Scots had surrendered their fort and town to the Spaniards. When Mackay was asked if it could be true, he laughed and said there was nothing in it. His confidence reassured the Directors, and when they sent news of the rumour to Rothesay Bay they urged the Councillors not to believe anything so inconsistent and fabulous. "We can believe no set of men in the world of any reasonable measures of discretion and resolution, and much less those in whose fidelity and courage we have placed such an entire confidence, could be guilty of so much groundless cowardice, folly and treachery."

As if the thought of cowardice had reminded them of Jolly and Montgomerie, the Directors called both men before the Court the next day. They were closely questioned, their memorials read, and their defence compared with the letters from the Council which Mackay had brought. From the moment they entered that panelled chamber in Milne Square, there can have been no hope for them. The charge of desertion was proven by their presence in Scotland, and after its distasteful encounter with Major Cunningham the Court was in no mood to be lenient. It was resolved, and written into the minutes by Rockerick Mackenzie, that their conduct in leaving the Colony had been "altogether groundless and unwarrantable". They were cast out, disgraced, and their share of the Company's stock withdrawn from them.

On Friday, September 22, Daniel Mackay left Edinburgh for the Clyde and his return to Darien. That day, the three Directors who were watching the Company's affairs at Greenock sent an express to the fleet, informing the Councillors that Mackay would join them on Saturday evening with late dispatches and two gabbards full of bread and rice. They too wrote of the rumour from London, and Mackay's derision. Why should Scots retreat before Spaniards, "of whom we never heard that our people were afraid"? The story was a malicious invention of the English, contrived by James Vernon to discourage the dispatch of provisions to the Colony.

The fleet sailed in the forenoon of Saturday, without warning, and without waiting for Mackay or the bread and rice. The Councillors had received the Greenock letter, and by the boat that brought it sent back what the Directors later complained was a "short and supercilious" note. It declared that a favourable wind at last could not now be ignored. When Mackay arrived at Rothesay the bay was empty, and the ships long since gone below the horizon. He pursued them unsuccessfully as far as Loch Ryan and then returned to Greenock in an angry temper. The Directors were outraged, writing furious letters in pursuit of the fleet, but the nation was delighted.

> Our sable night is gone, the day is won,
> The Scots are followed with the Rising Sun.

Twelve days later that sable night returned, and the day seemed clearly lost. Rumours of disaster could no longer be dismissed as English lies. Past sunset on Monday, October 9, a rider reached Milne Square from Leith where the London pacquet had arrived. He brought papers from James Foulis, Paterson's old friend and associate, and enclosed with them were copies of two letters sent from New York in August. They had been written by George Moffat, supercargo of the *Caledonia*, and addressed to his master Joseph Ormiston in London. They were brief and unemotional, but from what they said there could be no doubt that the Colony had been abandoned.

The Directors published a summary of the facts in the *Gazette*, and by the end of the week the news was known all over the Lowlands. Saturday was the birthday of the exiled Stuart king, and the Jacobites of Edinburgh, who waited in the wings throughout the whole tragi-comedy of the Company's history, now made a short and melodramatic appearance on stage. For here was a disaster that could be blamed on the asthmatic usurper, and if rightly exploited would embarrass his servants. But the demonstration was without purpose or organisation. Toasts were drunk in public to King James's health, some notable men stood about bonfires upon which unrecognisable effigies were burnt, a few pistols and fireworks were exploded in the dark and that was all. The country was too numb for a political weapon to be made of its bitterness and shock. When the numbness faded there was the pain of wounded pride and a fierce anger against the Caledonians, not the Councillors alone but all who had sailed with the first expedition. Fathers believed that they had been betrayed by their sons, brothers by brothers. No one would have disputed the tone of the letter which the Directors wrote to the survivors in New York, accusing them of a "shameful and dishonourable abandonment". There were many men, Sir James Oswald among them, who declared that if their sons did not return to Darien and their duty they need not come back to their homes.

Moffat's letters were still unread by most of the Directors when those meeting in a quorum at Milne Square on October 10 took immediate steps to save the Colony. They agreed that bills of account should be sent to New York and Jamaica upon which the Colony might draw, and had that sensible procedure been adopted from the beginning the first Caledonians would never have had any difficulty in buying provisions. It was also agreed that the first available ship should be chartered to carry Daniel Mackay to the Colony with fresh instructions for the second expedition and the captains of the *Olive Branch* and the *Hopeful Binning*. In the meantime a letter to the Councillors aboard the *Rising Sun* was hastily drafted and signed. It informed them of what they surely would know before they received it, that the settlement had been abandoned, and it warned them against any thought they might consequently have of returning to Scotland.

> If this find you not possessed of our shamefully deserted Colony, you are forthwith to make the best of your way thither, and endeavour (if you find it possessed by any other) to repossess yourself thereof by force of arms; but if that should prove altogether impracticable or impossible for you at this time, you are to set down in the nearest and most convenient place which you can fall upon, to wait a fit opportunity to do the same, which at no time, neither now nor hereafter, must be neglected.

More important than this letter was the man who carried it, and who was introduced by it as one of the new Council of Caledonia, "having frankly and generously offered himself to go wherever the Company's service might require him." Indeed he had, and had been waiting for more than a month to know whether the Directors would accept his offer. That acceptance, so long delayed, was made this day in anxious haste, and with the sudden realisation, perhaps, that here was a man who should have been employed twelve months before.

He was Alexander Campbell of Fonab, a tall West Highland laird with steady eyes and a gentle smile. Not yet forty, he had until recently been the lieutenant-colonel of Lord Portmore's Regiment of Foot, and before that a company commander in Argyll's. Thomas Drummond was his friend, and another had been Robert Campbell of Glenlyon, the bankrupt murderer of Glencoe whose body he had sadly buried at Bruges. With them he had led his company against the bloody redoubts of Dottignies, and with them he had broken his sword in anger when their regiment was surrendered at Dixemude. Honour, duty and loyalty were the simple milestones he followed, and he appears to have had neither malice nor jealousy. With their letter, the Directors gave him his commission and a draft for £1,000 Sterling on a

Jamaican merchant, with which he was to hire or buy a sloop for Caledonia. He said good-bye to his wife and daughter, and left at once for Bristol. There he hoped to find a ship that would take him to the West Indies.

The Court of Directors and the Council-General met regularly every day for the rest of the month. The loss of so many ships and supplies—so much expenditure without return—forced them to make another call on the stockholders and to take resolute action against all their debtors. The Moderator of the Kirk was asked to appoint a National Day of Fast and Humiliation, and having thus appealed for God's mercy they resolved that none be shown to the guilty men of Caledonia. If any Councillor of the first Colony could prove his loyalty he was to be re-admitted to the Company's favour,

> But such as shall be found to have deserted either for cowardice, temerity, or simplicity, to be suspended till advice thereof be sent hither and an answer returned; and if any of them be found guilty of treachery or evil practices against the honour and interest of the Company or Colony to be condignly punished with the outmost severity as in cases of Treason.

Of Robert Pennecuik's guilt there was to be no admission of doubt. In this arrogant, bullying man the Company found its scapegoat. Without offering proof, the Directors accused him of conspiring with the English and betraying the Colony. The Councillors of the second expedition were told to treat him with disgrace and infamy wherever he might be found, to strip him of office and command, and to punish him as his crimes deserved.

Though he might not have agreed, his miserable death had been a providential mercy.

"And we looked for Peace, but no good came..."
Caledonia, November 1699 to January 1700

One hundred and sixty people died on that voyage from Rothesay in Bute to Caledonia in Darien. Though the fleet made the crossing in half the time it had taken the first expedition, its losses were four times as great. Yet James Byres would write confidently to the Directors that "our dead and sick men are very far short of what may be thought agreeable to so long a voyage." Many of the children did not survive to see the faery wonder of the green West Indian Isles, and among them was Mary Jaffray, the Fire-master's daughter. Alexander Dalgleish also died. One of God's jewels, said Borland, and much lamented. He left his pregnant and bewildered wife to the care of his colleagues. Aboard the *Rising Sun* there were thirty-five dead, most of them officers and Volunteers. The sickness had begun while the ships waited at Rothesay, and once burning could not be checked.

Antigua was the first landfall, sighted soon after dawn on November 9, and before dusk the fleet came up with the rocky isle of Montserrat and dropped anchor. Byres went ashore by long-boat to the town of Plymouth, where he asked for water and provisions. "But the Governor," said Borland, "was so inhuman that he denied us the liberty of having any, pretending his orders from the Court of England for so doing." The Scots were told that their Colony had been abandoned six months before, but they would not believe it. They left the next morning and that night, in a squall of rain and rising seas, the *Hope*'s look-out lost sight of the flagship's lantern. She sailed alone for two despairing weeks before she found the others. "At length, through the good Providence of God, we all arrived safely together on the coast of Darien." It was November 30, and all that they had been told at Montserrat was true.

Gibson fired a signal gun as he had been ordered, and waited for a pilot to take his ships into the harbour. There the new colonists saw no fort, no flourishing town, no warehouses, no busy quays, no fine ships loading. There was a half-submerged wreck at the harbour-mouth, the burnt ribs of another on the southern shore, and two small sloops anchored off the peninsula.

The *Olive Branch* and the *Hopeful Binning*, under their masters William Jameson and Alexander Stark, had arrived at Caledonia in August. They were astonished to find nothing but ruins, discarded kettles and pots, moss-grown cannon balls and the mute agony of four hundred graves. The Indians brought them one of the men left behind by the first expedition, and from him they learned what had happened. Although Jameson and

Stark did not think that they could hold the peninsula against attack, they bravely landed the survivors of the three hundred settlers they had taken aboard at Leith, raised the Company's standard, and told the Indians that they were but the vanguard of a great force now on its way from Scotland. As they probably hoped it would, this information reached Carthagena and Santa Maria before the end of the month. While no move was made against the Colony by land, the sight of Spanish cruisers idling some miles offshore made all the Scots uneasy. The problem of what they could or should do was soon resolved for them by a stupid accident. The cooper of the *Olive Branch*, carrying a candle below decks one night in search of brandy, set light to it, himself and the ship. She quickly burnt to the water's edge, with all her stores and provisions.

Being men of prudence rather than rash courage, Jameson and Stark decided to leave Lieutenant Oliphant and a dozen of their fittest men ashore with the Indians, and to take the rest to Jamaica in the *Hopeful Binning*. The voyage to Port Royal was long and bitter, and those colonists who did not die aboard were dead soon after they reached the English island.

On November 22 one of the twelve men left behind, and now watching anxiously from Point Look-out, sighted two sloops coming up from Golden Island. When he saw the Company's flag on an ensign-staff he ran down to the beach, crying with joy. The first ship was the *Ann of Caledonia*, and the second was the *Society* which Thomas Drummond had hired at Saint Thomas and loaded with provisions, paying for them with a bill drawn on Delancey and Wenham in New York.

The *Ann's* rigging was cut, her canvas holed, and her decks splintered. A day or more away from the settlement, and separated from the *Society*, she had been attacked by a Spanish warship of 20 guns. Though he had only six light-pounders on the sloop, a crew of thirteen, and the handful of volunteers who had come with him from New England, Drummond would not surrender. For more than four hours the *Ann* carried on a running fight with the Spaniard, escaping at last into the night.

Now on November 30, his scarlet coat neatly patched, his sword at his side and his hat pulled low, Drummond was rowed across to the *Rising Sun*. He demanded his place as a Councillor of the Colony, presenting letters from Paterson and Samuel Vetch as his credentials, and said that the Colony could get all the provisions it wished from New York. The Councillors did not believe him. "The fund of credit he proposed," they sneered in their report to the Directors, "was his word of honour." Angered by their disbelief and by their frightened distress, he became vainglorious. "He told us that he now reckoned all things very right, the Colony resettled, and that we could take Portobello if we pleased." He left the yellow cabin with no clear promise that his rights as a Councillor would be honoured, but with the certain knowledge that he and James Byres would clash violently before long.

From the sides of their ships the new colonists stared with horror at the land they had reached. "Expecting to meet with our friends and countrymen," said Borland, "we found nothing but a vast howling wilderness, the Colony deserted and gone, their huts all burnt, their fort most part ruined, the ground which they had cleared adjoining to the fort all overgrown with weeds; and we looked for Peace but no good came, and for a time of health and comfort, but beheld Trouble."

A small party was sent ashore in the rain to clear the parade of the fort and rebuild some of the huts. There was an immediate outcry from others who said that they had not come to settle a Colony, but to reinforce one already established. The Councillors shared this opinion, with the dismal and additional responsibility of deciding what should be done about it. They were not cheered when Drummond told them that there could be no debate, the town should be rebuilt and the fort prepared for the attack which the Spaniards would certainly mount against them soon.

Four days after the fleet's arrival a general meeting of Councillors, Land and Sea Captains, and all the Company's senior servants was held aboard the *Rising Sun* under the presidency of James Gibson and in his cabin. He began with a discouraging report. From the ships' invoices he had studied, including the *Society's*, he believed that their provisions would not last more than six months, and that on short allowances. At a ration of one gallon to every three men, the brandy would not last four. The hot and angry debate which followed this startling announcement passed, without conclusion, into a quarrel over a motion put by Byres. He suggested that they retire at once to Jamaica, leaving two or three companies of soldiers to hold the peninsula. Against whom and with what hope, he did not say. When it was realised that this might at least represent a settlement, and could not be called desertion, it was agreed that five hundred men should remain and that the rest should leave when the fort was in a proper state of defence. Byres then proposed another motion, that Thomas Drummond—who must surely have angrily abstained from the last—had no right to sit or vote at these meetings, and should be told to leave. He lost the vote, and was furious when William Vetch proposed that the full government of the Colony should rest in a triumvirate, himself, James Byres, and Thomas Drummond. There was only one valid commission, shouted Byres, and that was his. All others had been made null and void by the desertion of the first Colony. When Gibson and Lindsay meekly agreed to this astonishing claim, and the rest of the meeting grew uneasy with the late hour and the direction of the argument, Vetch withdrew his proposal.

They met again the next day, at eight o'clock in the cool of the morning. Byres seemed to have forgotten his demand for absolute power, and accepted the formal acknowledgement of himself, Vetch, Lindsay and Gibson as the Council of the Colony. He said little, but raised his hand with the majority when it was agreed that the daily ration of meat and biscuit should be cut, and that the colonists who were to leave for Jamaica should be carried in the *Hope of Bo'ness* and the *Duke of Hamilton* with provisions for three weeks.

Since he and his fellow-ministers were not invited to such meetings, except to offer a conventional prayer for wisdom and guidance, Francis Borland had little respect for the Council. He had none at all for most of the settlers. He thought they were mean, selfish and godless, and sure to suffer the Almighty's punishment for their heinous sins and abominations. On the voyage from Scotland, and now here on the edge of the world, few attended public worship, and none realised that the sickness and mortality already experienced compelled them to give thanks to God for His mercies even in the midst of His wrath.

Disappointed by the failure of their ministrations at sea, and dejected by the indifference of the Council now that they had

reached land, the three men met to consider the course their
work should take, and to have their conclusions properly recorded
by Mr. Stobo. They met in a borrowed cabin aboard the *Hope
of Bo'ness* because it had been made plain to them that if they
wished to have a hut ashore they must build it themselves. They
agreed that Wednesday, January 3, should be set aside—with the
consent of the Council—as a solemn day of Prayer, Humiliation
and Thanksgiving, whereby all men could "confess with shame
and sorrow their own and the sins of others concerned in this
undertaking." These sins were atheistical cursing and swearing,
brutish drunkenness, detestable lying and prevaricating, obscene
and filthy talk, blasphemous mockery, "yea and among too many
of the meaner sort, base thieving and pilfering, besides Sabbath
breaking and contempt of all Gospel ordinances." Even those
who had called out for Divine forgiveness during the delirium of
a fever at sea had now returned to their errors like a dog to its
vomit.

They carried their demand for a Day of Prayer to the Council,
and were told that it was unnecessary but they might do as they
wished. "Even a Heathen could give better advice," said Borland
bitterly. But they persevered in the Lord. They went from ship to
ship, or trudged through the mud ashore, distributing the printed
sermons, the prayers, tracts and catechisms they had brought
with them. Most were thrown away unread, or used as spills to
light a pipe, and Borland noticed that the men who did this were
usually Highlanders "of the meaner sort". He did not relate their
apparent profanity to the fact that they spoke little or no English
and could not read, though he seemed to think that such ignorance was also a heinous sin and abomination.

The friendship which the Indians had generously offered to the
leaders of the first Colony was now destroyed by the Council of
the second. Byres despised them, and was openly contemptuous
of their simple gifts. They were a parcel of rogues, he said when
Jaffray complained that one had shaken a lance at him, and
should all be hanged. Robert Turnbull boldly protested, warning
Byres that the Colony could not resist the Spaniards or meet
them in the field without the Indians' help. He had never known
them to be treacherous, but if they were ill-treated and their
women molested the Scots would be wise to keep within the fort.

Byres stared at the young man with astonishment. Who was going beyond the fort? They had not come here to take towns. From thenceforward, any one who opposed Byres was accused by him of being "for the taking of towns".

The morale of all was lowered by the open quarrels and idle inaction of the leaders. John Wallace had died on the voyage, and the remaining engineer, Thomas Kerr, could get little work from men who asked why they should rebuild the fort for others who did nothing but watch them from the ships. George Winram's liquor-still rusted in the hold of the *Hope*. There was no gold for Robert Keil's crucibles or John Hunter's coining-mill. No Indians came to learn good Lallan from Robert Johnson, although, to Borland's dismay, they became fluent in the obscenities they were mischievously taught by the soldiers. The useless trade goods in the ships—"so much thin grey paper, so many little blue bonnets" —were a mockery when there were no provisions to buy with them. There were daily complaints against the rations, but at half a pound of beef and half of bread, however odorous and rotten, they were a luxury compared with what was yet to come. By the middle of December work on the huts and fort had almost stopped. A miasma of idleness and despair had quickly fallen on the Colony. Many were sick, and for want of the strength or will to dig the morning graves the living threw the dead into the bay. The wet green forests, the mountain-heads in a mist of rain, the clean sea rolling beyond the harbour-mouth, were deceptively innocent and beguiling, tempting the desperate to desert. There was a rumour that the men sent to Jamaica would be sold as slaves to the English plantations, and among the Highlanders, who had long memories of kinsmen thus betrayed and transported, the story was easily believed. Ten Planters stole an eight-oared boat from the *Rising Sun* and rowed away to Portobello.

From the Indians, who remembered him with respect, Thomas Drummond learned that the Spaniards were preparing for a great attack on the settlement, by land and by sea. He thought it insane to wait for this, when a bold stroke might not only prevent it but also raise the spirits of the Scots and check their mutinous discontent. Aboard the *Ann* on December 15, he wrote a brief and soldierly proposal, sending it to the Council by Robert Turnbull's hand. Let him be given 150 men "that would be willing to take their fate with me" and he would lead them to live and fight in the forests with their Indian allies. Except for arms, ammunition and some provisions they would be no further burden to the Colony, and would not return to it until it was safe from danger. This each man would solemnly swear, and sign his name to the oath in witness.

When he appeared before the Council to argue this proposal he explained that he would raid Portobello, perhaps even Carthagena and release the *Dolphin's* prisoners there. He reminded the Council that there were men of courage and loyalty in the Colony, that many of the officers had recently offered to resign their commissions and remain as ordinary Planters when the others left for Jamaica. Byres was infuriated and frightened. He told the other Councillors that they should not "pin their faith upon another man's sleeve". He said that there were not six weeks' provisions left and none expected from Scotland. How could they think of taking towns? William Vetch was ill again, his spirit too weak to call up the courage he had once shown in the streets of Dunkeld. He let the decision go as the majority wished, and the others were too cowed by the noisy vehemence of Byres' voice to ask how six months' provisions had suddenly become six weeks'. Drummond's offer was refused.

The next day a file of musketeers under an ensign marched into the fort and arrested Alexander Campbell, a carpenter working there. He was manacled and taken aboard the *Duke of Hamilton*, charged with "mutinous association and villainous design of murder". He appears to have been a simple man with more pride and self-respect than malice. Since the fleet arrived he had frequently declared that in such a noble undertaking as this there should be no difference between the food enjoyed by an officer and that given to a common man. When he heard that the Council had rejected Drummond's proposal he became bolder and more foolish. "A great many officers, volunteers, planters and seamen," he said, or was later charged with saying, "had a design for seizing the Councillors and hanging them if they would not divest themselves of the government in favour of the conspirators." Within the hour he was arrested and his court-martial ordered by the Council.

The Court met in Gibson's cabin on December 18 under the

presidency of Major John Ramsay, six captains, three lieutenants and three ensigns. Campbell was now frightened, by the naked swords of his escort, by the witnesses whom he had thought were his comrades, and by the hard faces of these officers whose privileges he had resented. He admitted that he had complained about the food, and had said that the Company's money aboard the flagship should be used to buy more provisions. He had heard, and repeated, the rumour that some of the colonists were to be sold as slaves, but he had been party to no conspiracy and had not wished to hang the Councillors or overthrow their authority.

His unsupported confession of innocence was outweighed by the depositions made against him. He had been "a great seducer of the Colony", deponed William Macleod, and had said that since the Councillors were enriching themselves by denying food to honest men, they should hang. Those of a like mind with him would have no difficulty in seizing the *Rising Sun*, "for once the old fox, meaning Captain Gibson, were hanged, they'd meet with no resistance." Sergeant Andrew Logan swore that Campbell had asked him to seize the *Hope* with the men of his company, and sail it to Ireland. Peter McFerran said that the signal for rebellion in the Colony was to have been the waving of a flag. And Sergeant William Robertson declared that Campbell had assured him that if Captain Drummond's proposal were rejected by the Council then those officers who supported it would join the conspiracy. This, to James Byres, would be the most important evidence of all.

Alexander Campbell was found guilty of all the charges laid against him. He was sentenced to death by hanging and was taken from the flagship to the *Duke of Hamilton*, there to await execution. He was undoubtedly a scapegoat, the expendable victim of cunning men and a complaisant Court. In all the evidence it is clear that he was the servant rather than the instigator of the grand conspiracy. There was, for example, an Ensign Spark who had been the intermediary, so witnesses implied, between ambitious officers and discontented men like Campbell. No action was taken against Spark, however, nor any others for the moment. It may be that the Court was reluctant to worsen a strained situation by advising further investigation.

Though it would discourage further plots, the execution of a mean carpenter could embarrass no one but himself. The Councillors were less tolerant. "We have lame and partial proof against several others," they wrote to Edinburgh, "but not so legal as they should be, so we must have patience." James Byres would not endure that patience for long.

During the two days he had left, Campbell was kept in the lamp-lit hold of the *Duke of Hamilton*, with irons on his wrists and ankles, and a corporal's guard to see that he did not end his agony now by breaking his head against the mainmast foot. Borland visited him frequently, and although Campbell may have found the minister's scalding sermons an unnecessary addition to his punishment he was happy to ask for forgiveness. Or so Borland wrote. "This poor man seemed to die very penitently.... He said that for some time before this, particularly since God had recovered him from a late sickness, he had left off prayer to the Lord, and therefore God had justly left him to this sad end." Though Borland seemed more pleased by this graphic illustration of Divine wrath than he was angered by the causes of Campbell's discontent, he and another minister compassionately asked the Council to commute the sentence to banishment. They were told that it was impossible.

There was more anger than penitence in the carpenter's last moment, and a brave defiance in his acceptance of it. Toward two o'clock in the afternoon of Wednesday, December 20, he was rowed ashore behind a drummer beating. In the south ravelin of the fort, looking across the harbour-mouth, his fellow-carpenters had built a scaffold. As he stood upon it, the noose about his throat, a company of soldiers drawn up in hollow square, and silent crowds on the ships and shore, he remembered those men for whom he was dying. "Lord forgive them who brought me on this lock!" he shouted, and jumped from the scaffold without waiting for the thrust of a drum-major's hand. Byres found another meaning for those last words. "We fancied the rascal expected relief to the last minute."

The next day or the day after, Thomas Drummond was arrested by order of the Council and taken from his sloop to the *Duke of Hamilton*. There he was locked in a cabin and allowed no visitors. Three other officers were also taken up, Captain Kerr the engineer, Ensign Spark, and a Lieutenant Logan who had come from New York with Drummond. A fifth man placed under guard was Alexander Hamilton. Having loyally returned to the Colony as Overseer of Supplies, he was the natural man to be held responsible for the shortage of provisions. The Council of four was now the instrument of one quixotic man. Vetch had persuaded himself, or had been persuaded by Byres, that his commission referred to the first Colony and that he had no real authority in the second. Lindsay seems to have been a soldier of limited wit, happy to have the weight of his conscience carried on another's shoulders. And Gibson, according to the ministers, accepted all that was done with indifference, thinking only of his pipe and dram. No formal charges were brought against the arrested men, no court-martial was ordered, but to all those who were curious about their ultimate disposal Byres talked of the evidence at Campbell's trial, of an officers' plot to overthrow the Council. There would be proof of Drummond's villainy soon, very soon. There is no record of any protest against the arrests. Weakened by fever and fear, unnerved by the sight of the carpenter's body hanging on its rotting rope, the Planters did nothing. Bound by their solemn oath to serve the Company, the Officers would not openly defy its rightful representative. Byres had come to the end of his patience. He had silenced Drummond's opposition to his proposal for a retreat to Jamaica, and by this, his only positive action, he had made himself king.

Two days before Christmas, having bought the sloop *Society* on a bill they hoped the Company would honour, the Councillors decided to send her away with their first report to the Directors. Though signed by all four men, the letter was the voice of James Byres. Admittedly "long and melancholy", it whined, complained, boasted and appealed. The first colonists were a disgrace to Scotland and a reproach to humanity. There was no gold, no silver, no Nicaragua wood, and all who had reported otherwise were fools and knaves. The ships' stewards were also proven knaves, never had there been such a collection of knaves in so small a community. Captain Drummond was in custody for offences whereof there would soon be proof.... Captain Kerr, also in custody, was not fit for service in the Colony and the Council intended to be quit of him. The fort could not be rebuilt without proper tools, and the Colony was thus defenceless. On the other hand, there was no great fear of the Spaniards. The Indians were worthless allies, small and weak, and one Scots grenadier would not find it hard to defeat ten of them at once. The Company knew—and here there was a hint that Byres was frightened by the authority he had assumed —that the undersigned were under no obligation to serve as the government of the Colony, but were honest men and awaited those whom the Directors might send to replace them. "Meantime, we shall not disgracefully lay down the baton so providentially put in our hands."

The Colony now sank into a paralysed inertia that was to last for six weeks. No work was done except that necessary for simple existence. The five hundred men selected for Jamaica, and all the remaining women and children, were sent aboard the *Hope of Bo'ness* and the *Duke of Hamilton*. Among them were most of the volunteers who had come from New York with Drummond, those who had sworn to take their fate with him in the jungle, all whom Byres suspected of being "for the taking of towns". While the weather blew steadily from the north, however, the ships could not leave the harbour, for they were as clumsy to windward as their predecessors had been. Nor was the *Society* allowed to sail, though she could have got through the sea-gate. For reasons that would be clear later, Byres delayed her departure.

Fever was again epidemic. There were never less than two hundred gravely sick men aboard and ashore. At first light each morning, the night's dead were turned over the ships' sides. The ministers, who had hoped that such God-sent suffering would turn men away from viciousness, were disappointed. Mr. Shields preached aboard the flagship upon the text *Behold your sins shall find you out*, but the colonists remained stubborn in their depravity. "I remember," wrote Borland, "the observation of the Reverend Mr. Shields, that he had conversed with many sorts of people in several parts of the world, and had served as a minister for several years in the Army in Flanders, but he had never seen or been concerned with such a company as this was." The ministers had kept apart from the political squabbles of the Colony. Though they detested Byres, and believed Drummond to be "the most diligent and useful man", they made no protest against his arrest. Byres now ignored them, and no longer invited them to open Council meetings with a prayer. They complained bitterly when they were not given huts ashore, but they would not lift a hammer or an axe to build one for themselves. To stop their mouths perhaps, someone at last gave Stobo and Borland the use of his own hut, but Shields remained aboard the *Rising Sun*. Even ashore there was no peace from the mockery and blasphemous contempt of the colonists, and when these three humourless men met they often went into the trees for their mournful deliberations. *Inter densas umbrosa Cacumina Sylvas*, wrote Borland, glumly remembering the dripping leaves above his head.

Their Day of Prayer, Thanksgiving and Humiliation was a dismal failure. Though each preached a long sermon on hellfire and damnation, few came to listen and most of those for the diversion only. They decided that it was neither practicable nor expedient to set up a Presbytery as they had been instructed, and they turned, with relief almost, to their second obligation, the conversion of the Indian. When Robert Turnbull heard of their wish to visit a Cuna village he acquired leave to accompany them with a file of soldiers. They could not have gone far without him, but that was not his reason. He was anxious to talk with Pedro, if that elusive captain were still alive, and to discover what was known of the Spaniards' preparations against the Colony.

They left early in the morning of January 16, crossing by boat to the far shore of the bay and travelling from thence on foot. They climbed so many steep hills and waded so many streams that the wearied Borland lost count of them. By nightfall, when they reached Pedro's village on the banks of the Greater Acla, they were exhausted and wet to the waist. Reports of the little chief's death, which had come to the first Colony before it left, were false, and he greeted his friend Turnbull with affectionate warmth. He welcomed the ministers too, and although their black broadcloth and white neck-bands were strange to him, he could see by their manner that they were important men. He fed them all on dried fish and meat, plantains and potatoes, and ordered fires to be lit by their hammocks. The Indians listened in polite silence to the ministers' sermons, but were indifferent to their meaning. Perhaps Turnbull was too tired to translate the scriptural homilies that thundered across the firelight, or had not the vocabulary to do the ministers justice, for they later complained that they could not labour in God's vineyard here without an interpreter. The Indians, they said, were a poor and naked people, idle and lazy, more inclined by temperament to adopt a Scotsman's vices than accept his religion.

What Turnbull had learned from Pedro put him in no mood to linger while Mr. Shields or Mr. Stobo explained the significance of the Sabbath to an uncomprehending audience that counted time by the moon. He wanted to talk with other headmen, and at dawn the next day he ordered a march, moving westward to the Lesser Acla. At every village the Scots were welcomed kindly, and at each Turnbull's anxiety to return to Caledonia was increased. Believing that they might reach it more quickly, and with less strain on the ministers, if they travelled by way of the coast, he led the party back to the Greater Acla and turned northward along its banks to the sea. The ministers stumbled wearily behind the soldiers, marvelling at wide savannahs of moving grass, the vermilion flash of startled birds, cool parks of stately trees. At the mouth of the river they saw Golden Island, serene in a seaward mist, and believed that they were but a short walk from their harbour. Some way along the shore to the east, said Borland, they came to a rocky point, and moved inland again to approach the shore on its other side.

> But here we travelled so long and by such crooked turnings and through such thickets of tall and dark woods that we quite lost ourselves, and were bewildered, that we knew not what way to move, nor how to extricate ourselves. Standing still, therefore, in our bewildered and melancholy condition, we heard the noise of the sea, and judged it to be our only surest guide to wind ourselves out of our present labyrinth. Therefore we turned our course directly toward the noise of the waves, and a very difficult and uncomfortable passage we had in striving to get through the thorny thickets of woods in our way, and with much ado at length we got safely into the open air by the sea.

Here was no sandy walk, however, but an angry coastline of breaking waves, and rather than move inland again Turnbull led the party along the edge of the water. "We were washen with waves ... and the various windings and bendings of the coast made our way much longer; sometimes we had steep rocks to pass over, which we must climb with our hands and feet." They had eaten nothing since leaving the last village on the Acla, and they had no water to drink. All were exhausted, but Shields was scarcely able to walk and became so feeble that Borland feared he would die. At last they found a spring, breaking from the rocks above and as heaven-sent, they said, as the well was to Hagar in the wilderness when her child was like to die. It gave Shields the strength to continue. By dusk they saw the bare top-sail yards of their ships above the trees. "The Lord leading the blind by a way they knew not," quoted Borland, with little gratitude to Turnbull, "preserving our going out and our coming in, and as our day was, so making our strength to be."

The Lieutenant went straight to the Council. From the information the Indians had given him, he said, he believed that the Barliavento Fleet and an army from Santa Maria would shortly attack the Colony. Byres was unimpressed. He would fight any Spaniard who came, but Caledonia was impregnable from the sea and nobody but a fool would attack it from the woods. A week later, under strong pressure from the company commanders, he agreed that some guns should be landed from the ships and mounted in the embrasures of the fort.

But he would not release Drummond or Thomas Kerr.

"This was now a smiling Providence upon us, but alas...!"
Caledonia, February 1700

From the Woods of Caledonia, Mr. Stobo wrote at the head of the letter, *February 2, 1700, Reverend Sir.* ... The three ministers were alone in the Shades of Love, away from the stench and profanity of New Edinburgh, composing a letter to the Moderator. They thought it their duty to inform him of the sad and afflicted state of the Colony. The source and fountain cause of all its miseries were the colonists themselves. *Our land hath spewed out its scum.* ... They were perverse, pernicious and mean, without religion, reason, honesty or honour. *We could not prevail to get their wickedness restrained, nor the growth of it stopped.* God has punished them with a sore and contagious sickness, taking away as a terrible example some of his own jewels and excellent ones. *This sickness, for some time abated, is now returned in its former rage....*

It was a bitter letter, composed by lonely men who were bewildered by the failure of their mission and wounded by the contempt of men they had hoped to inspire. They sat together under the trees, each comforted by the others' sympathy, offering a word, a phrase, a scriptural reference to strengthen the letter. Mr. Stobo's pen dipped regularly into the ink-horn, scratching line after line of complaint and accusation. They had done their duty as colleagues in a Collegiate of Relation, although it had been impossible to establish a Presbytery. They had preached every Sabbath, one aboard the flagship and two ashore, but such was the malignant obstinacy of the colonists that few came to listen. *Near on a third at least are wild Highlanders that cannot speak nor understand Scotch, which are barbarians to us and we to them.* The Indians were no better, though those who came to hear the ministers were at least decent in their behaviour. God's servants would persevere in their thankless work, they would stay until the end of the year they had agreed to serve, but... *We must now give you advertisement, and entreat you to intimate to the Reverend Commission that none of us are determined to settle here.* They asked for prayers and understanding. They signed themselves the Moderator's afflicted brethren in the Work of the Gospel. They sealed the letter and walked down to New Edinburgh, to something they had not thought fit to mention— the sound of axe and saw again, the sight of men now at work after a month of despairing lethargy.

The threat of a Spanish attack had frightened those colonists not marked down for Jamaica, and the enthusiasm of young officers like Turnbull had encouraged them to resist it. Four guns from the *Rising Sun* were now ashore, and were being dragged across the marsh to the fort as the ministers came down from the Shades of Love. Although Byres had not authorised it, seventy huts and two storehouses were also being rebuilt. The walls and roof of the guardhouse were restored, and the ministers had been informed that they might use the building as a church when it contained no prisoners. This, too, they had not told the Moderator. Not all the officers thought that resistance was advisable, and most of the men waiting to sail for Port Royal were hoping that they would be away before it became necessary. Major John Ramsay and several captains said that they wished to leave on the *Society*, and to take ship for Scotland from whatever port she touched. Sick in his cabin prison, Thomas Drummond asked the Council to free him so that he might go home for the good of his health. During the past five weeks, seeing no one but the guard at his door and the steward who brought him food, he had lost faith in the Colony and could think of his reputation only. He wanted to be the first to tell the Directors of his quarrel with Byres.

Much of the work being done was without the direction or sanction of the Councillors, and they frequently confused everybody by ordering all sea-captains to take on water, to secure their guns and clear their decks for sailing as soon as the wind blew from the south-east. Byres' braggart defiance of the Spaniards had changed to a surly disapproval of any attempt to resist them. It would be unlawful, he said, all war was unlawful and un-Christian. Alexander Shields was outraged by such blasphemy. He had soldiered with the Cameronians and knew that was lawful. He had seen them die with the Psalms on their lips and knew that was Christian. The Councillor told him that he was talking nonsense, contradicting the Gospels, and tempting men to become atheists. On Sunday, February 4, Byres honestly acknowledged that his own safety was more important to him than the security of the Colony. He announced that he would sail away with the *Society* as soon as the fly-boats could warp her out of the bay.

The thought had probably been in his mind since he first delayed the sloop's departure, now it had been translated into action by the arrival that morning of a Jamaican brigantine. She was loaded with dry-goods and Negro slaves, but her master had some beef and flour he was willing to sell. He was also anxious to be away as soon as he had caulked a leak, and the news he brought explained why. Four great warships had recently arrived at Portobello from Cadiz, the largest of 60 guns, and three more were expected from Carthagena. The streets of Portobello were sweet with the scent of new-made bread, thousands of loaves for the seamen and soldiers who were to fall upon Caledonia by land and by sea.

James Byres was aboard the *Society* before nightfall, with his baggage, his brother-in-law and his apprentice. He said that he would return soon with provisions from Jamaica, but the letters he carried from the Council referred the Directors to Mr. Byres himself should they have any questions that were not answered in the dispatches. Perhaps—and it may be charitable to assume this—the reference was to letters which Byres said he would write to the Company from Port Royal. No one protested against this shameless desertion, all would no doubt have agreed with Shields that it was "a step in our deliverance". It was Wednesday before the fly-boats got the sloop through the sea-gate, and there was one other passenger aboard, Mrs. Dalgleish. "She is big with child," said the Council's letter. "We are not in condition so to treat her as her circumstances and good behaviour require." They hoped that she would finally reach Scotland, and that the Company would pay her the stipend her husband might have earned.

From the cabin window of the *Duke of Hamilton*, Thomas Drummond watched the sloop until she was gone beyond the point, convinced that James Byres' voice would now be heard in Milne Square before his.

The remaining Councillors did nothing. They increased the daily allowance of flour by a quarter of a pound, and they worried about the brandy that was being stolen, suspecting James Milne, the steward of the *Rising Sun*. But they did nothing to organise the defence of the peninsula, and they stubbornly refused to release the arrested officers or to put more men ashore. For two weeks a Spanish cruiser, hull-down to the north, had been watching the Colony, and now it moved in closer, picking up a long-boat which the Scots had sent out to study it. From dawn to dusk the gold of its stern and the distant call of its trumpets could be seen and heard from Point Look-out. By the week's end, like a paralysed rabbit, the leaderless Colony was once more immobilised by fright.

For months the Spanish had known less about the strength of the Scots than the Caledonians knew of theirs. An Indian, holding up his fingers before Turnbull or Drummond, could say with accuracy how many ships he had seen, but a lock of hair shaken before the Campmaster at Toubacanti might mean five hundred men or five thousand. The Spanish commanders were also bound by rigid and inflexible rules. The long chain of command, its sea and land-borne links connecting Carthagena, Portobello, Panama, Vera Cruz and Mexico City with that moribund Sufferer in Madrid, made strong and independent action inadvisable where it was not impossible. Days passed before a Governor could read a Campmaster's report, a week, two weeks before a President heard from a Governor, a month before a President's dispatch was read by the Viceroy, and almost a year before the Viceroy might hope for an answer from Madrid.

The new Governor of Carthagena, Don Juan Pimienta, was more impatient than most with the long delays between the dispatch of information he had received and the return of orders in reply. When he heard that the *Hopeful Binning* had left Caledonia he advised the King that the twice-abandoned fort should now be occupied by Spanish soldiers, but even he would not do this without orders, and before his letter could reach Madrid the Scots were back. Pimienta was a small, dark-skinned salamander, neat and stiff in the Castilian manner, inexorable in purpose but scrupulously exact in the courtesies of war. He was no pen-and-ink soldier, and did not waste paper or insult his own intelligence by calling the Scots pirates and corsairs. He was as anxious as Don Quixote for a chivalrous passage of arms with them, respecting their valour and eager to gild his own by defeating them. His garrison and ships, however, were crippled by disease, and he believed that his dispirited soldiers would have to be dragged "to anything that looks like fighting". He asked for seasoned infantrymen and good sea-officers, knowing that by the time they arrived—if ever they arrived—the Scots might become too strong to be dislodged. He complained bitterly that the citizens of Carthagena tightened their purse-strings when ordered to loosen them in the King's service. His councillors were tradesmen who knew nothing of the disciplines of war, frightened men who confused themselves with ridiculous rumours. The Scots, they said, had mined a mountain above the neck of the peninsula and intended to explode it should the Spanish attack from that direction. Who could lay such a long fuse, asked Pimienta, who could be sure that such a vast mine of powder would not become damp and useless in this climate? Such inane fancies, he thought, "cause the writing of a great lot of paper to those who direct military affairs."

On January 15 the Conde de Canillas, President of Panama, was at last in no doubt about the strength and morale of the Colony, and was delighted to find that both were much lower than he had feared. At noon that day a sergeant and four Indians from Santa Maria brought him two Scots deserters—John Jardine a labourer, and William Strachan a tailor. Both had sailed with the first expedition as Planters, and both had returned with Drummond on the *Ann of Caledonia*. Shortly after Christmas they had decided that rather than exist any longer on a daily ration of two biscuits and a little codfish they would live or die in the forest. For a few yards of stolen linen an Indian agreed to take them where gold might be found, but he did not tell them that the gold was coin and that he hoped to find it for himself. He led them into the mountains and delivered them to Campmaster Carrizoli at Toubacanti. From thence they were sent to Panama City by way of Santa Maria.

They were miserable and frightened when they were brought before Canillas and his council that afternoon. None of the Spaniards could understand their thorny Scots, but an illiterate Irish adventurer, a marine called Michael Burke, acted as an interpreter. Canillas was gentle with the deserters, telling Burke that they might take whatever oath their church allowed, examining them separately and questioning them closely on both the first and second expeditions. By dusk he knew all that they were able to tell him about the ships, arms, supplies and defences of the Colony, the discontent and the desertions. They had left before Byres agreed to the landing of the flagship's guns, and Strachan said that his countrymen had not "mounted any artillery ashore, their whole effort being to build houses to shelter them; the old fortification is in bad shape, without gates." When the interrogation was over, the tailor and the labourer were taken away under guard. They were again lost in the darkness that hides the existence of most men. This one afternoon only of their lives endures on record, but it was decisive.

Canillas ordered an immediate attack on Caledonia, his couriers riding the treasure road to Portobello and from thence by ship to Carthagena. Though there was a terrible epidemic of fever in all the Spanish provinces, from Vera Cruz to New Granada, the President was confident that those seamen and soldiers who were not sick were enough to exterminate this puny and impudent settlement of pirates. He proposed the plan he had attempted a year before, the land attack which had ended in Montgomerie's skirmish and his own wretched retreat from Toubacanti, but this time it would be supported by a simultaneous assault from the sea by the Barliavento Fleet under its commander, Don Diego Peredo. Pimienta, and those of his soldiers whom he could drag to the business of fighting, were to leave Carthagena as soon as possible by the auxiliary transports of the Barliavento, and Canillas would join them off the coast of Caledonia with three ships and five hundred men from the garrisons of Panama City and Portobello. Three companies of militia, also from Panama City, were to be sent by oared galleys to Santa Maria from whence the foppish Governor of Darien, Don Miguel Cordones, would march them inland to reinforce Carrizoli's militia, slaves and levies at Toubacanti. With the four hundred men he would then command, Cordones was to strike north at Caledonia as soon as his scouts reported the arrival of the Barliavento.

At dawn on February 12 Pimienta went aboard Peredo's flagship, *San Juan Bautista,* and ordered her out to the harbour mouth where some launches were waiting to load the last of his field guns and carriages. To his speechless fury, an incompetent helmsman put the ship aground on a shoal in the lee of the castle, and it was sunset before she could be warped off by her own boats. Even then she dragged her anchor in the night breeze and went aground again. It was another twenty-four hours before the guns were hauled aboard and the flagship could at last sail in pursuit of her squadron.

Had all gone as Canillas wished, had the Barliavento answered Cordones' advancing trumpets one morning with a cannonade from the lee of Golden Island, the demoralised Scots would probably have surrendered without resistance. They were saved in time from this disgrace by an unlikely *coup de théâtre,* by The Hero's sudden appearance from the wings, sword in hand.

Alexander Campbell of Fonab arrived on Sunday, February 11, slipping past the watching cruiser in a Barbadoes sloop. It had taken him four frustrating months to reach Caledonia, and he brought it no more than a few provisions, a young naval officer called John Stewart, and the strength of his own indomitable spirit. A Jamaican sloop followed his into the bay, driven there by the cruiser, and her master told the Scots that Benbow's fleet was under sail to help them. Heartening though this nonsensical report was, the real encouragement came from Fonab's presence, the sight of his calm and upright head, his straight back and scarlet coat as he was rowed across to the *Rising Sun*. He was no stranger, most of the officers had served with him in Ramsay's Scots Brigade, and many of the Planters had trailed a pike or shouldered a musket behind him at Dottignies and Landen. The three miserable Councillors scarcely troubled to read his commission, but gladly gave him all responsibility for the protection of the Colony. His advice was simple, fight—and by fight he meant offence not defence. He took command in a storm of sleepless energy, ordering the instant release of the arrested officers, the landing of the men embarked for Jamaica, and their immediate employment on the fort and ditch. "So we see," wrote Borland, with no apparent confidence that all was now for the best, "that men propose but GOD disposeth of us and all our concerns, and it pleaseth Him."

When Thomas Drummond came ashore from the *Duke of Hamilton*, Fonab embraced him warmly. They had not met since they were captains together in Argyll's, and it may be that Campbell hoped his friend would share this command with him. But the galling indignity of his imprisonment had soured Drummond's loyalty to the Colony and the Company. He could think only of James Byres already at sea, and if not bound for Edinburgh then certain to be writing letters of scurrilous complaint against him. He was ill, and in this bitter mood was of no use to Fonab. When he asked leave to sail for Scotland as soon as possible, for an early opportunity to vindicate himself before the Directors, Campbell willingly gave it.

Within a day of his arrival Fonab proposed an attack on Toubacanti where, according to Turnbull's Indian friends, several companies of Spanish soldiers were assembling for an assault on the Colony. Campbell knew nothing of the country, of the difficulties of marching through it or fighting in it. He knew where the enemy was, and that was sufficient. His confidence inspired the younger officers, particularly Turnbull, who offered him thirty eager warriors he had trained as a militia, and who said that Captain Pedro would join them with as many more once he heard the Scots had decided to fight. On Tuesday morning, having had little sleep in the forty-eight hours he had been in the Colony, Alexander Campbell crossed the bay with two hundred Scots and Turnbull's Indians. The soldiers had been hurriedly selected by candle-light on Monday night, each captain choosing the fittest men in his command, and twelve of them were young Gentlemen Volunteers particularly attached to Turnbull in loyalty and affection. They marched with incredible speed through the mangroves and the thick forest to the south of the bay, men who had eaten nothing but rotting biscuits and codfish for months, who carried heavy muskets, ammunition-boxes and swords, whose wet clothes and long hair were caught by every snatching thorn. Yet before nightfall they had reached Pedro's village on the banks of the Acla. He was waiting for them, having been warned by a runner, his face painted black for war, his shoulders covered by the stained scarlet coat the Scots had given more than a year before. Fonab and his officers slept in Pedro's long-house that night, with fires beside their hammocks, and at dawn he joined them in their march with forty of his warriors.

The way was now even harder than it had been on Tuesday, for the ground rose steadily toward the ridge of the cordillera, and was barred by fallen trees, great boulders and the rush of bright green streams. Campbell kept the Scots together and on the march by the strength of his will and the power of his personality. None of them, except perhaps Turnbull, had ever been this deep into the forests or seen such country, so unlike their homeland hills or the dusty avenues of Flemish poplars where once they had campaigned. Sometimes they saw nothing but the red shoulders of the man in front, an angry branch snapping back as he passed. They sank to their knees in a millennium of vegetable decay, were blinded by leaf-splintered sunlight, and deafened by the raucous protest of hidden birds. Turnbull enjoyed all of it.

I was ordered to march on the front with the Volunteers (he wrote to his cousin later) and with Captain Pedro and about 30 Indians, the rest being divided among the party. We marched over a great hill and crossed the river that runs to the South Seas, and then one of our Indian spies came in and told us that the Spaniards were on top of the next hill, cutting down trees to strengthen themselves, so I sent and told Captain Campbell, and he marched up with the party and halted there a little.

It was noon and the heat intense. The "next hill" was a long mountain slope of timber, some miles from its foot to the flat summit of Toubacanti. Nothing could be seen but the shimmering movement of leaves. The Scots dropped exhausted where they stood, or bent over their grounded muskets in the sobbing agony of fatigue. The Indians' childish enthusiasm had changed to a melancholy despair, and they were in no humour for an assault on a stockade manned by Spanish soldiers. Pedro smiled hopefully and asked why they should not remain where they were in ambush, for the Spaniards must pass this way to Caledonia. Campbell angrily refused, a soldier was not a bandit but a brave man who advanced boldly upon his enemy with musket primed and bayonet fixed. He drove his Scots to their feet and put them to the march again. They could climb no more than two miles of the bitter slope before dusk and then, by a small spring, the Indians stubbornly refused to go any further. There would be no more water, they said, before Toubacanti was reached. That night the Scots ate the last of the biscuits and dried fish they carried in their pockets, slept as best they could on the earth, and were glad when dawn came. They stood in file, ready to march, but the Indians would send no scouts ahead. Turnbull was ashamed for his friends.

I used all the persuasion I could, promising them great rewards and telling them I would go with them myself. They told me I would be killed. I told them it was no matter though I was killed, so that the Commander could have perfect intelligence. Then they laughed at me, so I saw nothing would do with them. I turned myself to the leader and told him in their language that so, they were great brags of their stoutness in Caledonia, that now I saw they were all cowards. Then they were so mad that, calling all their Indians together, running up the hill as if they would engage the Spaniards themselves, but I got them pacified and they immediately ordered two of their Indians to go with me.

He advanced with the scouts and his twelve Volunteers, and two hours later he was within bow-shot of a Spanish working-party. He could not see them, but he heard them, as they had heard the noisy approach of his careless Volunteers. "I heard them cutting down trees, and speaking very fast, for their out-sentries had run in and told them of my march." He fell back into the trees for two bow-shots, placed his men in a defensive skirmish line, and pencilled a note to Fonab. If it were his pleasure, the Commander could attack at once, for the Spaniards had no intention of sallying out to fight. Moreover, since they had built their fort on the southern descent of the hill the Scots would have the advantage in assault. Campbell sent up reinforcements, and then arrived himself. He and Turnbull crawled forward until they could see the stockade in a clearing, and they were soberly impressed by it. Its walls were made from thick piles the height of a man, driven into the earth and interlaced with branches. It was star-shaped, with redoubts and bastions, faces, flanks and angles. Smoke drifted above it from a cooking-fire, and although the Scots could see the sunlit flash of steel, could hear the sound of excited voices, they saw no one and could not tell how weak or strong the garrison might be.

Fonab told Turnbull that he would attack at once, and the lieutenant asked where he might have the honour to advance. Campbell smiled and told him to take whatever position pleased him. In the van with his Volunteers, said Turnbull.

They went back to the waiting Scots and Indians. Fonab placed axe-men in his front line, drew his sword and called the advance. Away went Turnbull's Volunteers with a huzza, his Indians following. They ran into the clearing, halted, formed line and marched forward until they were twenty feet from the nearest breastwork. There they halted again and presented their muskets. Turnbull saw the Spaniards waving to him, ironically inviting him to bring his forlorn hope yet closer. He ignored them and calmly gave the order to fire. The Volunteers were priming for a second volley through the smoke of their first when the Spaniards replied from a salient to their left. Turnbull took a ball in his right shoulder but remained on his feet, ordering his little platoon to advance with the bayonet. "The company had no loss by falling, the Gentlemen making no stop, but went on bravely. Neither did the Spaniards show themselves to be coward, standing till our Gentlemen did grip their firelocks by the muzzle."

Now Fonab came out of the trees, running sword in hand with the main body of the Scots behind him. When they reached the palisades the axemen chopped and slashed, others thrust their bayonets through the branches or fired up into the faces of the shouting defenders. Pedro's warriors screamed on the flanks of the attack, hurling their lances over the walls. The little fight was shortly over. Once the axemen had cut a breach in the palisade, the Scots pushed in, lunging with bayonets and hacking with broadswords. The Spaniards made a brief stand by their cooking-fires and then threw down their arms and ran out of the far gate into the trees. A musket-ball in the joint of his right shoulder, his sword in his left hand, Fonab ordered a pursuit. Within an hour the sun had set, and his drummer beat a recall into the dusk.

Lying on the muddy earth of the fort was Don Miguel Cordones' jewelled sword. And also his splendid coat, laced and corded, embroidered on the left breast with a Golden Fleece, the badge of a Knight of the Order of Saint James.

It had been a brave little affray, entirely to Fonab's taste, surprise and courage having overthrown a superior enemy in a strong defensive position. Seven of the Scots were dead, lying at the breach or inside the stockade, and fourteen or more were wounded. The Indian dead were not counted, but Pedro had been wounded as he attacked the salient from which Turnbull was shot. There is no exact record of the Spanish losses, and reports of them later would be ridiculously exaggerated, but there were two or three dozen prisoners surrounded by black-faced, screaming Indians. When the Scots saw that Fonab and Turnbull were wounded (or so it was said, though it may have been the dead of their own rank that angered them) they turned on the prisoners and had already butchered some before Campbell could beat them away.

The dead were buried in the firelight, and when prayers had been said above them Fonab honoured two naked Indians whose courage he admired. The first was Diego's son, Steven, and the second an unknown man to whom Campbell gave his own name, Alexander. They were made captains in the service of the Company, and were each given a scarlet coat and a beaver hat, the late owners of which having no further use for them.

At sunrise on Friday the Scots marched for Caledonia. They left all but three of their prisoners behind. They burnt or destroyed what they could of the fort, and took away the arms, ammunition and provisions they could carry. They reached the south shore of the bay on Sunday, February 18, their drums beating a triumph. It was seven days only since Fonab had arrived in the Barbadoes sloop, and it was the end of his active control of the Colony. But though his aching wound, and the fever that followed it, would keep him to his bed, his spirit and his presence would still be the Caledonian's main strength.

The victory at Toubacanti was no more than Francis Borland had expected from the Almighty, but the disgraceful way in which the Colonists celebrated it filled him with gloom.

This was now a smiling Providence upon us, and our people now generally were lifted up with hopes and confidence that all things would succeed prosperously with them. But alas! we did not walk humbly and thankfully before GOD under this smile of His providence upon us. Instead of our glorifying the GOD of our Salvation, there was little to be seen among most of our men but excessive drunkeness, profane swearing, ranting, boasting, and singing. And so came of it, for shortly after our present smiles were turned into frowns, our clear sunshine was overcast with dark and threatening clouds. We were soon as much dejected and cast down as we had before been vain, proud and lifted up.

The first cloud in the clear sunshine was seen from Point Look-out on February 23. A tall ship, a great man-of-war was moving off Golden Island, a small schooner and a dispatch-boat in her wake. Before sunset they lay to with the wind in the west and seemed to be studying the mouth of the harbour. The warship, with a naked image on her sterncastle, was the *San Juan*

Bautista, and Don Diego Peredo was profoundly worried by Pimienta's rash enthusiasm for getting closer yet to land so that he might see what ships were in the bay. Heavy seas and winds on the previous day had sprung the flagship's foremast, and Peredo knew nothing and feared the worst of currents that might drag her on to the cliffs of the peninsula. By nightfall Pimienta stifled his curiosity—seeing nothing now in the moonless dark—and allowed Peredo to take the ship out to sea. She returned the next day, and the next, and was joined by others, the *San Francisco* and *El Florizant* with their attendant sloops, schooners and transports. They cruised far out to sea; only the small ships came in to stare at the harbour mouth like children, to put their helms over and run at some imagined alarm.

The sight of so many ships, the paradoxical threat of their continued inaction, dismayed the Colonists. "We daily expected their coming in to attack our fort and ships," said Borland, "Our people were filled with fears and sad thoughts of heart." No one was more fearful, or had sadder thoughts than the Councillors Gibson, Lindsay and Vetch. They were for capitulating at once, for the sending out of a sloop to sue for terms. Fonab had come to their meeting in great pain, but he forgot it in his anger. He would not surrender, he said, and neither would they while he was there. They were silenced by his contempt more than by his arguments, and for the moment they spoke no more of capitulation. Though they stubbornly retained the pretence of authority, the defence of the Colony was now in the hands of officers inspired by Fonab. His bright confidence, even in a fever, was infectious. When he was told that the musketeers had less than enough shot for one engagement, he advised the casting of more from all that useless English pewter. He could do nothing to increase the miserable rations of green biscuits and rotting fish, but he reminded the men that their comrades had no more than this in their bellies when they took the stockade at Toubacanti. He was disappointed in Drummond when he found that the fort was half a mile from the nearest spring, but he wasted no time in angry protest. He ordered casks to be filled with water and taken inside the palisades. There were three hundred sick in the huts of New Edinburgh, and he put the ships' surgeons ashore to restore those who could be cured in time to work and fight. John

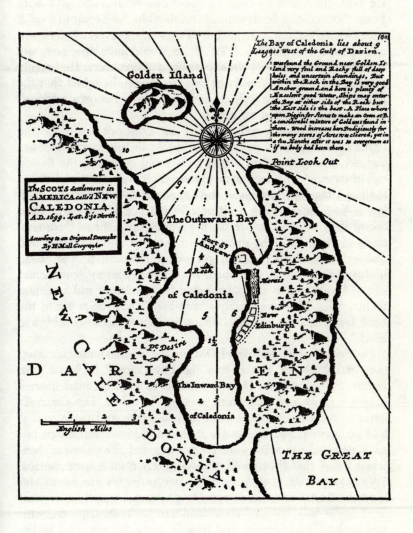

[60]

The Bay of Caledonia *lies about 9 Leagues West of the Gulf of Darien.*

we found the Ground near Golden Island very foul and Rocky full of deep holes and uncertain Soundings. But within the Rock in the Bay is very good Anchor ground and here is plenty of Excelent good Water, Ships may enter the Bay at either side of the Rock but the East side is the best. A Place where upon Diging for Stones to make an Oven at B. a considerabl mixture of Gold was found in them. Wood increases here Prodigiously for the many scores of Acres were cleared, yet in a few Months after it was so overgrown as if no body had been there.

Golden Island

Point Look Out

The SCOTS Settlement in AMERICA call'd NEW CALEDONIA. A.D. 1699. Lat. 8.30 North

According to an Original Draught By H. Moll Geographer

10

9

The Outward Bay

Fort St. Andrew

A Rock

of Caledonia

Morais

A

New Edinburgh

5   6

1½

Pt. Desire

The Inward Bay

of Caledonia

N E W

C A L E

D A R I E N

D O N I A

1   2   3
English Miles

THE GREAT BAY

Stewart, the young naval officer he had brought with him, was told that he could now build that fire-ship he so earnestly desired. He was given the fly-boat of the *Hope of Bo'ness*, and with James Spence, the boatswain of the flagship, he began to load it with twisted oakum, canvas, tarred shavings, barrels of resin and oil. Spence was offered £500 if he would take the boat out against the Spanish fleet when possible and necessary. He bravely agreed, but since he could not hope to survive he asked that the money be paid to his wife in Scotland. Upon his own responsibility, Fonab gave that assurance.

Every night the watchman on Point Look-out could see the lights of the Spanish ships, bright sparks in the darkness of sea and sky. Every day their signal-guns could be heard, the fluting call of trumpets. At each dusk the warships were a little closer to the bay than they had been at dawn. Ashore, men became careless in their uneasy fear. Spilt powder was accidentally ignited in one of the huts, and before the fire was stopped it had destroyed many of them. "Hereby many of our men lost all their goods and clothes," said Borland, "and several of the sick people being hastily pulled out to save them from the devouring flames, and exposed to the open air, it increased their sickness and hastened their death." This was clearly a warning. "Thus the anger of the Lord burnt against us round about, yet few of us duly laid it to heart."

On February 27 Nathaniel Old, master of the Jamaican sloop that had followed Fonab into the bay, agreed to leave with letters and dispatches. He was anxious to go. This mad quarrel between Dons and Scotchmen was not his affair. The Council's letter to the Directors was brief and soldierly, and reads as if it had been composed by Fonab. It said nothing of surrender, but gave news of the victory at Toubacanti and the colonists' confident belief that they could withstand any assault from the sea. "We have put ourselves here in the best order we can for receiving their fleet. So we are hopeful to give you as good an account of them as you have of their land army." This dispatch, with private letters to families and friends, from the ministers to the Moderator, was entrusted to one of the Land Captains, Thomas Hamilton. He went aboard the sloop at dusk, and was joined later by Thomas Drummond, who had promised Fonab that he would not leave Jamaica for Scotland before sending provisions to Caledonia. He too was anxious to be gone. It did not occur to him that he was leaving the Colony as James Byres had left it.

Nathaniel Old took his ship out on a west wind some hours before dawn, unseen by the Spaniards. Among the letters carried by Hamilton was one from Turnbull to his cousin. The musket-ball still in his shoulder, and unable to write, the young man had dictated it to a friend. "There is now lying before our bay twelve Spanish ships, several of them of considerable force. We know not what they intend. . . ."

❋ 5 ❋

A Nation's Humour

"The honour and interest of the nation is engaged"
Scotland, October 1699 to May 1700

EARLY IN OCTOBER a terrified English merchant, Samuel Tuckey, left Edinburgh at the gallop and did not feel safe until he had crossed the Border and reached Newcastle. There he took lodgings, at the White Hart by the post-house, and wrote an hysterical letter to the Lord Mayor of London. A week later this was placed upon James Vernon's crowded desk, and although the Secretary suspected that Mr. Tuckey's mind was probably disordered, it was not his practice to ignore any news that came from the north. He wrote at once to the Mayor of Newcastle, asking him to interrogate the anxious merchant. "He seems to have come lately in great fright from Edinburgh, and speaks of the ferment they are in now they begin to believe their expectations from Darien are vanished. He makes a very odd request, that three or four men with good horses should be sent for him, to secure his coming up to London; he imagining the Scots are lying in wait for him."

Vernon knew that the people of Scotland were "very clamorous and lay their disappointments at our door", but he believed they should blame their own stupidity and not his country for their misfortunes. The mobbing of frightened Englishmen like Tuckey troubled him less than the knowledge that the Jacobites could make irksome use of such discontent. He had already heard from Ireland that James Stuart's supporters there "base great hopes on the annoyance caused by the Darien affair." Those Scottish servants of the King who were in London were also alarmed, particularly Seafield. He had been there for a month, awaiting the King's return from Holland, and he feared that the behaviour of his countrymen would chill the hoped-for warmth of that reunion. All the news from Scotland was unsettling. "You cannot imagine," Cockburn of Ormiston wrote to Carstares, "what a general concern this nation is in.... Such a humour raging in the nation...." Not only was the Edinburgh mob pursuing innocent Englishmen into the wynds, the Company was demanding another Parliamentary Address of Protest to the King, and Seafield knew how distasteful that would be to William.

When George Moffat's letter from New York had been confirmed without doubt, when the numbing shock passed into anger and pain, the Councillors-General of the Company were hastily summoned to Milne Square. Though the order came at short notice forty-three of them attended, many of them the greatest peers in Scotland. They were full of passion and noble self-denial, swearing that none would spare his purse until the Company's credit was restored. They unanimously agreed that they should address the King, asking for the recall of Parliament in November "in full confidence and expectation of having the most natural and cordial assistance from those who had first established the Company and promised it protection." Because none could sustain such unanimity for long, they then began to quarrel about the wording of the Address. The moderates were opposed to any precipitate protest against the Proclamations, saying there should be time for reflection. The hot-heads, inspired by Lord Belhaven's emotive syntax, clamoured for a vote, "Delay, or proceed to address?" Carried for the latter. And then another long debate, who should sit on the Committee for Drawing the Address? When finally chosen, it was dominated by Belhaven and his supporters. Yet another debate then, who should be sent to the Moderator, asking for a National Day of Fast and Prayer? They sat through supper and candle-time, and went home late as the bells of St. Giles' were calling ten o'clock.

The Committee for Drawing met the next morning at Milne Square, and by noon had prepared a draft Address that included both the demand for Parliament's recall and a protest against the Proclamations. Belhaven took it to Ross's coffee-house where several of the Councillors were dining. They suggested some minor amendments, and in the afternoon it was approved by a full meeting of the Council-General. Belhaven was instructed to send it to Seafield in London, with a request that it be placed before the King.

In another room at Milne Square nine Directors, sitting as a Court, were preparing an angry letter to those deserters believed to be skulking in New York—to Paterson, Vetch and the Drummonds, to all Sea and Land Officers. Though it was signed "your affectionate friends and humble servants", it was full of bitter, unforgiving words like shameful, dishonourable, knavery and cowardice. It wondered how men of trust could leave "so valuable and impregnable a settlement as you all wrote it was." Despite that Address being prepared next door, it refused to accept the Proclamations as an excuse for deserting the Colony, any man who so pleaded was a knave and a coward. All of them —gentlemen and commons—were ordered back to Caledonia at once, and were warned that "the only remedy for a fault is to amend it the best way you can."

The letter was sent to New York by the hand of Daniel Mackay, and he had been at sea aboard the frigate *Speedy Return* for three weeks when the *Caledonia* dropped anchor in the Sound of Islay on November 19. There she stayed for a day, like an errant child reluctant to face its angry parents. Robert Drummond wrote a report to the Directors, sending it to Glasgow in a fly-boat with two young officers, one of them his cousin Laurence Drummond. It gave a brief account of the Colony's sad history, and it declared that because of the English Proclamations the Landsmen had believed that they would receive no help from home, and that the Company itself had been destroyed. It lied: it said that the colonists would willingly have returned to Caledonia had there been seamen and ships to carry them from New York. It blamed the Councillors for the abrupt and frightened withdrawal. "They never intimated their intention of coming away forty-eight hours before they weighed anchor, but concealed their intention from several of the Colony who questioned them upon it."

The only Councillor who had returned, and who had therefore to carry the obloquy of all, was William Paterson. When the *Caledonia* reached Greenock on Tuesday, November 21, he was carried ashore weak and ill. It took him fourteen days to travel the sixty miles to Edinburgh, and he spent many of them in bed at an inn or the house of a friend. Appearing at last before the unsympathetic Directors, he asked leave to prepare a full report before questions were put to him. He finished it within two weeks, and it remains one of the saddest and most honest accounts of that wretched Colony.

There was no welcome for the men who came back with the *Caledonia*. There was only abuse and disgust. After all they had endured, the miracle of being alive when three times their number were dead, they were bewildered by the contempt of their friends and the shame of their families. Sir James Oswald refused to see his son. From the Widow Finlay's in Glasgow, a morning's ride from his home, the boy wrote to Thomas Aikman, sadly protesting that he was not alone in what his father called "treachery and cowardice", and bitterly agreeing that it might have been better for all had he died in Caledonia.

I am mightily sorry that I should have angered my father, but necessity has no laws. I wish he would forget my fault when I am gone, I know not whither but certainly it is to more misfortune, for I see plainly that my life is composed of a labyrinth of my own out of which I will never get an outgate but by death's door. I design not to go back to Caledonia, but to somewhere else wherever my fate leads me, though it was one of my resolutions to go back and lay down my life cheerfully for my country's sake. Since it pleased God that I have preserved it still, and had not the good fortune (if I may term it so) to lose it in that place, and so have been happy by wanting the sight of so many miseries that have come upon myself and others of my relations which I have got notice of since I came to this town. I never intended, nor do I intend, to trouble my father any more... Only I hope you will acquaint him that I wish him long life, wealth and happiness, and more comfort in the rest of his children than he has had in me.

The nation's humour had become a desperate hunger for revenge. When the mob could not find an Englishman to frighten, it bullied these miserable Caledonians, recognising them by their fever-yellow skins and their threadbare scarlet. The news from

England caused riots and bonfires. The King—that "wise prince and steady to please his people" according to Seafield—had received the Address from the Council-General and had liked none of it. He coldly replied that he was sorry his northern kingdom had sustained such a sad loss, and that of course he would always protect and encourage its trade, but there should be no more talk of an immediate assembly of the Estates. "We will order that the Parliament shall meet when we judge the good of the nation does require it." The good of the nation, in William's opinion, would not require it before March 5. Though they were angered and humiliated by this contemptuous rejection of their Address, the Councillors made excellent use of it. They printed and circulated the King's reply, and they directed the fury it aroused into support for another Address, one which they hoped would be signed by thirty or forty of the most influential men in the nation. It would remind the King of the Company's rights and privileges, and advise him that the immediate calling of Parliament had never been more necessary.

William's patience with Scottish affairs, always short, now came to an ill-tempered end. On December 12 he wrote to his Privy Council in Edinburgh. He had never denied his subjects their just privileges, he had never discouraged their freedom to petition him in a dutiful manner, but to hear of a second Address in motion when he had said all there was to say in reply to the first was more than he was inclined to stomach. He particularly resented the fact that both Addresses were inspired by factious men who had never shown any affection for him or his Government. He ordered the Privy Council to make his displeasure known, and to take effectual steps within the law to stop the Address. The Company's friends were delighted to make that displeasure known, and they naturally emphasised the cavalier tone in which it was expressed. The effect was dramatic, and the reverse of what the King and his servants wished. There was another of those passionate manifestations of national unity which ennobled the Scots in the seventeenth century. All manner of men, as individuals and corporate bodies, demanded the right to sign the Address. As copies were sent to the shires and burghs it became a people's protest, a declaration of loyalty to Scotland's Company and Scotland's Parliament. The Lord Chancellor, the

Earl of Marchmont, realised that he could not proceed against
the subscribers without challenging a subject's right to petition
the King, that William could not insist upon such interference
without breaking the promises he had made when he accepted
the Crown of Scotland. "We have a very tender point in hand,"
Marchmont told Seafield, "and if I should adventure upon
prosecutions not sustainable by law, that would be to open a pack
and sell no ware." He decided to do nothing.

In its burning pride and indignation the country also remembered the lost crew of the *Dolphin*, albeit somewhat late. It was
perhaps a relief to recall that some of those first colonists were
worthy of sympathy and respect. Since September, when Daniel
Mackay brought news of the ship's capture, Mrs. Pincarton and
other tearful relatives had been asking the Company for news,
for help, for an appeal to the King. It was believed that the
wretched seamen were still in the dungeons of Carthagena, but
four of them were now in Spain—Pincarton, John Malloch, James
Graham, and a boy David Wilson. They had been taken to
Havana in September, and from thence to Cadiz with Benjamin
Spense. Pincarton had been bitterly angered by the Spaniards'
treatment of his men at Carthagena. "They were every day
carried out with their slaves," he wrote later, "to work at their
walls and clean their streets; and were likewise forced to cry and
beg from everyone that passed by, for God's sake, for some
charity to save their lives." When he heard that the first Colony
was gone from Caledonia he asked Pimienta to release him and
his crew. "He told me that the old Governor had wrote such
things against me that he could not let me go, but of necessity I
must be sent to Old Spain." When he left, seven of his men were
already dead and the rest had been sent as slaves to the Barliavento Fleet.

Despite her agonised persistence, the Council-General did not
consider Mrs. Pincarton's appeal until December, when it decided
to petition the King for his intercession on behalf of the prisoners. Wasting no opportunity of catching the royal sleeve,
it also reminded him of an earlier request for three naval frigates
now lying idle at Burntisland. The man who took this cheerfully
optimistic petition to London was Lord Basil Hamilton, the
proud and contentious brother of the Duke. He went reluct-

antly, declaring that he would rather attend to his private affairs in Scotland, that there were others more capable than he. Certainly there could have been few less acceptable to the King, and William childishly refused to see him. Through Seafield he announced that he was displeased with the Company for sending a man who had never had the courtesy to attend his Court, and whose lack of affection for the Throne and Government was notorious. Though insulted by this rebuff, and angered when he was treated like a messenger, Hamilton doggedly remained in London. He bit on his pride and sent an apology to Seafield, asking the King's pardon for any past offence in his conduct, but William hated the Hamilton clan and would not forgive or receive this stiff-necked member of it. He said he would read the petition if it were brought to him by Seafield, and when he replied to it, on January 10, he ignored Hamilton and wrote directly to the Privy Council of Scotland. He would certainly ask the King of Spain to release the *Dolphin's* crew, but as for those three frigates ... they were there to guard the coast of Scotland and he could not dispose of them without the advice of Parliament.

A compassionate Englishman in Cadiz, Martin Westcombe the Consul, heard by chance that the prisoners were there and went to see them. He was horrified by their suffering, and persuaded the Governor to release them from irons. He appealed to the Court in Madrid, saying that the misery and innocence of these men surely justified their merciful release. When next he enquired about them he was told that they had been sent to Seville, there to be tried as pirates and undoubtedly executed.

In Scotland at the beginning of February the Company chartered a sloop, the *Margaret* of Leith, and loaded her with provisions for the Colony. It occurred to the Directors that the second expedition, finding Caledonia deserted, might be in need of stronger encouragement than beef, codfish and flour. The young supercargo of the sloop, Patrick MacDowall, was given a letter addressed to all Land and Sea Officers. "We need not tell you," it said, "how far the honour and interest of the nation is engaged, there is no looking backward." The first colonists had behaved without religion or morality. Many of them had been impudent villains and treacherous knaves, and even those who had died at sea during the flight to New York had wantonly denied themselves the glory of perishing in Caledonia. Some of the young officers with the second expedition were related to the greatest families in the kingdom, and should therefore know that if they did not do their duty their dishonour would be all the more conspicuous. This should inspire them to exceed each other in virtue. The more illustrious a man's birth the more base his degeneration if he abandoned those qualities which distinguished his family from vulgar men. "It's a lasting disgrace to the memories of those officers who went on the first expedition that even the meanest planters were scandalised at the viciousness of their lives, many of them living very intemperately and viciously for many months at the public charge, whilst the sober and industrious among them were vigilant in doing their duty."

MacDowall also carried letters which his friend Paterson wrote to Alexander Shields and Thomas Drummond. Paterson had not yet recovered his health and was suffering, he said, from a cold and feverish humour that clouded his mind and made writing difficult. He saw the hand of God in everything, in the recent terrible fire that had destroyed much of the High Street, Cowgate and Parliament Close, in the loss of the Company's ships, in the desertion of the first Colony. But at least the Almighty had favoured him, his report had been accepted by the Directors. "In all my troubles," he told Drummond, "it's no small satisfaction to have lived to give the Company and the world unquestionable proof that I have not had any sinister nor selfish designs." He praised Drummond's industry and integrity, and that grenadier captain—if he ever received the letter—may have been astonished by such warmth and generosity, for he had never disguised his belief that Paterson was a fool and a meddler. Paterson also advised Shields to have tolerance, to bear with the infirmities of others, provided they were not rawheads, mushroom politicians, intriguing cabals and Tarpaulin Councillors. In a letter of farewell to MacDowall he urged the young man to behave prudently, to honour his father, and "to take care that these boisterous mariners shall no more domineer over us."

There was a feverish note of delirium in all the letters, from Paterson and the Directors.

It was March 5 before the *Margaret* sailed, the day on which the King had promised the Scots that their Parliament would be called. It was not called, and no word came from London. Toward the end of the month the National Address—which was now the Ark of the Covenant to an angry people—was carried to England by four members of the Council-General led by the Marquis of Tweeddale. They could not be ignored as Hamilton had been insulted, but when Seafield took them to Kensington Palace on the afternoon of Sunday, March 25, they saw how unwelcome they were and how little time the King was prepared to give them. A troop of Guards and a travelling-coach were waiting at the steps to take him to Hampton Court. He received them in his bed-chamber, and was alone except for the servants who were dressing him. He was cold and brief in his welcome as the four men bent to kiss his white hand, and although he took the Address he did not open it. He stared at them silently, as if that were all. Tweeddale mumbled something which Seafield, inclining his head, could not hear, but it was clearly a request for the Address to be read aloud, for the King gave it back to him. Tweeddale handed it to Sir John Home of Blackader who read it clearly in a challenging voice. Another silence, and then Tweeddale humbly asked what answer they might take back to Scotland.

"My lord," said William icily, "I suppose you know that I have ordered the sitting of Parliament to be on the 15th of May, and that it cannot possibly meet sooner. Therefore, I think you might have spared this trouble."

The audience was over and he moved toward the door. Blackader, who stood in his way, stubbornly refused to step aside. With controlled anger he asked the King to understand that the Address was not only a petition for a Parliament, it was also evidence of his countrymen's deep concern for the security of their Company and the safety of their kinsmen in Caledonia. The truth of that, said the King adroitly, would surely be known when Parliament met.

They followed him out of the bed-chamber and down the great staircase to the golden mist of a spring evening. They stood among his grooms and his servants as his coach was driven away to Hampton Court.

The Scots Parliament did not meet on May 15. Having had no

more than eight weeks' warning the King's Commissioner, the Duke of Queensberry, announced that his equipage—that magnificent train of carriages, footmen, outriders and guards which must carry him from Holyroodhouse to Parliament Hall—could not be ready before May 24. When the session did begin it was noisy and ineffectual, and the King's servants opened it with the cunning proposal that before all else Parliament should debate the grievous state of morality and religion in Scotland. Unable to deny theology its proper priority, the Company's party waited three days before moving "That our Colony of Caledonia in Darien is a legal and rightful settlement in the terms of the Act, and that Parliament will maintain and support the same." The motion was never put. On May 30 Queensberry complained of a sore throat, the result, no doubt, of that rank smell of charred wood in Parliament Close. He could scarcely speak, and he had no wish to risk his health by sitting too long in the Hall. Moreover, the motion raised issues upon which the King should be consulted. By his order Parliament was adjourned until June 20.

It would not meet again until the end of October, and long before then all would be lost.

"To the satisfaction of all sensible men, Scots or English"
London, January and February 1700

Of all the paper and ink expended in the little pamphlet war over Caledonia, Walter Herries' book is the only one that excites the imagination—not because it is trustworthy but because it acknowledges that men are human and that much of their behaviour is motivated by interest and not by the nobility of the ideals they profess to serve. He called his ribald, entertaining mixture of truth and fiction *A Defence of the Scots Abdicating Darien*, and he could not have been surprised when the Lord Justice Clerk ordered it to be burned as a seditious libel by the hangman of Edinburgh. In the New Year it was answered, on the Company's behalf, by an anonymous *Inquiry into the Causes of the Miscarriage of the Scots Colony*. This naturally outraged the English, and the House of Lords sat late in debate upon it. They listened as Lord Peterborough read several scandalous paragraphs aloud, and because it reflected upon the honour of King and Parliament they ordered it to be burned in the Palace Yard. They agreed to address the King, reminding him of the Address of both Houses in 1695, and declaring that the mischievous Colony on Darien was prejudicial to the trade of the English plantations in America.

Herries had been living in England since his return from Caledonia, his pregnant wife snugly housed in Rochester while he scribbled in a Fleet Street tavern. If not already James Vernon's paid hack he was certainly the Secretary's spy, hoping his loyal service would eventually win him a pardon for that impulsive sword-thrust into the body of Captain Graydon. His book had also been answered by Fletcher of Saltoun in an essay of noble and inexact logic, but this offered no serious challenge in the gutter where the surgeon preferred to brawl, and where most people formed their opinions. Herries was incensed by the *Inquiry*, however, because it contained a lively attack upon him, written in a venomous style he might well have envied. He believed, with some truth, that the Company had authorised its publication to encourage support for the National Address, and on January 7 he wrote to Vernon from Kent: "I design to answer the last scurrilous and rebellious pamphlet, I hope to the satisfaction of all sensible men, whether Scots or English. It contains nothing *ad rem* to confute what I have offered already; which I shall make appear, as likewise the malicious lies wherewith he basely asperses me."

Until he left for Rochester to attend his wife's lying-in, Herries had been convoying—as he put it—four Scots officers who had arrived in London at the beginning of January. They had left the Colony on the *Saint Andrew* and bought a passage from Jamaica to Bristol. One was Lachlan Maclean, the Highlander who had laid information against the Drummonds on the voyage to Madeira, and the others were Captains Forbes, Stewart and Stretton. Having heard how returned Caledonians were being received in Scotland, none of them was eager to return home. The King's Scottish Secretaries, Seafield and Lord Carmichael, were anxious to question them, and so was Lord Basil Hamilton, but they could not be found. With an impudent skill that a twentieth-century newspaperman would envy, Herries had hidden them in a tavern. He interrogated them closely, he told Vernon, and "took care that the material part of what they had said should be inserted in the public prints", that material part being damaging to the Company and favourable to the English. When he saw that Stewart and Stretton were loyal to the Company he released them to Hamilton, telling Vernon that they could do little harm since one was a madman and the other a fool. But Maclean and Forbes he brazenly took to Seafield and Carmichael, confident that the work he had begun for Vernon would now be continued by the Secretaries. He did not entirely abandon them, but left them in the care and under the watch of one of his own spies, a man with the remarkably apt name of Crouch.* Writing to Vernon from Rochester, he enclosed a fair copy of a report he had just received from this energetic subordinate.

Captain Forbes had been with me to-night. He says they did their message to the Secretaries to expectation, and are still at heart as yourself. Seafield asked whether the Proclamations hindered the settlement? They answered negatively. Whether they had vessels with victuals or not? Answer affirmatively, but no goods to buy withal, nor no credit. The Secretary was glad, for he had been reflected on by his country. He told them Herries had written a book some called scurrilous, he would have them read it and give their opinion. Captain Maclean replied that he had met with it at an inn, and had read it, and swore that there was never a lie in it. Fie! saith the Secretary, you must not say so, for you'll be thought as ill of as I am. By——! says Maclean, I won't deny the truth to please any man.

Referring so lightly to his own unpopularity, Seafield was clearly delighted to have such explosive ammunition to use against the Company, but Carmichael was uneasy, and he may have suspected that both men had been bought by Herries with money supplied by Vernon. During the next two or three days Crouch dined with the officers, and questioned them thoroughly. They told him that James Campbell, the Company's agent, had taken them to the Three Lions tavern in Bedford Court, the lodgings of Paul Domonique, Paterson's Huguenot friend. There they

---

* Possibly Nathaniel Crouch, a stationer and hack journalist.

also met Lord Basil Hamilton who reminded them of the honour of their country and told them to do or say nothing that would bring discredit upon it. Maclean's Highland temper was aroused by the suggestion that a Lowlander could teach him anything about honour. "Never a lord in Christendom," he swore, "shall make me conceal the truth!" He refused to meet Hamilton again, but Forbes went once more to the Three Lions where he was told that James Vernon would probably send for them both and question them on the Colony. They should not go. On a point of good manners, said Forbes in guile or simplicity, must they not accept such an invitation? Hamilton gave them up as lost, and returned to Scotland with Stewart and Stretton.

The authorship of the *Inquiry into the Miscarriage of the Scots Colony* has never been clearly established. It is sometimes attributed to Saltoun, but it has none of his architectural style, and he could not have committed some of its solecisms even in an attempt to hide his identity. Conversely bizarre is a suggestion that the author of the *Inquiry* also wrote a defence of the Darien settlement for which Fletcher was responsible. To the Government of England in 1700 the question of authorship was political not academic, and in January the King signed a proclamation offering rewards of £500 and £200 for the apprehension of the author and printer of "a false, scandalous and traitorous libel, intituled *An Inquiry etc.*, the design of which was to create a misunderstanding between our subjects of England and Scotland, and to stir up sedition." Before the month was out Andrew Bell had been arrested for printing it in England, and Patrick Campbell for publishing it in Ireland. Three more men were taken up for circulating it in London. Perhaps they kept their mouths shut under questioning, but more probably they did not. On February 3 Simon Chapman, Messenger to the Press, was given a warrant for the arrest of James Hodges. That afternoon, professing great astonishment and outraged innocence, Hodges was taken from his lodgings at the Pheasant and Crown in Drury Lane and thrown into the Gate House Prison.

He was a pleasantly enigmatic figure, and the records of this affair do little to show him in the round. He was possibly Scots, an able pamphleteer with an active pen that would dance through a lexicon to the music of a purse of guineas. Though he had been arrested by the Government, his first act upon reaching the Gate House suggests that he was until recently its paid scribbler. He wrote to William Lowndes, Secretary to the Treasury, declaring that he had been wrongly accused. Sparing no cliché, he said that he was as innocent as the day he was born. "I, who am so great a lover of the King and a friend to the Government, cannot be guilty of owning opinions contrary to the interest of both." He asked Lowndes to vindicate him, expressed gratitude for past kindnesses, and promised that when they next met he would show the Secretary something "that I have been preparing for your view, of another nature than the book whereof I am unjustly challenged to be the author."

The depositions of witnesses, when they were sent to James Vernon by the Attorney-General, scarcely supported this declaration of innocence. Anne Dunbar, a serving-girl at the Pheasant and Crown, said that she often went into Mr. Hodges room when he was writing. She asked him what the book was about, and "he said it was the Darien Company, and that it should make Scotland rejoice and England mourn, for Parliament had not done well by them, and if they had assisted the Company Scotland would have been richer than ever England was." He chattered frankly to her, though he would not let her touch the manuscript. When she saw it was gone from his room, he told her that the Duke of Hamilton had taken it to Scotland.

Elizabeth Clark said that she had known Hodges for many years in Scotland, and that when she came to London she had taken lodgings at the Pheasant and Crown upon his recommendation. "Last summer she observed he was writing a book, and he told her it was about the Scotch African Company, which he said he was obliged to send down to Scotland the night before Duke Hamilton went to Scotland, which she thinks was toward the end of the year." At Hodges request, she carried it to the Duke's lodgings in St. James's Street, and thought no more about it until some Scots in London told her that it was to be burnt by the hangman. "And being fearful of the same, she begged her landlady to desire Mr. Hodges to remove his lodgings." He told them both that he knew all about the burning and was not afraid.

There was also the strange evidence given by James Cuff, a

watchmaker at the Ship Tavern in Fleet Street. He and Hodges had fought together in the Duke of Monmouth's abortive rebellion of 1685, but they had not met again until recently. "We did go together into some house near the chocolate-house in Charles Street near Covent Garden, where I saw several papers written, which I did read some part, he not seeming to make a secret thereof but said it should soon be in print." Cuff offered to find a printer, but Hodges said he already had one. "What I read to the best of my memory was the very same book, *viz.* the book shown me by Mr. Secretary, and what I can plainly remember was expressed *An Answer to a libel entituled A Defence of the Scots Abdicating Darien.*" He thought little of the matter until he saw the King's Proclamation against the author and printer, and then he was shocked to receive four anonymous and threatening letters. Copies of them were pinned to his deposition.

The first began, *If you discover that business in relation to the Scots papers which you saw it shall be a dear £500 for you. . . .* It warned Cuff that if he injured the writer he would regret it and his father would grieve. The second, a day or so later, *I understand you have been prating concerning those papers you saw at Charles Street, notwithstanding I earnestly entreated you not to disclose anything.* Cuff was invited to meet the writer that evening at the Three Tuns by Holborn Bridge. When he did not go he received a third letter which accused Cuff of informing upon the writer, *I understand you was this morning where you will repent when it is too late.* A trap must then have been set to catch the writer, and failed, for the next morning Cuff received the fourth and final letter. *Your snare last night was not so well laid. . . I design not to trouble you any farther with lines after this, but I shall leave you to your own destruction.*

This evidence, though circumstantial, was enough at that time to have convicted Hodges. Much less had sent other men to the pillory or the gallows. But when the Attorney-General, Sir Thomas Trevor, sent the papers to James Vernon he said that he could see nothing in them upon which to base a charge. Vernon agreed, and Hodges was released from the Gate House. Some months later he was petitioning Seafield and William Carstares for their help in securing a pension from the King of £300 a year. "I will do the best I can to merit it, and to bestow it in his service. As my brother did serve him with his sword, I will endeavour to supply his room with my studies and pen."

Walter Herries also discovered that a hack with a reversible coat need never despair of the gratitude of great men. On July 8, James Vernon sent a brief note to the Admiralty. "His Majesty orders that the prosecution of Walter Herries (on account of the quarrel that formerly happened between him and his commander) shall be stopped."

"Wilful Willy, wilt thou be wilful still. . . ?"
Edinburgh, June 1700

Robert Pincarton and his four companions were brought from their cells below the great walls of the Alcazar in Seville. They had not seen the sunlight for weeks. Now it flooded over them, glowing on the exquisite arabesques and columns of the room in which they faced their Judges. They were ragged and emaciated, scarred by the irons that had hung on their wrists and ankles, and they believed that they had been abandoned by their country. Pincarton acknowledged none of the accusations made against him, if he could not save his life he could at least die with dignity. He was not a pirate, he said, he was by trade a sea-captain. He had no stock in the Company of Scotland, nothing but his bare wage of ten pounds a month. He had never wished to suppress the Indians or injure the subjects of Spain. He did not believe that the country of Darien had belonged to any European prince before the Scots came. There had been no wish to compete with Spanish traders in their own territories. "The cargo we had was most for the use of our own people, and was suitable for the English islands, for it consisted of linen cloth, white and blue, periwigs, Scots shoes for men and women, slippers, which is very seldom worn amongst Spaniards in that country."

He was found guilty, and so were John Malloch, James Graham and Benjamin Spense. All were sentenced to death. The boy David Wilson was freed upon his promise never to return to Darien. The Judges declared that the Council-General and the Directors of the Company of Scotland were equally guilty of piracy. An account of the expenses of the Spanish Crown in all its actions against the Colony should be presented to the King of England and Scotland, and payment demanded. The Governor of Carthagena was also reprimanded, and was told that he should have punished the crew of the *Dolphin* in a summary and exemplary fashion, and not troubled the King by sending their leaders to Spain.

The four men were taken back to the darkness below the walls, there to wait until the manner and date of their execution had been decided.

Two days later in Scotland, on May 30, the Duke of Queensberry's sore throat brought the brief session of Parliament to an end. By curious chance a pamphlet published that same day passionately voiced the people's anger with the King's servants, and their desperate desire to have their grievances remedied by Parliament. Culled from an earlier and duller pamphlet, it was called *People of Scotland's Groans and Lamentable Complaints Pour'd out before the High Court of Parliament*. For a hundred years, it said, the political leaders of Scotland had been the servants of England and had frequently treated the Scots as enemies, never more so than now. By all that was sacred, the noble representatives in Parliament were implored to save their ancient and gallant country. "We beg you to consider how our Sovereignty and Freedom is violated, and Laws trampled upon, our Trade interrupted: how our brethren have been starved and made slaves, our Colony deserted, our ships burnt and lost abroad; whilst our Petitions have been rejected, our Company baffled."

The most immediate response to this wordy jeremiad came from the King's servants whom it obliquely attacked. Hugh Paterson, a surgeon-apothecary, and James Watson, a printer, were arrested and sent to the Tolbooth for writing and publishing the libellous pamphlet. But this merely plucked a leaf and left the thistle to flourish. Angry members of Parliament, outraged by Queensberrys' high-handed action, drew up another Address to the King. Signed by peers, knights and burgesses, it expressed their "unspeakable grief and disappointment" and begged William to recall Parliament with liberty to sit as long as might be necessary to redress the grievances of the nation. When this reached Kensington Palace in mid-June even Seafield heard the warning echo of angry trumpets, sounding down four centuries of conflict with the English. Supporting a frightened dispatch from Queensberry, he and the Earl of Argyll advised the King to give his assent to an Act that would declare Scotland's right to Caledonia. William refused. "Could we have done it at all," he told Queensberry, "we would have done it at first, but the longer we think upon it we are the more convinced that we cannot do it." Privately he thought the Scots were fools about their Colony on Darien, and so he wrote to a Dutch friend. They caused him great annoyance and they delayed his departure to Holland, "for which I long more than ever".

There were many such fools in Scotland who now thought that the King could oblige his twin kingdoms by retiring to his homeland for ever. On June 10, the birthday of the exiled Stuart's son, the Jacobites openly celebrated with bonfires and drawn pistols. They published a crude lampoon in which William appeared as the stork which Jupiter gave to the frogs who had asked for a king. Colonel Ferguson, whose regiment garrisoned the Castle, told Carstares that "Treason is become so common that nobody takes any notice of it. They talk publicly that unless the King will grant them the legal settlement of Caledonia they will address him again with forty thousand hands at it." In the coffee-houses there was cryptic, smiling talk of a flame that burnt unseen in the heart of the city, awaiting the rising of a terrible wind.

That wind, or at least a small gust of it, arose on June 20. Captain Thomas Hamilton had died at sea, but the dispatches he carried arrived safely that day with news of a glorious victory at Toubacanti. The Directors ordered its immediate publication, and by nightfall Edinburgh was a playground for the mob. The pensioners of the Town Guard, who should have prevented this, understandably locked themselves in their guard-house by the Tron Church.

The riot began discreetly. In the forenoon the Duke of Hamilton, the people's hero and the Jacobites' darling, visited Peter Steel's tavern where he drank a toast to Toubacanti and demanded another National Address. He was cheered away in triumph, having maintained his popularity and secured his house from damage that night. Past noon, at the Cross Keys inn, a meeting of gentlemen who called themselves "True Caledonians" also drank several toasts, to Toubacanti, to the Company, and to the damnation of its enemies. They proposed and agreed that all the windows of the city should be illuminated with candles of joy, and they called upon the gathering crowd outside to enforce that resolution. By dusk huge fires were burning in the High Street and Canongate, the shadow of their ruddy flames crawling up the stone-faced lands and broken gables. Before dark the mob was shouting at windows still unlit, and throwing stones through those that did not respond. Over the shouting and screaming, the splintering of glass and explosion of fireworks, the bells of St. Giles insanely rang their way through a Jacobite rant. *Wilful Willy, wilt thou be wilful still. . . ?*

Three times the mob in Canongate attempted to break down the door of Lord Carmichael's house, then shattered its windows and tumbled the candles which his frightened servants had lit. Another crowd burst in upon the Lord Advocate, Sir James Stewart, and ordered the old man to sign a warrant for the release of the author and printer of *Groans and Complaints*. Further along the street, Seafield's wife crouched in terror among the fallen glass of her husband's fine windows, listening to a many-tongued voice that cried damnation to him and his royal master. In Holyroodhouse, however, the Duke of Queensberry slept soundly, undisturbed, he told his secretary the next morning, by the noise of any tumult. Had there indeed been a riot?

The mob at the lower end of the Royal Mile moved to join that in the High Street, encouraged by loyal gentlemen who leant from their glowing windows with cries of approval. The Earl Marischal, who may have seen the imminent return of King James behind the bonfires and the broken glass, sent out his servants with wine, and toasted Caledonia from his doorway. The crowd drank his lordship's wine, wished success to all his hopes, and then broke the windows of a house belonging to the Reverend Mr. David Blair, for no other reason, it seemed, than that it was his duty to read daily prayers when Parliament was in session. He was also called a rogue and a villain.

When the two mobs met at the Netherbow Port they took away the keys of the gate so that they might not be locked within the high city. Without waiting for the warrants which the Lord Advocate may or may not have signed under duress, they stormed the Tolbooth. They were lighting a fire at the base of its oak and iron door when the redcoat pensioners sallied out of the guard-house under Baillie Johnstone and some other magistrates. The unhappy veterans were driven off without much difficulty, "by a great many in gentlemen's habits," it was later reported, "who came up briskly with drawn swords." The door of the Tolbooth gave way, and the first man inside carried a bayonet, the second a sabre. Keeper Atchison prudently surrendered his keys, and Paterson and Watson were released and carried away in triumph. Other prisoners were also liberated, including some wild Highlanders who were there for cattle-lifting, but Atchison was allowed to keep two or three who had been charged with "bouggary and theft". In the noise and the scuffling, the red flame of torches, a turnkey was wounded by a bayonet thrust, and Gaoler Drummond was robbed of his hat, periwig, cloak, ring, and all the goods in his sutlery.

The mob then advanced on Parliament Hall. Some may have got inside, for the Underkeeper of the Wardrobe later reported that the gold fringe had been stolen from the Chair of State. At no time that night did the garrison of the Castle attempt a sortie against the rioters. The Portcullis Gate was closed, the guns of the Half Moon Battery were manned, and the Governor was convinced that he would shortly be under siege. He was profoundly dismayed by this thought. His provisions would not last two days, his men were unnerved, his batteries in a state of neglect. He watched the shudder of flames beyond the Landmarket, listened to the mob, and did nothing.

Before daybreak the rioters were exhausted or drunk, their only movement a sudden, purposeless whirl of malice, often directed against their own sympathisers. Hugh Brown, staggering home by the Netherbow, was stopped and told to drink a toast to Darien. He protested that he had drunk too much and could take no more, but the mob insisted that he swallow another cup. "Come, gentlemen," he said, "I'll do what none of you will do, that is, I'll spew a pint to the health of Caledonia." He did so, and was cheered for a loyal fellow. Thus ended the noble Toubacanti Riot. Early in the forenoon there was the crunch of steady feet on broken glass. Colonel Archibald Row's Fusiliers were marching into the city with bayonets fixed and muskets primed.

They arrived in answer to an order from the Privy Council, a few frightened members of which had gathered at Holyrood-house as soon as it was safe to do so. Queensberry came from his bedchamber to greet them, angry and apologetic. He bullied his secretary, and told the wretched man to write to London, taking all the blame for his master's undisturbed night. Now that the Fusiliers were in control of Edinburgh, the Council acted with firmness and decision. Two loaded guns were posted at the Netherbow, flying picquets from Row's regiment and the Town Guard imposed a nightly curfew, and an angry proclamation forbade "all illuminations or bonfires used for expression of public joy to be made in any burgh within this realm on any pretence whatsoever." Some of the rioters were taken up, including the cook who had burst into the Tolbooth bayonet in hand, and his sabre-swinging companion. But no gentleman was arrested, and a proposal in Council that the Earl Marischal, at least, should be sent to the Castle was regretfully rejected. It was believed that the rioters—who had destroyed window-glass worth more than £5,000 Sterling—had been inspired and directed by the Jacobites, and the Privy Council had no wish to provoke them to something worse by imprisoning their leaders.

A week later the joy and the fear were forgotten. At four o'clock in the afternoon of Friday, June 28, a special meeting of the Council-General and the Court of Directors was held at Milne Square. A terrible rumour had been current in the city since yester-evening. Now it was confirmed, and they listened in stunned silence as Roderick Mackenzie read a letter from Samuel Vetch in New York. Campbell of Fonab, it said, had arrived there on May 5. The Caledonians had surrendered to the Spaniards and entirely abandoned the settlement.

✲ 6 ✲

God's Wonderful Mercy

"Indeed, most of us had the sentence of death in ourselves"
Caledonia, March 1700

BY NIGHT TWO SPANISH SCHOONERS came in close to the harbour-mouth and sent their boats to make soundings. In the darkness, from the palisades, the Scots could hear the plash of oars and the murmur of voices. Three nights they came, and then were heard no more. Their masters reported to Pimienta that they had found twelve fathoms at the mouth, but heavy breakers and the guns of the fort would make an entry and a landing in the bay both difficult and hazardous. The Governor had never seriously considered so bold an attack.

At the end of February another schooner had found a small inlet four miles to the east of the peninsula, and her master told Pimienta that artillery might be landed there with little difficulty. Though another reported that the landing of field-pieces would not be as easy as the first believed, Pimienta decided to make the attempt. From Captain Prandie, an Indian who had once been the Caledonians' friend, he had heard of Cordones's defeat at Toubacanti, but he was sure that this was a small reverse only, and that he would soon be joined by a large force from Santa Maria. Deserters from the Colony, three starved and feverish men found on the sand at Caret Bay, told him that although there were five hundred armed men on the peninsula they were all weak from the want of food and medicine. On March 1, Campmaster Don Melchor de Guevara was put ashore at the inlet with three companies of foot, two hundred men. He was told to establish a beach-head to move inland as soon as he could.

He marched the next day, and his advance was slow. There were no natural paths through the trees and thickets, and his soldiers slashed and hacked their way forward with their swords. Several times they crossed the same winding river, holding their muskets and pouches above their heads as the water rose to their waists. Their eyes were blinded by tormenting insects, their clothes torn by thorns. They climbed the high ground toward the neck of the peninsula, and on the eastern slope of one hill they surprised an outlying picquet of four Scots who slipped away without resistance. On the summit of the hill a captured Indian told de Guevara that a large force of Caledonians was advancing against the Spaniards. Don Melchor was no infantryman, offence had been no part of his training as an engineer. He ordered his men to clear a field of fire on their front, and to build a rampart of the branches.

There they waited for one hour, another, and then a third. They listened to the sounds of the forest, the distant murmur of the sea, but no attack came. At last de Guevara ordered his command down the hill, cautiously and behind a skirmish line of fifteen men. No Scots were met at the bottom, but when the ensign leading the skirmishers had gone another two miles he suddenly saw the white sand of the bay, the bare yards of the Caledonians' ships, and the smoke of their fires. His blue and yellow uniform, bright against the trees, was seen by Captain Thomas Mackintosh whose company held the neck of the peninsula. A drummer had beaten to arms along the earthen rampart soon after the outlying picquet came in, and now a scarlet platoon crossed the ditch and advanced on the ensign with a hurrah. He and his men boldly stood their ground, fired two volleys, and then fell back to de Guevara's ambuscade. Met by a violent, unexpected flame of musketry, the Scots dropped down the slope of the hill and took what shelter they could behind the trees until Mackintosh came up with the rest of his company. Three times this stubborn Highlander led an attack against de Guevara's hidden infantry, and at the third repulse his men broke and ran to the safety of their ditch.

De Guevara walked over the little battlefield, sword in hand. He counted the bodies of seventeen Caledonians, and believed that there must be more undiscovered in the trees. He had no dead, and only thirteen wounded. He was pleased by his victory, by the arms the Scots had thrown away, but he did not advance. Had he done so, he might have carried the ditch that afternoon and driven Mackintosh back to the huts of New Edinburgh. Instead he retired, later arguing that his wounded needed care, that much of his powder was damp and his provisions spoiled. He fell back beyond the hill where he had made his empty stand, and did not feel secure until he had reached the bank of the River Matanzas near Caret Bay. There, with the instinctive reflex of an engineer, he began to build a fort.

On March 3 the warship *El Florizant* arrived off the inlet and Pimienta came ashore with three hundred picked infantrymen. Leaving seamen and gunners to disembark his artillery, he marched the soldiers to de Guevara's camp. Though he had no high opinion of the Campmaster's skill and valour, he approved of the fort. This was something demanded by the complicated formality of siege warfare. "I continued the work of entrenchment," he wrote in his diary, "laying out the form of this fortification and issuing orders which the Campmaster and other officers were to observe, both as to the watch and ward of the camp, and also in the distribution of the subsistence, arms and munitions." From the canebrakes to the west of the river two of Mackintosh's scouts watched with astonished curiosity, crawling forward until they were seen and fired upon by the Spanish sentries. They quickly fled, but they had alarmed the camp. Pimienta put his men in battle array until his Indians convinced him that his five hundred men were in no danger of attack.

His fort begun, Pimienta took the next step in the ritual dance of war and sent a drummer to the Scots, cordially inviting them to surrender. The generosity of the King his master, said his letter, obliged him to do this before his fleet entered their harbour and his soldiers stormed their trenches. He hoped they would accept his invitations, otherwise his men would give no quarter in the assault. Moreover, and this with disarming frankness, once his ships were inside the bay the prevailing wind would prevent them from leaving, and they would "be unable to go about the business in which I may need them." The drummer returned to Camp Matanzas the next day, and the letter he brought from the four Councillors had none of Pimienta's polished elegance. Without a good interpreter, it said, a clear understanding of the Governor's offer had been impossible, but if it meant that the Caledonians were to be attacked then they would fight. They were men of honour, confident in the Almighty's favour.

Such a response was no more than Pimienta had expected from chivalrous enemies. At the Caret Bay inlet he ordered ashore more men, guns and supplies. Another landing of infantry and artillery was made to the west of the harbour mouth, with orders to push their batteries forward until they commanded the seagate and the south shore of the bay. He was pleased to hear that Cordones might be with him soon from Santa Maria, with seven or eight hundred Spaniards, Negroes, Mulattos and Indians. He would then command more than two thousand men ashore and twelve ships at sea. He was in no hurry. There were rules to observe, the greatest captains of Europe had laid down the pattern for an assault on an entrenched and fortified position. Day by day he moved his outlying picquets forward, a cannon-shot in advance of their following companies. As the picquets approached so Mackintosh's ragged skirmish lines fell back. The weather was changing and the rains were coming. Powder was damp, and muskets hung fire in the weird mists of morning when a man in blue came face to face with a scare-crow in scarlet.

In pain from a wound that would not heal, light-headed from its attendant fever, Campbell of Fonab now had little authority in the Colony. Thomas Kerr commanded the defence, hampered by Vetch and Gibson. Lindsay was dying from waste and fever, but he came still to Council meetings, giving his colourless assent to all that the others proposed. More than a third of the Scots were sick and unable to stand, and the rest little better, forcing green biscuits and rotting fish down their throats each morning and evening. "The hand of the Lord was heavy upon us at this time," said Borland, "our sickness and mortality much increasing, and many daily dying, most of our able officers were taken away by death." Among these officers was Lord Mungo Murray, and because of his name, his rank, and the love his gentle nature inspired, he was not thrown into a communal grave by the marsh. He was buried inside the fort, below the Company's standard.

Toward the middle of the month Pimienta reinforced his picquets to company strength and sent them forward in attacks on the peninsula. From dawn until dusk the garrison in Fort St. Andrew, the sick in the huts, heard the heavy echo of shots on the damp air, the quick drum-beat of an advance, the long roll for retreat. The attacks came along the seaward side in the north, and from the shore of the bay in the south. There were ugly, confused struggles in the trees and in the water, voices crying in pain, the crash of volley-firing across the ditch. Thomas Mackintosh was mortally wounded in the last of these inconclusive engagements, and was carried away to die in his hut behind the rampart. There were no lieutenants or ensigns left alive in his company, and the command now fell to Lauchlan Bain, the young man from Mackay country who had asked to serve as a Volunteer until merit and opportunity won his promotion.

There was much consternation of heart among us at this time (said Borland) and sinking fears and little faith and hope: our condition now seeming most desperate like. Death on all hands stared us in the face, and indeed most of us had the sentence of death in ourselves, many among us said. They believed there was not a people in the world in more calamitous and desplorable circumstances that we were at this time.

The Ministers asked the Councillors to declare a Day of Prayer and Humiliation, but were roughly told that there was no time for such things. Primly hurt, they went alone to the Shades of Love, and there sent up their own mournful appeals to the Hearer of Prayer.

Shortly after dawn on March 18 the Spaniards came out of the mist in great strength, marching on the ditch with muskets presented and drums beating. There was no resistance. Lauchlan Bain had been given the opportunity he desired but could not find the courage to merit it. He ran, and his shocked and demoralised men ran with him. Cautiously the Spaniards crossed the ditch and advanced along the shore of the bay. To their front they could see the Scots retreating into the huts of New Edinburgh. Two miles away, across a low sandy sprit, they saw the Caledonian ships with gun-ports open. Though no shot was fired against them, they halted, threw up entrenchments and stood to arms behind them. Pimienta sent a company into the trees on his right, to find and hold an inlet on the north side of the peninsula where he might land his guns. He sent another along the high ground to Look-out Point, flanking the fort. The watchman was long gone, but the Spanish found his mean hut and his discarded scarlet coat. They began to build a gun emplacement, looking down on the ships and the fort.

That afternoon Vetch, Gibson and the dying Lindsay called a general meeting of all Land and Sea Officers. Sixteen tired and dispirited men gathered in Fort St. Andrew, and there was little argument when Vetch proposed that they capitulate on honourable terms. Their vote in favour was unanimous. Bitterly ashamed of his comrades, Fonab was not present. Perhaps he remembered that two or three of these officers were men of Argyll's who had broken their swords with him when they were shamefully betrayed into surrender at Dixemude. Nor would he sign the letter which the Councillors wrote to Pimienta, and had he agreed with it he would certainly have insisted that it was phrased with honesty. Weakly evading the word surrender, it said that because the Scots did not wish to be responsible for any ill-feeling between the Kings of Great Britain and Spain they would like to know what terms the Spanish might offer.

Pimienta received the letter next day at vespers, aboard the frigate *San Antonio* where he had gone to watch the disembarkation of two carriage guns. He waited a day before replying, until he had seen the field-pieces ashore and on their way to Look-out Point. The letter he then wrote was long and courteous, but its meaning was brutally blunt. Since the Scots were not officers of any crown or government acknowledged by his royal master, he could not talk of terms until they had surrendered. At his camp on the peninsula the next day, within sight of the Scottish outposts, he received yet another appeal. Still the Councillors prevaricated. *The lack of an interpreter. . . . Some person skilled in English, French or Flemish. . . . Also we send herewith an Act of Parliament. . . .* Pimienta seemed to enjoy the slow pavane of such exchanges as much as he relished the formal manœuvres of war. He replied that he had understood all the Caledonians' letters, and the French and Latin translations that had obligingly accompanied them. Any rupture between the Crowns of Spain and Great Britain would be the fault of the Scots. They were no more than dependents of a merchant company barely tolerated by their king, yet he would be generous, he would treat them as if they were William's officers and vassals.

He spent the rest of that wet day strengthening his hold on the eastern end of the peninsula. Leaving a strong guard of militia and levies to protect his tented camp, he advanced two hundred and fifty regulars to within cannon-shot of New Edinburgh. There they dug trenches and built gabions for two more carriage-guns that had been landed from the *San Antonio* and dragged overland from the neck.

At eight o'clock in the morning of March 21 a Spanish outpost in advance of the forward trenches challenged Thomas Kerr and a drummer. Both had white handkerchiefs tied to their sleeves. They were allowed no further than the sentinel's presented musket, and they waited in the chilling rain until Pimienta came out to them. It was early, and the Spaniard was in no mood for lengthy courtesies. Had the Scots officer come to submit? No, said Kerr, but he had the authority to suggest a truce for thirty hours. Soon after dawn to-morrow a senior officer would come with absolute authority to treat. He proposed an exchange of hostages during the truce, and Pimienta sent him away with two aides from his own staff. Within the hour two Scots captains were returned, "whom I ordered quartered in the advance post, all pleasant treatment and entertainment possible to be afforded them."

At seven the next morning a drummer once more approached the outpost, beating a parley. With him were William Vetch and James Main, the Colony's interpreter who had come in the hope that his French might be understood by Pimienta. Vetch said that the Scots were ready to surrender if they could leave with all their guns, ships and stores. Pimienta was astonished. It was, he thought, a most unworthy suggestion. All a vanquished garrison could expect was the honour of marching out with arms shouldered and colours flying, and that only after a valorous defence. All else was the rightful prize of the victors. He called up the captains he held and released them to Vetch, demanding the return of his aides. He went back to his breakfast, and when he was told that the Scots had been working on their fort during the truce he ordered a company to clear their outposts from New Edinburgh. He sent another to reinforce his gunners on Point

Look-out. Thus the hopeful armistice ended miserably, with a spatter of musketry in the trees and the death of three Scots below the hill.

The Caledonians were now contained in their fort and the shallow, water-logged trenches their outposts held beyond its moat. Though they occasionally sent out a fighting-patrol, toward the Spanish lines or Point Look-out, the men were weak from hunger and were easily beaten off. Still Pimienta made no grand assault. Two days after the truce ended, Carrizoli arrived from Toubacanti with a hundred Indians, and although they did little more than eat the supplies they brought they were followed the next day by Cordones with two companies of regulars from Santa Maria. These were less than Pimienta had expected, but he sent them forward at once.

March 28 & 29 (recorded Borland), the Spaniards near us. Some of their musketeers advanced forward near the skirts of the wood contiguous to our Fort, and fired both these days upon our Fort, the bullets flying over our heads, we had only one man wounded at this time. Our men on the other side were also firing toward them, they keeping themselves still darkened in the woods and behind the great trees.

It was a great loss to us that since the Spaniards had got so near our Fort they debarred us from our watering-place, which was about half a mile distant from our settlement, for none then were suffered or durst adventure to go out of the Fort to fetch water, the enemy lying hid in the woods. So our poor distressed people were necessitate to dig for water within the Fort, which is brackish, puddle-unwholesome water. This was most hurtful and pernicious to our men, especially considering how bad and unwholesome our old, sair and spoiled provisions now was. And as for other liquors at this time, to give to the sick and the dying, we had little or none, or any other sustenance that was suitable or comfortable, and moreover our Surgeon's drugs were now almost all exhausted, and our Fort indeed like a hospital of sick and dying men.

Seaward from the palisades the Scots could see the Spanish fleet, great castles of blue and scarlet and gold, their sails clewed, their pennants flying, and their upper gun-ports open.

They lay beyond range, and each day their boats ferried more men and more guns to the peninsula and the south shore of the bay. On March 29, an armed launch from the *San Juan Bautista* came in to the little bay below Pelican Point, presumably in support of the outposts there. The Scots fired upon it with cannon and muskets. It escaped without injury but the firing continued all day, a senseless, frustrated anger echoing across the water and the trees. Yet this little incident lifted the spirits of the Scots, particularly John Stewart, and he asked leave to send out his forgotten fire-ship. James Spence the boatswain took it out at eight o'clock that night, but before he could make the long tack about and come to windward of the Spanish fleet he was sighted by the look-out of the *San Juan Bautista*. Drums beat on the flagship, and in the flash of musketry and cannon from her high decks he saw two launches approaching to leeward. He let the fly-boat run before the wind and back into the harbour.

During the night of March 30 the Spanish made a landing in strength below Pelican Point. Seven launches from the fleet brought guns, mortars, timber and men. By dawn a gun-battery, well protected by gabions and fascines, had been built within pistol-shot of the moat. The Scots fired upon it all day, and although they did little damage to it they prevented its gunners from cannonading their rotting walls. Before dusk there was silence, a veil of smoke across the bay, and then a drum beat a parley from the Spanish lines. An officer advanced on the moat with his hat in his hand. The letter he carried from Pimienta asked the Scots to consider their weakness and the Spaniards' strength. Were they stubbornly resolved to resist his last assault by land and sea he could not prevent their total annihilation. The friendship between the King his master and their own compelled him to ask again for their surrender.

The letter was less than honest. Pimienta's diary recorded that most of his men were ill with fever and the rest exhausted. The rainy season was beginning, and he did not believe that he could take the fort by assault or support a long siege.

The Caledonians' reply reached him an hour later. From somewhere, perhaps from Fonab, the Land Officers and the Sea Captains had found the momentary courage to over-rule the Councillors. Pride and self-preservation would not permit them to give Pimienta their ships and guns. His terms, they told him, were shameful and unworthy, and if they were accepted the Scots could never return home. "Wherefore, we consider it better to die honourably than to live without honour." Though he was genuinely grieved by the reply, Pimienta admired its courage. It obeyed the chivalrous code he himself observed, and it called upon him to make an equally noble gesture.

I ordered Campmaster Don Melchor de Guevara to advance to their fort with a drummer to summon them and to say to them on my behalf that it was not my desire to deprive any man of honour, nor would my obligations permit me to do so, especially when I held them to be honourable men who had defended themselves as such; and that they might realise this to be the truth, to bid one of their commanding officers to return with him under the protection of my word to parley with me.

While de Guevara waited at the broken gate of the fort a meeting of Councillors and Officers discussed the offer he had brought. Lindsay was dead that morning, but had he still been alive he would have agreed with Vetch and Gibson. They said they would ask Pimienta for better terms, but even without them the Colony must surrender. From his sick-bed, Fonab sent a passionate appeal against such a decision. There should be no treating with the Spaniards, except as honourable men with sword in hand. But though he was ready for this, and might even have welcomed death in some bloody, slithering struggle once the Spaniards broke into the fort, there was no heart left among the others. Less than three hundred of the Scots could now stand at their posts. Fever was killing sixteen a day, more than Spanish musketry. The bread they had was green with worms, the fish so stinking that starving men could scarcely swallow it. The last of the pewter had been melted into shot, and there was little powder left that was not damp or impure. Surrender was inevitable, but the shame of it was bitter, and long after it was done even Borland would feel compelled to defend these men he had so often denounced and vilified.

If the impartial reader weighs these things, and candidly considers the case of these distressed people in the wilderness at this time, I think he shall have no just cause to reflect upon or find fault with our officers and chief men for accepting of a capitulation with the Spaniards in such circumstances. Whoever shall reproach and blame them for it, so they manifest little of Christian sympathy with them that are in affliction when they themselves live at ease. So I must tell them they know little of what it is to be in an American wilderness in such circumstances, and I would not wish them (were it lawful to wish evil to any person) to be in sadder circumstances in this world.

From the palisades a Scottish drummer beat an acceptance of the Spanish offer to treat. William Vetch put on his sword and walked down to the nearest outpost with James Main and de Guevara. There they waited until Pimienta came up with a cloud of officers. Vetch asked what terms the Scots might expect. "I answered," reported Pimienta, "that I would permit them to evacuate with all military honours, with all their chattels and vessels excepting the warship *Rising Sun*." Vetch said he must discuss this with his officers, and was given two hours. He returned within the time and pleaded with Pimienta not to take the flagship. Had the Governor insisted, the Scots would probably have surrendered the ship, but he graciously let them keep it. He was not altogether generous. That morning his frigates had driven away two strange ships that tried to enter the harbour, and he was afraid that reinforcements might be on their way to the Scots.

In the rain, and at noon on Sunday, March 31, the Articles of Capitulation were signed by Pimienta and counter-signed by Vetch and Gibson. James Main had written them in Latin so that they might be mutually understood. The Scots were to march out of the fort immediately, with drums beating and colours flying. They had two weeks in which to wood and water their ships, to load their guns and goods, and to embark themselves. They must then be gone on the first fair wind. Remembering their Cuna allies, the ministers asked for an assurance that the Spanish would not ill-treat them. Pimienta angrily replied that the King of Spain needed no advice on how to deal with his Indian subjects. When Alexander Shields protested, the Governor told him to mind his own business, *"Cura tua negotia!"* Unused to such a reproof in the language of his beloved classics, Mr. Shields meekly answered *"Curabo."*

The Caledonians abandoned the fort the next day, carrying their sick, their arms, their drums and their colours. Pimienta had no time to be shocked or surprised by their wretched appearance. He had too much difficulty in assembling three hundred of his own men to take possession of the fort. Some of them were seamen, wearing uniforms that had been stripped from the dead in the trenches. They marched in, raised the standard of Spain and retired, leaving one sentry at the gate and another on the palisades.

During the night of April 1 one of the strange ships that had been driven from Golden Island slipped into the harbour. Thomas Drummond was back. At Port Royal in Jamaica he had found two of the Company's ships, the frigate *Speedy Return* and the sloop *Content*. The first had brought Daniel Mackay from Scotland and was bound for the Colony, but there was no knowing where James Byres intended to sail the other. Since the man had not yet left for Scotland, and could do no harm to Drummond's reputation if he were further delayed, the grenadier decided that both ships should sail at once for Caledonia with all the provisions they could carry. Byres was reluctant, but he could not refuse. When Spanish warships drove them from the harbour mouth, Drummond said they should come by the lee of Golden Island that night and enter under darkness. He told the master of the *Content* to steer by the topsail yards of the *Speedy Return* and to follow her in without fear. The captain was willing enough, but when Byres saw the stern-lights of the Spanish fleet he picked up a billet of wood and threatened to kill the man if he took the ship any further. The master shrugged his shoulders and stood out to sea for Jamaica.

Drummond was as angry and as bitter as Fonab when he heard that the Colony had surrendered. He sullenly kept to the *Speedy Return* and would not speak to the colonists, though he gave them the provisions he carried. He also delivered the dispatches which Mackay had brought from Scotland, and there was a mocking irony in their threats, promises, orders and exhortations. They had been found in Mackay's valise. Somewhere between Jamaica and Caledonia, leaning over the stern to fish for sharks, the hot-tempered young lawyer had fallen into the sea. "And so," said Borland, "perished in a very lamentable manner, being torn in pieces by those ravenous and devouring sharks."

The embarkation was slow, for the Scots were weak and the work was hard. The long-boat of the *Rising Sun* ran upon the sunken rock and was abandoned for the want of strength to haul it off. Angered by the arrival of the *Speedy Return*, Pimienta would give no help. When Captain Andreas sent canoes to assist his friends, the Spaniards chained him in a hut. Vetch and Gibson would not protest, the one too sick and the other too indifferent, happy in his yellow cabin with his pipe and dram. But Drummond sent an angry message to the Spanish camp. If ever he had an opportunity treat Pimienta as Andreas was treated he would do it in good heart. The ministers also said nothing. It was as if they had suddenly realised how close they had come to the fires of the Inquisition and a painful martyrdom for the Kirk.

> Many of the poor, distressed Caledonians (said Borland) were sensible of God's wonderful, seasonable, and prevent- ing mercies that had thus delivered them from falling a pray to the teeth of their bloody, Popish enemies, with whom they expected to find no mercy.

By the evening of April 11 the Scots were all aboard. Like Paterson before him, Fonab had been carried aboard in a litter, weakly protesting. One man only refused to leave. He was Henry Erskine, brother-in-law to Haldane of Gleneagles and the dear friend of young Colin Campbell with whom he had been apprenticed to Pincarton on the first expedition. Captured with the *Dolphin*, he had returned to Caledonia as a boatswain's boy aboard one of the Spanish ships. Pimienta offered to restore him to his countrymen under the Articles of Capitulation, but he said that now he had been accepted into the Catholic Church he would remain with his new friends. The Scots mourned him as if he were dead.

The Caledonian ships weighed anchor the next morning, but the seamen were so weak they were unable to warp the clumsy vessels out of the bay. Their bloody Popish enemies now sent boats to help them, and for a day they lay under the guns of the Spanish fleet until a fair wind sprang up from the east and carried them away. By noon they were out of sight.

Before they left, the Protestant Scots had witnessed one last humiliating ceremony. The largest hut in New Edinburgh was consecrated to Saint Charles. There mass was said before Don Juan Pimienta and his officers, their musketeers kneeling on the earth outside its door.

"Lord, when Thy hand is lifted they will not see it"
From Caledonia, April to August 1700

The failure of the second expedition was more disastrous than the first. None of its four great ships returned. Thirteen hundred men, women and boys had left the Clyde in September, and almost a thousand were dead within the year. Of the remainder, a handful only came back to Scotland.

Francis Borland's survival was providential, though not for the reasons he might have argued. He lived to publish his journal. His compassion was confined in a cell of bigotry. He could not accept the meaningless tragedy of human waste, or even acknowledge that it might be the result of incompetence, selfishness and frailty. He saw it as a grand and terrible visitation, Divine punishment for a nation's sins, and he naturally accepted his own survival as an exculpation and a reward. Beneath the flesh of jejune theology, however, his journal has a firm skeleton of vivid reporting. He carefully recorded the horror of that middle passage from Caledonia to Jamaica during which the colonists endured more misery than they had believed possible, even on the peninsula.

As they had been exercised with sore sickness and mortality while in Caledonia, so now when we were at sea it much increased upon us, and no wonder it was, for the poor sick men were sadly crowded together, especially aboard the *Rising Sun*, like so many hogs in a sty or sheep in a fold, so that their breath and noisome smell infected and poisoned one another. Neither was there anything suitable or comfortable to give to the sick and dying, the best was a little spoiled oatmeal and water, and poorly were they attended in their sickness.

And it was most uncomfortable and dangerous work for the poor Ministers to go down among them, and visit them in their sad and dying condition, their noisome stench being ready to choke and suffocate any. Malignant fevers and fluxes were the most common diseases, which swept away great numbers from among us. From aboard one ship, the *Rising Sun*, they would sometimes bury in the sea eight in one morning, besides what died out of the other ships. And when men were taken with these diseases, they would sometimes die like men distracted, in a very sad and fearful-like manner; but this was yet more lamentable to be seen among these poor, afflicted and plagued people, that for all God so afflicted them, yet they sinned still the more, were as hard and as impenitent as before, would still curse and swear when God's hand was heavy on them, and their neighbours dying and dead about them.

Once they had cleared Golden Island it was difficult for the ill-manned ships to keep together, and before dusk on April 13 the *Rising Sun* was lost to the others. When she came up with them, some days later, the *Hope of Bo'ness* was leaking badly by the head. Her captain, Richard Dalling, brought her up on the flagship's quarter, calling across the water. Would Gibson take his passengers? The Councillor did so unwillingly, and they came aboard to die. With half of his crew at work on the pumps, Dalling put his helm over and sailed south-east by east for Carthagena. There he offered his ship to the Spanish in exchange for the freedom of himself and his men.

Bitterly disillusioned by the surrender of the Colony, Drummond told John Baillie, master of the *Speedy Return*, to steer for Jamaica as soon as his ship cleared the harbour and to shorten sail for no one. Aboard the *Ann of Caledonia*, Campbell of Fonab advised her captain to make for New York. She was there within the month, and his own advice probably saved Fonab's life, for his wound and its fever would have killed him in the Caribbean.

It was the first week in May before the other three ships sighted the blue and green hills of Jamaica. The *Duke of Hamilton* was the first to drop anchor off Blewfields, followed next day by the flagship, and one day more by the *Hope*. Two hundred and fifty of their crews and passengers had been thrown overboard in the middle passage.

There was little relief and no consolation at the English island. No credit could be obtained from Jamaican merchants, and without it the ships could not be refitted for the Atlantic voyage. The rotting, useless goods in their holds were wanted by no one. Some of their seamen and many of the Planters went ashore in the dark of night, and like the survivors of the first expedition they sold themselves to the plantations in return for food and clothing. There were good men and women on the island who did what they could for the Caledonians. Two English army surgeons brought rum and sugar and medicine, bravely going below decks to treat the sick and prepare the dead for decent burial. They asked no payment, and reluctantly accepted the gift of a few muskets. A rich and handsome widow called Ricaut sent beef she had bought from her own purse. Mrs. Isabel Murray, a Scots-woman who had turned her house into a hospital for the sick of the *Saint Andrew*—and buried some of them at her own expense —now gave up her bed to take more.

The dying continued quixotically. Sometimes there were no deaths for a week, and then five, eight or ten in one day. The only solace for the living was the rum they could buy or steal. "The intemperance of many of them," said Borland, rightly if smugly, "did hasten their deaths."

One hundred died in two months. Among them James Main, dead in the house of a friend at Port Royal. Two young men whom the ministers had been training as divinity students, thrown overboard from the *Rising Sun*. John Baillie, captain of the *Speedy Return*, and John Baillie, surgeon of the *Hope*. Lauchlan Bain, released from the shame of his cowardice on the peninsula. James Spence of the fire-ship, dying within hours of his small son. The Earl of Galloway's brother. The Laird of Culbin and his son, Ensign William Kinnaird. Robert Johnson, who had hoped to teach the Indians both Scots and English, following a wife and a son already dead in Caledonia. The eager young volunteers and their tutor from Glasgow University. George Winram the distiller, the goldsmith Robert Keil. John Hunter, who had minted no coins from the mythical ores of Darien. Captain Walter Duncan, master of the *Duke of Hamilton*. The Laird of Dunlop and the Laird of Minto. Thomas Kerr the engineer, and Alexander Shields. . . .

The death of their dear friend shocked and frightened both Borland and Stobo. Yet if God chose to punish the sinful with a just death, so he might reward himself by taking such excellent jewels as Shields and Dalgleish. The Cameronians' chaplain died within days of preaching his only sermon at Jamaica, upon the text Hosiah 14:19, *The ways of the Lord are right*. Having preached it, he left the ships and went to live in Port Royal "He had been heart-weary," said Borland, "and broken with this company of men, among whom he had laboured and conversed so long with so little success." He also had a premonition of his own death, telling Borland that it would come in the month of June, as indeed it did. But he had not expected it this year, for he had brought himself a passage on an English ship shortly sailing for London. Mrs. Murray spent £13 on his funeral and nobody promised to repay her, not even Shields' brother who was a Volunteer aboard the *Rising Sun*.

There was a great bitterness at so many deaths and so much sickness. Only the ministers saw the hand of God in this, others suspected the greedy fingers of John Munro of Coul. A doctor called Crawford, who had sailed with the *Unicorn* and now practised in Jamaica, swore that Munro had cheated the Company, robbing the surgeons' chests of the medicines the Directors had ordered.

Toward the end of June the Company's relief ship *Margaret* arrived at Port Royal, her foremast sprung in two places and her canvas torn. Her master, Leonard Robertson, had taken her up to the mouth of Caledonia Bay before it was seen that the Spaniards were now there. Since then he had been in no hurry to reach Jamaica. When Patrick MacDowall urged haste, saying the fugitive colonists must be in need of provisions, Robertson amiably told him that "To-morrow's a new day." A stiff gale at last maimed the ship and blew her into Port Royal. MacDowall did what he could for the survivors, distributing the *Margaret's* provisions where justified by the orders given him in Edinburgh. He also delivered the Company's letters of credit to merchants ashore, and he gave a barrel of meal to Mrs. Murray for her expenses in burying Alexander Shields and four young officers from the *Rising Sun*.

He was no more fortunate when he approached the Governor than others had been. Sir William Beeston was polite, but unhelpful. Now in receipt of letters from James Vernon, telling him not to hinder the sailing of any Scots ships, he did not think he was thereby obliged to assist them on their way. He had recently hanged some Spaniards who outrageously claimed that by pirating a New England sloop they had been taking reprisals against Caledonia. Although he thought the rogues deserved the noose, and was ready to hang a few more if necessary, it was all more trouble than the Scots were worth.

Aboard the Caledonian ships, in the lodgings which some officers had taken ashore, there were now bitter disagreements and angry recriminations. Colin Campbell, who had brought the *Saint Andrew* to Blewfields a year ago, and who insanely believed that he might yet take her to sea again, quarrelled with his friend Drummond. Each accused the other of quitting the Colony with shame and dishonour. William Vetch, too ill at times to leave his cabin on the *Hope*, bickered with Dr. Blair, the Company's agent, and intrigued with Leonard Robertson. James Gibson drunkenly upbraided MacDowall, claiming that when the *Margaret* came in she should have fired a salute to his flagship. MacDowall insolently taunted him. "If I had met him riding in Caledonia Bay he should have had all the guns we had." Even when the survivors diced for it, there were miserable squabbles over the property of those who had died, sometimes a few coins, a sword-belt, a linen cravat. Declaring that it was in payment of a debt owing him, Gibson took all that was left by Andrew Stewart, Lord Galloway's brother. And Vetch, according to Robert Turnbull, had two purses of money in his cabin for which there was no proper accounting. On the periphery of all these sad disputes there hovered the hopeful, ingratiating smile of James Byres. He was ostracised by all except Vetch, who weakly restored him to the Council. "It is but reasonably just," MacDowall wrote in his journal, "that such should have been the event of our Colony when such cowardly, dishonourable, self-opinionated puppies had the guiding of it as Byres is."

The Council of five—Vetch, Gibson, Drummond, Campbell and Byres—met infrequently and invariably in disunion. They were without spirit and purpose, determined only on returning to Scotland yet afraid of their countrymen's contempt. Their single unanimous resolution was an order for the arrest of Henry Paton, whose sloop had deserted the *Unicorn*. He was placed under guard until the Company could bring him before the Justices of Jamaica. He thought this would be never, and was content to remain on the island for the rest of his life.

In the frustrating heat, within sight of the mocking beauty of the Blue Mountains, angry discontent spread beyond the narrow circle of a few officers. Dalling had arrived from Carthagena with his crew, and he asked MacDowall to take them to Scotland in the *Margaret*. "I could not but tell them it savoured neither of too much honour nor honesty." Aboard that ship her mate had called upon the crew to sail her out as a buccaneer. MacDowall would have hanged him from the mainmast yard, but Robertson let the man go with a gentle reprimand. The *Rising Sun* lost many of her crew and passengers by desertion, and for a time she was ruled by a seaman called William Pearson and a group of starving delegates from the lower deck. "Gibson, that fine brave commander," said MacDowall, "allowing them to come to his roundhouse and make their demands with their caps on their heads, and afterwards without any orders than their own to release some of their number out of the bilboes." But the leaders of this sad and hopeless mutiny were winnowed by death, and the rest fell to drunken brawling among themselves.

"Lord," said Francis Borland, "when Thy hand is lifted, they will not see."

By some miracle of organisation and command that no one recorded, or perhaps in desperate fear alone, the ships at last put to sea. The *Speedy Return* sailed first, urged on by Drummond's stubborn resolve to be in Scotland before Byres. The *Content* followed her, with Colin Campbell who had now abandoned the rotting ship at Port Royal. On July 21 the *Rising Sun* weighed anchor and steered north about the island with her dying passengers, a sick and inadequate crew, and a master who rarely left his yellow cabin. She was followed the next day by the *Hope* and the *Duke of Hamilton*. Francis Borland was aboard none of these ships. Inspired by Mr. Shields' example, and "directed by the wise and well-ordered providence of the Lord", he had sailed on a New Englander the week before and was now on his way to Boston. It had pleased a holy and all-wise God, he later wrote, to save the lives of some of his ministers. "The Lord preserving, leading, healing, strengthening and upholding all the way. Thus when once Lot was got out of Sodom into Zoar, then without any longer delay the Lord rained destruction from Heaven."

Destruction from heaven, literal if not divine, first struck the *Hope*. She sailed westward, and before she cleared Negril Point she was leaking from midships to stern. Between Jamaica and Cuba she ran into heavy squalls that first beat her back and then veered, driving her toward a lee shore on the island of Camanos. Her decks were crowded with sick and dying, her crew could scarcely haul a sheet. She mounted the shoreward rocks by night, and the living still aboard her were taken off by the Spanish. William Vetch had at last died of his fever, and had been turned overboard within a few days of leaving Jamaica.

On August 14, in the Gulf of Florida, the *Rising Sun* ran into a gale that carried away all her masts and stove in most of her boats. Of the hundred and forty seamen and landsmen who had left Blewfields with her, twenty-eight had already died. The rest were now ready to accept death, with prayers or rum according to their courage. But the storm had aroused Gibson from his lethargy. It was a challenge he understood, had met before, and did not fear. He bullied his crew and the landsmen into erecting a jury-mast. Though the ship was leaking badly, he kept her afloat for ten days and brought her to the bar at Charleston in Carolina. She was too low in the water to cross it and make the nine miles upriver to where the *Duke of Hamilton* was already close-reefed and at anchor. For three days and nights the flagship's crew and passengers worked to lighten her, at the pumps, heaving guns and cargo overboard. On the fourth day a small galley, bound for New York, came downriver from Charleston. Though her master could not, or would not help, he waited long enough to take a letter which Gibson wrote to the Directors. It survives, stained and hastily-written, inexplicably unsigned. It gives a brief account of the ship's departure from Jamaica, the storm that dismasted her, and from the last paragraph it is clear that the bitter labour of three days had been for nothing.

> By what is said you may judge of our hard circumstances. Notwithstanding whereof, God in his infinite mercy has brought us this length. Our men were fatigued with pumping, the water being six feet above the keelson all the night and next day after our misfortune, and at writing.

James Byres, who had chosen to sail on the flagship rather than the *Content*, now decided that it was time to leave her. With fourteen others, including Alexander Stobo and his wife, he went ashore in the long-boat. None of them, understandably, reported what Gibson may have said at their departure. Three nights later a black hurricane came up from the Florida keys. It sank the *Duke of Hamilton* where she lay at anchor, and it plucked the flagship from the bar and threw her out to sea. She went down with James Gibson and all her remaining company. Some of her dead, her good Berlin oak and the golden convolutes of her stern came ashore with the tide, but she took the rising sun of her figure-head with her.

Alexander Stobo never returned to his ministry in Scotland. He established another in the land to which the Lord, in his charity, had safely delivered him. He sired a sturdy line which included Theodore Roosevelt, during whose term as President America built the canal that was the ultimate realisation of William Paterson's dream. Stobo had no regret, no pity for the Caledonians who were dead.

> They were such a rude company [he wrote to Borland] that I believe Sodom never declared such impudence in sinning as they. Any observant eye might see that they were running the way they went, hell and judgement was to be seen upon them and in them before the time. You saw them bad, but I saw them worse, their cup was full, they could hold no more. They were ripe, they must be cut down by the sickle of His wrath.

Francis Borland agreed. "They were a sad reproach to the nation from which they were sent."

❦ 7 ❦

As Bitter as Gall

"Now the state of that affair is quite altered . . . rest satisfied"
Scotland, 1700 to 1707

ALEXANDER CAMPBELL OF FONAB came home in July. His shoulder was still stiff from the Toubacanti bullet, but the hurt he felt was the wound to his pride. His country had been dishonoured and he openly blamed the Company, accusing it and its colonial Council of treachery. Though he despised them, the Directors and the Councillors-General honoured him. The nation would have allowed them to do no less. He was given a gold medal, the Company's arms on the obverse, and on the reverse a classical figure leading an attack upon the Spanish stockade. It was designed from his own modest sketch. Silver copies of this Toubacanti Medal were given to the few men who had survived the action, the siege, the fever, flux and the hard voyage home. Upon the Directors' suggestion, Fonab also received a special grant of arms from the Lord Lyon. *Dexter*, an Indian in his native dress, with bow and quiver. *Sinister*, a Spaniard in his proper habit. The arms of the Company were quartered with those of his Stewart and Glenorchy ancestors.

Fonab's return coincided with the trial of the Toubacanti rioters. Four men appeared before the Lords of Justiciary. The cook, who had been first through the door of the Tolbooth with a bayonet, was sentenced to a scourging, the others to the pillory. All were then to be banished from the city. The Earl of Argyll thought the punishment mild, he had received worse for truancy at school. On the day the sentences were carried out, a drunken crowd escorted the prisoners from the Tolbooth to the pillory by the weigh-house, throwing roses in their path. The hangman applied the scourge so gently that the angry magistrates threw him into prison, despite his protest that he had been threatened with death "if he laid on but one sure stroke". The hangman of Haddington, called to scourge him as he had not punished the cook, lost heart when he saw the crowd and turned back to his home.

The mood of the mob reflected the sullen anger of the gentry and the indignation of the Estates. After the initial shock there was a renewed enthusiasm for the Company, and a mad belief that the Colony could yet be re-established. "Our fondness for asserting our right to Caledonia," wrote Sir James Murray, the Lord Clerk Register, "does rather increase than abate, and it is now talked confidently that there are assurances from chief men of both Houses of Parliament in England that if we stand firm to that point . . . they will stand by us." Such was the madness of the fever, that England should be held responsible for Scotland's misfortunes and yet be willing to save her from them. Parliament met in the autumn. The Company's party, led by the Duke of Hamilton and Lord Belhaven, at once took up the business that had been so providentially interrupted by Queensberry's sore throat. They hotly demanded another Address to the King, once more asking him to assert the nation's right to its Colony, to redress its wrongs, to secure the release of its suffering subjects from the Alcazar in Seville. Every burgh and shire in the kingdom drew up its own Address, repeating these earnest pleas. The King had already answered them, however, and he was not to be moved. In his letter to the Estates at the beginning of the session he said that he was sorry the Company had sustained such losses. He would ask for the release of the *Dolphin's* crew, but he would not affirm Scotland's right to Caledonia. To do so would mean war with Spain. "Now the state of that affair is quite altered, we doubt not but you will rest satisfied with these plain reasons."

On September 20 the King of Spain happily obliged his cousin of Britain. The irons which had once more been shackled to Pincarton, Graham, Malloch and Spense, were struck away. Released from death, released from prison, they came home.

The Estates were not satisfied with the King's answer, and they did not rest. The angry threshing in Parliament Hall achieved little, although the debates were bold and theatrical. To support the canvassing for an Address, the Company had published all its early papers, particularly those relating to events in London and Hamburg. One day Lord Belhaven stood before the Estates with a copy held high above his head. "Let any Scotsman eat this book," he roared, "and he shall find it as bitter as gall in his belly!" He thought well enough of the whole speech to have it printed.

When the session ended, all that had been won was the King's empty assent to an Act extending the Company's existing privileges for another nine years. It was more ironic than generous. One of the last resolutions passed by the House had been put by Lord Tullibardine. It declared that those who had acquitted themselves faithfully in Caledonia—naming Fonab, Drummond and Pincarton—should be rewarded. Fonab was disgusted, and angrily asked for his name to be struck from the paper.

The year had limped away in bitterness and confusion, the Company impoverished and the people despairing. A warrant was issued for the arrest of Herries, should he ever cross the Border, and a lampoon called *Caledonia, or the Pedlar turned Merchant*, which he may have written, was burned by the hangman. Drummond and Byres appeared before the Directors, who heard them and their witnesses at great length, and finally released Drummond from all blame and censure. Byres was declared guilty of "several unwarrantable, arbitrary, illegal and inhumane actings and practices, manifestly tending to the great and irretrievable loss of the Company and the Colony, and to the dishonour of the nation." The condemnation was out of proportion to the man's simple knavery, but perhaps it cloaked the guilt of others unnamed.

William Paterson's faith in the Company was undamaged, though now he saw a different future for it. Recovered from his illness and his private grief, restored to the favour of the Directors and the goodwill of the people, he was writing *A Plan for Scotland's Trade*. Once more he proposed a Fund of Credit, and argued that all the country's merchants should join in one company to trade with the Indies, settle colonies, abolish poverty, and shame those subscribers who were now demanding the return of their money from the Company of Scotland. He told Queensberry of this scheme, and the Commissioner was professedly touched by "the poor man's diligence and affection to the King and country." He advised William to grant the patient scribbler an annuity of £100, and the advice was not disinterested. "He has been with me several times of late, and as he was the first man that brought the people here into the project of Caledonia, so I look upon him as the properest person to bring them off from the extravagancy of prosecuting it." But Paterson could not be bought, and his *Plan* was not what Queensberry had expected. Nor was the Company interested, though the Directors voted him a gift of £100. His dreams became extravagant. He thought of a Crown Colony, a joint undertaking by Scotland and England with a capital of two million pounds, but Edinburgh's interest was lacklustre and his garrulous enthusiasm once more a bore. He left for London, and was no more successful there. He barely supported himself by teaching mathematics to poor students, but he wrote busily of the happiness and prosperity that must come from a union of Parliaments.

Roderick Mackenzie's zeal for the impoverished Company became a blind loyalty, charged with an unforgiving hatred of its enemies. In March, 1701, he was carried to the Tolbooth accused of publishing a libellous cartoon. Its central figure was Scotia crowned, her supporters three men clearly identifiable as Hamilton and the Marquises of Atholl and Tweeddale. Ballooning from one side of her prim mouth were the words *Take courage ye to whom your safety and the glory of your country is dear*, and from the other the same exhortation in Latin. Below the garlands in her hands were the names of all the nobility and gentry who had supported the Company in the Estates, and all those who had opposed it. One of the King's servants was shown with the Devil on his shoulder, and another was falling into the retributive flames of Hell. Mackenzie denied all responsibility for the cartoon, but he remained in the Tolbooth until the Directors bought his release. He was angered by the indignity of his arrest, both personally and as the Company's servant. He was determined on revenge, and the first innocent steps toward it had been taken while he was still in his cell at the head of the Tolbooth's turnpike stairs.

The Company remembered that Africa was as prominent in its

title as the Indies. Already one small vessel had been sent to the Guinea Coast, but had returned with no more than seventy pounds of gold. Now it was hoped that the prosperity and reputation lost in the west might be recovered from the south. In May the *Speedy Return* and the *Content* sailed from the Clyde with barrels of flour and beer, tobacco, bullet-moulds, ivory-handled knives, looking-glasses framed in leather, gilt and silver buttons, worsted hose and scarlet ribbons. Thomas Drummond was the supercargo of the *Speedy Return*, and Robert was her master. Neither ship was seen again in Scotland.

They lay at anchor off the Madagascar coast some months later, loaded with slaves bought by the cargoes the Directors had hoped would be exchanged for ivory, gold and spices. When they had sold the slaves, the Drummonds caroused with the pirates to whom the island was a refuge and a buccaneering republic. One of them, John Bowen from Bermuda, persuaded Robert Drummond to lend him the Scots ships for a raid on homeward Indiamen, offering the loot in his own ship as payment. Although Drummond later withdrew from the agreement, Bowen sailed with the ships when the brothers were ashore. The *Content* was lost by fire on the Malabar Coast and Bowen scuttled the *Speedy Return* in favour of a merchantman he had taken. Neither of the Drummonds thought it wise to inform the Company of the peculiar disposal of its ships, and no more was ever heard of these hard and resolute brothers.

Months of silence were followed by years, and the Company sadly abandoned the ships as lost. A third was wrecked in the Malacca Straits, and having no money to buy or build another the Directors ordered their London agents to hire the *Annandale*, then lying in the Thames. Her Welsh master, John ap-Rice, agreed to sail to the Spice Islands under the Company's flag and privileges, and to keep the matter to himself until he was at sea, but the Governors of the East India Company heard of the agreement (from Captain ap-Rice himself, it seems) and the ship was seized in the Downs for the contravention of their charter. The anger this aroused in Scotland, sparked and blown upon by Mackenzie's passion, made the hanging of Thomas Green inevitable.

This young man brought the merchantman *Worcester* into

Leith Road on the last day of July, 1704. She belonged to a Londoner, Thomas Bowrey, and was lately returned from the mouth of the Hooghly. Little attention was given to her at first, although it was believed that she belonged to the East India Company and that she carried a cargo of immense value. Green took lodgings with Mrs. Bartley in Edinburgh, the Scots among his crew went home and the rest idled aboard or in the taverns of Leith. Within a week Mackenzie had convinced himself that the ship was indeed an Indiaman, that she should be seized as a reprisal for the *Annandale*, and that she had brought her cargo to Scotland in defiance of the Company's privileges. He persuaded the supine Directors to swear out a warrant for her, and joyfully volunteered to serve it himself.

> The chief and almost only difficulty that remained with me (he wrote) was how, with secrecy and dispatch to get together a sufficient number of such genteel pretty fellows as would, of their own free accord, on a sudden advertisement, be willing to accompany me upon this adventure, and whose dress would not render them suspected of any uncommon design in going aboard; nor had I power to compel any man.

He found his genteel and pretty fellows, some of them, perhaps, embittered survivors of the Colony. At sunset on Saturday, August 12, four of them were rowed out to the *Worcester* with Mackenzie, swords and pistols beneath their coats. The officers aboard welcomed them hospitably, and took them into Green's cabin for wine, brandy, lime-juice and cigars. Mackenzie was amused to be taken for a lord, and played the part as if it were a comic theatrical. By dark a second boat had come up on the ship's larboard quarter, and more genteel fellows climbed aboard. Unseen by the watch, now drunk from the punch sent up by Mackenzie, they posted themselves at the gun-room and on the main-deck, quarter-deck and forecastle. A third boat hailed a Scots naval frigate nearby and got her captain's promise of help should it be needed. There was little resistance, however, when Mackenzie's men drew their swords and pointed their pistols across the punch-bowl. A carpenter waved a blunderbuss, but it was taken from him and the *Annandale* was avenged.

When Green heard of the seizure he at once protested and

sent his brother to London with the news. Bowrey protested too, but both were ignored. For twelve weeks Green watched in impotent anger as his ship was stripped of her guns, sails and rudder, her cargo placed under seal, and her master's cabin turned into an ale-house for Mackenzie's "stout, pretty fellows". On December 15 he and his crew were arrested for piracy. His surgeon, who had escaped down the Newcastle road, was brought back with a bloody nose.

Though Scotland had been delighted by the taking of the ship, it soon became clear to the Directors that the charges made against her by Mackenzie were not supported by any valid proof. They might have released her, but by a strange fortuity the Secretary was able to present them with a more terrible charge. From his conversations with the *Worcester*'s steward, he said, from the drunken talk of some of her crew there was no doubt that Green had taken the *Speedy Return*, killed the Drummonds and burnt the ship. The evidence, where it has any substance, crumbled under the slightest touch of reason, but it hanged Thomas Green, John Madder and James Simpson.

What was left of the Company's honour and nobility died with those men on Leith sands. Two years later it was itself destroyed by Article Fifteen of the Treaty of Union by which one Parliament of Great Britain replaced those of Scotland and England. There were some Scots who would not surrender their noble undertaking without bitter protest. Robert Blackwood urged the Scottish Secretary "to have the nation's just grievances with relation to our Company's sufferings redressed by a suitable recompense, and that our Company's privileges be kept still entire." But the English Commissioners, treating with the Scots in the Cockpit at Westminster, insisted that the security of England and the prosperity of the united kingdoms made this impossible. English gold, which bought the vote of the Estates for the Treaty, also stopped the mouths of those who wished their Company to endure. England agreed to give Scotland nearly £400,000 Sterling for the liquidation of its public debts, for the improvement of its monetary standard, and for the repayment of the capital stock of the Company with interest at five per cent. A special committee of the Commissioners found that the sum due to the shareholders was £232,884 5s 0⅝d.

"This Company," wrote Paterson, "hath rather been calculated and fitted for and towards bringing a Union than for subsisting in an ununited state ... no good patriot would have been angry when even the miscarriage of that design hath contributed to the Union." This was perhaps true, and the Treaty removed most of those commercial grievances that had made the Company necessary. By Article Four, the subjects of the United Kingdom now had "full freedom and intercourse of trade and navigation to and from any port or place within the said United Kingdom and the dominions and plantations thereunto belonging." Few good patriots, however, agreed with Paterson, and may be admired for their continued dream of a Scotland independent in government and independent in trade. Within the context of the time both were impermissible, but upon that issue of independence Scotsmen would yet fight and die.

It was two years before Roderick Mackenzie at last put away the Company's ledgers, and locked the great oaken press that had housed them for so long. Most of England's money had been distributed—to shareholders glad to receive what they had thought was irrecoverably lost, to the widows of the dead, to angry and impoverished officers like Turnbull and Colin Campbell, to seamen and soldiers in desperate want, to brewers and bakers, gunsmiths and goldsmiths, to tanners, hosiers, fleshers and printers. Idle in the Clyde, the *Caledonia* was bought by William Arbuckle. The tall buildings in Milne Square were sold. Within a month of the Treaty being ratified, a committee of Directors drew up an inventory, an *Estimate of Plenishings in the Office* so that their value might be known. There was a clock and an escritoire, sixty-six chairs, some desks, tables and chests, a bound copy of the Acts of the Scottish Parliament, a dictionary and a book of maps. Their total value was £22 7s.

Because he held no stock, because his claims were overlooked or forgotten, Paterson received nothing until seven years later when an Act of Parliament granted him an indemnity of £18,000. It came to him when he was in great need, and it eased the last few years of his life.

Darien is now a scar on the memory of the Scots, and the pain of the wound is still felt even where the cause is dimly understood. There is little more. Upon the coast of the Isthmus there is a

finger of land that some call Punta Escoces. There is an overgrown ditch where Scottish musketeers once stood, where the
descendants of Andreas and Pedro now float their canoes. And
the rising sun flies unrecognised in the standard of a Scottish
bank.

Appendices

⋙ Principal Characters ⋘

ALLISTON, Captain Robert, buccaneer. Paterson's friend. Piloted the first expedition from Crab Island to Darien.

AMBROSIO, Captain. Indian leader on Darien. Ally of the Scots.

ANDREAS, Captain. Indian leader. First to welcome the Scots and allied to them by treaty.

ARGYLL, Archibald Campbell, 10th Earl, later 1st Duke of. Chief of Clan Campbell. The King's servant, but a large shareholder in the Company. Encouraged the officers and men of his regiment to serve in the Colony.

BALFOUR, James, merchant. Joint-founder of the Company. Lobbied support for the Act. Served in London as a Director. Ancestor of Robert Louis Stevenson.

BELHAVEN, John Hamilton, 2nd Baron. Director of the Company in London and Scotland. Violent supporter of it in the Estates.

BELLAMONT, Richard Coote, 1st Earl of. Governor of New York, Massachusetts and New Hampshire. Sympathetic toward survivors of first expedition, but adhered to the English Proclamation against them.

BLACKWOOD, (Sir) Robert, merchant. Joint-founder of the Company. Lobbied with Balfour. Served in London as a Director.

BORLAND, the Reverend Francis. Served with the second expedition as minister, only one of four to return. Wrote an account of the Colony.

BYRES, James, merchant. Councillor of the second Colony, later deserted it. An enemy of Thomas Drummond. Condemned by the Directors for treachery.

CAMPBELL of Fonab, Colonel Alexander. Councillor of the second Colony. Won a victory over the Spanish at Toubacanti and strongly opposed surrender. Later accused the Company of treachery.

CAMPBELL, Captain Colin. Land officer, later appointed to the Council of the first Colony. Took the *Saint Andrew* to Jamaica after Pennecuik's death.

CAMPBELL, Colin, seaman volunteer. Apprenticed to Pincarton on the *Unicorn*. Kept a journal.

CAMPBELL, James, merchant. The Company's agent in London.

CANILLAS, Conde de. President of Panama. Led an expedition against the first Colony, retired without fighting. Sent support to Pimienta in the attack on the second Colony.

CARRIZOLI, Campmaster Don Luis. Commanded the Spanish militia at Toubacanti. Joined Pimienta in the successful attack on the second Colony.

CHIESLY, James, merchant. Joint-founder of the Company, took Paterson's scheme to Edinburgh.

CHIESLY, Sir Robert, Lord Provost of Edinburgh. Merchant and Director of the Company. Paterson's principal correspondent during the attempt to set up a London Court of Directors.

CUNNINGHAM, Major James. Councillor of the first Colony which he deserted.

DIEGO, Captain. Indian leader. Allied by treaty with the Scots.

DRUMMOND, Captain Robert. Commander of the *Caledonia*, which he brought home from New York. Later commanded the *Speedy Return* on an African voyage. Brother of

DRUMMOND, Captain Thomas. Once a grenadier officer of Argyll's Regiment. Took part in the Massacre of Glencoe. A Councillor of the first Colony, returned to it from New York.

Quarrelled with and imprisoned by Byres. Sailed to Africa as supercargo on his brother's ship.

ERSKINE of Carnock, Colonel John. A director of the Company, and sent with Gleneagles and Paterson to Hamburg to open subscriptions there.

FLETCHER of Saltoun, Andrew. Scottish patriot. Soldier, writer, supporter of the Company and a friend of Paterson. Asked Lionel Wafer to serve the Company. Replied to Walter Herries' attack on the Colony.

GIBSON, Captain James. Master of the *Rising Sun* and Councillor of the second Colony. A Director of the Company and its representative in Amsterdam. Lost with his ship off the coast of Carolina.

GREEN, Captain Thomas. Master of the *Worcester*. Charged with piracy against the Company's ship, *Speedy Return*, and the murder of the Drummonds. Hanged on Leith sands.

GUEVARA, Campmaster Don Melchor de. Spanish officer, led the first attack on the peninsula. Sent by Pimienta with terms for the surrender of the Colony.

HALDANE of Gleneagles, John. A Director of the Company, sent with Erskine of Carnock and Paterson to Hamburg. Discovered James Smith's embezzlement of the Company's money.

HAMILTON, Lord Basil. Furious supporter of the Company. Carried its Address to the King in 1700.

HAMILTON, James Douglas, 4th Duke of. Supporter of the Company in the Estates, led the defence of it in Parliament 1700.

HERRIES, Walter. Once a surgeon in the English Navy, accompanied the first expedition to Darien, deserted it and returned to London. Attacked the Colony in a book. Probably became a paid agent of the English.

HODGES, James, pamphleteer. Probably employed by the Duke of Hamilton to write a reply to Herries' book. Arrested by the English, but dismissed for want of conclusive evidence.

JOLLY, Robert, sea-captain and merchant. Councillor of the first Colony. Quarrelled with and arrested by Pennecuik. Left the Colony and was later stripped of his office and privileges by the Company.

LINDSAY, Major John. Probably an officer of Argyll's Regiment. Ineffectual member of the Council of the second Colony. Died in Darien.

LONG, Captain Richard. Quaker master of the *Rupert*. Sent by James Vernon to spy on the Scots.

MACDOWALL, Patrick. Supercargo of the relief ship *Margaret*. Found the survivors of the second Colony at Jamaica. A friend of Paterson. Kept a journal.

MACKAY, Daniel. Lawyer. Sailed with the first expedition as a Councillor. Returned with dispatches. Followed the second expedition in the *Speedy Return*. Lost overboard between Jamaica and Caledonia.

MACKENZIE, Roderick. Secretary of the Company, first in London and later in Edinburgh. A relentless enemy of the English. Served the Company well. Responsible for the arrest of Green on a charge of piracy.

MACLEAN, Captain Lachlan. Company commander with the first Colony. Returned to London where he attacked the Company.

MARCHMONT, Sir Patrick Hume of Polwarth, 1st Earl of. The King's Commissioner to the Scots Parliament. An opponent of the Company.

MONTGOMERIE, Captain James. A kinsman of the Earl of Eglinton. Member of the Council in the first Colony, won a skirmish against the Spanish. Quarrelled with Pennecuik and left Darien with Jolly. Censured by the Company.

MOON, Richard. Jamaican ship-master and friend of Paterson. Brought provisions to the first Colony.

MUNRO of Coul, Doctor John. Employed by the Company to equip the expeditions with medicines and supplies. Refused to sail with the second expedition. Accused of peculation.

MURDOCH, William. First mate and later commander of the *Unicorn*. Took Jolly's side against Pennecuik, and left the Colony in protest.

NANFAN, John. Lieutenant-Governor of New York, and a kinsman of Lady Bellamont. Refused the survivors of the first Colony anything more than provisions to take them home, but was outwitted by Thomas Drummond.

OSWALD, Roger. Served in the first Colony as a Volunteer. Survived, but was disowned by his father. His letters contain a vivid account of life on Darien.

PANMURE, James Maule, 4th Earl of. Member of the Council-General of the Company. Jacobite in sympathies.

PATERSON, William. Originator of the scheme for a Scots colony on the Isthmus of Panama. Drew up the proposals on which the Act establishing the Company was based. A Director of both the London and Edinburgh Courts. The company's emissary to Hamburg. Disgraced by the Smith scandal. Served in the first Colony as a Councillor. Became an ardent supporter of the Union of Parliaments.

PATON, Henry. Second mate of the *Unicorn*. Ordered to come to her assistance in the Caribbean, he deserted her. Later arrested in Jamaica.

PEDRO, Captain. Indian leader and son-in-law of Ambrosio. Turnbull's friend, fought with him and Fonab at Toubacanti.

PENNECUIK, Captain Robert. Commander of the *Saint Andrew* and Commodore of the Company's fleet, member of the Council of the first Colony. Once an officer in the English Navy. Quarrelled with everybody, particularly the Drummonds. Died at sea after the desertion of the Colony.

PIMIENTA, Don Juan. Governor of Carthagena. Organised the attack on the second Colony by land and sea. Accepted its surrender.

PINCARTON, Captain Robert. Commander of the *Unicorn* and a member of the first Council. Aboard the *Dolphin*, he was captured by the Spanish and was their prisoner for nineteen months.

ROSE, Hugh. Secretary and Clerk to the first Colony. Kept an official journal of the voyage and landing.

RYCAUT, Sir Paul. English Resident at Hamburg. Successfully prevented the Scots from opening a subscription book there. Spied on their shipping.

SANDS, Captain Edward. Jamaican shipmaster, Moon's colleague. Brought supplies to the Colony.

SEAFIELD, James Ogilvy, 4th Earl of Findlater and 1st Earl of. The King's servant and principal enemy of the Company, as Secretary of State for Scotland, President of Parliament and Commissioner. Submitted to the mob and agreed to the hanging of Thomas Green.

SMITH, James. A friend of William Paterson and a subscriber to the London book. A Director of the Company and sent by it to London, where he embezzled funds entrusted to him by Paterson.

SHIELDS, the Reverend Alexander. Minister to the second Colony. Served in Flanders as chaplain to the Cameronians. Resolute Covenanter. Died in Jamaica, having deserted the survivors.

SPENSE, Benjamin. Sailed with the first expedition as an interpreter. Captured by the Spanish on Cuba, sent to Spain and imprisoned with Pincarton.

STOBO, the Reverend Alexander. Minister to the second Colony. Deserted the *Rising Sun* in Carolina and never returned to Scotland.

TWEEDDALE, John Hay, 2nd Earl and 1st Marquis of. Lord Chancellor of Scotland. As Commissioner gave the Royal assent to the Act creating the Company, 1695. Dismissed by the King. Died 1697 and succeeded by his son

TWEEDDALE, John Hay, 2nd Marquis of. Member of the Council-General of the Company and Paterson's patron.

TULLIBARDINE, John Murray, Earl of. Joint Secretary of State for Scotland, 1696–98. Suspected of Jacobite sympathies, he veered between support for the Company and opposition to it.

TURNBULL, Lieutenant Robert. Company officer with the first expedition. Returned to Caledonia with Thomas Drummond from New York. Fought with Fonab at Toubacanti. Captain Pedro's friend.

VERNON, James. English Secretary of State. Originator of "Mr. Vernon's Line" and the Proclamation forbidding the American plantations to give aid or supplies to the Scots Colony. A resolute and cunning opponent of the Company.

VETCH, Captain Samuel. Son of a respected Covenanting minister. A dragoon officer who became a company commander in the first expedition. Later a Councillor. Friend of the Drummonds and one of their party against Pennecuik. Remained in New York, and was believed to have appropriated some of the Company's goods.

VETCH, Captain William. Brother of Samuel. An officer of the Cameronians. Prevented by illness from joining the first expedition as a Councillor. Sailed with the second. Surrendered the Colony to the Spanish against Fonab's advice. Died at sea aboard the *Hope*.

QUEENSBERRY, James Douglas, 2nd Duke of. King's Commissioner to the Estates, 1700. Opponent of the Company, and successfully prevented its party in Parliament from addressing the King. Slept through the Toubacanti Riot.

WAFER, Lionel. Buccaneer surgeon. Lived and worked with the Indians in Darien. Wrote a book about them and the country, a manuscript copy of which Paterson gave to the Directors. Was later called secretly to Edinburgh by the Company, but was dismissed when the Directors had closely questioned him.

❋ Ships ❋

Vessels owned or chartered by the
Company of Scotland

THE FIRST EXPEDITION

Saint Andrew (Captain: Robert Pennecuik), launched at Hamburg and originally called *Instauration*. Abandoned at Port Royal, Jamaica.

Caledonia (Robert Drummond), launched at Hamburg. Returned to Scotland 1699.

Unicorn (Robert Pincarton), originally the *Saint Francis*, and re-named *Union* by James Gibson when he bought her in Amsterdam. Abandoned in New England.

Dolphin (Thomas Fullarton), originally a French ship, the *Royal Louis*, bought by Gibson in Amsterdam. Lost to the Spanish at Carthagena.

Endeavour (John Malloch), bought by Dr. John Munro at Newcastle. Sunk in Caribbean.

RELIEF SHIPS

Ann of Caledonia, originally the *Anna*, bought by Thomas Drummond in New York and sailed back to Caledonia.

Dispatch (Andrew Gibson), wrecked off the coast of Islay, February 1699.

Olive Branch (William Jameson), reached Darien in August 1699. Burnt in Caledonia Bay.

Hopeful Binning (Alexander Stark), also reached Caledonia in August 1699. Retired to Jamaica after the loss of the *Olive Branch*.

Society, chartered at Saint Thomas by Drummond on his return to the Colony.

THE SECOND EXPEDITION

Rising Sun (James Gibson), built at Amsterdam. Lost in a hurricane off Charleston with all hands, August 1700.

Duke of Hamilton (Walter Duncan), chartered, sunk by a hurricane in Charleston harbour, August 1700.

Hope of Bo'ness (Richard Dalling), chartered. Surrendered to the Spanish at Carthagena, April 1700.

Hope (James Miller), bought by the Company. Wrecked off Cuba, August 1700.

RELIEF SHIPS

Speedy Return (John Baillie), sailed from Clyde with Daniel Mackay, and took Thomas Drummond from Jamaica to Darien. Scuttled on the Malabar Coast by the pirate Bowen.

Content (Ninian Warden), chartered by Thomas Drummond for his second return to Colony. Bought by Company, lost by fire off the Malabar Coast.

Margaret (Leonard Robertson), brought Patrick MacDowall, supercargo, to Jamaica. Provisions she carried distributed among survivors of the second Colony.

Other vessels

Maidstone (Ephraim Pilington), a Jamaican sloop.

Neptune (Richard Moon), a Jamaican sloop.

Three Sisters, a New England merchantman, sent to Darien with supplies from Scots sympathisers in New York.

Rupert (Richard Long), English merchantman which came to spy on the Scots.

Maurepas (Duvivier Thomas), French ship wrecked in Caledonia Bay.

Adventure (John Howell), a Glasgow vessel which the Drummonds attempted to seize at New York.

San Juan Bautista (Don Diego Peredo), flagship of the Spanish blockading fleet.

San Antonio, Spanish warship.

El Florizant, Spanish warship.

Annandale (John ap-Rice), merchantman seized by the English East India Company to prevent it sailing under Scots colours.

Worcester (Thomas Green), English merchantman seized in the Firth of Forth by Roderick Mackenzie on behalf of the Company.

❧ Chronology ❧

1693

JUNE 14TH. Scots Parliament passes *An Act for Encouraging Foreign Trade*. Companies may be formed to trade with any country not at war with the Crown.

1695

MAY 9TH. At the opening of the fifth session of the Scots Parliament, Lord Tweeddale announces that the King will approve legislation for the establishment of a colony, and the formation of a trading company.

William Paterson's draft for such an Act is carried to Scotland by James Chiesly.

JUNE 15TH. The Bill is first brought before the Estates and referred to the Committee for Trade.

JUNE 26TH. Lord Tweeddale touches the Act with the sceptre and gives it the Royal Assent.

AUGUST 29TH. First regular meeting of "the gentlemen concerned with the Company" in London.

NOVEMBER 13TH. Subscription book for the Company of Scotland Trading to Africa and the Indies is opened in London. Entire issue of £300,000 is subscribed.

DECEMBER 3RD. House of Lords debate the Scots Act.

DECEMBER 5TH. London Directors of the Company are ordered to appear before the Lords.

DECEMBER 17TH. Lords and Commons go to the King, presenting an Address of protest against the Scots Company. William III declares himself "ill-served in Scotland".

1696

JANUARY. The London Directors have been examined by a Committee of the House of Commons. The House demands their impeachment. Subscribers withdraw and the English venture collapses. William Paterson leaves for Scotland.

FEBRUARY 26TH. The Company opens a Subscription Book in Edinburgh. Proposed capital for Scotland to be £400,000. A rush to take up stock.

JULY 23RD. Paterson hands over to the Company all his papers relating to Darien. Proposes a trading *entrepôt* on the Isthmus.

AUGUST 1ST. Subscription Books are closed. The proposed capital had been reached, and the first call upon it made.

OCTOBER. Paterson leaves to open a Subscription Book in Hamburg. James Smith embezzles money entrusted to him by Paterson.

1697

JANUARY. Paterson still in Amsterdam with Erskine and Haldane. Fail to interest Dutch merchants in the Company.

FEBRUARY. Paterson and Erskine leave for Hamburg.

APRIL. Final efforts to open a Subscription Book in Hamburg are defeated by Sir Paul Rycaut, English Resident.

SEPTEMBER. Paterson is examined by a special committee of the Company. He is exonerated, and acquitted of complicity in Smith's embezzlement, but is stripped of office in the Company.

NOVEMBER. The Company's fleet assembles in the Forth: *Caledonia*, *Saint Andrew* and the *Unicorn*, joined later by the *Endeavour* and the *Dolphin*.

1698

JANUARY TO JUNE. Ships are equipped and loaded. Councillors, officers and Planters selected.

JULY 14TH. The first expedition sails from Leith, anchors at Kirkcaldy.

JULY 19TH. Fleet sails northward from Kirkcaldy.

AUGUST 26TH. All the ships have arrived safely at Madeira.

SEPTEMBER 2ND. Fleet leaves Madeira.

SEPTEMBER 28TH. First landfall in the West Indies.

OCTOBER 3RD. Council takes possession of Crab Island in the name of the Company.

OCTOBER 7TH. Fleet sails for Darien.

NOVEMBER 2ND. First landing in Caledonia Bay.

NOVEMBER 5TH. Sick are put ashore. More men land to clear the ground and build huts.

NOVEMBER 15TH. Arrival of Richard Long in the *Rupert*.

DECEMBER 4TH. Treaty of friendship with Captain Andreas.

DECEMBER 11TH. Arrival of the *Maurepas*.

DECEMBER 28TH. The settlement declared a Colony of the Company of Scotland.

DECEMBER 29TH. Alexander Hamilton leaves for Scotland with dispatches, journals etc. Major Cunningham also leaves the Colony.

1699

JANUARY. The Barliavento Fleet anchors at Portobello. Spanish Governors consider steps to drive out the Scots.

The *Dispatch* leaves Leith with supplies, is wrecked on the coast of Islay.

FEBRUARY 5TH. The *Dolphin*, with Robert Pincarton aboard, is driven into Carthagena, strikes a rock and is taken by the Spanish.

FEBRUARY 6TH. Montgomerie's skirmish. The Conde de Canillas, President of Panama, abandons his attack on the Colony.

MARCH 11TH. The Council sends Lieutenant Maghie to Carthagena to protest against the imprisonment of Pincarton and his crew.

MARCH 25TH. Alexander Hamilton arrives in Edinburgh.

APRIL 10TH. Daniel Mackay leaves the Colony with dispatches for Edinburgh.

APRIL 21ST. Robert Jolly, James Montgomerie and William Murdoch leave the Colony.

MAY. The *Olive Branch* and the *Hopeful Binning* sail from the Clyde with provisions and 300 men and women.

MAY 18TH. Colony hears of the English Proclamations against the Colony. The Council prepares to abandon the settlement.

JUNE 22ND. Caledonia is totally abandoned except for six sick men.

JULY. The *Endeavour* is sunk soon after leaving Caledonia. The *Saint Andrew* reaches Jamaica.

AUGUST 4TH. The *Caledonia* reaches New York.

AUGUST 14TH. The *Unicorn* reaches New York.

AUGUST 18TH. Second expedition sails from the Clyde, anchors again in Rothesay Bay, waiting for a favourable wind.

SEPTEMBER 22ND. Daniel Mackay leaves Edinburgh for the Clyde to join the second expedition. There have been rumours of the desertion of the Colony which he denies as ridiculous.

SEPTEMBER 23RD. Second expedition sails without waiting for Mackay or extra provisions.

OCTOBER 9TH. Rumours of the desertion are now confirmed by letters from New York.

OCTOBER 12TH. The *Caledonia* sails from New York.

Alexander Campbell of Fonab leaves Scotland for England, where he is to find a ship that will take him to the Caribbean and the Colony.

The Council-General of the Company agrees to ask Parliament to send an Address to the King, asking for his protection. Also send one in the name of the Company.

Daniel Mackay leaves for the Colony on the *Speedy Return.*

NOVEMBER 21ST. The *Caledonia* reaches the Clyde.

NOVEMBER 30TH. The second expedition arrives at the settlement. Finds Thomas Drummond there with two sloops.

DECEMBER 4TH–5TH. Meeting of the Council and all officers. Agree to send 500 men and all the women to Jamaica.

DECEMBER 12TH. The King expresses his disapproval of all Addresses to him, and orders his Privy Council in Scotland to make his displeasure known.

DECEMBER 20TH. Alexander Campbell hanged for mutiny.

DECEMBER 21ST. Thomas Drummond arrested by Byres and held a prisoner aboard the *Duke of Hamilton.*

1700

JANUARY 10TH. The King agrees to ask Spain for the release of the *Dolphin's* crew.

Robert Turnbull returns to the Colony from a visit to the Indians with reports of an imminent Spanish attack.

FEBRUARY 7TH. Byres deserts the Colony.

FEBRUARY 11TH. Arrival of Campbell of Fonab.

FEBRUARY 15TH. Fonab defeats the Spaniards at Toubacanti.

FEBRUARY 23RD. Spanish ships appear off the mouth of the harbour.

FEBRUARY 27TH. Thomas Drummond leaves the Colony.

MARCH 1ST. Don Melchor de Guevara lands to the east of the Isthmus, drives back a Scottish attack.

MARCH 3RD. Don Juan Pimienta lands with more men. He invites the Scots to surrender, and when they refuse, moves forward against the neck of the peninsula.

MARCH 5TH. The *Margaret* leaves Scotland with provisions and supplies for the Colony. Patrick Macdowall, supercargo, carries letters.

MARCH 18TH. Spanish cross the ditch at the neck and advance on the fort. The Council ask for terms.

MARCH 22ND. Truce ended and the fighting continues.

MARCH 25TH. In London, four members of the Council-General of the Company present an Address to the King. He tells them he has said all there is to say on the matter of the Company's grievances.

MARCH 30TH. Pimienta offers to treat with the Scots again.

MARCH 31ST. Articles of Capitulation are signed. The Scots have two weeks to leave with their ships, guns and supplies.

APRIL 1ST. Thomas Drummond returns to the Colony.

APRIL 12TH. The Colony is abandoned for the second time. Pimienta takes possession of it.

The *Hope of Bo'ness* sails to Carthagena. Her master surrenders the ship to the Spanish.

MAY. The *Rising Sun, Duke of Hamilton*, and *Hope* reach Jamaica and anchor off Blewfields.

MAY 24TH. The Scots Parliament assembles but the Duke of Queensberry, Commissioner, prevents the Company's party from pressing for an Address to the King. He adjourns Parliament on the 30th.

JUNE 20TH. News of the victory at Toubacanti reaches Edinburgh. Rioting breaks out, mob in control of the city that night.

JUNE 28TH. Letter from New York informs the Company of the desertion of the second Colony.

JULY 21ST/22ND. The ships leave Jamaica. The *Hope* is wrecked soon afterwards off the coast of Cuna.

AUGUST 14TH. The *Rising Sun* dismasted in a gale in the Gulf of Florida, sails on northwards.

AUGUST 20TH/24TH. The *Duke of Hamilton* and the *Rising Sun* reach Charleston in Carolina.

SEPTEMBER 3RD. Both ships are sunk by a hurricane.

SEPTEMBER 20TH. Pincarton and three other prisoners released from prison in Seville.

OCTOBER 29TH. Scottish Parliament reassembles. Company's party begins its fight to declare Darien a legal settlement, and entitled to Parliament's protection.

1701

MAY. The *Speedy Return* and the *Content* are sent to trade on the African coast.

1703

Late in the year the *Speedy Return* and the *Content*, now in the hands of the pirate John Bowen, are destroyed off the Malabar Coast.

1704

JANUARY 31ST. The Company's chartered ship, the *Annandale* is seized in the Downs at the instigation of the East India Company.

AUGUST 12TH. The *Worcester* is seized in Leith Road as a reprisal for the taking of the *Annandale*.

1705

APRIL 11TH. Thomas Green, captain of the *Worcester*, is hanged on Leith Sands with his mate and gunner, having been found guilty of pirating the *Speedy Return*.

1707

MAY 1ST. The Treaty of Union of the two Kingdoms of Scotland and England takes effect. By Article XV, the Company of Scotland is dissolved.

Acknowledgements

ONCE MORE I AM IN DEBT to those Scots men and women who have made this book possible, by their aid, their advice and their hospitality. The original material from which it has been written is largely in Edinburgh, but a single sentence here and there is often the result of a wide journey into the Highlands and Lowlands. Wherever I went I found an eager and courteous desire to help, even where my curiosity must have appeared trivial and inconsequential. I am deeply grateful to all my correspondents and friends in Scotland, England and America, though they should not be held responsible for the use I have made of the information they placed before me, or the conclusions I have drawn from it. Particular acknowledgements must be made to the following:

The late Sir William Arbuckle, whose encouragement of my work continued until a week or so of his sad death. Miss Helen Armet, the Archivist of the City of Edinburgh, for her help in determining the exact site of the Company's office. A. M. Broom, of the National Register of Archives (Scotland), for access to private muniments. The Earl of Cromartie, for his hospitality and the freedom of his papers at Castle Leod. John Cushman, of New York, for his kindness in finding books for me. R. N. Forbes, of the Royal Bank of Scotland, for access to the invaluable papers the bank holds. R. E. Hutchison, of the Scottish National Portrait Gallery, for his generous help with the illustrations. John Imrie, of the Scottish Record Office, as always tireless on my behalf. Captain Kit S. Kapp, who has sailed his yacht *Fairwinds* into Caledonia

Bay and knows it better, perhaps, than anyone since the Scots left. J. R. Ker, for valuable introductions in Scotland. R. W. Munro, a stern critic but, as always, generously helpful. Thomas I. Rae, of the National Library of Scotland, for his continued kindness and guidance. William Stewart, Burgh Librarian of Hamilton, for access to Roger Oswald's letters. Finally, to my son, Simon, for his gift and discovery of the contemporary maps that are reproduced in this book, and to my son, John, for his seaman's knowledge of the Caribbean.

In the United States I am obliged to the Library of Congress and the John Carter Brown Library for photo-copies of *Caveto Cavetote* and *Proposals for a Fond*, the only existing copies of these pamphlets, I believe, being in their care. I am also indebted to the staffs of the British Museum Reading Room, the London Library, the National Library of Scotland, the Public Record Office, the Scottish Record Office, the Royal Bank of Scotland, and the Public Libraries of Banstead, Surrey, and Hamilton, Lanarkshire.

Sources and Bibliography

ANY WRITER ON THIS SUBJECT owes a profound debt to the scholarship of George Pratt Insh. In the early part of this century his discoveries recovered most of the original papers of the Company from dust and oblivion, and he found the work of research so fascinating an historical odyssey that he wrote a second book about it and gave it that title. His history of the Company of Scotland, published thirty-six years ago, is concerned less with events in Darien than those in Scotland, and the reasons for his brief and unsatisfying account of the second Colony, for example, remain inexplicable. Though I have returned to the original manuscript sources, and have gone to others unconsulted by Insh, it would be a gross impertinence for me to pretend that his work has not been of inestimable value, a guide-line without which my own would have been harder and longer.

Though the Bannatyne Club's *Darien Papers* (1849), and Insh's *Darien Shipping Papers* (1924) contain basic manuscript material, including the journals of Rose and Pennecuik as well as Directors' and Councils' letters etc., they barely touch the great store still unpublished and which would make a library in themselves. There is young Colin Campbell's journal in the National Library, Pennecuik's letters in the Dalhousie Papers, Jolly's vindication and Wafer's amusing report of his visit to Scotland in the Hamilton Papers, Oswald's letters in the Robertson-Aikman Muniments, and so on.

The relevant Spanish papers from the Archives of the Indies and elsewhere were published as a great appendix to Hart's general account of Darien, forty years ago. I acknowledge the enormous value of these, without which it would be impossible to understand the last days of the Colony. The account of the attempt to establish the Company in London is based upon the Journals of the House of Lords and the House of Commons, as well as Paterson's letters in the *Darien Papers*. Events in Hamburg come from Rycaut's letters in the Lansdowne MSS, and as published in the *Darien Shipping Papers* by Insh. Much of the material involving England and the English Colonies comes from the Calendar of State Papers, both Domestic and American.

The spelling of many names varies considerably throughout the manuscripts. Pennecuik is sometimes Pennycook. Pincarton may be Pinkerton or Pinkarton. Benjamin Spense is Spencer, Spensor or even Penso. I adhered to that spelling which pleased me, as other writers have chosen that which pleased them.

The use of private letters and journals, scattered throughout manuscript sources has, I think, made this the first detailed account of events in the Colony. Without a full knowledge of what happened there it is almost impossible to understand the traumatic effect of the disastrous undertaking. No mention has hitherto been made of the connection between the Massacre of Glencoe and the Darien Settlement, the fact that many of those involved in the former also served in the latter, and that the memory of the massacre aggravated the contention and disunion of the Colony's leaders.

It must also be said, I think, that forty years ago when Insh and others were writing about the Company, the story had no relevance to contemporary Scottish affairs. This is certainly not true to-day. In the current political and social mood of Scotland there are strong and recognisable echoes of the temper of that kingdom toward the end of the seventeenth century. It may seem bizarre to present events in Scotland to-day as source-material for a book on something that happened more than two and a half centuries ago, but I do so with all sincerity. The undertow of history is strong.

Manuscripts

SCOTTISH RECORD OFFICE: Leven and Melville Papers; Dalhousie MSS; Ogilvie of Inverquharity MSS (Bennet of Grubet Portfolios); Church of Scotland Papers; Regimental Rolls, 1689–91.

NATIONAL LIBRARY OF SCOTLAND: Darien Papers 1–50; The Earl of Leven's MSS (DP47); Colin Campbell's Journal (MS846); Tweeddale or Yester Papers.

THE ROYAL BANK OF SCOTLAND: Journals of the Court of Directors, 1696–1707; Instructions of the Court of Directors, 1696–1701; Acts etc., of the Council-General of the Company of Scotland, 1696–1707; Registers, inventories of ships and goods; List of Land Officers and Ship's Officers.

BRITISH MUSEUM: Lansdowne MSS.

PUBLIC RECORD OFFICE: MS Journal of William Blathwayt; Regimental Rolls, 1691–98.

HAMILTON PUBLIC LIBRARY: Robertson-Aikman MSS, Oswald letters.

LENNEXLOVE: Hamilton Muniments, 41 and 121.

CASTLE LEOD: Cromartie MSS, letters from David Nairne.

INVERARAY: Argyll Papers, regimental lists of the Earl of Argyll's Regiment.

Published Papers

The Darien Papers: being a selection of original letters and official documents relating to the establishment of a Colony at Darien by the Company of Scotland Trading to Africa and the Indies, 1695–1700. Edited by John Hill Burton for the Bannatyne Club, Edinburgh 1849.

Darien Shipping Papers, relating to the ships and voyages of the Company of Scotland Trading to Africa and the Indies, 1696–

1707. Edited by George Pratt Insh for the Scottish History Society, Edinburgh 1924.

Original Papers and Letters relating to the Scots Company trading to Africa and the Indies. Edinburgh, 1700.

Extracts from the Records of the Burgh of Edinburgh, 1689–1701. Edited by Helen Armet, Edinburgh 1962.

The Writings of William Paterson. Edited by Saxe Bannister, 2 vols., London 1858.

Calendar of State Papers (Domestic) 1695–1702.

Calendar of State Papers (America and the West Indies) 1695–1700.

Journal of the House of Commons, X and XI.

Journal of the House of Lords, XV.

House of Lords MSS, 1695–1697 and 1699–1702.

Historical Manuscripts Commission, 12th Report, App. Pt. VII; 14th Report, App. Pt. III (Marchmont Papers); 15th Report, App. Pt. IX (Hope Johnstone MSS).

Carstares Papers, 1774.

Extracts from the correspondence of the Hon. Alexander Stanhope, British Minister to Madrid, 1690–99. London 1844.

Correspondence of James, 4th Earl of Findlater, 1st Earl of Seafield, Lord Chancellor of Scotland. Edited by James Grant for the Scottish History Society, Edinburgh 1910.

Documents relating to the Colonial History of New York, Vol. IV.

The Annandale Family Book. Edited by Sir William Fraser, Edinburgh 1874.

Analectica Scotica, Vol. I. Edited by James Maidment, 1834.

The Diary of the Proceedings in the Parliament and Privy Council of Scotland, 1700–07, by Sir David Hume of Crossrig. Bannatyne Club 1828.

Contemporary Pamphlets, etc.

The History of Darien, by the Reverend Francis Borland, some-time Minister of the Gospel at Glassford who went along with the last Colony to Darien. Glasgow 1715.

A Defence of the Scots Settlement at Darien, with an Answer to the Spanish Memorial against it, by Phil-Caledon (Fletcher of Saltoun?). Edinburgh 1699.

A Defence of the Scots abdicating Darien, including an answer to a Defence of the Scots settlement there, by Walter Herries. Edinburgh 1700.

An Enquiry into the Causes of the Miscarriage of the Scots Colony at Darien; or an Answer to a libel entituled A Defence of the Scots abdicating Darien (by James Hodges?). Glasgow 1700.

A Short and Impartial View of the Manner and Occasion of the Scots Colony's coming away from Darien, in a letter to a person of quality, by P.C. 1699.

A Poem upon the Undertaking of the Royal Company of Scotland, etc., for James Wardlaw. Edinburgh 1697.

Proposals for a Fond to Cary on a Plantation. 1695.

Caveto Cavetote: being an Answer to a late Scotch letter concerning a late Scotch Act etc. London 1695.

An Exact list of all the men, women and boys that died on board the Indian and African Company's Fleet during their Voyage from Scotland to America, and since their landing in Caledonia. Edinburgh 1699.

Caledonia; or the Pedlar turned Merchant. A tragi-comedy as it was acted by His Majesty's subjects of Scotland in the King of Spain's province of Darien. London 1700.

Memoirs of the Secret Services of John Macky, Esq., during the Reigns of King William, Queen Anne, and King George I. London 1733.

Journey through Scotland, in familiar Letters from a Gentleman here to his Friend Abroad. London 1732.

A Just and Modest Vindication of the Scots Design for the having established a Colony at Darien. Edinburgh 1699.

Journals

Scottish Historical Review, January, April and July 1906. "The Early history of the Scots Darien Company", by Hiram Bingham.

—, July 1914. "Letters of Lieutenant Robert Turnbull to the Hon. Col. John Erskine."

—, July 1928. "The Founders of the Company of Scotland", by George Pratt Insh.

General Bibliography

ARCINIEGAS, Germán: Caribbean, Sea of the New World. New York 1946.

ATHOLL, Katharine, Duchess of: A Military History of Perthshire, 1660–1902. Perth 1908.

BANNISTER, Saxe: William Paterson, the merchant statesman and founder of the Bank of England: his life & trials. Edinburgh 1858.

BARBOUR, James Samuel: A History of William Paterson and the Darien Company. 1907.

CHAMBERS, Robert: Edinburgh Papers ("Edinburgh Merchants and Merchandise in Old Times"). Edinburgh 1861.

CUNDALL, Frank: The Darien Venture. Hispanic Society of New York 1926.

DALRYMPLE of Cranstoun, Sir John: Memoirs of Great Britain and Ireland. 1771.

DEFOE, Daniel: The History of the Union between England and Scotland. London 1786.

DONALDSON, Gordon: The Scots Overseas. London 1966.

HART, Francis Russell: The Disaster of Darien. Boston 1929.

HOWARTH, David: The Golden Isthmus. London 1966.

INSH, George Pratt: The Company of Scotland Trading to Africa and the Indies. London 1932.

—: Historian's Odyssey, the Romance of the Quest for the Records of the Darien Company. Edinburgh 1938.

—: Scottish Colonial Schemes, 1620–1686. Glasgow 1922.

MACKENZIE, W. C.: Andrew Fletcher of Saltoun, his Life and Times. Edinburgh 1935.

MEANS, Philip Ainsworth: The Spanish Main, 1497–1700. London 1935.

NISBET, Alexander: A System of Heraldry, Speculative and Practical, with the True Art of Blazon. Edinburgh 1816.

PREBBLE, John: Glencoe. London 1966.

SCOTT, John: A Bibliography of printed documents and books relating to the Darien Company. Revised by George P. Johnston. Edinburgh 1904.

SMOUT, T. C.: Scottish Trade on the Eve of the Union, 1660–1707. Edinburgh 1963.

TAYLOR, Joseph: A Journey to Edenborough in Scotland in 1705, by Joseph Taylor, late of the Inner Temple, Esq., from the original MS. Edinburgh 1903.

TEMPLE, Sir Richard Carnac: The Tragedy of the *Worcester*. London 1930.

THOMSON, Edith E. B.: The Parliament of Scotland, 1690–1702. St. Andrews 1929.

WAFER, Lionel: A New Voyage and Description of the Isthmus of America. Hakluyt Society, Oxford 1934.

WALLER, G. M.: Samuel Vetch: Colonial Enterpriser. South Carolina 1960.

WARBURTON, Eliot: Darien; or, The Merchant Prince, A historical Romance. London 1852.

Index

THE CEVENNES JOURNAL

*Notes On A Journey
Through The French Highlands*

by

Robert Louis Stevenson

On hundred years ago — in September 1878 — Robert Louis Stevenson travelled by donkey through the Cevennes region of France. For personal memory — and, as it happens, for literary posterity — the young Stevenson recorded copious notes on his journey as he travelled. Some of these witty and incisive impressions were subsequently published in *Travels With A Donkey*. The remainder, however, has never found its way into print until publication of this volume of *The Cevennes Journal*, planned to coincide with the centenary celebrations of that famous journey. This travelogue, which also includes several of Stevenson's previously unpublished sketches of the region, provides both a unique socio-historical document and an important piece of literature.

168 pages.　　　Cloth.　　　Illustrated.　　　Price £4.95.

ISBN 0 906391 01 6

THE LUDWIG INITIATIVE

A Cautionary Tale of North Sea Oil

by

George Rosie

What happens when the richest and one of the most powerful men in the world decides he wants to build a massive oil refinery in a strategic corner of Scotland? What impact has the biggest privately-owned corporation in the world had on political decision-making from local to Cabinet level in Britain? How was every apparently insurmountable obstacle thrown in the way of the project somehow overcome? George Rosie of *The Sunday Times* provides in this book a startling account of how the Cromarty Petroleum Company — the corporate vehicle of billionaire Daniel K. Ludwig — out-manoeuvred all opposition to the building of five hundred million dollars' worth of oil refinery in Scotland. The political implications of Ludwig's initiative extend far beyond local or national politics and highlight the tensions between a multinational corporation and a nation state.

160 pages.   Cloth.   Price £4.95.

ISBN 0 906391 00 8